PICTURING THE PAST

ENGLISH HISTORY IN
TEXT AND IMAGE
1830–1870

ROSEMARY MITCHELL

CLARENDON PRESS · OXFORD

*This book has been printed digitally and produced in a standard specification
in order to ensure its continuing availability*

OXFORD
UNIVERSITY PRESS

Great Clarendon Street, Oxford OX2 6DP

Oxford University Press is a department of the University of Oxford.
It furthers the University's objective of excellence in research, scholarship,
and education by publishing worldwide in

Oxford New York

Auckland Bangkok Buenos Aires Cape Town Chennai
Dar es Salaam Delhi Hong Kong Istanbul Karachi Kolkata
Kuala Lumpur Madrid Melbourne Mexico City Mumbai Nairobi
São Paulo Shanghai Taipei Tokyo Toronto

Oxford is a registered trade mark of Oxford University Press
in the UK and in certain other countries

Published in the United States
by Oxford University Press Inc., New York

© Rosemary Mitchell 2000

ISBN 0-19-820844-8

TO MY PARENTS

ACKNOWLEDGEMENTS

My greatest debt is to my sub-editor and former supervisor, Dr E. Jane Garnett of Wadham College, for her unwavering support and judicious criticism for more than a decade. Many thanks are also due to my other supervisor, the late Professor Francis Haskell, formerly of the Department of Art History in Beaumont Street, and to the late Professor Colin Matthew, first Editor of *The New Dictionary of National Biography*: I have benefited greatly from their attentive readings of my drafts. I am also grateful to all those who heard, read, or discussed with me aspects of this book, especially Father Peter Phillips, Dr Kim Reynolds, Dr Mark Curthoys, and Dr Annette Peach. To all my former colleagues at the *New DNB* and to many other supportive friends, especially Richard Dennis, I would also like to offer thanks for their sympathetic encouragement. Thanks are also due to the editors at OUP who have seen this book through to publication: Dorothy McLean and Michael Watson. I am, of course, profoundly grateful to my parents, to whom this book is dedicated.

Many thanks are offered to the kind members of staff of many libraries and archives, who assisted me in the discovery of manuscript letters and other source materials. Permission to quote from manuscripts—of which full details can be found in the bibliography—has been generously given by the following: Harris Manchester College Library, Manchester Public Libraries, Reading University Library, John Murray, the University College London Library, the Bodleian Library, His Eminence the Cardinal Archbishop of Westminster.

I am most grateful for permission to use illustrations from books in the Bodleian Library, the History Faculty Library, and the English Faculty Library, all in Oxford. The excellent illustrations were provided by the Photographic Department of the Bodleian Library and Mr Michael R. Dudley, formerly of the Ashmolean Museum, Oxford.

CONTENTS

LIST OF FIGURES

ABBREVIATIONS

The place of publication, unless otherwise stated, is London.

BM	*Bentley's Miscellany*
DNB	*The Dictionary of National Biography*, ed. L. Stephen and S. Lee, 63 vols. (1885–1904)
Engen, *Dictionary*	R. Engen, *A Dictionary of Victorian Engravers* (Cambridge and Teaneck, NJ, 1979)
Engen, *Wood Engravers*	R. Engen, *A Dictionary of Victorian Wood Engravers* (Cambridge and Teaneck, NJ, 1985)
ER	*The Edinburgh Review, or Critical Journal*
HWJ	*The History Workshop: A Journal of Socialist and Feminist Historians*
JMA	John Murray Archives
JPS	*Journal of the Printing Historical Society*
JWCI	*Journal of the Warburg and Courtauld Institutes*
MCL	Manchester, Central Reference Library
New DNB	*The New Dictionary of National Biography*, ed. H. C. G. Matthew and B. Harrison (forthcoming, 2004)
PH	*Publishing History: The Social, Economic and Literary History of Book, Newspaper, and Magazine Publishing*
QR	*Quarterly Review*
RH	*Recusant History*
VN	*Victorian Newsletter*
VPN	*Victorian Periodicals Newsletter*
VS	*Victorian Studies*
WI	*Wellesley Index to Victorian Periodicals, 1824–1900*, ed. W. E. Houghton and J. H. Slingerland, 5 vols. (Toronto, 1966–89)
Wood, *Dictionary*	C. Wood, *The Dictionary of Victorian Painters* (Woodbridge, 1978)
Word and Image	*Word and Image: A Journal of Verbal/Visual Enquiry*

INTRODUCTION

Picturing the English Past in Nineteenth-Century Britain—Historical Consciousness and National Identity

'THE TASTE FOR HISTORY'

I have been thinking a great deal about the plan of reading history in the most useful manner . . . The great preliminary matter is if possible to create a taste for the study . . . Pictures and prints I have found . . . a very good mode of fixing attention . . . it is not to children alone that such illustrations are useful . . . The taste for history being once formed the course of reading becomes a subsequent and easier subject of consideration . . . I would take the outline from one historian of modern date and resort to old chronicles for illustrations of such facts as are told with more naivete or piquancy of detail by co[n]temporaries . . .[1]

Lord Montagu's request to Walter Scott for advice on the historical education of his son may intrigue the modern reader. Why ask a historical novelist rather than a historian for advice on reading history? Why does Scott find it necessary to stress so heavily the importance of visual stimuli in acquiring the taste for history? Why does illustration mean imagery in one instance, and selections of material from primary sources in another? The answers to these questions can be found in an examination of the historical culture of early nineteenth-century Britain, a culture in which the history of the nation was of great and increasing importance. Scott's reply shows that he considered both text and image to play fundamental roles in the development and expression of this culture. He was not alone in pondering this issue. English history, presented in text and image, is the subject of this book, which will examine the relationship of the two genres, and the challenges and changes to their combined use as a means of embodying the national historical consciousness in mid-nineteenth-century Britain. The rise, predominance, and decline of a particular understanding and representation of the national past, which will be described as picturesque, will form the central theme of this monograph.

---

[1] W. Scott, *The Letters of Sir Walter Scott*, ed. H. J. C. Grierson, 12 vols. (1932–7), viii. 102–5. W. Scott to Montagu, 5 Oct. 1823.

The nineteenth century has commonly been perceived as the period in which a truly historical consciousness first developed. A sense of loss and discontinuity with the past fed a historical curiosity unprecedented in the history of the Western world. The causes of this sense of dislocation are complex, endlessly debatable, and vary from country to country, class to class, person to person. However, such cataclysmic political events as the French Revolution and the Napoleonic Wars and such more gradual changes as the emergence of a consumer society and the beginnings of industrialization clearly contributed. Most historiographers and cultural historians believe this new historical culture to be rooted in the contemporary cultural movement known as Romanticism, viewing this new historical awareness as 'one thread in the multicoloured skein of Romanticism . . . the most significant of all'.[2] Clearly, the demand for empathic understanding and the fascination with the visible relics of the past—whether architectural and archaeological, or literary, or pictorial—which characterize this new historical awareness link it to Romantic philosophies. So, too, does a democratic attention to the lives of the common people and other social, religious, and cultural groups generally marginalized by earlier historical writers and painters.

This new historical awareness was a democratizing force not only in its choice of subject-matter but also in its large audience and wide impact: it was not the preserve of a social or scholarly élite. Disseminated through a dynamic print culture—there was a huge expansion in the publication of books and other reading materials—it permeated the middle classes by mid-century and became a mass phenomenon by the end of the century. We owe to it the emergence of the modern heritage movement and many forms of popular historical representation, from the historical novel to the historical film. For part of its popularity was due to the fact that it was a historical culture in which the visual was as significant as the textual: the nineteenth century saw a revolution in the reproduction of images, with the development of new media such as lithography and photography,[3] and a widespread enthusiasm for visual phenomena such as panoramas, dioramas, and magic lanterns.[4] This ready availability of text and image were fundamental to the development of a historically minded mass audience by the end of the century.

---

[2] S. Bann, *Romanticism and the Rise of History* (New York, 1995), 4. Hugh Honour's classic introduction to *Romanticism* (Harmondsworth, 1979), for instance, devotes two of its nine chapters to the movement's 'sense of the past'.

[3] See Ch. 1 for bibliography relating to these new reproductive media.

[4] The importance of the visual in 19th-cent. British culture has long been unappreciated, except by art historians who have tended to examine only the prestigious varieties of imagery: such diverse works as R. Altick, *The Shows of London* (Cambridge, Mass., 1978), P. Greenhalgh, *Ephemeral Vistas: The Expositions Universelles, Great Exhibitions, and World's Fairs, 1851–1939* (Manchester, 1988), and R. Hyde, *Panoramania* (1989) begin to explore some of the more ephemeral aspects of Victorian visual culture.

Until recently, however, most studies of nineteenth-century historiography merely scratched the surface of this historical culture. Most studies of nineteenth-century English historiography tended—and still tend—to concentrate almost exclusively on the texts of leading nineteenth-century historians, marginalizing the popular, the fictional, and the visual aspects of the historical consciousness. In the tradition of G. P. Gooch's seminal work *History and Historians in the Nineteenth Century* (1913), many admirable publications continue to focus on such major historical writers as Thomas Babington Macaulay and Thomas Carlyle;[5] and even studies which take a thematic approach—exploring such significant issues as Whig constitutionalism and the relationship of past and present in Victorian historiography—rarely consider the works of any but prominent Victorian historians.[6] Many works, therefore, fail to consider less than first-rate writers, however popular and influential they might have been, or to examine alongside each other both factual and fictional representations of history. When historical fiction is examined, it is generally by literary critics who do not necessarily relate historical novels to contemporary history-writing.[7] Scholars of Victorian historiography, meanwhile, have also tended to keep narrowly to their own domain, rarely considering the examination of the works of any novelist except Walter Scott as a real contribution to understanding nineteenth-century presentations of the past.

In recent decades, new methodological and interdisciplinary approaches have broadened our understanding of nineteenth-century historiography. The publication of Hayden White's *Metahistory* (1973) and Roland Barthes's essay on 'The Discourse of History' inaugurated a period of intense interest in historical writings as literary constructions, which reopened—though in a more sophisticated form—the dialogue between literature and history characteristic of the nineteenth century itself.[8] It has also led to a more extended re-examination

[5] e.g. J. Clive, *Macaulay: The Shaping of an Historian* (Cambridge, Mass., 1987); J. D. Rosenberg, *Carlyle and the Burden of History* (Cambridge, Mass., 1985).

[6] R. Jann, *The Art and Science of Victorian History* (Columbus, Ohio, 1985); J. W. Burrow, *A Liberal Descent: Victorian Historians and the English Past* (Cambridge, 1981); P. Blaas, *Continuity and Anachronism: Parliamentary and Constitutional Development in Whig Historiography and in the Anti-Whig Reaction between 1890–1930* (The Hague, Boston, Mass., and London, 1978); T. Lang, *The Victorians and the Stuart Heritage: Interpretation of a Discordant Past* (Cambridge, 1995); A. D. Culler, *The Victorian Mirror of History* (New Haven, Conn., 1985).

[7] J. C. Simmons, *The Novelist as Historian: Essays on the Victorian Historical Novel* (The Hague and Paris, 1973); A. Sanders, *The English Historical Novel 1840–1880* (1979); A. Fleischmann, *The English Historical Novel from Walter Scott to Virginia Woolf* (Baltimore, 1971); H. Shaw, *The Forms of Historical Fiction* (Ithaca, NY, and London, 1983). Honourable exceptions to this tradition which attempt a thematic approach include A. Chandler, *A Dream of Order: The Medieval Ideal in Nineteenth Century English Literature* (1971) and R. Chapman, *The Sense of the Past in Victorian Literature* (1986).

[8] H. White, *Metahistory: The Historical Imagination in Nineteenth Century Europe* (Baltimore and London, 1973); R. Barthes, 'The Discourse of History', trans. S. Bann, in E. S. Shaffer (ed.), *Comparative Criticism: A Yearbook* (Cambridge, 1981), 3–20.

of the philosophical foundations of the discipline and the nature of historical writing.[9] The significance of scientific disciplines in shaping the Victorian historical consciousness is considered in such works as P. J. Bowler's *The Invention of Progress: The Victorians and the Past* (1989). Meanwhile, the textual emphasis of previous historiographical research has been counterbalanced by such developments as the emergence of new museum studies, which have highlighted the significance of exhibitions of all kinds in shaping and educating the popular historical imagination.[10] Museum studies have contributed to recent discussions of the idea of heritage, which have rightly addressed the issues of an audience for historical representation and the arrival of a popular historical consciousness.[11] Art historians, meanwhile, have been giving ever closer attention both to visual representations of the past and historical images as artefacts: key works for these approaches are, respectively, Roy Strong's *And When Did You Last See Your Father?* (1978) and Francis Haskell's *History and its Images* (1993).[12] All these new approaches offer valuable precedents for this study of representations of English history through text and image, but the work of Stephen Bann in *The Clothing of Clio* (1984) and his successive publications is the most obvious precursor.[13]

By considering illustrated history books, historical novels, and history textbooks, I hope to avoid the textual emphasis still historiographically predominant and to raise awareness of the significant visual element in nineteenth-century historical representations. The discussion of fiction alongside non-fiction is a recognition of the fact that interest in all things historical pervaded both genres. The variety of representations of English history in the period was striking: in order to convey an adequate impression of this diversity, a range of historical authors and illustrators is examined, some who are still well-known and others once popular but now obscure. Illustrated works where author and illustrator closely collaborated are compared with works over which the publisher held more sway, sometimes selecting already well-used illustrations from an earlier work. By considering this range of material, low-brow as well as high-brow, and including

[9] An excellent introduction to this ongoing debate, with contributions by most leading historiographers, can be found in B. Fay, P. Pomper, and R. T. Vann (eds.), *History and Theory: Contemporary Readings* (Oxford, 1988).

[10] P. Vergo (ed.), *The New Museology* (1989) makes a good introduction to this growing discipline.

[11] D. Lowenthal, *The Heritage Crusade and the Spoils of Modern History* (Cambridge, 1997), P. Mandler, *The Fall and Rise of the Stately Home* (New Haven, Conn., 1997), R. Samuel, *Theatres of Memory, i. Past and Present in Contemporary Culture* (1994) are among the more significant recent publications in an immense literature.

[12] R. Strong, *And When Did You Last See Your Father? The Victorian Painter and British History* (1978); F. Haskell, *History and its Images: Art and the Interpretation of the Past* (New Haven, Conn., and London, 1993).

[13] See S. Bann, *The Clothing of Clio* (Cambridge, 1984), *The Inventions of History* (Manchester, 1990), and *Romanticism*, among other works. Bann, of course, pays particular attention to 19th-cent. French historical culture.

widely used educational works—such as David Hume's *History of England* and Mrs Markham's textbook history—I approach Victorian perceptions of history in a more catholic manner than has employed before.

With such a variety of historical publications to choose from, it has been necessary to establish a chronological framework for this study. By concentrating on illustrated historical works largely published between 1830 and 1870—during the heyday of this new historical culture—it is possible to outline important evolutions in the techniques, form, and rhetoric of historical texts and images. Early nineteenth-century developments in printing techniques and reproductive media were encouraging the production of ever cheaper publications, many of which contained illustrations. Most of the works considered here would still have been too expensive for the average working man or woman (although some undoubtedly reached them in abridged and pirated forms), but few households from the lower middle classes upward would not have been able to purchase at least several among them. The result of this study will be, therefore, a fresh conception of the Victorian middle-class historical consciousness, a consciousness poised to become even more widespread and truly popular in the later nineteenth century.

NATIONAL IDENTITY: IMAGINING THE COMMUNITY

The development of this historical consciousness will be seen here through the lens of another cultural phenomenon dominant in nineteenth-century Britain: nationalism. The linkage of historical consciousness and national identity—both of which were common to most Western civilizations in the nineteenth century—is not coincidental. Many, probably the majority, of the materials which fed the early nineteenth-century British appetite for history dealt with the national past. This offers a stark contrast with the preference given to ancient (Greek and Roman) history in the eighteenth and even the seventeenth centuries (although classical history was and continued to be a comparative model and a source of *exempla* for those reflecting on the course of English history).

Equally, the significance of historical representations in the formation of nineteenth-century national identities is undeniable—a point well made in recent studies of the 'invention of tradition' in national communities.[14] All theorists and historians of nationalism and national identity agree that, whatever the significance of other factors such as geography, representations of the national past, a sense of history and myth, are indispensable components in the construction of nationhood. As the foremost advocate among theorists of nationalism for the significance of historical and mythical representations in the creation of

---

[14] This phrase was popularized in E. Hobsbawm and T. Ranger (eds.), *The Invention of Tradition* (Cambridge, 1983), which contains (among other essays) significant studies of Romantic nationalisms in Scotland and Wales by (respectively) Hugh Trevor-Roper and Prys Morgan.

a sense of nationhood puts it, nationalism provides '[a] sense of election, [a] unique history, [a] special destiny' to its participants.[15]

This monograph will offer an original study of the development of this nation's identity through publications on English history in the early and mid-nineteenth century, showing how the history of a national community was constructed in texts and images. English nationalism was not the subject of academic analysis until very recently: just over a decade ago, it was still possible for Gerald Newman, author of *The Rise of English Nationalism* (1987), to remark that 'it is strange to think how greatly English nationalism has eluded our scholarly attention'.[16] The situation is now much altered: studies of nationalism and national identities, which have been enjoying a considerable vogue since the 1970s, have recently included many analyses concentrating on the making of the United Kingdom and the relationships of England, Scotland, Ireland, and Wales. The issue of English nationhood—once unexamined because of its very pervasiveness—has now been raised, and it is in this context that this study is situated.

However, a study which emphasizes and concentrates on the development of English national identity in the nineteenth-century period is still unusual. As in the works of early theorists of nationalism—such as Ernest Gellner, Elie Kedourie, Eric Hobsbawm, Benedict Anderson, and Anthony D. Smith[17]— nationalism figures in this monograph as a peculiarly modern phenomenon, linked to Romanticism and dating from the later eighteenth century. (In the large literature on nationalism produced in the 1970s and 1980s, many of the reasons given for its emergence were the same as those given for the new historical consciousness.[18]) This perception of nationhood as a modern phenomenon has been challenged recently by scholars examining British national identities, who tend to emphasize the significance of earlier periods for the growth of English nationalism. Newman, for instance, places the emergence of English cultural nationalism firmly in the early eighteenth century. Synthesizing the work of prominent medieval scholars and early modernists[19] (and echoing uncannily his nineteenth-century predecessors), Adrian Hastings in *The Construction of*

---

[15] A. D. Smith, *National Identity* (1991), 176.

[16] G. Newman, *The Rise of English Nationalism: A Cultural History, 1740–1830* (1987; 1997 edn.), p. xvii.

[17] E. Kedourie, *Nationalism* (1960; Oxford, 1993 edn.); E. Gellner, *Nations and Nationalism* (Oxford, 1983); E. Hobsbawm, *Nations and Nationalism since 1780* (Cambridge, 1990); B. Anderson, *Imagined Communities: Reflections on the Origin and Spread of Nationalism* (1983; 1991 edn.); J. Breuilly, *Nationalism and the State* (Manchester, 1993).

[18] Eric Hobsbawm, for instance, emphasizes the development of capitalism and industrialization, while other theorists look to the French Revolution, or—in the case of Benedict Anderson— hold that nationalism found its roots in the political upheavals of the Americas, being an import from the New World to the Old.

[19] Such as J. Campbell, 'The United Kingdom of England: The Anglo-Saxon Achievement', in A. Grant and K. J. Stringer, *Uniting the Kingdom? The Making of British History* (1995), 31–47, and Peter Furtado, 'National Pride in Seventeenth-Century England', in R. Samuel (ed.), *Patriotism: The Making and Unmaking of the British National Identity*, 3 vols. (1989), i. 44–56.

Nationhood (1997) traces the course of English nationalism over a millennium, arguing that a sense of English national identity was emerging as early as the Anglo-Saxon period and that the English nation-state was the prototype for the Western world.[20] Liah Greenfield also confirms the primacy of England as a nation-state, although she does not suggest such longevity, claiming that the idea of nation originated in sixteenth-century England.[21] While concentrating her attention in *Britons: Forging the Nation* (1992) on the creation of a British identity in the eighteenth century, Linda Colley admits the prior existence of a sense of English nationhood.[22]

Clearly, dates for the emergence of the English national identity are almost as various as the historians promoting them. It is obviously undeniable that some sense of English and even British nationhood was available to a large part of the people of the British Isles before the nineteenth century. In fact, early theorists of nationalism were as aware of this circumstance as historians of 'new British' history: Hugh Seton-Watson long ago suggested that England was among the 'old, continuous nations' where a national consciousness preceded nationalism, forces which arrived simultaneously in the 'new' nations of the nineteenth century.[23] Equally clearly, this sense of English national identity was always a protean one, always in flux: thus the contention of the earlier theorists that nationalism in the nineteenth and twentieth centuries was qualitatively and quantatively different from prior manifestations remains, I think, irrefutable. The existence of British national identities (or ethnic communities, as some theorists prefer to call them) should not blind us to the unique characteristics of nineteenth-century English cultural nationalism—or the importance of studying it in depth.

Rather than contribute to the vexed debate the origins of English nationalism, therefore, this books offers a close analysis of national historical representations during one crucial period. A fevered search for starting-points and origins seems to me to be of only limited value: surely as important as asking 'when is a nation?' is to ask 'how is a nation?'. Walker Connor's interpretation of nationhood as 'a process not an occurrence'[24] presents an intelligent way forward which addresses both issues simultaneously. This study aims similarly at the conceptualization of a more flexible approach to the issue of national identity, one which acknowledges that it originates, fluctuates, proliferates, and changes in response to a complex range of factors. It can be seen as one among an increasing number of studies of the cultural production of national identity from a variety of disciplinary standpoints. In one such publication, Homi K. Bhabha has rightly emphasized that national identity is always in a state of becoming rather than

---

[20] A. Hastings, *The Construction of Nationhood: Ethnicity, Religion and Nationalism* (Cambridge, 1997), 35–65.

[21] L. Greenfield, *Nationalism: Five Roads to Modernity* (Cambridge, Mass., 1992), 14–19.

[22] L. Colley, *Britons: Forging the Nation 1707–1837* (1992; 1994 edn.).

[23] H. Seton-Watson, *Nations and States* (1977), 6–10.

[24] Quoted in J. Hutchinson and A. D. Smith (eds)., *Nationalism* (Oxford, 1994), 159.

being, and has highlighted the inevitable ambiguities with which national identities are always riddled because their history is only 'half-made' and meanings are partial and '*in medias res*'.[25] The texts and images analysed in this book must be seen not simply as various expressions or reflections of a sense of national identity (or its absence), but as attempts to create a nation (or to question and deconstruct representations of it).

Thus the fundamental assumption of this book—an anti-essentialist one—is that the cultural manifestations of nationality and national identity are in no way 'natural', inevitable, or monolithic. The notion of a nation in the process of becoming by means of its narrations and representations, myths and symbols, and never unambiguously or comprehensively present, clearly owes much to the perspectives of the 'first generation' theorists of nationalism of the 1970s and 1980s. These scholars argued that national identity was a constructed cultural phenomenon, an insight which is fundamental to the work of such postmodernist scholars as Bhabha: they affirmed that nations are created by nationalism, and not vice versa, and described them as 'imagined communities' and nationalism as an 'invented doctrine'.[26]

This book draws on and reinforces other insights offered by these early theorists of nationalism. It highlights, for instance, the dependence of the nineteenth-century English national identity on the emergence of a bourgeois intelligentsia and an active and interactive literary and print culture. This nationalism is presented here as a primarily cultural and linguistic movement, such as Benedict Anderson delineated in his influential portraits of 'imagined communities' in the Third World: it is the creation of an educated and literary-minded middle class, sharing and using the same vernacular language, and a 'print-capitalism' to provide them (and a wider working-class audience, should they choose to address it) with the means to exchange and inculcate their ideas of nation.[27] But—as this study suggests—it is important to recognize that, in the case of Britain, this educated middle class was by no means organized or homogeneous, nor should its publications be seen as uniform and co-ordinated expressions of one vision of national identity. As A. D. Smith has recently stressed, any consideration of the development of national identity must touch upon tangential and less deliberate, as well as direct and conscious, expressions of cultural nationalism, and the reception given by a wider educated audience to whom such expressions are disseminated.[28]

This diffuse and varied cultural nationalism—expressed through a literary and print culture—is considered in relation to that political manifestation of nationalism called the nation-state. In this study, it will be apparent that the development of national institutions—especially educational ones—resulted in an adoption of

---

[25] Homi K. Bhabha, 'Introduction: Narrating the Nation', in H. K. Bhabha (ed.), *Nation and Narration* (London and New York, 1990), 1–7. The challenging arguments of this introduction are sadly impaired by Bhabha's excessive use of postmodernist jargon.

[26] The first phrase is Anderson's, the second Kedourie's.

[27] Anderson, *Imagined Communities*, 37–46.   [28] Smith, *National Identity*, 91–8.

cultural nationalism. The contribution of the mid-nineteenth-century extension of the British government, the process of bureaucratization and professionalization, to the development of a sense of national identity certainly does not lend itself to the models developed by theorists looking at the interaction of nationalist movements and the state: this state neither provokes nationalism by opposition, nor openly promotes it. English cultural nationalism was not really the brain-child of an intelligentsia excluded from political power and ambitious to acquire it,[29] nor could the state be said to be the deliberate and vigorous implementer of a form of official nationalism.[30] A. D. Smith's description of ethnic communities such as England and their evolution through 'bureaucratic incorporation' into nation-states has offered us one way in which to understand the gradual process by which the English state emerged;[31] I would like to suggest that it was in such a half-conscious, subtle, understated, and indirect manner that Victorian national institutions began to incorporate and redefine this cultural nationalism of the middle classes.[32]

NATIONAL NARRATIVES

Students of historiography from Herbert Butterfield onwards have outlined the fundamental features of the English national narrative which is held to have dominated the nineteenth-century popular historical consciousness in Britain. Before turning to a closer examination of this narrative, some comment on the use here of 'English' rather than 'British' as a national descriptor is, perhaps, appropriate. Despite the revival (or rather invention) of Celtic cultures which arose in the late eighteenth and early nineteenth centuries, it is more than justifiable to consider the representation of English national history as a discourse about the history of Britain: it is clear that this is exactly what contemporaries did do. Moreover, many recent studies of Celtic national identities and historical consciousness confirm the hegemony of the English historical narrative. Kate Trumpener, for instance, in her *Bardic Nationalism* (1997), argues that English Romantic literature of the late eighteenth and early nineteenth centuries systematically imitated, appropriated, and politically neutralized the antiquarian and nationalist literature of Scotland, Wales, and Ireland, subsequently exporting the

---

[29] Kedourie, for instance, speaks of nationalism as 'a theory . . . invented . . . by literary men who had never exercised power' (*Nationalism*, 65), and John Breuilly considers the significant role of the 'unsuccessful professional', alienated from the modern state (*Nationalism*, 48–51), in the creation of cultural nationalism.

[30] Anderson, *Imagined Communities*, 133–40.

[31] A. D. Smith, 'The Origins of Nations', *Ethnic and Racial Studies*, 12 (1989), 349–56. Bureaucratic incorporation is contrasted here with another route to nationhood, via the rediscovery of an ethnic past.

[32] It seems unlikely, however, that the late 19th-cent. growth of popular imperialism can be viewed through this conceptual framework, but this issue lies outside the scope of this study.

results of this process to the Empire.[33] Similar arguments have appeared in the
works of historiographers: Marinell Ash's *The Strange Death of Scottish History*
(1980) and Colin Kidd's *Subverting Scotland's Past* (1993), for instance, suggest a
crisis in Scottish national historiography which resulted in the emergence of a
'sociological and Anglo-British mode of historical politics'.[34] Indeed, this book
reinforces the arguments of these two scholars of Scottish historiography: David
Hume's *History of England* and Walter Scott's historical fictions—the latter often
viewed as the height of Scottish Romantic expression—both stand witness in
their different ways to the hegemony of the English historical vision. This is still
more clear-cut in the case of Wales, where the Romantic Welsh national identity,
strongly historicist in its conception, was supplanted by a more contemporary,
urban, Nonconformist and liberal persona in response to English criticism in the
form of the Blue Books.[35] The Irish, of course, proved less pliable, and the many
uncomfortable confrontations of English historiography and a confusing variety
of Irish historiographies in the nineteenth century never resulted in a final victory
for either side.[36]

David Cannadine argues that 'during the heyday of the *British* state, nation,
and Empire, it was the *English* version of Whig history which was the prevailing
mode'.[37] He rests his case on the tendency for late nineteenth- and early
twentieth-century histories of Britain to be described in their titles as histories
of England. In fact, histories of England were as frequent in every form—from
textbooks to multi-volumed histories—well before the late nineteenth century, as
will be apparent in the course of this book. Thus this powerful national narrative
was already poised to dominate and define the historiography of the British Isles.
Predominant it was but, as will be apparent in this work, the national narrative—
and the English national identity—was never as homogeneous, well-defined, and
inflexible as some scholars assume. Nor was it, of course, wholly the creation of
nineteenth-century historians, although they undoubtedly added new aspects to
it (including a healthy dose of Teutonic racism). The writers, illustrators, and
publishers considered here adopted and adapted a pre-existing and protean discourse concerning the national past.

This often told and always evolving story of England was a narrative of gradual
constitutional progress, in which ancient freedoms were renewed and confirmed
by the growth of parliamentary government and the provisions of common law

[33] K. Trumpener, *Bardic Nationalism: The Romantic Novel and the British Empire* (Princeton,
1997).

[34] C. Kidd, *Subverting Scotland's Past: Scottish Whig Historians and the Creation of an Anglo-
British Identity, 1689–c.1830* (Cambridge, 1993), 7.

[35] P. Morgan, 'Early Victorian Wales and its Crisis of Identity', in L. Brockliss and D. Eastwood
(eds.), *A Union of Multiple Identities: The British Isles, c.1750–c.1850* (Manchester and New York,
1996), 93–107.

[36] See R. F. Foster, *Paddy and Mr Punch: Connections in Irish and English History* (1993).

[37] D. Cannadine, 'British History as a "New Subject": Politics, Perspectives, and Prospects', in
A. Grant and K. J. Stringer, *Uniting the Kingdom? The Making of British History* (1995), 17.

(the ancient constitution). These political developments were frequently linked with and dependent on economic, social, and religious ones: constitutional progress was allied with increasing economic prosperity, harmony between the different social classes (all, however, knowing their stations), and—last but by no means least—the triumph of Protestantism.

Indeed, Protestantism is now viewed as perhaps the most crucial component in the making of the English national identity before the late nineteenth century. Somewhat ironically—given the emphasis many theorists of nationalism have placed on its role as a secular replacement for religion—the importance of religion in the development of national identities is now the subject of several studies.[38] Both Edwin Jones, in his recent work *The English Nation: The Great Myth* (1998), and Linda Colley in *Britons* prioritize Protestantism as the major component of our national identity, while Adrian Hastings stresses the importance of the vernacular Bible in the creation of a sense of English nationhood.[39] From the sixteenth century, the establishment of Protestantism separated England from Catholic Europe:[40] the year was governed by a Protestant calendar, in which such events as the failure of the Gunpowder Plot (5 November) replaced saints' days,[41] and a whole literature—in which John Foxe's *Book of Martyrs* took pride of place—proliferated in which England featured as the elect nation among nations. It was Protestantism which gave the impetus to the development of Whig constitutionalism: proponents of both harked back to Anglo-Saxon England, highlighting respectively a pure English Church prospering before the arrival of Augustine and Roman Catholicism, or the ancient English constitution and laws established before the Norman Conquest and outliving its tyrannies.

The constitutional aspect of this Whig interpretation of the English past appears to have taken definite shape in the seventeenth century. J. G. A. Pocock, in his seminal *The Ancient Constitution and the Feudal Law* (1957), found its origins in the learned debates of seventeenth-century legal antiquaries such as Edward Coke and Matthew Hale, who drew in turn on the radical ideologies

---

[38] See e.g. H. W. Smith, *German Nationalism and Religious Conflict: Culture, Ideology, Politics* (Princeton, 1995), which examines German Protestant and Roman Catholic constructions of historical national identity.

[39] E. Jones, *The English Nation: The Great Myth* (Stroud, 1998), 31–60, where the author argues that the basic elements of the national narrative—which he identifies as Protestantism and erastianism (Church and King)—were current as early as the 16th cent. In *Britons*, Colley makes Protestantism the subject of her first chapter (pp. 11–54). Hastings, *Nationhood*, 14–19, discusses the biblical idea of nation and its impact on Western nationalism.

[40] The crucial period when Protestantism and national identity became irrevocably linked is the subject of dispute: while David Loades e.g. identifies the reign of Mary I, Anthony Fletcher suggests that the origins of English Protestant nationalism can be found in the opposition of the country gentry to Charles I's Arminian policies. D. Loades, 'The Origins of English Protestant Nationalism' and A. Fletcher, 'The First Century of English Protestantism and the Growth of National Identity', both in S. Mews (ed.), *Religion and National Identity* (Oxford, 1982), 297–307 and 309–18.

[41] D. Cressy, *Bonfires and Bells: National Memory and the Protestant Calendar in Elizabethan and Stuart England* (1989).

of the Civil War controversialists and moulded them into a more conservative interpretation of the English past. In this portrayal of English constitutional history, common law and Parliament—guarantors of the freedoms of the individual —originated in some unspecified way in the distant Anglo-Saxon past and survived the tyrannies of the Norman Conquest (the Norman Yoke).[42] Animated by the principles of liberty which these institutions embodied, the English people continued to resist absolute monarchy from the thirteenth to the seventeenth century, repeatedly securing confirmation of their immemorial and customary rights in 1215, 1628, and (eventually) 1688.[43] Naturally, Tory opponents argued that Parliament and the law derived from the will of the King, to whom all should ultimately defer. This weak link in the Whig constitutional interpretation was repaired by the accretion of a Gothic origin for the English love of liberty: the freedom-loving Germanic peoples and their primitive democratic institutions— as described by Tacitus—were presented as the ancestors of the English and their constitution and law.[44]

By the mid-nineteenth-century, this vision of the national past was shared by all major political parties and religious denominations, the dominant social classes, and—significantly—the élites of the Celtic minorities included in Great Britain. But it was, of course, infinitely restated, reinterpreted, challenged, and adapted: the myriad historical representations of the period exhibit a wide range of differing emphases in their imaging of the 'imagined community'. As the changing aspects of nineteenth-century editions of David Hume's *History of England* show, even a received standard text was neither unconditionally accepted nor retained in its original form. Charles Knight's *Popular History of England*, for instance, put far more emphasis on the development and benefits of English constitutionalism than W. H. Ainsworth, who offered a more Gothic vision in his historical romances: as a novelist, his priorities were rather different and his works were devoted to a highly visual reconstruction of the appearance of the national past. Other representations of the English past could amount to challenges in historical publications emanating from sections within the national community who were marginalized by the national narrative: Catholics at odds with the Protestant national identity, and women, excluded on the grounds of their sex from direct participation in the politics of their nation. The new historical consciousness and the Romantic nationalism of the nineteenth century breathed new life into the elements of the national narrative, making it more prevalent and populist.

---

[42] The classic treatment of the Norman Yoke is in C. Hill, *Puritanism and Revolution: Studies in the Interpretation of the English Revolution of the Seventeenth Century* (1958), 50–152.

[43] J. G. A. Pocock, *The Ancient Constitution and Feudal Law* (1957; Cambridge, 1987 edn.). This new edn. contains a retrospective essay analysing developments in this field of scholarship since the 1950s.

[44] S. Kliger, *The Goths in England: A Study in Seventeenth and Eighteenth Century Thought* (Cambridge, Mass., 1952); R. J. Smith, *The Gothic Bequest: Medieval Institutions in British Thought, 1688–1863* (Cambridge, 1987).

An important recent discussion of this process is Peter Mandler's admirable exploration of the Victorian idea of heritage. This shares many insights with my own presentation of the English historical consciousness of the 1830s and 1840s. Mandler rightly argues for the early nineteenth-century emergence of a primarily middle-class vision of the English past, which depended on technological advances in the print industry and the explosion of published matter for its dissemination. Less justifiably, he contrasts it with what he defines as the aristocratic 'polite vision' of the eighteenth-century, which alluded to the classical past, and the élitist chivalric pretensions of the nineteenth-century aristocracy, founded on a Romantic view of the Middle Ages. This popular enthusiasm for the English heritage focuses, according to Mandler, on 'the Olden Time', a period from the fifteenth to the seventeenth century. Then, it was believed, England was both Protestant and home to a new, dynamic commercial middle class—but also domestic and traditional in its social manners and customs, all classes joining together to celebrate such events as Christmas and May Day and to preserve the nation in times of crisis.[45] He illustrates his argument with examples of both text and image, from the publications of Charles Knight, W. H. Ainsworth, and the illustrator Joseph Nash.

This exploration of the English historical culture of the 1830s and 1840s perceptively highlights the centrality of the middle classes and a new print culture in the dissemination of historical representations which both domesticized and popularized the Whig historiography of constitutional progress. Nevertheless, it is clear that Mandler's description of the cult of the 'Olden Time'—valuable as it is—offers only one reading of early Victorian historical representations of the national past. Understandably, given his broader chronological consideration of the heritage movement, he is unable to explore in great depth the variety of historical publications current in the 1830s and 1840s, or to indicate the differences between the representations of the national past produced by Ainsworth and Knight, whom he rightly identifies as significant historical popularizers. This work will offer a more extensive and complex portrait of English picturesque historiography, analysing diverse historical publications which hint at less interpretative unity and a less confined chronological range among middle-class producers and readers of history than Mandler's study suggests.

A MODEL OF HISTORIOGRAPHICAL CHANGE

Mandler concentrates on the ideological content of the intended audience of the national historical culture of the 1830s and 1840s: these aspects will not be neglected in this study. However, this author aims to ground her central argument on the form and rhetoric of the representations of the national past here

---

[45] P. Mandler, ' "In the Olden Time": Romantic History and the English National Identity', in Brockliss and Eastwood, *Union of Multiple Identities*, 78–92.

examined. The studies of individual illustrated works of English history are read, each as a discrete work, both for their role in the national historical discourse and for the perspective which they offer on the historiographical evolution of the mid-nineteenth century: the predominance and the beginnings of the decline of an historical paradigm here described as picturesque. This mode of historical consciousness was preceded by one described as philosophical and succeeded by one referred to as scientific. The terms picturesque, philosophical, and scientific are not invented descriptions and are all used in (as well as of) the works here examined: they therefore reflect contemporaries' own interpretations of the historiographical changes of the period. These evolutions from philosophical to picturesque to scientific will be illustrated in Chapters 2 and 3, where successive nineteenth-century revisions of David Hume's *History of England* and a variety of popular nineteenth-century history textbooks will be examined. From the evidence provided by these test cases, it will be immediately clear that this evolution is by no means as straightforward or simplistic as this model of historiographical change suggests: each historiographical mode originated in the preceding one and shared characteristics with it; the time-frame for each overlaps (indeed, the picturesque is with us still); and some of the works considered here will show features which belong to more than one historiographical approach. Nevertheless, I believe that this model offers a valuable framework for interpretation of changes in the nineteenth-century historical consciousness, one which has the merit of corresponding to contemporary perceptions of this phenomenon.

Philosophical history stemmed from the Enlightenment and was predominantly rational, secular, and universalist in its emphasis. The philosophical historian was more likely to engage with the classical than the medieval or recent past; indeed, many Enlightenment historians regarded the medieval past as barbaric and unintelligible. Although British (largely Scottish) Enlightenment thinkers were interested in the evolution of societies from their rude state towards civilization, they were not so interested in the specifics of historical change within their own society: their perspective was primarily a comparative and sociological one, and they envisaged themselves as part of a rational, enlightened, and cosmopolitan élite, centred in Paris. The visual dimension of this historical perspective was a limited one: the Grand Tradition of history painting—classicist, didactic, idealized, even allegorical—still presided over representation of the past. In many ways, this form of historical consciousness was an inadequate vehicle for the English national narrative: although the ideas of sociological progress and historical relativism were inherent in it, the cosmopolitan, secular, and universalist emphasis of philosophical history did not mesh well with a discourse which presented the English as a special people with a distinctive constitutional and religious history which separated them from their European neighbours. Nevertheless, this approach to the past (at its most didactic) was highly influential in early and mid-nineteenth-century Britain, predominantly through the impact of David Hume's *History of England* in its many revised editions and the early nineteenth-century textbooks based upon it: these works are considered in Chapters 2 and 3. Indeed, that David Hume—religious sceptic and doyen of the Scottish Enlightenment—should choose to write a history of England rather than, for instance, a work of classical history such as *The Decline and Fall of the Roman Empire* indicates the potential within philosophical historiography for the emergence of a picturesque approach. The attempt to create an English school of history painting in the late eighteenth century is similarly indicative of a transition: in these paintings can be seen the first faint interest in accurate historical detail.

Picturesque history was a far more suitable vehicle for the development of a sense of national identity. It dealt much more with the specific national past—the Middle Ages and the early modern period in particular, but also recent history—than with classical antiquity. While philosophical history had a universalist ethos, that of picturesque history was highly particularist and localized. This was in part because it drew on the publications of late eighteenth-century antiquaries, whose close studies of English historical relics and the English localities had made them the poor relations of the philosophical historians.[46] Indeed, picturesque history not only drew on the works of underdogs, it also focused on underdogs, showing a Romantic fondness for rebels and rejects, historical failures and the neglected of history.[47] As such, it was more inclusive of the histories of groups previously marginalized in philosophical historical discourse: not only the histories of the Celtic fringes, but—for instance—non-established religious denominations (such as Roman Catholics) and women. These will be the subjects of Chapters 6 and 7, where—through the works of John Lingard, the Catholic historian, and Agnes and Elizabeth Strickland, biographers of the queens of England and Scotland—I shall examine how these historical writers attempted to write their constituencies into the national narrative.

This inclusiveness was, of course, most evident in the efforts of picturesque historians to write the common man into the historical narrative: this democratizing drive made picturesque history genuinely populist as no previous form of historical representation had been. Its proponents exhibited a greater interest in the lives of the English people as a whole than Enlightenment historians' tepid attention to 'manners and morals' had allowed: in this popularizing impulse—explored in Chapter 5 in the historical publications of Charles Knight—can be found both the origins of the national heritage movement and of the academic disciplines of social, economic, and cultural history. However, analysis of Knight's

---

[46] For English antiquarianism from the 16th to the 19th centuries, see S. Piggott, *Ruins in a Landscape* (Edinburgh, 1976) and R. Sweet, *The Writing of Urban Histories in Eighteenth-Century England* (Stroud, 1994).

[47] See M. Butler, 'Romanticism in England', in R. Porter and M. Teich, *Romanticism in National Context* (Cambridge, 1988), 37–67, where Butler portrays Romanticism as originating in the mid-18th cent. with the country movement of middle-class provincials, disenchanted with urban life and the French hegemony of culture: they adopt the protest language of 'patriots' and promote the history of people and marginal literatures and groups. At the French Revolution, the movement becomes conservative and nationalist rather than radical and 'patriotic'.

illustrated *Popular History of England* (1855–62) also suggests the limitations of picturesque history, as it displays the author—a popular publisher with a mission to educate the working classes—struggling to convert the traditional national narrative into a genuine social history of the English people.

While the imperative of philosophical history was strongly analytic and didactic, picturesque historiography emphasized the accumulation of historical evidences (often revealingly described as illustrations) and the practice of empathy as a pathway to historical understanding. Authenticity was the watchword of the picturesque historian, who always stressed his or her careful attention to primary sources and attempted to incorporate them in the text, in either verbal or visual form. But this conception of authenticity was a limited one which could tend to focus on the trappings of the past rather than its spirit: intent on a visualization of the appearance of the past and its events, the picturesque historian generally preferred dramatic reconstructive narrative to critical use of sources.[48]

As the adjective implies, picturesque history had a strongly visual dimension. It will be clear that the nineteenth-century application of the term picturesque— like its current usage—suggests a rather looser meaning than that assigned to the concept of the picturesque by aesthetic theorists such as William Gilpin, Uvedale Price, and Richard Payne Knight in the later eighteenth century. But the Victorian picturesque historian's perspective on the past was clearly a diluted version of picturesque aesthetics. The picturesque historian valued (and even fetishized) the historical remains and relics which had fascinated connoisseurs of the picturesque in the previous generation, exhibiting a strong 'sense of place' and a fascination with the national landscape. Indeed, it has been plausibly claimed that, for the Victorian, the past was 'a visual rather than a verbal faculty, cultivated in the landscape more often than in the library'.[49]

Similarly, an emphasis on appearance rather than ideological content seems common to both picturesque art and picturesque history. The picturesque historian used both text and image in conjunction in the endeavour to produce a picture of the past composed of authentic historical details. These historical representations—which can be described as historical reconstructions—suggest a fixation with the appearance of the past which sometimes seems to validate Charles Dellheim's contention, in *The Face of the Past* (1982), that the nineteenth-century attachment to things historical was a merely decorative one. Yet Dellheim's position is, I believe, an extreme one which underestimates both the importance of the reconstructive project to contemporaries and the serious contribution made by picturesque historiographers to the development of popular history. In Chapter 4, an analysis of the 1840s historical novels of W. H. Ainsworth—a

[48] Simmons, *Novelist*, 39.

[49] C. Delheim, *The Face of the Past: The Preservation of the Medieval Inheritance in Victorian Britain* (Cambridge, 1982), 37. The development of tourism in England itself, as opposed to the earlier Continental 'Grand Tours', began in the late 18th cent. See I. Ousby, *The Englishman's England: Taste, Travel and the Rise of Tourism* (Cambridge, 1991) for its influence on perceptions of the English landscape.

disciple of Walter Scott—will illustrate the picturesque enterprise at its most flamboyant, while hinting at its tendency to become static in appearance and simplistic in content. Ainsworth's novels—illustrated largely by George Cruikshank, who worked in close collaboration with the author, and focusing on celebrated national monuments in the heart of England—exhibit the picturesque reconstruction at its most flourishing and successful.

Picturesque history encouraged both factual and fictional representations of the past—not to mention blends of the two—in the effort to arrive at striking realizations. The division between fiction and non-fiction, which is so marked a feature of the modern book world, was not so obvious in the mid-nineteenth century. This is evident from the ease with which the writers here discussed moved between the two genres: Agnes Strickland, for instance, one of the authors of *The Lives of the Queens of England*, also wrote a couple of historical novels—of which *The Pilgrims of Walsingham, or Tales of the Middle Ages* (1835) was one. Charles Knight, the publisher of many works of an educational and informative nature, did not disdain to write a historical novel himself: *Begg'd at Court: A Legend of Westminster* (1867). Many historical works in the period were linked as vital inspirations to historical novels, and shared with such fictions a concentration on dramatic narrative and the amassing of descriptive detail: Thomas Carlyle's *The French Revolution* (1837), a powerful and episodic presentation of its subject, is considered to be a major influence on Dickens's *Barnaby Rudge* (1841) and *A Tale of Two Cities* (1859).[50] In the 1830s and 1840s, the close relationship between factual and fictional works was particularly pronounced, as history was still seen as a primarily literary mode, a part of *belles-lettres*. The emphasis on a rather antiquarian style of historical reconstruction, as an empathetic and subjective experience, invited the historian to use his imagination to the fullest and to function as a creator in a similar way to the novelist.

However, from as early as 1850, the predominance of picturesque historiography was challenged by a new historical mode—the scientific. In Chapter 7, ironic critiques of picturesque representation of the national past—manifested in the illustrated historical novels of W. M. Thackeray and Gilbert A'Beckett's *Comic History of England*, illustrated by John Leech—offer signs of this crisis in the historical consciousness, triggered partly by an obsession with historical authenticity. In *Metahistory*, Hayden White suggested a cyclical progression in nineteenth-century history-writing, in which mythical perceptions of history are replaced by histories constructed as romances, comedies, and tragedies, which are in turn undermined by satires, leading to a reversion to myth again. Although I do not believe that this limited literary model offers an adequate framework for analysing the totality of historiographical change in the nineteenth century, it does afford an insight into the ironic mode used by Thackeray, A'Beckett, and Leech.

The scientific historian shared his picturesque rival's concern for authenticity but in a more profound and accentuated form: s/he valued the physical remains

[50] See W. Oddie, *Dickens and Carlyle: The Question of Influence* (1972).

of the national past—especially historical documents—but brought to historical evidence a critical perspective derived from the new scientific disciplines current in the nineteenth century, giving priority to analysis rather than empathy, conservation rather than reconstruction or restoration. This change was fuelled by developments which the picturesque historian had encouraged, such as the formation of bodies like the Public Records Office to deal with documents, and the organization and publication of sources such as the Rolls series. It was also connected to increasing awareness in Britain of the school of historicism associated with Leopold Ranke and the German universities. History was beginning to develop as an academic discipline, practised by university-based professionals trained as historical researchers and taught by the staff of scholastic institutions.[51] Representation of the national past—once both produced and consumed by the educated middle classes, a populist affair—was gradually becoming the responsibility of the state: in Chapter 3, for instance, it will be shown how history textbooks written by women amateurs for a domestic audience, for instance, were replaced by historical readers intended for schools established by successive educational reforms.

Scientific history soon began to dissociate itself both from fictional representations of the national past, and—exhibiting a strongly textual imperative—any visual representations which were not simply reproductions of historical artefacts. These developments are apparent in Chapters 2 and 3: student editions of Hume's *History*, sparsely illustrated, exhibit the further adaptation of the standard text to serve as an examination textbook, while other textbooks also adopted a 'scientific' mode of presentation and dropped many old and popular anecdotes and most illustrations. The national narratives of these textbooks were dominated by a preoccupation with the inculcation of 'facts' and were highly political and constitutional in their content: institutions were the focuses of scientific history. Obviously, the apparent impartiality and the scientific format of such works was artificial, a form of rhetoric, despite the very real advances made in the academic world in the treatment of sources: a sometimes rampant national narrative (foreshadowing the intensification of imperialism) sits somewhat uncomfortably within an apparently objective format.

Although picturesque history continued to flourish in many fictional and visual forms, it had suffered a severe blow and was no longer viewed as the natural vehicle of the national narrative. These developments are evidenced in the historical fictions examined in Chapters 9 and 10: here Ainsworth struggles

---

[51] See G. P. Gooch, *History and Historians in the Nineteenth Century* (1952), 266–72, 317–34, for these changes. Gooch identifies Thorpe and Kemble, the authors of *The Saxons in England* (1848) as the first truly professional historians in 19th-cent. Britain. An excellent work, more recent than Gooch's standard text, P. Levine, *The Amateur and the Professional: Antiquarians, Historians and Archaeologists in Victorian Britain, 1838–1886* (Cambridge, 1986) traces the development of the historian from an amateur antiquarian to a professional academic. R. Soffer, *Discipline and Power: The University, History and the Making of the English Elite, 1870–1930* (Stanford, Calif., 1994) deals with the later period of historical professionalization.

unsuccessfully to adapt his picturesque historical fictions to the new post-1850 climate—with fewer illustrations, sometimes produced with scant attention to the text—while Charlotte Yonge attempts to meet stricter demands for authenticity in her historical tales for children and young people. Other greater novelists were exploring historical and ahistorical areas which fell outside the national narrative: both Gaskell's *Sylvia's Lovers* (1863)—set in provincial Yorkshire—and Eliot's *Romola* (1862-3)—set in Renaissance Italy—could be interpreted as partial returns to myth which, in their different ways, critique the idea of English national history.

However, before turning to the case-studies which constitute the body of this book, it is necessary to outline the circumstances in which the illustrated texts here examined were created and published. Chapter 1 will analyse the relationship of text and image in the mid-nineteenth-century book and the roles of author, illustration, publisher, and audience in the production and reception of the illustrated history book, textbook, or historical novel.

1

Publishing the Past: Text and Image, Author, Illustrator, and Publisher

ILLUSTRATION AND TEXT AND IMAGE

That the study of two different artistic media presented in one format—as in the case of the illustrated text—still requires some initial explanation is perhaps surprising in this multi-media age. Nevertheless, despite the development of cultural studies in general, and text and image studies in particular, over the last few decades, the acceptance of these disciplines, and the integration of the insights which they afford us, into more traditional areas of research has been slow. Thus J. Hillis Miller prefaces his 1992 work on *Illustration* with a lengthy discussion of the nature and development of cultural studies, explaining and supporting the importance of text and image studies.[1] The implications of the explosion in creative and reproductive media of the last 200 years, highlighted originally by such critical thinkers as Roland Barthes and Walter Benjamin,[2] are only now beginning to be explored by scholars from all disciplines.

Until recently, the nineteenth-century illustrated book was studied mainly by art historians, who tended to consider the text very marginally, and to concentrate on the image and its creator in isolation from the text. Full of biographical and bibliographical information, the works of such writers contain little on the relationship of text and image, concentrating instead on such issues as the illustrator's artistic style: tracing the transition from the caricature-like vignettes of the 1830s and 1840s to the classically based black-and-white 'Sixties' style, for instance, is often a preoccupation.[3] This is clearly a peculiarly unsatisfactory approach to nineteenth-century illustration, which was directed at readers familiar

---

[1] J. H. Miller, *Illustration* (Cambridge, Mass., 1992).

[2] R. Barthes, 'The Photographic Image' (1961) in *Image–Music–Text*, trans. S. Heath (1977), 15–31; W. Benjamin, 'The Work of Art in the Age of Mechanical Reproduction', in *Illuminations*, ed. H. Arendt, trans. H. Zohn (1970), 219–53.

[3] P. Muir, *Victorian Illustrated Books* (1971) and G. N. Ray, *The Illustrator and the Book in England from 1791 to 1914* (Oxford, 1976), both invaluable works, are nevertheless not entirely free from this approach. P. Goldman, *Victorian Illustration: The Pre-Raphaelites, the Idyllic School, and the High Victorians* (Aldershot, and Brookfield, Vt., 1996) and D. Wootton, *The Illustrators: The British Art of Illustration 1780–1996* (1996) are more recent works in this tradition.

with literary paintings carrying not only a title to pinpoint their source but frequently a substantial quotation.[4] Fortunately, the study of illustrated books in general has begun to diversify: Edward Hodnett, a leading writer on illustration who attempted to explore the text as well as the image, justly criticized works which 'ignore completely or treat superficially the central functional aspects of the illustrations'. He commended recent studies which draw on more than one discipline and attempt to receive the text and image as they were intended to be perceived—by a general reader, reading the illustrated book in question for the first time.[5] William Cole has voiced similar criticisms in the flagship journal for text and image studies, *Word and Image*, calling for the recognition of the illustrated book as 'the product of a collaborative effort', involving artist, writer, and publisher.[6] Works such as J. R. Harvey's seminal *Victorian Novelists and their Illustrators* (1970) have pioneered analytic study of the illustrated texts of novelists such as Charles Dickens and W. M. Thackeray. It is still rare for less prestigious or non-fiction works to receive the same attention, but several recent works signal change here: Brian Maidment's *Reading Popular Prints 1790–1870* (1996), for instance, presents a sophisticated reading of mass-produced popular imagery (often accompanied by rudimentary texts) which attends both to the intended audience and the variety of 'representational possibilities' inherent in a popular print. These new approaches inform this book. Here text and image will be examined in conjunction: the focus will be on the illustrated book as the proper centre of attention, and consideration will be given to the circumstances shaping its creation, the response to it, and the messages implicit in it.

TEXT AND IMAGE: THEORIES OF RELATIONSHIP

It is abundantly obvious that the Victorian reader took illustrations very seriously. Contemporaries remarked on the explosion in the publication of illustrated works: a reviewer in *The Quarterly Review* of June 1844 mentioned the 'rage for ornamented, or as they are now termed "illustrated" or "pictorial" editions of books', adding that, forty years previously, illustrated books were of 'comparatively rare occurrence'.[7] Such critics expressed their views on the relationship which should exist between text and image in illustrated books and —unlike the traditional twentieth-century student of illustration—they tended to

---

[4] See R. D. Altick, *Paintings from Books: Art and Literature in Britain, 1760–1900* (Columbus, Ohio, 1985) and R. L. Flaxman, *Victorian Word-Painting and Narrative: Towards the Blending of Genres* (Ann Arbor, Mich., 1983).

[5] E. Hodnett, *Image and Text: Studies in the Illustration of English Literature* (1982), 1–3.

[6] W. Cole, 'The Book and the Artist: Rethinking the Traditional Order', *Word and Image*, 8 (1992), 381.

[7] [E. Eastlake], 'Illustrated Books', *QR* 74 (1844), 168. Elizabeth Rigby married the artist and later President of the Royal Academy, Charles Eastlake, in 1849: she wrote several histories and surveys of art and was an important contributor to *The Quarterly Review*.

prioritize the text. The illustrator W. J. Linton,[8] writing a review of some new illustrated editions of poetry and stories in 1849, expressed the common opinions of his age on the role of illustrations in books:

Like a written commentary, or as the variation in music, the pictorial illustration of the book should either expound for the student the doubtful or abstruser passages of the text, or carry on the original idea through avenues of richer beauty . . . It should bear some relation to its subject, throw some light, some splendour, upon it. We may venture to say—*an illustration should be illustrative*; surely not too great a requisite . . . it should brighten with light or honour; or explain, or clear, or elucidate.[9]

This theory of the relationship of text and image was the prevalent one, even when very different sorts of text and illustration were involved: a reviewer in *The Spectator* of 1857 opined that

an illustrated book, in the stricter sense of the term, is a book in which the pictorial art serves to give the reader a clearer and enlarged comprehension of the written matter—as, for instance, by views of actual spots, portraits of historical personages, or accurate records of any costume, etc, with which the author concerns himself. This kind of illustration, when well done, is both valuable and interesting.[10]

This assumption that the text is ideologically, if not chronologically, prior to the illustrations, was an accurate one in many cases, particularly those concerning illustrated works of a high quality—such as, for instance, George Eliot's *Romola* (1862–3) and Elizabeth Gaskell's *Sylvia's Lovers* (1863). The reviewer of *The Spectator* would have applauded, too, a work such as the 1845–8 edition of the Stricklands' *Lives of the Queens of England*, where 'portraits of historical personages' were carefully selected to be 'valuable and interesting'.[11]

   This theory of the relationship of text and image is defined by Roland Barthes as the traditional view of illustration, one in which 'the image functioned as an episodic return to denotation from a principal message (the text) which was experienced as connoted since, precisely, it needed an illustration'.[12] This pattern has been, according to Barthes, reversed in the case of the newspaper photograph of today, where the text is essentially the illustration, interpreting the photograph and directing the audience's reception of the image. In fact, the use of the text as 'illustration' of an image is apparent in many nineteenth-century illustrated works, despite the privileging of the text proposed by contemporary critics: one example, found in the field of fiction, is a obscure novel by W. H. Ainsworth entitled *Boscobel* (1872), where the images were prior to the

---

   [8] W. J. Linton (1812–98) was a well-known artist and engraver, socialist, and poet. He was a friend of many famous figures, such as Thackeray, W. S. Bell, and John Leech. He worked on many important periodicals like *The Illustrated London News*, and engraved many illustrations, including those of Leighton for George Eliot's *Romola*. He wrote several manuals on wood-engraving (Engen, *Wood-Engravers*, 161–4).
   [9] [W. J. Linton], 'Illustrative Art', *WR* 51 (1849), 92.
   [10] [Anon.], 'Illustrated Gift-Books', *The Spectator*, 30 (1857), 1245.
   [11] See Ch. 6.   [12] Barthes, 'Image', 25.

novel, and were its greatest inspiration.[13] A more flexible approach to the illustrated text than that adopted by nineteenth-century commentators is required in
a work such as this, which considers a wide range of publications, many of which
rarely receive attention in traditional studies of Victorian illustration.

Clearly, it is best for the writer on text and image to consider, with equal
attention, the effect that each medium can produce upon the other, the relationship between the two being both complex and variable. As one recent commentator, W. J. T. Mitchell, puts it: 'The dialectic of word and image seems to be a
constant in the fabric of signs which a culture weaves around itself. What varies
the precise nature of the weave, the relationship of warp and woof.'[14] Mitchell
presents the history of culture as a 'protracted struggle for dominance between
pictorial and linguistic signs', in which each attempts to claim and to privilege
a certain 'nature' to which it alone has access. However, both are equally con-
ditioned by the other and, despite separate conventions, relate to the other in
a complex relationship of 'mutual translation, interpretation, illustration and
embellishment'.[15] Hillis Miller arrives at similar conclusions, describing the
tortured competition of word and image and their many 'skirmishes', and asking
if they are not 'different forms of the same thing, as blue and red are both light?'.
Rather than attempting to evolve a rigid theory of the relationship of text and
image which prioritizes one or the other, he concludes that 'vigilant and detailed
rhetorical reading' of each mixed-media example offers the best approach.[16]

Certainly such an open-ended approach is illuminating in the area of the
nineteenth-century illustrated text: texts and images appeared in a bewildering
variety of combinations. Many an illustration, for example, appeared with a text
which was not that for which it was originally intended (if, indeed, it was originally drawn as an illustration for any text). An extreme case of this phenomenon
can be found in the 1848 Virtue edition of David Hume's *History of England*,
where a plate which appeared with the caption 'King James Discovering the
Gunpowder Plot', had clearly appeared originally as Henry VIII protecting
Cranmer.[17] Equally, many texts which were not originally illustrated appeared
later with illustrations, while texts which were originally illustrated later appeared
with different illustrations—Hume's *History of England* and Mrs Markham's
History of England (1823) are examples of each of these manifestations.[18] Such
illustrations were like Barthes's press photograph: despite their apparently objective and fixed nature, the message can be altered by the texts around it and the
audience to whom it is addressed.[19] In the field of the Victorian popular press,
work by Patricia Anderson on Charles Knight's *The Penny Magazine* (1832-45)
demonstrates how the mass circulation of images—particularly apparent in the
works of this keen exploiter of illustrations—affected their appearance and

---

[13] See Ch. 10.
[14] W. J. T. Mitchell, *Iconology: Image, Text, and Ideology* (Chicago and London, 1986), 43.
[15] Ibid. 43-4.   [16] Miller, *Illustration*, 73-5, 151.   [17] See Ch. 2.
[18] See Chs. 2 and 3.   [19] Barthes, 'Image', 15-16.

meaning.[20] In fact, we could conclude that both theories of illustration discussed by Barthes are vital to an understanding of nineteenth-century text and image, despite the formal definitions of Victorian theorists. They are, however, representative of two opposing extremes: the relationship of text and image, and the interplay of meaning between them, is often very subtle, and thus the question of priority, in terms of ideological content and influence, is sometimes difficult to establish.

TEXT AND IMAGE: HISTORY, FACT, AND FICTION

The limitations of traditional studies of illustration can be attributed in part to the tendency of their authors to focus largely on high-quality works of fiction. This book, accordingly, examines three basic forms of illustrated text—history books, history textbooks, and historical fiction—in order to combat the tendency of many scholars to consider these categories of literature in isolation from each other. Concentration on the illustrations of fictional works by earlier writers has resulted in a variety of mistaken impressions: one is that one type of image—that which presents a parallel version of an event or moment within the text—was entirely dominant in the nineteenth-century illustrated text. Another type of image, however, was equally prevalent: photographs of places, events, or people, or copies of portraits, views of sites, or historical artefacts—in other words, supplementary images which claim to be authentic in some way.

At present, these two types of illustrations are generally restricted to particular genres of text, the first appearing in historical stories and novels, while the second appears in non-fiction works of history. In the mid-Victorian period, however, both sorts of illustrations appeared in both types of text—a clear indication of the lack of division between fiction and non-fiction at this period. The 1848 Virtue edition of Hume's *History of England*, for example, carried imaginary reconstructions of anecdotal scenes, such as Alfred burning the cakes, as well as views of historic sites and pictures of tombs, which were intended to be more objectively informative.[21] Ainsworth's *The Tower of London* (1840) was illustrated by Cruikshank with views of parts of the Tower as they were in 1840, as well as with scenes from the novel.[22] Stephen Bann, examining illustrations to the works of French historians such as Michelet, classified these two types of illustrations as 'metaphoric' (the imaginary reconstructions) and 'metanymic' (the copies of portraits, views, etc.), according to the way in which they relate to the text: while metaphoric illustrations offer a comparative version of the text, the metanymic illustrations select a part of the text in order to represent it—a character who appears in the text, or a place.[23] This theoretical distinction, derived from examination of the nineteenth-century illustrated book, is clearly a useful one for this

[20] P. Anderson, *The Printed Image and the Transformation of Popular Culture, 1790–1860* (Oxford, 1991), 50–83.
[21] See Ch. 2.   [22] See Ch. 4.
[23] S. Bann, *The Clothing of Clio* (Cambridge, 1984), 43–7.

study, and will be frequently used as shorthand to describe these two types of illustration.

However, when considering the two different types of illustrations, it is as well not to suggest too great a contrast between them. Metaphoric illustration in the nineteenth century grew increasingly more 'authentic' in the manner of metanymic illustration, by incorporation of elements from portraits, costume books compiled from manuscripts, and genuine views of buildings as they were either then or in the past: Cruikshank's plates to Ainsworth's novels and James Doyle's to the 1855 edition of John Lingard's *History of England* are excellent examples of this tendency.[24] This tendency is described by Roland Barthes as the 'reality effect': the employment of minor descriptive details into a realistic fiction or an 'objective' historical narrative, which serve no rhetorical or narrative purpose, but which create a sense of a concrete reality under description (or as Barthes puts it, a 'referential illusion').[25] Equally, it is wise not to accept uncritically the claims of authenticity offered by metanymic illustrations, which had all the apparent objectivity of photographs and just as much, or even more, subjective conditioning, both in their creation and their publication. Identifications of portraits were often mistaken, with regard both to sitters and painters, and views of historic sites were frequently executed as picturesque landscapes, rather than objective and accurate records. It is easy to overlook small but significant 'improvements' made to metanymic illustrations, such as those to Joseph Strutt's plates when they were reproduced in Mrs Markham's *History of England* (1823).[26]

AUTHOR AND ILLUSTRATOR

In the study of nineteenth-century illustrated books, the circumstances of publication should not be neglected. Such variables as the relationships of author, illustrator (and engraver), and publisher, the capacities of the media used, and the audience for which a work was intended all contributed to the formation of an illustrated text. The relationship between the author and the illustrator—if, indeed, there was one—could range from the most profound sympathy to the most acrimonious disagreement. Hostility, rivalry, or lack of communication often existed between author and illustrator. Authors were often fearful that an illustrator would not be able to reproduce the images of their minds in any recognizable form: Richard Westall, the illustrator of Scott's *The Lay*, wrote to the author to say that his rich and minute descriptions made the writer himself a painter and thus 'more difficult to paint from, as you have embodied your own

[24] See Chs. 4 and 7.

[25] R. Barthes, 'The Reality Effect', in Tzetan Todorov (ed.), *French Literary Theory Today: A Reader*, trans R. Carter (Cambridge, 1982), 11–17.

[26] Joseph Strutt was trained as a wood-engraver and he devoted his life to antiquarian and literary researches. He also exhibited paintings in the Royal Academy. See *DNB* lv. 65–7, and also Ch. 3 below.

ideas and presented them to the mind so completely that little is left for the pencil to perform'.[27] Writers could resent the superior wages earned by the illustrator of their work: Charles Reade, in the case of *A Good Fight* (1859), complained that he was paid less than Charles Keene, who illustrated this short novel.[28] In some cases, the illustrator's work was the more important element of a book: Scott asked Turner to produce the illustrations to *The Provincial Antiquities of Scotland*, but Turner was clearly the important partner here, as both Scott and subscribers to the work recognized.[29] *The Pickwick Papers* was originally viewed as a vehicle for the work of the illustrator, Robert Seymour, rather than that of the author, Dickens.[30] Within this book, there is the example of the pre-existent images of Ainsworth's novel, *Boscobel*, already mentioned.

Superior talent in an illustrator was not always a benefit, and an artist of more moderate abilities might well be an ideal collaborator—Hablot K. Browne, illustrator to both Dickens and Ainsworth, is perhaps an example. Changes in trends in illustration could disadvantage an author: Dickens deserted Browne in the 1850s, but the 'Sixties style' of his later illustrators, who chose what seemed to him tame and undramatic subjects, was often unsatisfactory.[31] However, there were many fruitful collaborations: those of Ainsworth and his illustrators are examined here. The extent, and the limits, of Ainsworth's collaboration with George Cruikshank were evidenced by the eventual controversy of the two over the true 'authorship' of works such as *The Miser's Daughter* (1842): the joint efforts of the partners made it difficult to pinpoint the originator of several parts of this and other works.[32] A perfect collaboration, however, could only realistically be expected in the case of a writer-illustrator such as Thackeray: Thackeray's illustrations are considerably more integrated with his text than most illustrations were in other works.[33] Even so, Thackeray sometimes felt that his visual realizations fell short of his conception because of his limited artistic ability.[34] While some mid-century collaborations were occasionally very close, in general (and certainly later in the nineteenth century), relationships between author and illustrator were probably more relaxed, reasonably amicable, workaday arrangements,

[27] S. Pantazzi, 'Author and Illustrator: Images in Conflict', *VPN* 9 (1976), 42. R. Westall to W. Scott, 5 Aug. 1805.

[28] Pantazzi, 'Author and Illustrator', 44.

[29] G. Finlay, *Landscapes of Memory: Turner as Illustrator to Scott* (1980), 49–68.

[30] J. R. Cohen, *Charles Dickens and his Original Illustrators* (Columbus, Ohio, 1980), 37–50. This was not a happy arrangement for Dickens, as he was autocratic towards his illustrators, nor for the illustrator, who committed suicide while working on this novel.

[31] J. R. Harvey, *Victorian Novelists and their Illustrators* (1970), 164–6. Harvey claims that, after realizing that Marcus Stone would not collaborate with him in the same way as Browne did, Dickens lost interest in illustration.

[32] See Ch. 4.

[33] See C. Coates, 'Thackeray's Editors and the Dual Text of Vanity Fair', *Word and Image*, 9 (1993), 39–50. Coates argues that the illustrations almost create a narrative of their own, which 'augments, advances, divides and disrupts the written text' (p. 43).

[34] See P. K. Sweeney, 'Thackeray's Best Illustrator', in P. L. Shillingsburg (ed.), *Costerus: Essays in English and American Literature: Thackeray* (Amsterdam and Columbia, SC, 1974), 83–112.

not unlike that of Anthony Trollope and John Millais: here the text was written first and some subjects were suggested by Trollope, but Millais—as the better known of the two at the start of the association—enjoyed a fairly free hand. With an artistic style basically in sympathy with Trollope's serious presentation of everyday life, his designs were sometimes hasty but generally conscientious, with the occasional failure to realize the author's comic characters.[35]

These examples are all concerned with metaphoric illustrations—representations of imaginary or imagined events and persons from the texts. However, many illustrations were straightforward reproductions of apparently authentic images: that is, of artefacts contemporary with the period discussed, and originally produced by another artist or craftsman—for instance, a portrait or an effigy from a tomb. In the case of images such as these, of which the artist was a mere copyist, the writer often had the predominant role in the selection of illustrations. One of the Strickland sisters, authors of *The Lives of the Queens of England*, recorded, in a letter to Thomas Phillipps, that they had 'superintended the copying of a beautiful portrait of Mary of Modena—the artist came last night to take directions'.[36] Many of the illustrations for their works were contemporary portraits which seem to have been located by the sisters themselves, on visits to country houses.[37] Elizabeth Penrose, who wrote under the name of 'Mrs Markham', almost certainly decided that the illustrations for her famous textbook, *A History of England* (1823), should derive from the works of the antiquary Strutt, who was the author of well-known works such as *A Complete View of the Dress and Habits of the People of England* (1796). The references to particular illustrations within the text confirm this impression.[38]

However, many illustrated works contained illustrations and/or text which were already extant before their appearance together in a particular work or which were produced for that work, but in isolation, without contact with the author and/or illustrator, possibly because s/he was dead. These works—which include here, for instance, editions of David Hume's *History of England*—are usually given little or no attention by writers on text and image, although they constitute a large part of the illustrated books published in the nineteenth century. In such cases as these, the link between text and image was generally provided by the publisher.

PUBLISHER, AUTHOR, AND ARTIST

The publisher has frequently been neglected in the study of the nineteenth-century production of illustrated books. In fact, it is only recently that literary scholars such as J. A. Sutherland, have begun to explore more systematically the

---

[35] M. Mason, 'The Way We Look Now: Millais's Illustrations to Trollope', *Art History*, 1 (1978), 309–40.

[36] Oxford, Bodleian Library: Phillipps-Robinson MSS, d. 128, fo. 220ᵛ. E. Strickland to T. Phillipps, 12 Sept. 1840.

[37] See Ch. 6.   [38] See Ch. 3.

relationship of author and publisher: his *Victorian Novelists and Publishers* (1976) is a pioneer work on the influence of publishers and their practices on Victorian fiction. There is no standard work which explores that of illustrator and publisher, although recent works on nineteenth-century illustration are beginning to show more interest in the publishing context of illustrated books.[39] It has been possible here to examine some of the sources which present themselves for further study of this collaborative triangle. It is hoped that some light is shed on the process by which the work of writers and illustrators, famous and otherwise, appeared in conjunction at publication.

Once again, the relationships were varied. Clearly, however, the influence of the publisher was in direct proportion to the insignificance of the author and illustrator. There is no need to concern oneself with the influence of the publisher of Ainsworth's *The Tower of London* (1840), for instance: the author was a best-seller at the time (and a shrewd editor of periodicals who understood the publishing world), while the illustrator was the best-known illustrator of the decade, George Cruikshank. The whole enterprise was managed by the two, who employed the publisher, Bentley, on commission.[40] This was, however, a very rare occurrence indeed. A less successful, though still important writer, Charlotte Yonge, had a friendly and co-operative association with her publisher, Alexander Macmillan, in which Yonge felt free to suggest illustrators for her work, and subjects for illustrations, which her judicious publisher sometimes accepted, but sometimes not. He ignored her suggestions for illustrations for her historical novel, *The Dove in the Eagle's Nest* (1866), for instance.[41] Obviously, in this relationship the publisher was paramount, though sympathetic. By contrast, the Strickland sisters had many problems with one of their publishers, Henry Colburn, and he succeeded in defrauding them quite substantially.[42] Tracing the relationship of author and publisher is often difficult, unless letters remain, as the memoirs of nineteenth-century publishers are usually bland, self-laudatory, and unlikely to include either the details of publications, or references to less successful ventures.

The relationship of publisher and illustrator is still more difficult to trace. Occasionally, an unexpected *aperçu* gives the reader some sense of the likely balance of power. The Dalziel brothers, who ran the leading wood-engraving firm of the 1860s, mention William Harvey, one of the most important illustrators of the 1840s:

As an illustrator he held the town for many years, and . . . did much to popularise black and white work; but even in his own time what changes took place! He said that in his early days if merely a frontispiece were wanted for a book, John Murray [the publisher]

---

[39] P. Goldman, *Victorian Illustrated Books, 1850–1870: The Heyday of Wood-Engraving* (1994); D. Wootton, with L. Coleman and A. Horne, *The Illustrators: The British Art of Illustration 1780–1996* (1997).

[40] See Ch. 4.   [41] See Ch. 9.

[42] See Ch. 6, and J. Sutherland, 'Henry Colburn, Publisher', *PH* 19 (1986), 59–84.

would invite him and John Thomson, the engraver, to dinner at Albemarle Street that they may discuss the subject fully . . .[43]

This suggests that the publisher often had considerable, perhaps decisive, influence with regard to most illustrations, even when the illustrator was quite an important figure. It also suggests that in the later part of the century, popular (and therefore, publishers') interest in illustrations declined, and the illustrator was left to his own discretion more often. Certainly, a publisher of the 1840s such as Charles Knight, with an enthusiasm for images, appeared to exercise considerable influence over illustrations for his pioneering works, such as *Old England: A Pictorial Museum* (1844). Knight collected around him a circle of wood-engravers, such as John Jackson, Stephen Sly, the Whympers, Ebenezer Landells, and Edmund Evans, who drew and/or engraved historic sites and monuments on his instructions.[44] These illustrations were subsequently at Knight's full disposal, and he reused them in other works as seemed appropriate.

Knight was not unusual in this respect. The considerable power over illustrations which was frequently enjoyed by publishers could, in certain instances, extend to the text. If author and/or artist were dead, or the work out of copyright,[45] the publisher was able to manipulate and transform a work as he chose. Hume's *History of England*, for instance, as the next chapter will show, appeared in numerous different forms in the nineteenth century, with different illustrations and often much changed text. Despite copyright—perhaps in defiance of copyright—publishers often seem to have done almost exactly as they chose. Mrs Markham's *The History of England* (1823) seems to have very much at the mercy of its owner, John Murray. It was purchased, apparently on a half-profit basis, from Elizabeth Penrose; after her death, Murray published it several times, sometimes in a revised form and with different illustrations, and, when copyright lapsed in 1865,[46] so did T. J. Allman, a rival publisher. Illustrations were,

---

[43] E. and G. Dalziel, *The Brothers Dalziel: A Record of Fifty Years' Work* (1901), 15.

[44] See Ch. 4. See also Engen, *Wood-Engravers*, 46, 133–4, 239–40, 284–6, 149–50, 81–4, for short biographies of Knight and these artists, and lists of their work.

[45] An excellent contemporary summary of 19th-cent. publishing practices is to be found in S. S. Sprigge, *The Methods of Publishing* (1890): it deals clearly with different methods of publication, such as half-profit and royalties systems. Useful introductions to the law of copyright in this period are: I. Parsons, 'Copyright and Society', in A. Briggs (ed.), *Essays on the History of Publishing* (1974), 31–60; J. Feather, 'Publishers and Politicians: The Remaking of the Law of Copyright in Britain, 1775–1842: Part I: Legal Deposition and the Battle of the Literary Tax', *PH* 24 (1988), 49–76, and 'Publishers and Politicians: The Remaking of the Law of Copyright in Britain, 1775–1842: Part II: The Rights of Authors', *PH* 25 (1989), 45–72. During the period concerned, basic copyright extended for 28 years after publication, or until the author's death, whichever was the longer period; in 1842, it was changed to 42 years after publication, or 7 years after the author's death, whichever was the longer.

[46] Elizabeth Penrose died in 1837, but copyright apparently ran for 42 years from publication. The half-profit agreement can be deduced from her husband's letters to Murray: he managed the publication of her works and acknowledged the receipt of cheques before and after her death. See, for examples, London, John Murray Archives: Penrose MSS, J. Penrose to J. Murray, 31 July 1829, 24 Nov. 1834, in which letters he acknowledges receipt of £89. 4s. 5d. and £93 respectively.

however, more in the power of the publisher than texts. It seems very likely that
publishers held a stock of images initially produced for a particular publication,
but which were used in later, and sometimes very different, ones. Both textbook
histories and Hume's *History of England* frequently contained George Vertue's
portraits of monarchs, initially produced for Paul de Rapin-Thoyras's *History of
England* (1726-31).[47] Anne Manning, a historical novelist who published *The
Cottage History of England* (1861), a textbook history, announced in her preface
that the illustrations had 'done good service already, and it is only on that account
that such very excellent ones can be afforded to so cheap a work'.[48] They had
already appeared in Anne Rodwell's *A Child's First Step to English History*
(1844).[49] Since the publishers of this work were Harvey and Darton, and those of
Manning's work, Hall, Virtue and Co., it seems probable, too, that illustrations
were passed around between publishers, or bought up from bankrupt publishing
houses.[50]

PRINTING AND THE PUBLIC

Finally, the writer on text and image must not ignore two other important
influences on the publication of illustrated books: these are the printing methods
of the nineteenth century, and the public for which a work was intended.
Improvements in the mechanics of printing made possible the publication of a
vast quantity of literature, of all kinds and in all forms.[51] It is obvious, too, that the
development of methods for the cheap and rapid reproduction of images, such as
wood-engraving, lithography, and steel-engraving—and, later, photography
and related media—vastly increased the number of illustrations which appeared
in works of all kinds.[52] It also highlighted perennial problems concerning the

---

[47] See Chs. 2 and 3.

[48] A. Manning, *The Cottage History of England* (1861), p. iv.   [49] See Ch. 3.

[50] Publishing houses were not remarkable for longevity in the 19th cent.: amalgamations were
frequent, and bankruptcies a regular occurrence. See B. Warrington, 'The Bankruptcy of William
Pickering in 1853: The Hazards of Publishing and Bookselling in the First Half of the Nineteenth
Century', *PH* 27 (1990), 5–25, for an example of the problems faced by publishing houses.

[51] Much work has been done on the manner of publication of works in the Victorian period,
particularly the effect of part publication and serial publication on fiction. A good recent work is
L. K. Hughes and M. Lund, *The Victorian Serial* (Charlottesville, Va., and London, 1991). Most of
the fictional works examined here have been considered in their book form—for instance, as a one-
or three-volumed novel. Book design, another area in which this author has not strayed, can be
approached through R. McLean, *Victorian Book Design and Colour Printing* (1963; 1972 edn.) and
M. Sadleir 'Aspects of the Victorian Novel' (1937), *PH* 5 (1979), 7–47.

[52] Useful works here include G. Wakeman, *Victorian Book Illustration: The Technical
Revolution* (Newton Abbot, 1973); M. Twymman, *Lithography 1800–1850* (Oxford, 1970);
B. Hunnisett, *Steel-Engraved Book Illustration in England* (1980); W. Chatto and J. Jackson,
A Treatise of Wood-Engraving, Historical and Practical (1839); E. M. Harris, 'Experimental
Graphic Processes in England, 1800–1859', *JPS* 4 (1968), 33–86, *JPS* 5 (1969), 41–72, and *JPS* 6
(1970), 55–89; and Allen Staley et al., *The Post Pre-Raphaelite Print: Etching, Illustration,*

translation of the original design for an illustration into the medium used for its reproduction: what effect does the choice of medium have on an image, and how does the intervention of the engraver or lithographer affect an artist's original design (assuming there is one)?[53]

This book will not dwell on these aspects of the production of illustrated books, unless they are particularly relevant. But it is important when examining the relationship of text and image, to be aware of such matters as the difference between intaglio and relief methods of engraving: the latter method, which is the one employed by wood-engraving, allows the text and image to be printed on the same page, thus encouraging a very close correspondence of text and image. Just how sophisticated an illustrated work using wood-engraving could become is apparent in the illustrations to some of Dickens's, Ainsworth's, and Thackeray's novels.[54] On the other hand, wood-engraving is not a medium in which delicate details can be very satisfactorily rendered, while steel-engraving—which offers more precision—can appear very hard. The potentialities and drawbacks of various media influenced, no doubt, the illustrations of the period. Illustrators could be surprised and even distressed by the appearance of their designs in their final form: Frederic Leighton, for instance, complained about the engraving of several of his illustrations for *Romola* by Joseph Swain,[55] and Thackeray experimented with a number of reproductive media to try and achieve the effect he desired.[56]

Assessing the influence of the reading public on a work is extremely difficult, particularly when it is a relatively low-profile publication: the reception given to a work is often unknown. Literary criticism has centred much attention on the polyvalent nature of texts, questioning whether authorial interpretations ought to be considered as more than one among many other interpretations, and concentrating interest on the reader's response. More recently, these considerations have also influenced interpretations of images. The debate on the nature of denotation and connotation of images among critics such as Barthes and Bryson, for instance, has alerted the student of images to the importance of the cultural

Reproductive Engraving, and Photography in England in and around the 1860s (New York, 1995). Lists of 19th-cent. artists and engravers can be found in C. Wood, *The Dictionary of Victorian Painters* (Woodbridge, 1978); R. Engen, *A Dictionary of Victorian Engravers* (Cambridge and Teaneck, NJ, 1979); R. Engen, *A Dictionary of Victorian Wood Engravers* (Cambridge and Teaneck, NJ, 1985); J. Buchanan-Brown, 'British Wood-Engravers, c.1820–1860: A Checklist', *JPS* 17 (1982/3), 31–61.

[53] S. Lambert, *The Image Multiplied: Five Centuries of Printed Reproductions of Paintings and Drawings* (1987), offers a good introduction to some of these issues, within the context of the print trade.

[54] See J. Stevens, ' "Woodcuts Dropped into the Text": The Illustrations in *A Tale of Two Cities* and *Barnaby Rudge*', *Studies in Bibliography*, 20 (1967), 113–33; Chs. 4 and 8 below; J. Stevens, 'Thackeray's Capitals', in Shillingsburg, *Thackeray*, 113–40.

[55] *Frederic Leighton 1830–1896* (New York, 1996), 130.

[56] N. Pickwood, 'Thackeray and his Book Illustrations' (D. Phil. thesis, Oxford, 1978), 2 vols., i. 23–5, 37, 46–9, 52–3.

milieu of the audience and the extent to which this influences interpretations of the image.[57] Clearly the intended meaning of a text or image is not the only message that might be received from it, as the audience's own cultural, social and personal concerns will influence their interpretation, giving rise to secondary meanings. The difficulty of communicating the full and intended message of a text or image to the public, however willing they may be to understand it, should not be forgotten. This should encourage the modern writer on text and image to pay equal attention both to the intentions of authors and illustrators, *and* to the response of the audience: this, where possible, is the aim of this study. The responses of critics and readers, when attainable, have frequently been examined: they could be most influential. In the case of later historical novels, for instance, critical opinion encouraged the decline of the picturesque historical novel of the 1830s and 1840s.[58] The vast majority of the works considered are those which, it is postulated, might well have reached an average middle-class home, either as purchases, library loans, or the contents of periodicals:[59] this is the audience which would have shaped these works. It seems likely, however, that the gap between writers and artists and the audience was not unduly wide in the nineteenth century. The illustrated works examined here were probably reasonably well understood by their intended middle-class audience. This was, after all, an age which found its main amusement in its reading matter, and discussion and analysis of books was a popular activity.[60]

However, if it is difficult to assess the response of the public to a work, it is easier to estimate the effects of decisions to orientate a work towards a particular section of the reading public. This decision could be made by an author, or by a publisher. The decision to orientate a non-fictional work towards the juvenile market, for instance, could be the primary influence in favour of including illustrations; equally, if the intended audience was an adult one, illustrations could be more easily dispensed with. Despite the rage for illustration in the nineteenth century, many publications, especially 'serious' multi-volumed works

[57]   See R. Barthes, 'The Rhetoric of the Image' (1964), in *Image–Music–Text*, trans. S. Heath (1977), 32–51, and N. Bryson, *Vision and Painting: The Logic of the Gaze* (1983), 60–2, for their opposing interpretations of denotation and connotation.

[58]   See Chs. 9 and 10.

[59]   Good introductions to the reading publics of the mid-19th cent. and their reading matter can be found in R. D. Altick, *Writers, Readers and Occasions: Selected Essays on Victorian Literature and Life* (Columbus, Ohio, 1989), 141–73. The standard works on the reading public of the period are Q. D. Leavis, *Fiction and the Reading Public* (1932) and R. D. Altick, *The English Common Reader: A Social History of the Mass Reading Public 1800–1900* (Chicago, 1957). Important works on the lower class reading public and its fiction are M. Dalziel, *Popular Fiction one Hundred Years ago: An Unexplored Tract of Literary History* (1957) and L. James, *Fiction for the Working Man, 1830–50: A Study of the Literature produced for the Working Classes in Early Victorian England* (1963).

[60]   Note, however, M. Steig, 'The Critic and the Illustrated Novel: Mr Turveydrop from Gillray to *Bleak House*', *The Huntingdon Library Quarterly*, 36 (1972–3), 55–67, where he argues that sophisticated allusions in Dickens's illustrated novels might have escaped the contemporary audience.

such as histories of England, did not carry illustrations: Sharon Turner's *The History of the Anglo-Saxons* (1799–1805) appeared without illustrations in the original, and in the 1807 and 1840 editions. John Lingard's *History of England* (1819–30) only appeared twice before 1860 with illustrations.[61] Even the popular *History of England* (1849–55) by Macaulay, who had earlier argued that a historian should 'paint with skill', illustrating changes in manners with 'appropriate images', appeared unillustrated in the first, the 1864, and the 1867 editions.[62] It took a strong combination of tradition, easily available illustrations intended for the work, absence of authorial control, and, most importantly, a strong readership among young people, to encourage the inclusion of illustrations in Hume's *History of England*.[63] In the case of later historical novels, it is clear that the tendency to orientate many works—even ones originally intended for an adult market—towards children, led to the inclusion of illustrations.[64] Often the decisions made by a shrewd publisher on the manner of republication of a work are the best clue to its initial reception or its present status. This hypothesis is aptly tested in Chapter 2 of this book.

[61] See Ch. 7.

[62] T. B Macaulay, 'History' (1828), in *Miscellaneous Essays and the Lays of Ancient Rome* (1926), 36–9.

[63] See Ch. 2.   [64] See Ch. 9.

2

The History of *The History of England*: The Evolution of a Standard Text and its Illustrations

'It is Hume who is read by everybody, Hume is the historian, whose views and opinions insensibly become our own':[1] here William Smyth, professor of modern history at Cambridge, rightly identified the most influential work of history in early nineteenth-century Britain. David Hume's *History of England* (1754–62) went through numerous editions in the course of the century, and it was also one of the few multi-volumed histories to be almost always illustrated. As such, it forms an ideal introduction to perceptions of national history in text and image in nineteenth-century Britain: the evolution of historiography through philosophical, picturesque, and scientific phases can be traced through changes to its text and images.

At first glance, however, the *History of England* was an unlikely candidate to be the standard national narrative of the early and mid-nineteenth century: for a start, its author was not an Englishman but a Scot. But Hume, like many of his contemporaries in the Scottish Enlightenment, was anxious to further the interests of his country through the Union of 1707 and full Scottish participation in a modernized Great Britain: he was one of those Scottish historians who abandoned the historiographical traditions of Scotland to write the history of her more progressive neighbour.[2] This decision was all the easier because Hume was a philosopher, influenced by the cosmopolitan spirit of the Enlightenment and sceptical of religious and national shibboleths. This scepticism did not desert him when he wrote the *History of England*: the work of an atheist, and mistakenly perceived by many critics as Tory in bias, it was by no means an entirely appropriate embodiment and expression of a national historical narrative based on Protestantism and Whig progressivism.[3] At the turn of the century, however,

---

[1] W. Smyth, *Lectures on Modern History from the Irruption of the Northern Nations to the Close of the American Revolution*, 2 vols. (1840), i. 126.

[2] C. Kidd, *Subverting Scotland's Past* (Cambridge, 1993), 205–15.

[3] This long-lived identification of Hume's *History* as a Tory interpretation has frequently been exposed as an over-simplification of an essentially non-partisan and complex narrative. See

there was no other text covering so many centuries of English history and enjoying such prestige.[4] Moreover, the author of the *History* was dead, the work was out of copyright, and it had already been subject to continuations by authors other than Hume: the *History* was clearly open to adaptation. Accordingly, nineteenth-century editions of the work reveal the influence of publishers in shaping, and their concern in responding to, an evolving historical consciousness, and changing ideas of authenticity.

'HISTORY FOR THE MILLION'

In the 1930s David Hume's *History of England* was described by T. P. Peardon as 'for over a hundred years the most widely read and influential' of English histories.[5] The author of the most recent full-length study of Hume's historical works agrees, pointing out that in as many years after Hume's death in 1776, fifty editions of the *History* were published.[6] As the standard history of England in nineteenth-century Britain, Hume's work became increasingly the textbook for the older child and the young adult, as well as the reference work for the mature reader. When Richard, the son of the famous fictional textbook writer, Mrs Markham, becomes, at the age of 10 years, 'very inquisitive about the history of his country', it is to Hume that he turns (and, finding it too difficult, incites his mother to write her own version).[7] Francis Palgrave, the medieval historian and Deputy Keeper of the Public Records from 1838, was a critic of Hume's *History*: he nevertheless recognized it as the 'History for the Million', 'the standard work'.[8] He acknowledged that it was the fundamental source for all early nineteenth-century history textbooks: 'All who, since Hume, have earned any commanding reputation, are more or less his disciples; and all our juvenile and educational histories and conversations, and outlines, are, in the main, composed out of Hume's material . . .'[9] Palgrave pointed to Mrs Markham's *History of England*

V. G. Wexler, *David Hume and the History of England* (Philadelphia, 1979), 49–54, 93–6; E. C. Mossner, 'Was Hume a Tory Historian? Facts and Reconsiderations' and M. Grene, 'Hume: Sceptic or Tory?', in D. Livingston and M. Martin, *Hume as Philosopher of Society, Politics and History* (Rochester, NY, and Woodbridge, 1991), 106–17 and 118–33. The *History* is superbly placed within the context of the early 18th-cent. Tory and Whig historiographical debate in D. Forbes, *Hume's Philosophical Politics* (Cambridge, 1975), 233–307.

   [4] For instance, Catherine Macaulay's *History of England* (1763–83)—a Whig rebuttal to Hume's *History*—covered only the 17th cent. and had, moreover, too many links to late 18th-cent. radical republicanism to figure as a safe standard history. See B. Hill, *The Republican Virago: The Life and Times of Catherine Macaulay, Historian* (Oxford, 1992) and B. B. Schnorrenberg, 'The Brood-Hen of Faction: Mrs Macaulay and Radical Politics, 1765–75', *Albion*, 11 (1979), 33–45.

   [5] T. P. Peardon, *The Transition in English Historical Writing 1760–1830* (New York, 1933), 19.

   [6] N. Phillipson, *Hume* (1989), 137.

   [7] E. Penrose ['Mrs Markham'], *A History of England from the First Invasion of the Romans to the End of the Reign of George IV* (1823; 1846 edn.), pp. vii–viii.

   [8] [F. Palgrave], 'Hume and his Influence upon History', *QR* 73 (1843), 537.   [9] Ibid. 541.

(1823) as 'the strongest case of the treacherous seductions of Hume', remarking that it was very clear that, on deciding to write the work, Mrs Markham had 'resorted at once to the historian whom she had been taught to consider as her philosopher and guide'.[10] William Smyth also recognized the fundamental role of Hume's *History* as an educational text; he remarked that 'Hume is the author who, from his conciseness, the charms of his style, and the weight of his philosophical observations, is always preferred, and is . . . universally and thoroughly read.'[11]

As the century advanced, however, the *History* was viewed less as a reliable history and more as a textbook, as a model of style, not of accuracy. Considering that, from the 1820s, criticism of Hume's *History* was rife in periodicals and contemporary works of history such as Henry Hallam's *The Constitutional History of England* (1823), it is perhaps surprising that it was still retained as *the* history of England for youth. Commentators with an axe of their own to grind suggested particular reasons: the Catholic critic of *The Dublin Review* of 1842 suggested that 'his style and his toryism' led Protestant schools and families to retain Hume's *History* as a textbook, although 'his credit as a historian was gone for ever'.[12] But the main reason was a more pragmatic one: no other multi-volumed history had attained, in the early nineteenth century, the unique importance that Hume's *History* had achieved in the late eighteenth century. Moreover, tradition was a strong influence in the choice (and the survival) of textbooks: a conservatism of a less political variety than that suspected by the critic of the *Dublin Review* was at work. When, in 1856, Charles Knight published the first volume of his *Popular History of England* he quoted a revealing comment made in a speech of 1854 by Lord John Russell, who—as a rampantly Protestant Whig—clearly found much to vex him in the *History* of Hume: 'We have no other *History of England* than Hume's. The cool, scoffing philosopher . . . still retains his place on our shelves and our tables . . . when a young man asks for a *History of England*, there is no resource but to give him Hume.'[13] Knight went on to state his own aim: to create a transitional national history 'between the school-history . . . and the library-history of Hume himself' for the young reader of about 17 years old[14]—a clear indication that, even then, the reign of Hume's *History* was not yet quite over.

Because of the importance of Hume's *History* as a textbook, it is not surprising that it was frequently illustrated. Many multi-volumed histories—such as, for instance, Sharon Turner's works and T. B. Macaulay's *History of England* (1849–55)—did not carry illustrations, but Hume's *History*, as a work frequently in the hands of youth, often did. There was, however, another obvious reason

[10] [F. Palgrave], 'Hume and his Influence upon History', *QR* 73 (1843), 591.

[11] Smyth, *Lectures*, i. 127.

[12] [P. McMahon], 'Dr Lingard's *History of England*', *The Dublin Review*, 12 (1842), 306–7.

[13] C. Knight, *The Popular History of England: An Illustrated History of Society and Government*, 8 vols. (1856–62), i, pp. i–ii.

[14] Ibid. i, p. ii.

why the *History* carried illustrations in the early part of the nineteenth century: there was already a sizeable number of illustrations specifically designed for it, or inspired by it. The Historic Gallery of Robert Bowyer in Pall Mall, inspired by John Boydell's Shakespeare Gallery, contained the paintings which, when engraved, formed the most important corpus of illustrations for Hume's *History*.[15]

However, these works were not the only resource upon which the nineteenth-century publisher could draw. Before Hume's *History* was even written, there existed the small beginnings of a native history-painting school, which was producing not only works portraying traditional classical subjects but also depictions of events from English history, both distant and more recent.[16] This 'revolution of history painting', as Edgar Wind described it, was related to a revived passion for patriotism.[17] A sense of pride in the national past was fostered, for instance, in William Kent's canvases for Queen Caroline, painted about 1730, which portrayed scenes of national triumphs from fourteenth- and fifteenth-century English history. These were followed by such works as Robert Edge Pine's *Earl Warren, Making Reply to the Writ Commonly Called Quo Warranto* (1771), John Hamilton Mortimer's *King John Delivering the Magna Carta to the Barons* (c.1776), and John Singleton Copley's *Charles I Demanding in the House of Commons the Five Impeached Members* (1782–95), which encapsulated moments from the Whig narrative of liberty and the rise of parliamentary government.[18]

Book illustrations to English history already existed in, for instance, the form of illustrations to the 1743–7 edition of Paul de Rapin-Thoyras's *History of England* (1726–31), an essentially Whig narrative displaced as the standard history of England by Hume's work. This publication was illustrated by Charles Grignion, Hubert François Gravelot, and (most importantly) the antiquary George Vertue, and contained a set of carefully researched portraits of monarchs essential to the illustration of later editions of Hume's *History* and many textbook histories. It also included early versions of subjects from English history which become stock choices for painters and illustrators alike—subjects such as *The Trial of the Marriage of Henry VIII*, which was painted by Robert Smirke for the Bowyer Gallery.[19] In addition, the publisher seeking illustrations for a

[15] R. Bowyer, *A Series of One Hundred and Ninety-One Engravings (in the Line Manner) by the First Artists in the Country Illustrative of 'The History of England'* (1812). I have considered these engravings to represent the contents of the Bowyer Gallery, though it seems possible that other paintings may have at least appeared briefly on the walls of the Gallery, which closed in 1806.

[16] See R. Strong, *And When Did You Last See Your Father? The Victorian Painter and British History* (1978), 14–29, 80–5 and P. Cannon-Brookes (ed.), *The Painted Word: British History Painting 1750–1830* (Woodbridge, 1991), 7–43, for much of the following.

[17] E. Wind, 'The Revolution of History Painting', in E. Wind, *Hume and the Heroic Portrait: Studies in Eighteenth-Century Imagery*, ed. J. Anderson (Oxford, 1986), 116–27.

[18] John Sunderland has explored J. H. Mortimer and R. E. Pine's links to radical anti-monarchical Whig politics in the 1760s and 1770s in 'Mortimer, Pine, and Some Political Aspects of English History Painting', *Burlington Magazine*, 116 (1974), 317–26.

[19] Strong, *Painter*, 14; Bowyer, *History*.

Fig. 1. After G. Vertue, engraved W. Ridley, *Edward III*, from
D. Hume (with T. Smollett and T. A. Lloyd), *The History of
England*, 12 vols. (1793–4), iii, facing 210

nineteenth-century edition of the *History* could look to other illustrated editions
of Hume besides that of Bowyer.[20] An important example was Charles Cooke's
illustrated edition of 1793–4, continued by Tobias Smollett and T. A. Lloyd and
'embellished with historical engravings and portraits of all the British Monarchs,
from William the Conqueror to his present Majesty George III. Habited in the
respective dresses of their time' (a claim hard to substantiate). This work contained the Vertue portraits (Fig. 1), engraved by W. Ridley, and an interesting
selection of illustrations of scenes from English history, such as *Rowena*

[20] T. S. R. Boase, 'Macklin and Bowyer', *JWCI* 26 (1963), 171–4.

Attending upon Vortigern by Thomas Stothard, a Bowyer stalwart, and *Edward, while Prince of Wales, Killing the Assassin who Attempted his Life* (Anon.).[21]

The publisher of Hume's *History* could also look to the sister project of the Historic Gallery (Boydell's Shakespeare Gallery) for paintings of scenes from the history plays.[22] He could also turn to other suitable paintings (including the historic canvases exhibited in the Vauxhall Gardens in the 1740s) which often appeared in other illustrated editions of the works of Shakespeare, whose status as a national and nationalist icon was confirmed in the late eighteenth century by the Shakespeare Jubilee celebration of 1769.[23] Eighteenth-century perceptions of history, at a mundane and anecdotal level, were still enormously influenced by Shakespeare's history plays, so that the use of these images would pose few problems. Boydell's Gallery included such works as *The Meeting of the Two Princes* and *The Smothering of the Princes in the Tower*, both scenes from Shakespeare's *Richard III*, painted by James Northcote.[24]

The Bowyer Gallery paintings were, nevertheless, the most important set of images of English history available at the close of the eighteenth century. As they were also archetypical of the English history-painting school, and of illustrations to history books of the period, they deserve some further consideration. The paintings of scenes from English history were commissioned for the 1793–1806 folio edition of Hume's *History*. The artists included James Northcote, Henry Fuseli, Richard Westall, Francis Wheatley, John Francis Rigaud, and Gavin Hamilton, among others. These works were all executed in the style which Roy Strong has termed 'Gothick-picturesque' (where a charming effect, rather than accuracy of historical detail, was the chief consideration), although some show slight signs of antiquarian research. They gave publishers of Hume in the early nineteenth century a sure set of illustrations.[25] The 1793 prospectus for the Gallery stated that the paintings were intended 'to rouse the passions, to fire the mind with emulation of heroic deeds, or to inspire it with detestation of criminal actions':[26] this was clearly a neo-classical view of history which linked the past to the present as the unproblematic source of moral exempla and edifying

---

[21] D. Hume (with T. Smollett and T. A. Lloyd), *The History of England*, 12 vols. (1754–62; 1793–4 edn.), i, title-page, facing 40, 226 (William I); ii, facing 285 (John); iii, facing 261. The Smollett continuation was used in all edns. which I examined, so it has been considered as if integral to the original text.

[22] A full-scale study of the publishing career of John Boydell is S. J. Bruntjen, *John Boydell, 1719–1804: A Study of Art Patronage and Publishing in Georgian London* (New York and London, 1985). Bruntjen rightly points to Boydell's crucial encouragement of an English school of history painting, and his attempt to 'integrate nationalistic themes with the neoclassical theory of history painting' (p. 244).

[23] T. S. R. Boase, 'Illustrations of Shakespeare's Plays in the Seventeenth and Eighteenth Centuries', *JWCI* 10 (1947), 83–108; R. D. Altick, *Paintings from Books* (Columbus, Ohio, 1985), 42–51. The relevant paintings from the Boydell Gallery can be found listed in [Anon.], *A Catalogue of the Pictures in the Shakespeare Gallery, Pall-Mall* (1810).

[24] *Shakespeare Catalogue*, 49–50, 51–2.

[25] Boase, 'Bowyer', 148–77; Strong, *Painter*, 16–29.   [26] Boase, 'Bowyer', 169.

Fig. 2. After T. Stothard, engraved J. Parker, *Queen Elizabeth at Tilbury*, from [R. Bowyer], *A Series of One Hundred and Ninety-One Engravings (in the Line Manner) by the First Artists in the Country Illustrative of 'The History of England'* (1812), plate 121

anecdotes. *The Surrender of Calais*, for instance, by Robert Smirke, combined an ideal of conjugal felicity with a lesson on the quality of mercy, while Thomas Stothard's *Queen Elizabeth at Tilbury* (Fig. 2) stimulated patriotic loyalty and courage, and Northcote's *Feckenham by the Order of the Queen Visits Lady Jane Grey in the Tower* promoted adherence to the Protestant faith.[27] The viewer of these works would surely have seen them as teaching public and private virtue in the same way as history paintings depicting scenes from Greek and Roman sources, to which they were sometimes blatantly related. The appearance of Henry Tresham's *The Resolute Conduct of the Earl of Warwick* exposed its proximity in theme and composition to neo-classical works: a almost naked and

[27] Bowyer, *History*, plates 53, 121, 107.

well-muscled earl seems to sacrifice a horse to the gods, casting an angry eye towards the sky.[28]

Such intentions on the part of Bowyer and the artists reflected the more sophisticated, but not dissimilar, aims of Hume himself, who viewed his philosophical reflections in the *History* as contributing to the education of the citizen. As Phillipson points out, he felt that 'history seemed particularly well suited to teaching morality in the modern age', by offering an arena for the exercise of an impartial and disinterested judgement of right and wrong.[29] On the basis of such opinions, Hume's approach to history has often been characterized as lacking any sense of historical relativism: Hume has been portrayed as a philosopher who believed in 'nothing new under the sun', holding that human nature remained basically the same from age to age and disdaining historical particularism.[30] While this description fails to take account of Hume's role in the Scottish Enlightenment, which produced pioneering sociological and economic perspectives on the evolution of societies, it is clear that, at least initially, Hume intended his study of the past to serve immediate political and polemical purposes and directed his research and writing accordingly.[31] Hume's *History of England* certainly does not exhibit the keen antiquarian appetite for any and all social and cultural details characteristic of the picturesque historian. And while the philosophical approach to history remained dominant, the paintings of Bowyer's Gallery would continue to provide an appealing set of illustrations. T. S. R. Boase comments on the poor grasp of historical costumes and setting exhibited by the artists, here pinpointing both the importance of the influence of the paintings and one of the reasons for their decline:

In the nineteenth century these illustrations did much to form the visual image of English history. They provided a corpus from which other illustrated histories freely borrowed. Their costumes and settings were, however, too fanciful for the new standards of historical accuracy that, stimulated by the revival of interest in the Middle Ages, began to be expected.[32]

The revision of Hume's text and the replacement of Bowyer's illustrations, and of other images conceived with the same aims and executed in the same manner,

---

[28] Bowyer, *History*, plate 75.   [29] Phillipson, *Hume* (1989), 77.

[30] D. H. Fischer, *Historians' Fallacies: Towards a Logic in Historical Thought* (1971), and J. B. Black, *A Study of Four Great Historians of the Eighteenth Century* (1926), both argue that Hume fell victim to the fallacy of the universal man; S. K. Wertz, 'Hume, History and Human Nature', in Livingston and Martin, *Hume*, 77–92, and Wexler, *Hume*, 105–7, oppose this argument.

[31] Leo Braudy has suggested, however, that Hume's non-party and philosophical programme increasingly disintegrated as the *History* progressed, leaving the historian with little more than chronology to structure his narrative when he embarked on the last (medieval) stage of his work. See L. Braudy, *Narrative Form in History and Fiction: Hume, Fielding and Gibbon* (Princeton, 1970), 31–90. This interpretation of Hume's experience of writing history suggests how philosophical historiography could precede and engender picturesque approaches.

[32] Boase, 'Bowyer', 171, 176.

thus signalled the decline of the historiographical imperatives implicit in Hume's original text and the Bowyer Gallery illustrations.

It would be misleading to imply that these scenes from English history were the only illustrations provided by Bowyer in his set of engravings. Significant though they are, Bowyer followed the tradition of earlier illustrated histories by including the inevitable Vertue portraits of English monarchs in, for instance, such a plate as *The Family of Tudor*, drawn by Ryley. These were supplemented by other collections of portraits, such as *Eighteenth Century Painters*, drawn by Smirke, who was the habitual composer of allegorical surrounds for such groups, and topographical plates, such as Thomas Hearne's *Castle-Acre Priory*. There were also numerous plates of coins, such as J. Landseer's *Coins of the Reign of Mary I*.[33] These illustrations, which were supplementary rather than complementary, related to the text in a way which can be described as metanymic rather than metaphoric. They show the influence of eighteenth-century antiquarian studies and county histories, exhibiting the characteristics of a nascent picturesque and Romantic historical sensibility which dwelt on the local, the individual, the particular. By their appearance in a popular history (albeit in an enormously expensive edition), they anticipated the new approach to illustration which was to predominate in early nineteenth-century Britain. The use of the Vertue portraits no doubt promoted their continuance as standard history and history textbook illustrations, while the interest in other authentic contemporary portraits continued the tradition of such ventures as *Richardson's Collection* (1792–1812), a selection of portraits chosen to complement James Granger's *Biographical History of England* (1769–74): this tradition thrived, in the early nineteenth century, in the form of works such as Edmund Lodge's *Portraits of Illustrious Personages of Great Britain* (1821–34).[34] In fact, by means of its dual status in the nineteenth century as both a gentleman's recreation and a standard school history, Hume's *History* may have aided the dissemination of the illustrations from antiquarian classics to those textbooks for the poorest, the ephemeral historical 'readers' of the late nineteenth century.

One class of illustrations which, however, did not survive the transition were the complex allegorical plates, such as Smirke's *Allegory of Lady Jane Grey*: here her portrait, and the elements of a lamb prepared for sacrifice, a knife, a smoking altar ornamented with a bas-relief of men bowing before a female idol, possibly representing the Virgin Mary, and thus the Catholic faith, and a pillar supporting a statue of Hercules (successful might? or Jane's choice between pleasure and the duty of queenship?), provide the basis for moral and philosophical reflection.[35] These plates clearly continued the tradition of seventeenth- and eighteenth-century allegorical history painting or even the more modest tradition of the emblem. It seems likely that such representations of history suffered severely from any movement away from the philosophical perception of history as

[33] Bowyer, *History*, plates 85, 187, 97, 104.   [34] Strong, *Painter*, 61.
[35] Bowyer, *History*, plate 105.

teaching by example, and were challenged by the demands of picturesque historiography, reliant on realistic representation, authentic detail, and historical realization.

'GRADUAL ADVANCEMENT'?: CONTINUITY AND CHANGE, 1834–1848

The examination here of nineteenth-century illustrated editions of Hume's *History* considers six editions: one published in 1834–6, one in 1838, two in 1848, one in 1859, and one in 1880. The Valpy[36] edition of 1834, with a continuation by T. S. Hughes,[37] is a classic example of early nineteenth-century attitudes to Hume's text and the standard illustrations of the Bowyer type. The text was unedited, and was accepted, largely uncritically, as an accurate and admirable history of England. Endorsing an Enlightenment agenda in rolling prose reminiscent of Hume's own rhetoric, the prospectus to the work announced that:

To trace with accuracy the gradual advancement of a country from primitive barbarism to a state of refinement in the arts and learning, is the grateful yet arduous task of the historian; and that this important task has been successfully accomplished by the labors [sic] of HUME and SMOLLETT, is sufficiently demonstrated by the high character which their Historical Works have long and deservedly maintained.[38]

The edition was illustrated by seventy-six steel-engravings, which were 'selected from the best authorities, comprising Portraits of the Sovereigns of England from the Norman Conquest to the present time, and a selection of Historical Illustrations from Bowyer's History of England, and from paintings of the most eminent masters, commemorative of important events in English History'.[39] The tendency of A. J. Valpy to rely on established and traditional illustrations is indicated by an attached advertisement, promoting the sale of an edition of Shakespeare's works, with 170 illustrations from the Boydell collection.[40] This impression is quickly confirmed: the portraits of the monarchs in the *History* prove to be the set produced by Vertue, which were reproduced in Bowyer's edition,[41] and the plates illustrating scenes from English history are frequently

---

[36] *DNB* lviii, 84–5. A. J. Valpy was a London editor and printer, who specialized in the publication of works considered as classics of English literature.

[37] *DNB* xxviii. 188–9. T. S. Hughes was a clergyman, historian, and religious writer, whose chief work was the continuation to this edn. of Hume's *History*.

[38] D. Hume (with T. Smollett and T. S. Hughes), *The History of England*, 21 vols. (1834–6), i, Prospectus, 1–2. In the 'Biographical Sketch of David Hume', merely as an addendum, Hume's 'partiality for the house of Stuart, and his laboured apologies for the acts of oppression and cruelty' which they had committed, as well as his lack of religion, were bemoaned, but the writer insisted on crediting him with 'laborious research and love of truth' which had raised him 'to the highest reputation as an historian'. Hume, *History* (1834–6), i, p. xii.

[39] Ibid. i, Prospectus, 3.   [40] Ibid. i, Prospectus, 4.

[41] e.g. Hume, *History* (1834–6), i, facing 222 (William Rufus); iii, facing 67 (Henry V). The inclusion of the Vertue portraits in Bowyer's edn. probably sealed their inclusion here. The engravers were a Mr Freeman and a Mr J. Rogers. The latter was a line and stipple engraver,

Fig. 3. After R. Smirke, *The Trial of the Marriage of Henry VIII*, from
D. Hume (with T. Smollett and T. S. Hughes), *The History of England*,
21 vols. (1834–6), iv, frontispiece

from the Bowyer illustrations, as in the case of *The Landing of Julius Caesar* (by
Burney), *The Trial of the Marriage of Henry VIII* (Fig. 3), and *The Martyrdom
of Cranmer* (both by Smirke).[42] Those which are not are nevertheless derived
from the same late eighteenth-century school of history painting—for instance,
Mortimer's *King John Delivering Magna Carta to the Barons* and Northcote's
The Death of Wat Tyler.[43]

primarily working on book illustrations, in particular, portraits: he engraved the illustrations for
Robert Chambers's *The Dictionary of Eminent Scotsmen* (1835), and portraits of Queen Victoria
and Prince Albert. Engen, *Dictionary*, 167–8.

[42] Hume, *History* (1834–6), i, frontispiece; iv, frontispiece and title-page; Bowyer, *History*,
plates 6, 92, 109.

[43] Hume, *History* (1834–6), ii, frontispiece; iii, frontispiece.

The 1838 edition, published by J. Rickerby, with a continuation and an essay on the study of history by Henry Stebbings,[44] also included an unedited text. Stebbings's essay, however, represented the beginnings of a genuine attempt by publishers of Hume's *History* to present the text critically. The essay advised a careful reading of authorities, with a consideration of their prejudices and bias.[45] The inclusion of Hume's autobiography (a rather mechanical feature in many editions) can thus be seen as affording an opportunity to the reader to understand Hume's character and failings before embarking upon his *History*.[46] Hume's authority as a historian could no longer outweigh his failings so easily. The modern reader may be perplexed by this method of approaching the problem of the increasingly unacceptable nature of the *History*, on the grounds both of his religious and political opinions and of his lack of research and poor critical methods. Why not replace the text with that of a contemporary historian of repute, rather than retain and revise a text which no longer met with approval? Many of the contemporary critics of Hume's *History*, however, commended the approach which this edition foreshadowed. In his *Lectures on Modern History*, William Smyth decided that no lecturer could serve English history better than 'by following Mr. Hume, step by step, . . . and showing what were his fair, and what his unfair inferences . . . what his mistakes, and . . . his omissions.[47] Palgrave's article on Hume's *History* included an imaginary conversation between two characters: while one argued that Hume's *History* was too full of fundamental misconceptions and mistakes for correction, the other suggested, with revealing pragmatism, that a competent reviser would have 'a far better chance of profit or fame by annexing their information to his pages, than through an independent production of their own'.[48] The reviewer of J. H. Burton's *Life and Correspondence of David Hume* agreed that 'Hume's History should not be our only history; or, at least, it should be accompanied by some copious and authoritative commentary, as a check.'[49] He added that it was a pity that 'no competent person' had been persuaded to prepare an edition of the *History* with 'this kind of commentary'.[50]

Clearly, the main disadvantage of this standard work, which needed correction, was the infidelity of the writer. This criticism had been levelled against Hume's *History* as soon as it was published: the increasing importance of a historiography in which national identity and Protestant Christianity were closely linked could only lead to further attack. The Protestant evangelical reformer and educationalist, Hannah More, in her *Hints Towards Forming the Character of a Young Princess* (1805), focused her objections to Hume's atheism on his treatment of the Protestant Reformation. After accusing him of including the

---

[44] *DNB* liv. 124–5. H. Stebbings was a poet, preacher, and historian, who did much work for *The Athenaeum*.

[45] D. Hume (with T. Smollett and H. Stebbings), *The History of England*, 10 vols. (1838), i, Introduction, pp. 20–3.

[46] Ibid. 55–64.   [47] Smyth, *Lectures*, i. 128.   [48] [Palgrave], 'Hume', 538.

[49] [W. Empson], 'J. H. Burton's *Life and Correspondence of David Hume*', *ER* 85 (1847), 19.

[50] Ibid. 40.

'injurious relations' of annalists hostile to the Reformation, she continued: 'He ascribes such a slender superiority to one religious system above another, that the young reader, who does not come to the perusal with his principles formed will be in danger of thinking that the reformation was really not worth contending for.'[51] She concluded that it was 'injurious to a young mind' to read an account of the Reformation by an author who did not see 'a divine power' accompanying it.[52]

This criticism of Hume intensified in the first half of the nineteenth century. Palgrave was among the critics who voiced their disapproval: ' "INFIDELITY FOR THE MILLION" is the heading for Hume's history . . . The first object of Hume is to nullify religion. All the workings of Providence in worldly affairs are denied, or blurred, when he cannot deny them.'[53] Palgrave claimed (not unfairly) that Hume had estimated the merit of a person or institution in proportion to the absence of Christianity, and gave an example of Hume's obscuring of religious matters by showing how he had, in his account of Charles I's death, omitted all the indications of the King's religious commitment which were present in his two sources, Whitlock and Herbert.[54] If the Anglican Palgrave was concerned by Hume's lack of religious faith, so too was the Catholic critic of *The Dublin Review*, who denounced Hume's historical philosophy as 'little more than the well-rounded flippancies of a cold-hearted metaphysical cynic, infidel and slave, endeavouring to turn to ridicule whatever plain, honest and religious freemen venerate'.[55] Not surprisingly, the problem of Hume's 'infidelity' was one of the first concerns of this 1838 edition of the *History*, in which the first real signs of change were apparent. In his introductory essay, Stebbings—not for nothing a Doctor of Divinity—made a comment which would have caused Hume turn in his grave (had he believed in any form of immortality): 'Let History be read wisely and it will "justify the ways of God to man".'[56]

If there were perceptions of a need to provide a commentary to the text, there were not yet any changes in the pattern of illustration in this edition, which remained based on the Bowyer school. As usual, the Vertue portraits were included,[57] and the plates illustrating scenes from English history derived from the late eighteenth century: Hamilton's *The Death of Prince Arthur* and Northcote's *The Murder of the Princes in the Tower*, from the Bowyer and Boydell Galleries respectively, were both included.[58]

---

[51] H. More, *Hints Towards Forming the Character of a Young Princess*, 2 vols. (1805), i. 157–8.
[52] Ibid. i. 158.   [53] [Palgrave], 'Hume', 563–4.   [54] Ibid. 566, 579–85.
[55] [McMahon], 'Lingard's *History*', 302.   [56] Hume, *History* (1838), i, Introduction, 49.
[57] e.g. ibid. ii, frontispiece (Richard I); iv, facing 15 (Richard III). The first of these two plates, when compared with Richard I's portrait in the Bowyer engravings (Bowyer, *History*, plate 33), shows, by the inclusion of an axe, that the engravings for the 1838 edn. were derived from the Vertue originals and were not copied from the Bowyer edn.
[58] Ibid. ii, title-page; iv, title-page. Bowyer, *History*, plate 41; *Shakespeare Catalogue*, 51–2. Although the use of the Vertue heads was uniform, each publisher's selection from the common pool of Bowyer and Boydell paintings was different, although certain favourites—such as Hamilton's *The Death of Prince Arthur*, for instance—appeared more frequently than other, less popular, works.

The pattern of illustrations for the 1848 edition published by the mass-producing firm of Thomas Kelly[59] was equally traditional. The Vertue portraits were once again an important element,[60] and several of the numerous scenes from English history derive from the Bowyer engravings: Loutherbourg's *The Battle of Hastings* and Francis Wheatley's *The Death of Richard II* were included.[61] Other works contemporary with these appeared too: Benjamin West's *Alfred the Great Divides his Loaf with a Pilgrim* (1779), for example.[62] Others were reproduced from the 1793–4 Cooke edition of Hume's *History*: *William the Conqueror Pronouncing Malediction against his son Robert* and *The Earl of Richmond Chosen King after the Battle of Bosworth* are both examples.[63] Some problems have been experienced in tracing the derivations of others of the illustrations—Kelly told the reader than that they were by 'first-rate artists', but declined to name these paragons—although the images are all clearly in the late eighteenth-century style. A possible explanation is that many of the plates are free variations on eighteenth-century originals. In the case of the plate *The Death of Prince Arthur* (Fig. 4), it is clear, when it is compared with Hamilton's Bowyer version of the subject, that the figure of John is derived from this source, although the Kelly print has an outdoor setting while the Hamilton painting's background is a Gothic building complete with full moon and bat.[64] The illustration *Lady Gray Petitioning Edward IV for her Lands*, in which the king wears a very eighteenth-century lace collar and Elizabeth Grey has a round-necked gown, shows some similarity to J. F. Rigaud's 1796 version of the same subject.[65] The very traditional nature of the illustrations was only varied by the inclusion of a plate showing a Druid, and an Ancient British man and woman.[66] Nor is the text any less traditional: it is an unedited version, with a continuation by J. C. Campbell.

The 1848 Virtue edition contained Stebbings's essay and the autobiography of Hume, but otherwise the text itself remained unaltered except for the updating of the continuation.[67] This equivocal treatment of the standard history—retaining the text, yet hinting at the relativity of its truth—was far more pronounced in the illustrations, which were at once transitional and also new. They formed what might be politely termed a medley, partly because the publisher, George Virtue,

[59] Thomas Kelly (1777–1854), an archetypal early Victorian businessman who rises from the industrious apprentice to be Lord Mayor of London, established a firm publishing large numbers of standard works including Bibles and Foxe's *Book of Martyrs*. He is said to have sold 5,000 copies of Hume's *History*, making £4,185. See H. Curwen, *A History of Booksellers, the Old and New* [1873], 364–71.

[60] D. Hume (with T. Smollett and J. C. Campbell), *The History of England*, 3 vols. (1848), i, facing 62 (Henry II), 164 (Richard II).

[61] Ibid. i, facing 30, 172. Bowyer, *History*, plates 20, 58.

[62] Hume, *History* (Kelly, 1848), i, facing 16.

[63] Ibid. i, facing 44, 211. Hume, *History* (1793–4), i, facing 265; v, frontispiece.

[64] Hume, *History* (Kelly, 1848), i, facing 90; Bowyer, *History*, plate 41.

[65] Hume, *History* (Kelly, 1848), i, facing 200.   [66] Ibid. i, facing 1.

[67] This was by a W. Farr, probably William Farr the statistician, a major contributor to *The Lancet*. See *DNB* xviii. 226–7.

Fig. 4.   After G. Hamilton, *Murder of Prince Arthur*, from D. Hume (with T. Smollett and J. C. Campbell), *The History of England*, 3 vols. (1848), i, facing 90

seems to have used whatever came to hand. And much did come to hand, as he was the founder of a firm specializing in the publication of illustrated books, and was once calculated to have issued over 20,000 copper- and steel-engravings.[68] However, this mixture of images also reflected changing attitudes to the illustration of history books. Some of the old 1790s illustrations were still included—for instance, Northcote's *The Murder of the Two Princes*, Stothard's *King Henry VIII's First Meeting with Anne Boleyn*, and Opie's *Queen Isabella Seized at Nottingham Castle*[69]—as well as the Vertue portraits, in some number.[70] But much new material was added. A Romantic sense of the historicity of place seems to have led to the insertion of many views of towns and castles, taken in the seventeenth, eighteenth, and nineteenth centuries—such as, for instance, Thomas Allom's *Holyrood Chapel* or W. H. Bartlett's *Dover*.[71] There were also

[68] *DNB* lviii. 374–5 and Curwen, *Booksellers*, 372–8. The firm was later continued by his better-known son, James Sprent Virtue, with his brother.

[69] D. Hume (with T. Smollett and W. Farr), *The History of England*, 3 vols. (1848), i, facing 194, 289, 346. Bowyer, *History*, plate 51; *Shakespeare Catalogue*, 51–2, 106–8.

[70] e.g. Hume, *History* (Virtue, 1848), i, facing 394 (Edward VI).

[71] Ibid. i. 444; ii, facing 13. Bartlett (1809–54) was a London-based topographical watercolourist and illustrator: he had been articled to John Britton, who sent him to make topographical drawings for his *Cathedral Antiquities of Great Britain* and *Picturesque Antiquities of English Cities*. Allom (1804–72), an architect and topographical watercolourist, was a regular employee of Virtue and Co. and Heath and Co. as a topographical illustrator, and is now remembered for his watercolours of buildings. Wood, *Dictionary*, 38–9, 22–3.

other signs of the new historiography prevailing in the 1840s: an interest in social history greater than was shown by Hume's occasional appendices to the odd chapter[72] led to the inclusion of such illustrations as that of the costume of the reign of Charles II.[73] But most interesting of all is the use of genuine images of historical artefacts (often to fill the space left at the end of a chapter)—as opposed to imaginary reconstructions of scenes—such as, for instance, illustrations of the shrine of Edward the Confessor, and the tomb of Edward III.[74] Illustrations appeared, too, which were straightforward copies from authentic portraits other than those of reigning sovereigns: *Thomas Howard, Earl of Surrey* by Holbein, and *Henrietta Maria* by Van Dyck, for example.[75] There was a copy, too, of the Hampton Court painting of the *Field of the Cloth of Gold*, probably painted in the 1550s, and of a plate showing *The Burning of a Lollard* from Foxe's *Book of Martyrs*.[76] This use of 'authentic' images, reproductions of contemporary portraits and paintings, architecture and artefacts, represented the future of illustration in Hume's *History*. The scheme of illustration in this edition, as a whole, was a tribute to the influence of the enterprises of Charles Knight, the most innovative English publisher of illustrated works in the 1830s and 1840s.

Such illustrations were the visual manifestation of the predominant historiography, Romantic and picturesque. This new approach was, in fact, praised cautiously by Palgrave, who, although concerned that the study of 'archaeology' (i.e. tangible remains of the past apart from documents) with reference to 'art or decoration . . . manners and customs . . . incident and romance' might cease to be secondary to 'proper' history, nevertheless appreciated the increasing understanding of the Middle Ages which it had brought about.[77] Knight had established the trend for the publication of lavishly illustrated works of picturesque history, in which he could carry out his 'plan of rendering wood-cuts real illustrations of the text, instead of fanciful devices—true eye-knowledge, sometimes more instructive than words'.[78] The extremely high proportion of illustrations to text was made possible by the development of wood-engraving as a cheap and plentiful means of reproducing images. Virtue's edition of Hume's *History* was by no means as fully illustrated as some of Knight's publications, but it contained considerably more pictures than earlier editions. Moreover, the variety of

---

[72] Forbes suggests that Hume's theoretical identification of the history of civilization with political history was almost total; however, he proved unable to exploit the sociological perspectives of the Scottish Enlightenment in his narrative. Thus he remained a philosophical historian occasionally dependent on chance as an explanation of change rather than a pioneer of materialist historiography. The problem of writing social history without adequate critical apparatus was to present itself to his 19th-cent. successors too. See Forbes, *Hume's Philosophical Politics*, 296–8, 308–23 and Ch. 5 below.

[73] Hume, *History* (Virtue, 1848), i. 826.   [74] Ibid. i. 44, 222.

[75] Ibid. i. 393, facing 611.

[76] Ibid. i. 328, 242; J. Foxe, *The Acts and Monuments of John Foxe*, ed. S. R. Cattley, 8 vols. (1837), iii, facing 238. This plate represented the burning of John Badby.

[77] [Palgrave], 'Hume', 568.

[78] C. Knight, *Passages of a Working Life During Half a Century: with a Prelude of Early Reminiscences*, 3 vols. (1864), ii. 262.

illustrations, a mixture of imaginative reconstructions such as the Bowyer's Gallery paintings alongside views of towns and original portraits, was similar to the pattern of illustration which Knight practised. The illustrations bear witness to Virtue's determination to copy Knight's abundance of images, and show, too, the manner in which publishers resorted to pre-used illustrations to fill their pages: the illustration of *King James I discovering the Gunpowder Plot* had clearly appeared before as *Henry VIII protecting Cranmer* (the king is obviously drawn from a Holbein portrait).[79] The fact that many of the 'space-filler' wood-engravings were engraved by the firm of Whymper confirms this apparent link between Knight's enterprises and this edition, as this firm was chiefly employed by Knight in the 1840s.[80] The evidence of a changing attitude to history-writing and the illustrations of history books in this 1848 edition is further confirmed, in the case of the illustrations, by an article in *The Quarterly Review* of 1844. In this article, Lady Eastlake is critical of the old Bowyer illustrations on the grounds of their failure to illuminate the text and their historical inaccuracy: '[Illustration] implies something which tends to explain or throw light upon the text . . . what light is thrown upon Hume's text by the magnificent nonsenses in Bowyer's edition? a book as superb and as useless, and as devoid of real beauty as Macklin's Bible. It outrages all probability, and sets at defiance all consistency in manners and costume.' By contrast, Knight's *Pictorial History of England*, written by G. L. Craik and Charles Macfarlane, has 'real illustrations of the text'.[81]

'APPROPRIATE FURNITURE': HUME'S *HISTORY* IN DECLINE, 1859–80

The two later editions of Hume's *History* showed a further evolution in the direction of factually accurate, 'authentic' history in text and image. The text of Hume's *History* was now clearly unable to meet the demands of a positivist national historiography. This historiography required not only high standards of factual accuracy, based on archival research and rooted in the development of history as a professional discipline; it also encouraged the production of texts suitably packaged for the education and examination of a wide range of potential citizens—civil servants, army officers, university students, elementary school pupils—in a state-approved version of the national past. In these later editions of the *History*, Hume's historical methods and conclusions were found increasingly unacceptable and suffered extensive revision and even subversion.

---

[79] Hume, *History* (Virtue, 1848), i. 581.

[80] Engen, *Wood-Engravers*, 285–6. Josiah and Ebenezer Whymper or Whimper founded the firm at Lambeth in the 1830s. They also worked for Murrays and *The Illustrated London News*. Apprentices included well-known illustrators such as Charles Keene and Frederick Walker, and the brothers were close friends of the prolific illustrator, John Gilbert.

[81] [Eastlake], 'Illustrated Books', *QR* 74 (1844), 194.

It was hardly surprising that, in the light of historical research conducted since the beginning of the century, Hume's *History* should have received criticism for both its factual content and its interpretative bias. For Hume, as for other eighteenth-century philosophical historians, archival research and the critiquing of sources had not been a high priority.[82] Henry Hallam, in his popular work *The Constitutional History of England* (1823), had frequently found occasion to dispute Hume's use of his sources. He referred, for instance, to Hume's inclusion of Elizabeth I's famous verse on transubstantiation, commenting disdainfully that Hume 'always loves a popular story' and adding that the 'inquisitioners of that age were not so easily turned around by an equivocal answer'.[83] He also attacked Hume over his misrepresentation of a Latin letter of Charles I to Rome, which implied Charles's willingness to be favourably disposed to Roman Catholicism, in the event of receiving assistance against his enemies.[84] The quality of Hume's historical research was disputed by George Brodie, the author of *A History of the British Empire* (1822), who claimed that Hume lacked 'the unremitting industry', which 'sifts and collates authorities'. While admitting that many of Hume's deficiencies were apparent only after the emergence of documents not available to him when he was writing the *History*, Brodie comments that: 'From the short period . . . devoted by him to that portion of British history, I conceive it to have been morally impossible for him to have become master of necessary materials.'[85] William Smyth was also critical of Hume's 'inaccurate representation of the very authorities which he quotes'.[86] Palgrave voiced similar criticism: 'Hume may have turned over the leaves of the chroniclers, but he never rendered them the objects of study, and never distinguished between primary and secondary sources.'[87]

The critic of *The Edinburgh Review*, meanwhile, attributed Hume's inaccuracies and distortions, not only to his political prejudices and his atheism, but also to his 'craving after theories, or pictures which were to produce effect'.[88] Against the background of such criticisms the two later editions of Hume's *History* here discussed should be viewed: they included real revisions of the text and forceful attempts to bring Hume's prevailing argument into line with the Whig progressive interpretation of the national past predominant in mid-nineteenth-century England.

In 1859, John Murray, the publisher of many leading educational works, brought out a volume called *The Student's Hume*, which described itself as

---

[82] Although Wexler does point out that Hume carried out more research in primary source material than is often believed; he stresses, however, that his archival work was directed and limited by his immediate polemical aims. See Wexler, *Hume*, 37–40, 97–101.

[83] H. Hallam, *The Constitutional History of England from the Accession of Henry VII to the Death of George II*, 3 vols. (1823; 1867 edn.), i. 108–9 n. *a*.

[84] Ibid. i. 410–11, n. *q*.

[85] G. Brodie, *A History of the British Empire from the Accession of Charles I to the Restoration . . . including a Particular Examination of Mr Hume's Statements Relative to the Character of the English Government*, 2 vols. (Edinburgh, 1822), i, p. iv.

[86] Smyth, *Lectures*, i. 133.   [87] [Palgrave], 'Hume', 555.   [88] [Empson], '*Life*', 19.

'abridged and incorporating the corrections and researches of recent historians and continued to 1858'. The editor of this work held—not surprisingly, in the decade of Macaulay's greatest popularity—that Hume's apparent bias in favour of the royal prerogative made him partial in his account of the reigns of James I and Charles I.[89] Politically, of course, Hume was certainly not a Tory: his historical position was based on a pragmatic acceptance of the legitimacy of a settled and peaceful government and a healthy scepticism concerning the existence of the ancient constitution and liberties of the English people, which Whig historians traced to the Anglo-Saxon period.[90] But this distinction had at no time disarmed his critics: Brodie, for example, in his *History of the British Empire*, felt that Hume's presentation of the state of government and public opinion under Charles I was 'altogether erroneous',[91] and Smyth commented that Hume's account of the Stuarts was 'little better than an apology'.[92] Now, the editor of *The Student's Hume* criticized similarly Hume's careless treatment of the Anglo-Saxon period, both from his lack of knowledge of authentic documents and his tendency to dismiss its people as barbarians. The reader was informed that corrections had been made by reference to the works of Sharon Turner, Palgrave, Lappenberg, and John Mitchell Kemble.[93] Hume's treatment of the Anglo-Saxon and medieval periods had early been a target for Palgrave's criticism: in *The Quarterly Review* of 1826, the historian had deplored Hume's tendency to treat the whole medieval period as one whole, to quote later chroniclers where earlier ones were available and to use secondary sources where primary ones were obtainable.[94] Palgrave later renewed the attack, exhibiting his own consciousness of historical relativism by criticism of Hume's use of anachronistic language: he quoted, as an example, Hume's reference to 'Anglo-Saxon gentlemen', commenting that 'gentleman is a complex idea, entirely belonging to our own times'.[95] All the blame, however, lay not with Hume, he conceded, as new sources and 'sounder criticism' had emerged since his day.[96]

Notes were also added to this new edition of Hume's *History*, as well as appendices of important documents, such as the Bill of Rights, and lists of authorities. Thus, at last, there was extensive alteration and correction of the original text. While, for instance, Hume's original text asserted that Alfred the Great 'founded, at least repaired the University of Oxford', *The Student's Hume* told the reader that 'for this pretension, there seems to be no satisfactory evidence'—despite Alfred's niche in the Whig pantheon of heroes. It also refuted the claim that the king was responsible for new laws, such as the law of frankpledge, and new institutions, such as trial by jury, presenting him more modestly as the enforcer,

---

[89] D. Hume, *The Student's Hume*, ed. anon. (1859), preface, vi.

[90] For full analyses of Hume's position, as manifested in his *History*, see Wexler, *Hume*, 26–89, and Forbes, *Hume's Philosophical Politics*, 260–307.

[91] Brodie, *History*, i, p. v.   [92] Smyth, *Lectures*, i. 127.   [93] *Hume* (1859), p. v.

[94] [F. Palgrave], '*The History of England* by Hume: A New Edition, 1825', *QR* 34 (1826), 249–50.

[95] [Palgrave], 'Hume', 558.   [96] Ibid. 538.

Fig. 5. *John. From his Tomb in Worcester Cathedral. Isabella from her Tomb at Font-evraud,* from D. Hume, *The Student's Hume,* ed. anon. (1859), 135

rather than the promulgator, of laws.[97] The illustrations reflected this new and more scientific attitude: nearly all were from coins and medals from the British Museum, as we are informed in the preface.[98] Other illustrations, portraits of kings and queens, were from their effigies—King John's, for instance, was from his tomb at Worcester Cathedral (Fig. 5)[99]—rather than from the traditional Vertue portraits. Moreover, in comparison with the Virtue edition of 1848, this edition of Hume's *History* was very sparsely illustrated.

The dearth of illustrations continued in a new edition of *The Student's Hume* published in 1880, again by John Murray. In the 1859 edition, there were, scattered in the table of contents, no less than four illustrations, including one of the mitre of Thomas à Becket, for example. In the 1880 edition, there were none.[100] In the 1859 edition, there was an illustration of a section of the Bayeux Tapestry, and a description of it in the main text; in the 1880 one, there was no illustration, and the description was relegated to a footnote, although new information was added to explain that it was probably intended for the cathedral of Bayeux.[101] It may seem strange that, when Hume's *History* was being tailored

[97] Hume, *History* (Kelly, 1848), i. 17; *Hume* (1859), 45–7.
[98] *Hume* (1859), p. vi.   [99] Ibid. 135.
[100] Ibid. pp. vii–xiv; D. Hume, *The Student's Hume,* ed. J. S. Brewer (1880), pp. ix–xxxvi.
[101] *Hume* (1859), 69; *Hume* (1880), 69.

so much for a (largely) youthful audience, illustrations should be dispensed with in so many cases. This can, however, be related to developments in the illustration of children's textbooks in the 1860s and 1870s, which are discussed more fully in the next chapter.[102]

Once again, the text of *The Student's Hume* was drastically revised. As editor, Murray had selected John Sherren Brewer, an historian best known for his monumental work, *The Letters and State Papers of the Reign of Henry VIII*, part of the Rolls Series:[103] such a choice testified to the increasing importance of a scientific and professional approach to the construction of the national narrative. Naturally, Brewer showed much attentiveness to recent research, and an anxiety to include accurate facts:

I have been guided to the best of my ability, by historical truth, by the investigations of *recent, trustworthy* historians . . . the popularity of the work must depend on its merits for accuracy and ability . . . I am fully convinced that the road to success is by careful investigations and temperate narrative, showing the reader that there is another side to the question than that which some recent writers have presented . . . Wherever there was *fair* evidence for Hume's statements, I have retained them, and still more frequently Hume's estimate of motives and characters *when he had the facts before him* . . .[104]

It is no surprise after reading this declaration, to discover many alterations of the text. If the 1880 edition is compared with the 1859 one, we discover an increasingly sceptical attitude towards the very tales and legends which provided the anecdotal subjects of the 1790s illustrations. The tale of Alfred and the cakes was prefaced with a cautionary 'if we may trust this old story' in the 1880 edition, and the story of Alfred's visit to Guthrum's camp in disguise disappeared altogether.[105] Thomas à Becket, the *bête noire* of Hume and the rationalists, as well as of the firmly Protestant historians of the mid-nineteenth-century era, was given the benefit of the doubt in the wake of the Oxford Movement and the onset of scientific history. Whereas the 1859 edition still tells us, with a touch of scepticism, that Becket 'affected the greatest austerity', the 1880 one tells the reader that he 'practised' it. While the 1859 edition accused him of pride and ambition 'under the disguise of sanctity', the 1880 one asserted that: 'no one who enters into the genius of that age can reasonably doubt of his sincerity . . . the assertion of an authority resting on some higher sanction than the will of the king was needful and important'.[106] This anti-monarchical reflection neatly contained a more favourable interpretation of the martyred archbishop within this predominantly Whig revision of the *History*. There was a shift in the interpretation of the English

---

[102] See Ch. 3.   [103] See *DNB* vi. 294–5.   [104] *Hume* (1880), pp. v–vii.

[105] *Hume* (1859), 42–3; *Hume* (1880), 44–5. Also see Ch. 3 for a fuller discussion of the question of anecdotal history.

[106] *Hume* (1859), 110–15; *Hume* (1880), 109–15.

Revolution back a little towards Hume's standpoint, but this was largely the result of Brewer's intense admiration for the work of S. R. Gardiner.[107]

A STANDARD WORK OF THE LAST GENERATION:

HUME'S *HISTORY* BECOMES OBSOLETE

In a late and deplorable novel of C. M. Yonge's called *That Stick* (1892), the newly married Lady Northmoor, formerly a teacher, explores the library of her new home, a country mansion, and finds it full of 'the standard books of the last generation . . . the "tea, tobacco, and snuff" of an old library where the books are chiefly viewed as appropriate furniture'. Among these works is an edition of Hume's *History* in nine volumes. Recalling her schoolroom acquaintance with *The Student's Hume*, she asks her husband if there is much difference between the two and receives the answer: 'Rather to the Student's advantage, I believe'— clearly a truth which refers to the quality and quantity equally. Among the other tomes here gathering dust is Boydell's edition of Shakespeare, the paintings for which inspired the Bowyer Gallery.[108] Hume's *History* in its original form, with its best known illustrations, was obviously a relic of the past. The authority of Hume's *History* and of the original 1790s illustrations had been undermined in the course of the nineteenth century as new attitudes to and perceptions of history—political, religious, social, and artistic—arose: the evolution of the *History* sketches an outline of these changes. By the 1890s, though, not only the original text and images, but *The Student's Hume* itself, had become obsolete. The *History* which had shaped, and been shaped by, the nineteenth-century consciousness of history, went out of print in 1894.

[107] *Hume* (1880), p. vi. Gardiner's painstaking lifetime's study of 17th-cent. English constitutional history laid the foundations for modern study of that period, demolishing the extreme view of both Whigs and Royalists. E. P. Gooch, *History and Historians in the Nineteenth Century* (1952), 335–40.

[108] C. M. Yonge, *That Stick* (1892), 72–3.

3

True Stories and Solid Facts: The Evolution
of the English History Textbook

The historiographical evolution of Hume's *History of England*, examined in the
last chapter, was similar to—but was not mirrored by—the transformation of the
nineteenth-century English history textbook. These more obscure works passed
through the same historiographical revolutions, influenced in succession by
philosophical history, picturesque history, and scientific history: they evolved
from story-books with pictures, intended for consumption in a domestic and
informal setting, to closely printed, fact-laden texts, suggestive of the wider context of a nascent national education system. However, the circumstances of their
production meant that most English history textbooks were slow to respond to
new historical trends: textbooks were generally published as cheaply as possible
and often for a wide audience, with the result that revisions and new versions of
both text and illustrations were reluctantly adopted. Accordingly, the picture of
the national past presented to children was not only (at first) derived partially
from Hume's *History*, but even more persistently adhered to conservative forms
and content than editions of that long-lived work.

The historiographical evolution of the nineteenth-century English history
textbook might have been explained by a contemporary as the pursuit of truth.
Throughout the century, the issue of authenticity was a dominant preoccupation
for the textbook writer. This is apparent in an early work such as Mrs Markham's
The New Children's Friend (1831): after Mrs Markham—the assumed persona
of Elizabeth Penrose[1]—had narrated a potted history of the Isle of Wight, her
daughter Mary commented that she liked 'make-believe stories very much, but
still, after all, there is nothing like true stories'.[2] The writers of mid-nineteenth-
century textbooks were similarly convinced of the appeal of real-life historical

---

[1] *DNB* xliv. 342–3; R. A. Mitchell, 'Elizabeth Penrose', *New DNB*. The daughter of Edmund
Cartwright, she was born in 1780, and married the clergyman, John Penrose, in 1814. In 1823, she
published *A History of England*; it became the most popular textbook of English history for the
next forty years. Her husband wrote some of the chapters of the *History*, and managed the publishing arrangements for her. See JMA: Penrose MSS, J. Penrose to J. Murray, 12 Feb. 1842, [n.d.,
c.1843?].

[2] E. Penrose ('Mrs Markham'), *The New Children's Friend*, 2 vols. (1832), ii. 151.

tales to the juvenile mind. In the Preface to *The Child's First Step to English History* (1844), Anne Rodwell announced that her history textbook was written because 'intelligent children evince at a very early age, a desire to learn and hear of things that are true'.[3] This emphasis on the high status of factual, as opposed to fictional, versions of national history affected the textual and visual means used to transmit history to the young, leading to the production of works specifically adapted to the infant mind. Gradually the nineteenth-century child was separated from his predecessors, whose British history had been learnt largely from such sources as Shakespeare's history plays, literary sources with a strong emphasis on narrative and intended for a wider audience. The evolution of the concept of 'truth' or authenticity in narrative and visual form, touched upon in the last chapter, and of the moral and nationalist rhetorics of the text and images in textbooks published between 1817 and 1880, are the themes of this chapter.

'THINGS THAT ARE TRUE': PHILOSOPHICAL HISTORY DOMESTICIZED

To the modern reader, the emphasis of early nineteenth-century textbook writers on the 'true story' may appear paradoxical, in view of their narrative technique and content: historical anecdotes, with heavy-handed moralizing, are narrated in the manner of bedtime stories. Indeed, the term 'textbook'—necessary though it is for the sake of concision and convenience—is both anachronistic and inappropriate. The context which we now associate with the textbook—a state-regulated school environment, professional teachers, established academic disciplines, examinations, and set syllabuses—did not exist for most of the period considered here. The early nineteenth-century history textbooks here discussed were read within an educational environment which appears to our eyes to be amateurish and informal: they were read in home schoolrooms and small private schools, under the supervision of relatives, governesses, and other *ad hoc* tutors, at a time when history was still part of *belles-lettres* and was expected to exhibit the narrative techniques of literature.

Indeed, as already shown by the quotations in this chapter, the contents of their textbooks were still referred to as stories and tales—albeit true ones—rather than as accounts or descriptions. J. I. Whalley identifies two formative textual precedents for the late eighteenth-century history textbook, the precursor of these works: the first was British philosophical history-writing, offering moral instruction by the examples of 'good' and 'bad' kings and other figures of political significance: works such as Hume's *History*. The second was 'folk history', replete with the standard anecdotes, such as that of Alfred and the cakes, and focusing on dramatic events such as the loss of the White Ship: the stuff of Shakespeare and the medieval and Tudor chroniclers, the old familiar tales which even Hume

---

[3] A. Rodwell, *The Child's First Step to English History* (1844), p. v.

had not entirely forsaken.[4] The kind of national history created by the fusion of these two approaches was to fill the pages of English history textbooks for more than half a century, as has been recognized by Valerie Chancellor.[5] In early nineteenth-century textbooks, these two approaches combined to create the 'true stories' narrative, which married philosophical truth and moral teaching to all the literary apparatus needed to tell a good tale.

These two approaches were as important in shaping the illustrative tradition of the textbooks. Illustrations for late eighteenth-century textbooks tended to be simply portraits of monarchs: G. G. and J. Robinson's *A Compendious History of England from the Invasion to War with France* (1794), for instance, had imaginary cuts of the kings by leading wood-engravers, Thomas and John Bewick. These were perceived less as an illustration of the text than as an *aide-mémoire*, as the verses printed beneath them indicated.[6] However, such precedents dovetailed with the usual focus on the individual and his/her personal life and concerns apparent in early nineteenth-century textbooks. But more significant precedents for illustration of these works can be found. Just as Hume's *History* was a major textual source for this moral yet anecdotal approach, so too were its illustrations. As has already been seen, the anecdotal nature of its text was exaggerated in the eyes of the early nineteenth-century reader by the illustrations produced for it in the late eighteenth century, in particular the paintings of Bowyer's Historical Gallery in the 1790s.[7] Even Bowyer's moral intentions—to inspire virtue and the detestation of criminal passions—gave rise to subjects which were 'personal and anecdotal ones'.[8] The preoccupations of his artists with neo-classical or Romantic concerns meant that there was little interest in accuracy of costume or setting, but the subjects of such paintings were to appear frequently in early nineteenth-century textbooks. Of the Bowyer subjects, *Augustine Preaching before King Ethelbert* (Tresham), *Alfred in the House of the Neatherd* (Wheatley), the *Death of William Rufus* (Burney), the *Death of William, Son of Henry I, on the White Ship* (Rigaud), the *Death of Prince Arthur* (Hamilton), *The Surrender of Calais* (Smirke), *Queen Margaret and the Robber* (Smirke), the *Death of Wolsey* (Smirke), *Queen Elizabeth at Tilbury* (Stothard: see Fig. 2), *Charles I Taking Leave of his Children* (Stothard), and *Oliver Cromwell Declining the Crown* (Stothard)[9] all became textbook favourites. In some textbooks the works from Bowyer's Gallery were simply reproduced, while in others illustrators drew on the subject-matter and/or the composition. Additional influences on early

---

[4] J. I. Whalley, *Cobwebs to Catch Flies: Illustrated Books for the Nursery and the Schoolroom 1700–1900* (1974), 75–6.

[5] V. E. Chancellor, *History for their Masters: Opinion in the English History Textbook 1800–1914* (Bath, 1970), 12, 67–8. Chancellor spends little time, however, considering the implications of the organization of the text by anecdotal episodes, and does not set out to give more than cursory attention to illustration.

[6] Whalley, *Cobwebs*, 75.   [7] See Ch. 2.

[8] T. S. R. Boase, 'Macklin and Bowyer', *JWCI* 26 (1983), 176.

[9] R. Bowyer, *A Series of One Hundred and Ninety-One Engravings . . . Illustrative of the 'History of England'* (1812), plates 12, 15, 28, 30, 41, 53, 76, 121, 145, 146.

nineteenth-century textbook illustrations were provided by other literary history paintings, such as those of Boydell's Shakespeare Gallery, as well as by earlier illustrations of Shakespeare. Such influences reinforced the literary and anecdotal approach of the textbook, as they linked English literature, traditional tales, and national history together.

Thus the narrative techniques of the early nineteenth-century history textbook were essentially those of the story-teller and the dramatist, despite their intention to transmit 'true stories' which claimed the status of fact. For—while the moral emphasis of philosophical history was considered essential—the standard texts were thought to be too dry and repulsive in an unadulterated form: they had to be rendered in a more attractive medium. The author of *Anecdotes of Kings, selected from History, or Gertrude's Stories for Children* (1837) was clearly persuaded of the necessity of writing historical events in a form which would appeal to a juvenile audience.[10] In this work, the fictional characters, George and Egbert, complain to their mother that history is 'so dry'. Her response is to tell the tale of Prince Edward (later Edward I), who, while on the Crusades, is stabbed by an assassin with a poisoned dagger; his wife Eleanor of Castile, with great presence of mind, sucks the venom from the wound. George is convinced that such an exciting tale could not be an episode from English history; Mrs Stanhope assures him that it is indeed a true story 'with little or no embellishment'. Soon Egbert is asking for another story, and 'let it be as true as the last was: I like true stories best'.[11]

This conversation serves to emphasize the appeal of fact presented within a fictional mode: it seems clear that the claim of truth was at once a historian's justification of his/her text and the rhetorical device of a fairy-tale, intended to engender interest and to suspend disbelief. A similar exchange occurs in Mrs Markham's *The History of England*: after her eldest son, Richard, has struggled unsuccessfully with Hume, his mother agrees to create a history to 'entertain and instruct you', to be read aloud in the evenings instead of the usual stories.[12] Textbook history was shaped by the form of the stories which it was presumed to imitate and replace. Clearly, the setting envisaged for not only the reading but even the production of the text was a domestic one, where a mother or aunt—a sort of historical Mother Goose—transmitted her own version of true stories from the national past, as a superior substitute for the bedtime story. The maternal fiction, at least, could be far from the truth; most of the early nineteenth-century history textbook writers here examined were childless and/or unmarried women: they were often established writers, and few of them were writing primarily for children known to them.[13] A work which allows us to glimpse the realities behind

---

[10] [Anon.], *Anecdotes of Kings, selected from History, or Gertrude's Stories for Children* (1837), p. v.

[11] Ibid. 2, 16–17.   [12] Penrose, *History* (1846), pp. vii–viii.

[13] The biographer of Sarah Trimmer remarked that her subject, the mother of twelve children, 'is the only one, of all our popular writers on education, that had a mother's experience'. See C. L. Balfour, *A Sketch of Mrs Trimmer* [1854], 12; also [A. Worsley?], *A Sketch of Emily Taylor*

this familial fiction is Maria, Lady Callcott's *Little Arthur's History of England* (1835), which purported to be written for a young friend. Unusually enough, the claim was valid: it was indeed written for 'a particular child', as an educational birthday present.[14] Callcott, however, leaned on the fiction of the narrating mother, rather than upon the fact of a literary 'aunt' preparing a present for a child: the Preface was addressed to mothers,[15] and she thought that an illustration of 'King Alfred learning from his mother . . . will come [in] very nicely'.[16] That these details are all divulged in letters to her friend and publisher, John Murray, hints at the commercial context in which the book was created.

In such textbooks, the religious and constitutional aspects of the national narrative were downplayed: the national past was viewed as a source of exempla for good and bad conduct within the child's immediate domestic circle. Although this was partly an attempt to ensure that textbook morality was attuned to children's everyday experience, it is also a reflection of social and cultural realignments of social classes and the defining of private and public spheres and spaces. The virtues advocated in early nineteenth-century history textbooks were familial duty, personal integrity, and social benevolence: the *domestic* qualities of the eighteenth-century gentry. As Chancellor has pointed out, most early nineteenth-century textbook writers addressed their texts to the (fictional) children of the aristocracy and gentry, despite their own social status, which was usually middle class:[17] an indication, perhaps, of the eighteenth-century embourgeoisement of the upper orders. The civic imperatives of Hume's *History*—unlike its anecdotes and its tone of moral instruction—do not generally inform the early nineteenth-century history textbook. Written largely by women within their own homes and framed as domestic narratives, early nineteenth-textbooks devoted little attention to the cultivation of public and political virtues.[18] The redefinition of public life—as a sphere established by the nation-state, administered by professionals and linked inevitably to the private life of the individual through increasing state intervention—was a later nineteenth-century phenomenon: the philosophical history textbook and (to a lesser extent) its picturesque successor dealt in the heroism of the private individual.

Heroism was certainly presented as a very domestic affair in the early nineteenth-century history textbook. Mrs Markham, for instance, in *The New Children's Friend* (1832), told the story of a father and his loving daughter during the French Revolution: Stephanie secures the release of her father from a prison, even offering herself as a substitute. Mary Markham exclaimed, 'how delightful

by a Friend (private circulation, 1872), G. Battiscombe, *Charlotte Mary Yonge: The Story of an Uneventful Life* (1943).

[14] JMA: Callcott MSS, M. Callcott to J. Murray, 24 Apr. 1835. The identity of the child is, however, unknown.

[15] M. Callcott, *Little Arthur's History of England* (1835; 1856 edn.), p. iii.

[16] JMA: Callcott MSS, M. Callcott to J.Murray, [n.d., May 1835?].

[17] Chancellor, *History*, 22, 25–6.

[18] See Ch. 6 for further discussion of women's writing of history.

it would be to render you any such great service!' Her mother replied, 'The occasions for great services do not often occur; but there are opportunities every day of performing the lesser duties of affectionate and dutiful attention; and with them, your papa and I shall be fully satisfied.'[19] Authors frequently utilized a historical example of heroism to advocate a domestic virtue, with little sense of the ensuing descent from the sublime to the ridiculous. In the *Anecdotes of Kings*, young George's failure to wait at the gate for his uncle's arrival, as instructed, provokes his brother into recounting a tale of Alexander the Great, and his mother one of Mutius and Porsenna, to illustrate the importance of dutiful conduct to one's superiors.[20] One cannot help wondering if George's natural (and sensible) reluctance to stand waiting in the rain deserves such a weight of classical condemnation.

As anecdotal episodes from the lives of sovereigns seemed to form perfect encapsulations of personal moral instruction, it is not surprising that textbook writers exploited them so frequently. An episodic narrative of essentially isolated tales resulted almost inevitably from the rejection of the organizing themes of Hume's philosophical *History*—the evolution of a society and its civic institutions—and the absence of the central thesis of the progress of the nation-state, which was to structure the later nineteenth-century history textbook. A typical example of the techniques of the writers can be found in the treatment of the lives of the Norman and Plantagenet kings, which were frequently used to demonstrate the problems of family life when members of the domestic circle were undutiful.[21] Anne Rodwell, for instance, in *A Child's First Step*, characterized Henry I as 'both a cruel and a bad brother . . . In vain Henry tried to be happy, nothing could give ease to the heart that had been the cause of so many bad and cruel deeds.'[22] Rodwell warned also of the error of filial disobedience—one of Ethelwulf's sons 'who would not mind him as a child, grew up, as you may guess, a very bad man'.[23] Occasionally, there is an exemplar of good conduct: diplomatically, recent monarchs were often presented as domestic paragons. Mrs Markham waxed lyrical over George III: 'I believe I may confidently affirm, that a better father, husband, son and brother never existed.'[24] Simple morals and straightforward advocacy of virtues suitable for the child abounded: the life of Henry VIII was presented, not as a study of complex megalomania, but as a lesson in 'how much harm may be done by giving way to bad temper'.[25] Social virtue was seen as a matter of individual interpersonal actions, private acts of benevolence in many

---

[19] Penrose, *Friend*, i. 240.   [20] *Anecdotes*, 122–35.

[21] The critical moment in the 19th cent., when the growing cult of domestic virtue and the embourgeoisement of the monarchy created a public debate of unparalleled proportion, was during the Queen Caroline affair in 1820. See L. Davidoff and C. Hall, *Family Fortunes: Men and Women of the English Middle Class, 1780–1850* (1987), 149–55.

[22] Rodwell, *Step*, 42–5.   [23] Ibid. 13–14.

[24] Penrose, *History* (1846), 468. As her reign advanced, Victoria replaced her grandfather as the royal representative of domestic virtue in history textbooks. Chancellor, *History*, 42–3.

[25] Rodwell, *Step*, 120.

cases, such as Queen Philippa's intercession on behalf of the burghers of Calais and Sir Philip Sidney's donation of his water bottle to a dying soldier at the battle of Zutphen.[26] Public acts of heroism were played down: war was perceived as a great ill, and war heroes were frequently criticized. Mrs Markham, for instance, commenting on the reign of Henry V, who, she felt, made war without an 'adequate object', remarked that: 'History is indeed a sad catalogue of human miseries, and one is glad to turn away from the horrors of wars and bloodshed to the tranquillity of private life. Shall I tell you something about the domestic habits of the English in the fifteenth century?'[27]

The temptation to present history as a series of stories, of episodic personal anecdotes, was reflected and reinforced by the illustrations of these early nineteenth-century textbooks. In several important textbooks, such as Sarah Trimmer's *A Series of Prints Designed to Illustrate English History* and its accompanying text, *A Description of a Set of Prints of English History* (1817), or Emily Taylor's *Historical Prints* (1821), illustration—as the titles suggest—was a priority, and shaped the episodic form of the text by its innate inability to provide continuous narrative. These illustrations clearly aimed to provide a miniature Bowyer's Gallery for a juvenile audience—as Taylor's explanation of their purpose seemed to suggest: 'forming and fixing interesting associations with the principal facts of all our history in the minds of young people.'[28]

Trimmer's *Prints* followed the precedent of the Gallery closely in the choice of subjects for illustration: Vortigern and Rowena, Canute rebuking his courtiers, the death of William Rufus, the loss of Prince William and the White Ship, Pandolf receiving King John's submission, the burghers of Calais, Elizabeth I at Tilbury, and Charles I taking leave of his children were common to both, among other subjects. The style of Trimmer's illustrations was entirely eighteenth-century and thus also comparable to the paintings of the Gallery: in the manner of history paintings, little attention, if any, was paid to authentic historical detail. Costumes, furniture, and architecture all reflect the classically based styles of the eighteenth century. All the figures wear eighteenth-century stage dress—Lady Jane Grey at her execution wears an eighteenth-century gown and sash, and a frilly collar which is a feeble excuse for a ruff. The furniture is always more Chippendale than historic: King Alfred sits in his study on a cabriolet-legged chair and has an elegant folio stand to hand (Fig. 6), while Thomas à Becket is buried in a classical obelisk, which faces a wall-monument supported by cherubs.[29] Despite their pretensions to imitate history paintings, these anecdotal textbook illustrations achieved, by minimalism of detail, limited setting, and even an occasional lack of perspective, a very domestic and miniaturized version of national history.

---

[26] e.g. Penrose, *History* (1846), 143, 316.   [27] Ibid. 186–7.

[28] E. Taylor, *Historical Prints, Representing Some of the Most Memorable Events in English History* (1821), p. iii.

[29] S. Trimmer, *A Series of Prints Designed to Illustrate English History* (1817), prints 42, 7, 14. Published with S. Trimmer, *A Description of a Set of Prints of English History* (1817).

Fig. 6. *King Alfred*, from S. Trimmer, *A Series of Prints Designed to Illustrate English History* (1817), plate 7

CHANGE WITHIN THE TRADITION:
THE PICTURESQUE HISTORY TEXTBOOK

Early nineteenth-century textbook writers and illustrators, therefore, worked within this model, but with an increasing concern for authenticity. Herein lay signs of a shift towards picturesque historiography, devoted to the antiquarian rediscovery of the national past, which was to dominate the mid-century English history textbook. To the twentieth-century viewer, the concept of authenticity shared by these textbook writers and illustrators may seem very rudimentary and credulous. The traditional interpretations of Shakespeare and folklore history were complemented, but rarely replaced, by reference to contemporary (and even non-contemporary) chroniclers, whose own bias and limitations remained unexamined. This uncritical attitude to literary and documentary sources— which resulted in a undifferentiated patchwork of facts and excerpts—was paralleled in the illustrations by the use of well-known antiquarian publications, particularly those of Joseph Strutt. Such works were exploited with no apparent

attention to the degree to which the images they contained were already interpreted and edited by the antiquarian author and illustrator, and were, to this
extent, inauthentic. The authors and illustrators of textbooks were probably
unaware of the degree to which Strutt's thematic approach, for instance, led
him to abstract details from entire images with little recognition of the influence
of the subject on the nature of the image, and to combine groups of such details in
rather surreal collages with an uncertain system of chronology. As the illustrators
in general continued to produce metaphoric illustrations, into which details from
Strutt were 'pasted', it is evident that such concerns would not naturally have
arisen. The textbook authors and illustrators were both subject, too, to the
antiquaries' failures to identify the dates and origins of works of art, or to recognize that a signature was not always a guarantee of authenticity: practically every
sixteenth-century painting was customarily attributed to Holbein, and there
was no apparent recognition of the significance of artistic schools.

An example of this combination of traditional philosophical approach with a
new interest in authenticity, which heralds the arrival of the picturesque history
textbook, can be seen in Emily Taylor's *Historical Prints* (1821). Conservative
though it was in its episodic and anecdotal approach, the author claimed to have
consulted modern historians, 'the best guides', including John Lingard, whose
History of England was indeed only just appearing, the first volume being
published in 1819.[30] Taylor made use of the traditional anecdotes, including
Alfred and the cakes and the loss of the White Ship, after which Henry I never
smiled again.[31] But seeds of doubt were sown: she admitted that there were 'many
romantic tales' of Fair Rosamund. However, she did exist, Taylor insisted, and
did live at Woodstock.[32] She was also doubtful about the traditional account of
the death of Prince Arthur, indicating that there was no positive proof that King
John was the murderer.[33] Mrs Markham was similarly dualistic in her approach:
she repeated the traditional anecdotes, but frequently questioned their accuracy.
She admitted that the tale of Prince Arthur and his keeper Hubert was not 'strictly
true', adding that Shakespeare and the writer of *Stories from English History*
had failed to appreciate that Arthur was not a child at the time, but a young man
able to bear arms.[34] The tale of the institution of the Garter was, she commented,
'generally believed to be a mere fabrication',[35] and the traditional account of
Clarence's death was, she remarked, 'difficult to believe'.[36] Writing twenty years
later, Rodwell still repeated the same structuring and moralistic anecdotes,
but was similarly aware of new interpretations. Her text referred to the Strickland
sisters' very recent reinterpretation of the reign of Mary I;[37] one suspects that the
sympathy shown by young Jane (one of Rodwell's imaginary juvenile audience)
for the exiled king, when her mother describes the reign of James II, could be
traced to the same source.[38]

[30] Taylor, *Prints*, p. iii.   [31] Ibid. 6–7, 19–20.   [32] Ibid. 24.   [33] Ibid. 28.
[34] Penrose, *History* (1846), 110.   [35] Ibid. 152.   [36] Ibid. 210.
[37] Rodwell, *Step*, 127.   [38] Ibid. 169.

Like the texts, the illustrations to early nineteenth-century textbooks showed signs of aspirations towards greater authenticity, contained sometimes uneasily within the traditional anecdotal framework. Taylor's *Historical Prints*, which was one of the textbooks to set a trend in illustration for the subsequent thirty years, is very illuminating. Most of its illustrations are of the same subjects as Trimmer's *Prints*: Canute rebuking his courtiers, the death of William Rufus, the coronation of Henry VI, and the marriage of Henry VII and Elizabeth of York, for example, are illustrated in both. Many of the illustrations showed compositional similarities which suggested that Taylor's illustrator might well have seen the earlier work—for instance, those of the Black Prince attending King John, and the deaths of the Protestant martyrs Latimer and Ridley.[39] This makes the difference between the prints themselves all the more apparent. The subtitle of *Historical Prints* declared that, in the 'memorable events' depicted, 'the costumes of the times are carefully preserved', and the prints do indeed display clear signs of the artist's reference to well-known antiquarian works. In print 5, *Alfred Framing Laws* the king was derived from the figure of an eighth-century monarch in Joseph Strutt's *Dress and Habits* (1796–9).[40] The three clergy in *Henry the Second Doing Penance*' (Fig. 7), were drawn from another plate in the same work of *Ecclesiastics of the Tenth and Eleventh Centuries* (Fig. 8).[41] A print showing Edward I presenting his infant son to the Welsh owed its central figure to an illustration of Edward's coronation in *Dress and Habits*.[42] Another definite source for Taylor's prints was Francis Grose's *A Treatise of Ancient Armour and Weapons* (1786). Prints 14, 15, and 16 showed William I wearing a helmet which was derived from a plate in Grose's *Treatise*, where it was described as a helmet which belonged to the King.[43] In print 48, a horse appears in the same armour as one shown in another plate from this work.[44]

The anecdotal and traditional aspects of Trimmer's and Taylor's prints continued to influence the pattern for the illustration of many textbooks which were published during the 1830s and 1840s, when picturesque history was at its height. Taylor's *Historical Prints* may be compared with Anne Rodwell's *The Child's First Step* (1844). Taylor's work contained ninety-six prints in total; Rodwell's had forty-six illustrations. Of these, forty-one were of the same subjects as Taylor's prints. Coincidences of composition in many of the illustrations, including Richard I pardoning his brother John, Prince Edward rescuing his father

[39] Taylor, *Prints*, prints 11, 31, 18, 49, 62, 73; Trimmer, *Prints*, prints 9, 19, 11, 30, 36, 43. In the case of the latter (and no doubt others), the viewer must be aware of the possibility of a visual source common to both—such as John Foxe's *Book of Martyrs*, for example.

[40] Taylor, *Prints*, print 9; J. Strutt, *A Complete View of the Dress and Habits of the People of England*, 3 vols. (1796–9), i, plate 3.

[41] Taylor, *Prints*, print 23; Strutt, *Dress*, i, plate 25.

[42] Taylor, *Prints*, print 37; Strutt, *Dress*, i, plate 60.

[43] Taylor, *Prints*, prints 14, 15, 16; F. Grose, *A Treatise of Ancient Armour and Weapons* (1786), plate 9.

[44] Taylor, *Prints*, print 48; Grose, *Treatise*, plate 25.

Fig. 7. *Henry the Second Doing Penance at the Tomb of Becket*, from E. Taylor, *Historical Prints, Representing Some of the Most Memorable Events in English History* (1821), print 23

(Fig. 9), and the Duke of Gloucester entreated to accept the crown, confirm the impression that Taylor's work was known to the illustrator of *The Child's First Step*. This seems all the more probable in the light of the fact that the publishers of both textbooks were Harvey and Darton, the leading early nineteenth-century publishers of educational works for children: the firm may well have commissioned an illustrator to modernize the style of the old set of prints for further use.[45] This example suggests that the continuity of the anecdotal style was reinforced by mundane considerations of convenience and expense, either on the part of the illustrator or the publisher.

Such a view is confirmed by the arrangements for the first edition of Lady Callcott's *Little Arthur's History* (1835), the text of which was saturated with the Romantic nationalism characteristic of picturesque history. Lady Callcott initially hoped to provide original designs for the work, but when the young artist, John Callcott Horsley, whom she had chosen to produce them rejected her offer,

---

[45] Rodwell's illustrations are even more firmly attached to the traditional anecdotal tradition by their close resemblance to some of the Bowyer Gallery paintings. The composition of *Queen Elizabeth at Tilbury* (Fig. 2) and *Charles I Bidding Farewell to his Children* are so close to the paintings by Stothard of these subjects that it is probable that the artist had these well-known images before him as he worked.

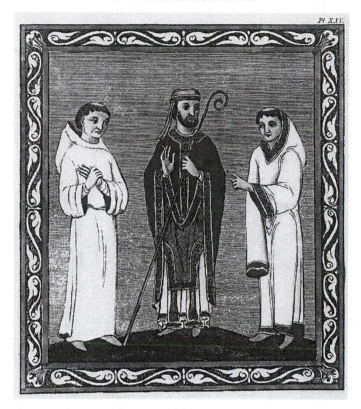

Fig. 8. J. Strutt, *Ecclesiastics of the Tenth and Eleventh Centuries,*
from J. Strutt, *A Complete View of the Dress and Habits of the People of
England,* 3 vols. (1796–9), i, plate 25

she took the advice of her artist husband and fell back mainly on copies from the
Bowyer and Boydell Galleries. One consistent aim in her selection of designs,
however, shows how strongly domestic and anecdotal concerns continued to
dominate illustration of textbooks in the 1830s and 1840s: she was determined to
include 'the points where children are the heroes of the stories'.[46]

The drive for authentic illustration, which was apparent in Taylor's *Historical
Prints*, was continued in a very different direction in Mrs Markham's *History of
England*. This extremely popular work, with its quintessentially philosophical
and domestic narrative, was nevertheless pioneering in the field of illustration.
Probably for the first time, a textbook was illustrated with metanymic illustrations. As the illustrations characteristic of picturesque historiography were
metaphoric ones with authentic details incorporated, this suggests a peculiarly
radical approach to the inclusion of images, close to that apparent in the later

[46] JMA: Callcott MSS, M. Callcott to J. Murray, 4 and 22 May 1835.

Fig. 9. *Edward Rescuing his Father*, from A. Rodwell, *The Child's First Step to English History* (1844), 59

nineteenth-century textbook. Was Mrs Markham really so ahead of her time in her attitude to illustration? Elizabeth Penrose's text reflected her interest in, and control of, the choice of illustrations.[47] In the Advertisement to the *History*, she commented that: 'the little engravings with which these volumes are accompanied will be easily recognized as taken from Mr Strutt's works and other books of acknowledged authority.'[48] This interest and involvement is clear within the body of the text. When Mary Markham asked to see a picture of Edward V, her mother described an old manuscript illustration of Caxton and the royal family, and

---

[47] Letters between John Penrose and John Murray show that arrangements concerning the illustrations were left almost entirely in the hands of the Penroses by the publisher. John Penrose suggested that wood-cuts on the same page as the text would be 'an incomparable improvement' for a new edn. of another of Elizabeth Penrose's works, *A History of France*, and he sent four new drawings for it; he offered to send the drawing of the illustrations used in the 1st edn. of *A History of England*, published by Constable in 1823. Ibid.: Penrose MSS, J. Penrose to J. Murray, 30 Nov. 1825 and 20 Aug. 1829.

[48] Penrose, *History* (1846), p. iv.

Fig. 10. After J. Strutt, *A Saxon Ship of the Ninth Century*, from E. Penrose ('Mrs Markham'), *A History of England* (1846), 15

added a few comments on two painters of the time, Holbein and Mabuse.[49] A link between text and illustration was formed by the portrait of Henry VII and his wife, attributed to the latter of these artists, which appears at the head of a subsequent chapter.[50] George Markham asked whether Richard III looked like 'that gentleman in the picture with the long shoes', referring to an earlier illustration.[51] Later, describing Tudor fashions, Mrs Markham remarked that the 'little drawing of Lady Hunsdon', the illustration for that chapter, would give 'a good idea of the dress of the ladies'.[52]

However, it is important to emphasize that Mrs Markham's illustrations were derived principally not from original sources, but from the works of Joseph Strutt. It is true that, unlike the *Historical Prints*, Markham's illustrations are more or less straightforward reproductions of selected subjects from Strutt's plates, instead of attempts to render imaginary versions of events more historically accurate. Both the illustrations and, in part, the text show that the decision to use such apparently authentic images was not accompanied by any understanding of source criticism, visual context, or artistic conventions and styles. In chapter 4, for instance, Mrs Markham applied her critical eye to the proportions of a Saxon ship of the ninth century, doubting whether this illustration is an 'exact representation' (Fig. 10).[53] The illustration was abstracted from Strutt's *Manners* (1775–6), and copied as it was—except for the addition of a sea-scape and some

[49] Penrose, *History* (1846), 220.   [50] Ibid. 231.   [51] Ibid. 178, 228.
[52] Ibid. 304, 315.   [53] Ibid. 15, 20.

perspective alterations achieved by shading.[54] This shows little respect for the integrity of the source, in the interest of simply rendering the illustration intelligibly rather than accurately. Despite the fact it is not a metaphoric representation of the text, it is treated as if it could be: its independence and integrity as an image from the past is much undermined.[55] The gentleman and lady of Mary I's reign, also from Strutt's *Manners*,[56] suffered a slight alteration to make these two separate figures seem like a couple in conversation—an alteration reminiscent of Strutt's own methods. This sort of visual editing was common in Markham's *History*, and reflects both the interest in genuine artefacts of the national past and the essentially uncritical and amateur attitude to them characteristic of picturesque historiography. Other works of Strutt besides *Manners* served as sources and were similarly edited. A picture of the Quintain was derived from *Sports and Pastimes* (1801),[57] and was rendered less static than it appeared in the original; an Anglo-Saxon nobleman, who came from Strutt's *Dresses and Habits*,[58] was shown standing instead of sitting. It is but fair to say, however, that many images were straightforward reproductions—some fifteenth-century rustics and women servants, for example, were derived without alteration from *Dress and Habits*.[59] This particular response to the need for greater authenticity— reproduction of images derived from manuscripts (at one remove), rather than imaginative reconstruction of anecdotal events—pioneered the illustration of later Victorian textbooks. Possibly the visual modernity of Markham's *History*, which has been described as 'almost the only textbook of English history used in schools and families for nearly forty years',[60] helps to explain the longevity of its appeal.

Paradoxically, the other universally popular nineteenth-century textbook— the first edition of Maria Callcott's *Little Arthur's History of England*—contrasts with Mrs Markham's *History of England* in its combination of a more progressive text characteristic of picturesque historiography with conservative and uninspiring illustrations, as has already been shown. As a letter of 1834 to her friend Caroline Fox makes clear, Lady Callcott initially conceived of *Little Arthur's History of England* as a traditional episodic series of 'true stories':

I am going to put in the cake-tasting of Alfred, and moreover make a little niche somewhere for King Arthur. You shall see how I can make a patch-work. I am making an

---

[54] Penrose, *History* (1846), 15; J. Strutt, *Horda Anjel-cynna, or, A Compleat View of the Manners, Customs, Arms, Habits etc of the Inhabitants of England*, 3 vols. (1775–6), i, plate 9, fig. 1.

[55] Penrose, *History* (1846), 35; Strutt, *Manners*, i, plate 17, fig. 1.

[56] Penrose, *History* (1846), 273; Strutt, *Manners*, iii, plate 12, figs. 5 and 6.

[57] Penrose, *History* (1846), 162; J. Strutt, *Gli-gamena Anjel-deod, or, The Sports and Pastimes of the People of England* (1801), plate 10.

[58] Penrose, *History* (1846), 29; Strutt, *Dress*, i, plate 4.

[59] Penrose, *History* (1846), 168, 174; Strutt, *Dress*, ii, plates 106, 117.

[60] *DNB* xliv. 342. By 1843, it was in its 10th edn.; further edns. followed in 1846, 1853, 1862, 1865, 1871, 1872, and 1873.

experiment you know—not meaning to read any authorities till I see how my memory would serve to *tell* the history to an intelligent child. I shall *then* read and correct—maybe print.[61]

But the patriotic tone of Callcott's *History* exhibited a Romantic nationalism absent from Mrs Markham's *History* and other philosophical history textbooks (a development which may be partially attributed to Callcott's earlier travels in both India and South American countries then in the midst of their battles for independence[62]). While still inculcating domestic virtues—'Is any man the worse citizen for being a good son, or brother, or father, or husband?'—Callcott's aim was consciously national and patriotic, as well as domestic and social. Romantic historiography, after all, popularized not only the cult of the individual but also the celebration of the cultural uniqueness and right of self-determination of the nation. Callcott stressed that history was next after scripture as an essential guide to the patriot.[63] Sir Thomas More, for example, is eulogized for his happy family life: 'You may think what a happy family this was, and how much all the children and the parents loved one another.'[64] But he was commended still more for his ability to sacrifice family to country in his service as chancellor and his willingness to die for his beliefs: 'You know that God gives men duties to do for the country they live in, as well as for themselves.'[65] Other authors shared Callcott's aim to educate patriots[66]—heroism, once again, was becoming a matter of public action (in addition to private virtue). The attitude of horror at the details of wars, particularly unnecessary ones, even if they were successful, was mitigated by national pride: many textbooks carried illustrations of Nelson and the Duke of Wellington as their sole visual contribution to the history of the nineteenth century.[67]

   The illustrations of the 1856 edition of Callcott's *Little Arthur* repay attention, as in their entirety they reflect the whole range of nineteenth-century historiographical evolutions here explored. All were metaphoric recreations of anecdotal scenes: some of the illustrations, derived from the first edition, were poor near-copies of paintings from Bowyer's Gallery—for instance, Charles I bidding his children farewell[68]—but many, evidently more recent, were executed with attention to historical detail in costume and in the classically based 'Sixties

[61] Quoted in R. B. Gotch, *Maria, Lady Callcott: The Creator of 'Little Arthur'* (1937), 289.

[62] See E. Mavor (ed.), *The Captain's Wife: The South American Journals of Maria Graham 1821–23* (1993) for her opinions on Brazilian and Chilean politics in the early 1820s.

[63] Callcott, *Arthur*, p. iv.   [64] Ibid. 142.   [65] Ibid. 143.

[66] Chancellor, *History*, 112–38. This chapter examines the increasingly nationalistic and jingoistic attitude of later Victorian textbook writers, an attitude the seeds of which are apparent in some of the textbooks examined here.

[67] Ibid. 130–2. See Iain Pears, 'The Gentleman and the Hero: Wellington and Napoleon in the Nineteenth Century', in R. Porter (ed.), *Myths of the English* (1992), 216–36, for a discussion of the portrayal of Wellington as the gentlemanly epitome of the English character, a British counterpoint of the apotheosis of Napoleon, a type of the Romantic hero beloved of picturesque nationalist historiography.

[68] Callcott, *Arthur*, 148.

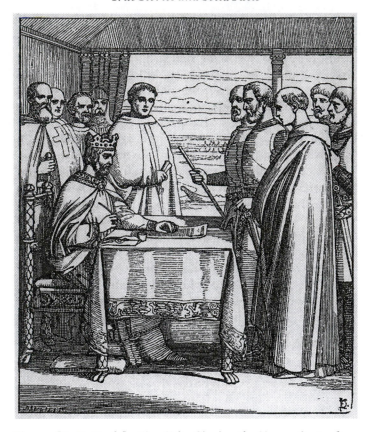

Fig. 11. [J. E. Doyle], *King John Signing the Magna Carta,* from
M. Callcott, *Little Arthur's History of England* (1856), 71

style'.[69] These illustrations are essentially transitional, reflecting the picturesque
approach in their metaphoric form, historical details, and emphasis on the individual, but also suggesting the new scientific historiography associated with
bureaucratic development of the nation-state. They lack the more intimate quality of the other textbook illustrations, bringing to mind the similarly transitional
Westminster murals of the 1840s. Included are some unusual subjects, such as
Alfred supervising the building of the English navy, which echoes Callcott's
patriotic sentiments (and celebrates the emergence of the defensive apparatus
necessary to a nation-state). The signature appears to be that of James Doyle,
who illustrated his own *A Chronicle of England to AD 1485* (1864) and an edition

---

[69] Illustration in the 1860s was dominated by considerations of style. Naturalism, the influence
of German illustrators, and an almost sculptural interest in form combined to produce a distinctive
style, of which John Millais's work is archetypical. See F. Reid, *Illustrators of the Sixties* (1928).

of Lingard's *History of England* (1819–30) in a very similar manner in the 1850s.[70] It is therefore most probable that he was the illustrator of this textbook. Although, as a keen amateur historian, he may well have had access to many antiquarian works, it is likely that he would have relied, like many fellow artists, on J. R. Planché's *History of British Costume* (1834), of which more below. In the illustration of King Richard I taken prisoner, the armoured figure of the Duke of Austria owed much to the effigy of Geoffrey de Magnaville, shown in Planché, while in the illustration of King John signing the Magna Carta (Fig. 11), the King's costume was a conflation of the effigies of John and Richard I.[71]

'THE GROUNDWORK OF ACCURATE FACT': THE EMERGENCE OF THE SCIENTIFIC HISTORY TEXTBOOK AFTER 1850

By 1850, the drive for authenticity in Victorian textbooks was both intensifying and changing with the advent of a new, more scientific approach to history: history, now evolving into a professionalized discipline, was soon to be perceived as a fundamental part of the state educational system. The effect of a new interest in the documentary sources of national history and their systematic and critical examination, and the development of history as an academic discipline, has been assessed in the case of textbooks by Valerie Chancellor: she postulates that later Victorian textbooks aimed at neutrality of opinion, offering 'facts not judgements'.[72] While it is clear that such neutrality was (and is) more apparent than possible, she rightly pinpoints a change in the author's attitude to his/her text, an alteration in the rhetoric of the textbook. Once part of the liberal education of the upper- and middle-class family, a formative influence on judgement and taste, morals and manners, history now became the essential factual basis of the patriotic citizen's education. Influenced initially by the creed of Romantic nationalism, the textbook narrative of the English past soon became subject to institutional control, the object of examinations for civil servants and children alike. Chancellor gives due weight to the emergence of public examinations in the 1850s and 1860s.[73] The extension of schooling to all classes by the 1870 Elementary Education Act, and to the provinces by the informal University Extension Scheme,[74] was also an important factor, as too was the reform of the Universities.[75]

---

[70] See ch. 7.

[71] Callcott, *Arthur*, 66, 71; J. R. Planché, *The History of British Costume* (1834), 86, 79.

[72] Chancellor, *History*, 11.

[73] Examinations were only introduced for candidates for the civil service in 1870, but after 1855 the qualifications of candidates were to be checked fully by their potential superiors.

[74] This began in 1876–8. See J. F. C. Harrison, *Learning and Living: A Study in the History of the Adult Education Movement* (1961), 219–45.

[75] P. Slee, *Learning and a Liberal Education: The Study of Modern History in the Universities of Oxford, Cambridge and Manchester, 1800–1914* (Manchester, 1986), 20–117.

From the 1850s, history textbooks altered in style and content, though more significantly in the former than the latter. Most were written by professional teachers for pupils to read in classrooms,[76] and, particularly after 1870, aimed at covering the factual ground necessary to aid the reader to pass an examination. Many appeared in a series of 'readers', orchestrated by publishers who assumed still more control of the production of the history textbook. The familial fiction was discarded; the encouragement to empathize was minimal; the format was characterized by numbered sections and the use of bold print for names and dates, and the narrative was very bald. Nevertheless, anecdotes of the traditional kind were often still included, though frequently with a critical qualification.

Textbook illustrations were not so obviously altered as the text, partly because, while history becoming an accepted academic and professional discipline, art history was still the province of amateurs and was not to achieve the same status in Britain until well into the twentieth century. A fully critical response to the visual reproduction of historical artefacts (and to many of the artefacts themselves) was simply not attainable, and the drastic solution to this academic dilemma proved to be, in fact, the marginalization and even the total elimination of illustrations. In some cases illustration was retained but with changes, albeit mainly in the form of a more systematic pursuit of the innovations introduced by picturesque historiography: the lifting of historical details from antiquarian works, an unusual feature in Taylor's *Prints* when they first appeared in 1821, now extended to all metaphoric illustrations, regardless of the age group for which they were intended. Metanymic illustrations, such as those in Markham's *History*, increased in number dramatically: no doubt viewed as a more objective form of illustration, they were the dominant images of the new scientific textbook. Both approaches to illustration, however, were part of a common search for a degree of authenticity, and therefore both benefited from the advent of works which popularized the visual contents of Strutt's and other antiquaries' volumes. Prominent among these were Planché's *History of British Costume*, which aimed to 'condense and sift' Strutt's material, F. W. Fairholt's *Costume in England: A History of Dress* (1846), S. R. Meyrick's *Specimens of Ancient Furniture* (1836), and Richard Lodge's *Portraits of Illustrious Personages of Great Britain* (1823–34). The contribution of such works to the spread of authentic historical images has already been recognized in the case of history paintings by Roy Strong,[77] but has not been discussed in the case of textbook illustrations.

A typical example of the text of the new type of textbook was W. Legg's unillustrated *A Reading Book in English History* (1864), a work divided into numbered paragraphs and with a set of questions for its conclusion. In the Preface, its reviser, R. K. Brewer, set out his intention that it should be an 'aid both to

[76] Chancellor, *History*, 25.
[77] R. Strong, *And When Did You Last See Your Father? The Victorian Painter and British History* (1978), 62–73.

teachers and schools' and 'a pleasant reading book to the young, but a sufficient guide to candidates for Middle-class examinations'.[78] An earlier and more
transitional work such as E. Farr's *The Collegiate, School and Family History
of England* (1848) is, however, particularly interesting. This work purported to
be a textbook both for private and public pupils, families and schools, but it was
the last target at which it was really aimed. It was advertised in the Preface as a
substitute for the inaccurate 'History commonly used in schools, and which
professes to be an improved edition of the work originally written by [Oliver]
Goldsmith'. It was not aimed at educating just gentlemen, but 'loyal and good
subjects, and peaceful and useful members of the community':[79] accordingly,
the national narrative is highlighted, with much greater attention being given
to constitutional and political matters. The fiction of the mother indulging in an
evening *conversazione* with her children was discarded by most textbook authors,[80]
as writers such as Farr began to appeal to a wider community of school children.
Their material was presented in a straightforward classroom manner—often,
as in Stacey Grimaldi's *A Synopsis of English History* (1871), arranged by kings,
with a list of the events of each reign at the head of the chapter, or even, as in
C. H. S. Nichols's *Outlines of English History* (1850), without any text at all
to link dates, details of kings, remarkable events, and celebrated figures. The
statement of purpose in Farr's Preface reveals the new orientation of moral intent
in the textbook: history was now viewed, above all, as a tool in the education
of citizens.

The content of textbooks after 1850, however, did not differ as much as their
format from the earlier works: another indication of the persistence of tradition
in the English history textbook. Many of the anecdotes entrenched in the early
nineteenth-century textbooks continued to appear in later works—and many old
favourites, such as Markham's *History* and Callcott's *Little Arthur's History*,
continued to be used (albeit in revised forms) as the basic texts of juvenile history
courses. Revised rather than substantially original material was the order of the
day. Most authors increasingly recognized the inadequacy of the old anecdotes
and showed a tendency to distinguish firmly between fact and fiction characteristic of the post-1850 period. E. M. Sewell (who ran her own small school on
the Isle of Wight) wrote, in the Preface to *A Catechism of English History* (1872):
'Historical stories are attractive at the moment; but unless the groundwork of

---

[78] W. Legg, *A Reading Book in English History*, ed. R. K. Brewer (1863), preface.
[79] E. Farr, *The Collegiate, School and Family History of England* (1848), pp. iii–v.
[80] One of the few works to maintain the familial fiction (*Uncle William's Concise History of
England for the Use of Schools and Families* 1880s?) carries a significant frontispiece of the mother
of Alfred the great instructing her children, but makes use of the fiction beyond the title-page. The
fiction was also maintained in the 1865 edn. of Markham's History, ed. Mary Howitt, in the
additional sections of the work, she wrote that she had 'for the sake of consistency, maintained
the little fiction of Authorship by supposing the wife of the worthy Mrs Markham's son to continue
the narrative to her children, and I hope in so doing I have written in the spirit of the original'. See
E. Penrose ('Mrs Markham'), *A History of England*, ed. Howitt (1865), preface.

accurate fact is well laid, they can never make a real historian.'[81] After perusing less rigorously written works than *A Catechism*, readers would find that they had forgotten 'the important facts', recalling 'only the amusing anecdotes or descriptions of dress and manners'.[82] Sewell treated the traditional anecdotes ruthlessly: the tale of Edwy and Elgiva was dismissed as 'a painful story',[83] while that of Edward, Eleanor, and the poisoned dagger was included, but with the authorial comment that 'the story, however, rests on no good authority'.[84] Sewell's friend, C. M. Yonge—although she became the writer of many historical tales—was almost equally committed to the purist stance. In the Preface to *The Kings of England* (1852), she wrote: 'There has . . . been less attempt than is usual in such work, to gather together numerous anecdotes . . . [from] the beautiful, half-traditionary stream that flows along beside the graver course of our history.'[85]

But many textbooks did include the anecdotes, pausing only to add an editorial caution. The introductory phrase 'It is said' was sufficiently common to be deplored by one contemporary pupil who recalled, with pleasure, her still more conservative textbook. M. V. Hughes, educated initially at home in the 1870s, commented:

My English history was derived from a little book in small print that dealt with the characters of the kings at some length. I learnt how one was ruthless alike to friend and foe and another was so weak that the sceptre fell from his nerveless grasp. I seemed to see it falling. The book had no doubts or evidence or sources, but gave all the proper anecdotes about the cakes, the peaches and new ale, never smiling again, the turbulent priest and the lighted candle. I am glad that I had this at the credulous stage, and in this unhesitating form. They were much more glowing than if they had been introduced by the chilling words 'it is said that'.[86]

When she went to school, she seems to have progressed from a philosophical history textbook to the quintessential picturesque work, which retained the storytale appeal of her first favourite:

My new history book was 'Little Arthur', which one could read like a delightful story. The general spirit of the author about unpleasant things seemed to be that they happened so long ago that they probably never happened at all. Anyway, we gained a fair idea of the flow of events and the stories of leading people without boredom.[87]

These quotations capture perfectly the combination of empathetic and visual experience of the past with the rather contradictory sense of a 'delightful story', almost more fiction than fact, which the traditional approach could induce in the reader.

It is no surprise, therefore, to find a reluctance to discard the anecdotes (or the texts which encapsulated them) in many later textbooks. The revised 1875

---

[81] E. M. Sewell, *A Catechism of English History* (1872), p. iii. [82] Ibid., p. iv.
[83] Ibid. 11. [84] Ibid. 47. [85] C. M. Yonge, *The Kings of England* (1852), p. iii.
[86] M. V. Hughes, *A London Child of the 1870s* (1934; Oxford, 1977 edn.), 42.
[87] Ibid. 62.

edition of Mrs Markham's *History* repeated the tale of Edwy and Elgiva, but added to the account: 'It is right to notice, however, that the evidence on which this horrible tale rests is to some extent imperfect.'[88] In the 1875 edition, the original homily on immoderate ambition, which succeeded the death of Godwin, was replaced by the critical (and patently nationalistic) comment that 'some modern writers think it [the story] was probably an invention of the Normans, who had obvious motives for vilifying the sturdy English earl'.[89] The much altered 1860 version of Taylor's *Historical Prints, England and its People*, is similarly cautious with the traditional anecdotes. Alfred and the cakes and Henry V and Judge Gascoigne appear in unadulterated forms, but Rosamund's murder by Queen Eleanor is recounted 'as the stories say', and though Prince Arthur was rumoured to have been murdered by King John, the reader was cautioned once again that it is difficult to judge the truth here.[90] The tale of Edward and the poisoned dagger was included, although Eleanor is only 'said' to have sucked the wound.[91]

Textbook illustrations were often similarly unchanged in content: sometimes, the appearance of the traditional style of illustrations was the sign of a writer or publisher saving time and/or money by simply recycling existing illustrations, long after their original appearance. Anne Manning's *The Cottage History of England* (1861) was a late work to use this type of metaphorical illustration exclusively, but the reasons for this choice were given in the Preface. The author justified her work by its cheapness, hoping that: 'it will find its way from the book hawker's basket into many kitchens and cottages . . . As for the illustrations, they have done good service already, and it is only on that account that such very excellent ones can be afforded to so cheap a book . . .'[92] The illustrations had indeed done good service—they were the same ones used in Rodwell's *A Child's First Step* and, no doubt, other similar works. As such, their conjunction with the text was occasionally uneasy: the illustration of the Battle of Lewes, for example, was originally used to illustrate the Battle of Evesham, as is blatantly obvious from its central motif of Prince Edward saving his father (Fig. 9).[93]

Other textbooks had new illustrations, which had, however, very traditional subjects. This was particularly apparent in the case of works for younger pupils, which were more likely to be read in a domestic setting and could therefore retain the approach of the early and mid-nineteenth-century textbook. *The Children's Picture-Book of English History* (1859), like Callcott's *Arthur*, kept the traditional anecdotal subjects, including Canute rebuking his courtiers, the escape of Maude from Oxford, and Oliver Cromwell dissolving the Long Parliament. But

    [88] Penrose, *History* (1846), 26; E. Penrose ('Mrs Markham'), *A History of England*, ed. anon. (1875), 24.
    [89] Penrose, *History* (1846), 43–4; Penrose, *History* (1875), 39.
    [90] Taylor, *Prints*, 6–7,47, 24, 28; E. Taylor, *England and its People: A Familiar History* (1821; 1860 edn.) 10, 132, 68, 80.
    [91] Taylor, *Prints*, 34; Taylor, *England*, 89.
    [92] A. Manning, *The Cottage History of England* (1861), pp. iii–iv.
    [93] Ibid. 59; Rodwell, *Step*, 59.

the artist had clearly consulted the popularizing purveyors of antiquarian illustrations: the illustration of the Druids in the *Picture-Book* clearly owed much to an
illustration from Bernard Montfaucon's *Antiquité expliquée*, reproduced in both
Planché's and Fairholt's works.[94] C. M. Yonge's *English History for the Little
Ones* was a work very similar to the *Picture-Book*—an anecdotal account with
illustrations showing little sign of research. But even these did show indications
of some consultation of visual sources. It is probable that Ethelbert and his wife,
in an illustration of Augustine preaching, were derived from plates in Planché.[95]
A hood, which was worn both by a woman listening to Peter the Hermit, and by
Maude as she escaped from Oxford, also echo a plate in Planché's work.[96] The
lukewarm researches of this illustrator for very young children indicates that even
the most unpretending of works were now obliged to nod in the direction of historical authenticity.

Textbooks also responded to the more positive results of new critical work on
historical sources, particularly recent research on Anglo-Saxon and constitutional history. D. Beale's *The Student's Textbook* (1858), for example, concentrated much attention on constitutional changes, as these had been given
'peculiar prominence . . . in recent examinations'.[97] In the Preface of the 1875
edition of Markham's *History*, it was announced that it had 'undergone scrupu-
lous revision . . . Many passages relating to the early period of the Saxon annals
have been rewritten, in order to make them conform more closely to the testimony of the original authorities and to the results established by modern
research.'[98] Accordingly, the account of the Heptarchy was greatly increased, in
deference no doubt to the new Teutonic emphases of the national narrative.[99]
The tale of Henry II and Thomas à Becket was enhanced by a quotation from an
acknowledged chronicler, and Henry II's legal reforms were given more space
and detail.[100] The text of *England and its People*—under which rousing nationalist and democratic title a revised version of *Historical Prints* appeared—also
showed an awareness of recent research. In *Historical Prints*, the Magna Carta
had been commended for the moderation it showed, which 'commanded the
admiration of succeeding generations'.[101] In *England and its People*, this comment was revised to 'certainly [it was] more for the good of the nobles than the
people at large, but still it provided for the liberties of all to a great extent'.[102]

In a similar way, textbook illustrations tended to include many more
metanymic images of the kind used by Knight, Planché, and Fairholt, in some

---

[94] [Anon.], *The Children's Picture-Book of English History* (1859), 14; Planché, *History*, 12;
F. W. Fairholt, *Costume in England: A History of Dress* (1846), 18.

[95] C. M. Yonge, *Aunt Charlotte's Stories of English History for the Little Ones* (1873), 13;
Planché, *History*, 22, 41.

[96] Yonge, *History*, 37, 45; Planché, *History*, 67.

[97] D. Beale, *The Student's Textbook of English and General History* (1858), p. iii.

[98] Penrose, *History* (1875), p. vi.

[99] Penrose, *History* (1846), 10–11; Penrose, *History* (1875), 10.

[100] Penrose, *History* (1846), 83, 86–7; Penrose, *History* (1875), 75, 78.

[101] Taylor, *Prints*, 30.   [102] Taylor, *England*, 83.

cases derived from observation of the original artefacts rather than antiquarian works. Revised editions of Markham's *History*, for instance, continued to follow the pattern of reproduction of 'authentic' images practised in the early editions. The Murray edition of 1853 advertised on the title-page its 'numerous woodcuts' and included both the original and a large number of new illustrations. Many of the latter came from the pencil of George Scharf,[103] who, it seems probable, was employed by Murray to render the best-selling textbook even more popular: these included a view of Stonehenge in its present state, Lord Burleigh's monument from St Martin's church in Stamford, and the shields and portrait of Richard I.[104] There were also two plates probably derived from Planché: these were illustrations of early English helmets and of Earl Rivers presenting his book to Edward IV.[105] The 1865 Allman edition of Markham's *History* relied much more heavily on Planché's work to provide new illustrations, probably because of lack of access to the 1853 Murray illustrations. The illustrations of British weapons, the military habits of the Anglo-Saxons, female costume of the reign of Edward IV, and a powder flask of the time of Mary I all derived, as did many other illustrations, from the pages of Planché.[106]

This trend towards the reproduction of these so-called authentic images, usually as many as possible, was apparent in other later Victorian textbooks. The fifth edition of Taylor's *England and its People* (1860) was another work which owed its metanymic reproductions to Planché's *History*. Illustrations of Druids from the Autun bas-relief, a Saxon abbot and an archbishop, Norman barons, a lady in a gorget, and an eighteenth-century lady, among others, derived from Planché.[107] It seems likely that Taylor herself suggested Planché as a suitable source for new illustrations, as she appears to have drawn upon his text: she quoted a contemporary poet's criticism of the gorget which is to be found in Planché too.[108] Another textbook which presented an array of such images was T. Birkby's *The History of England* (1870): illustrations included British, Roman, and Saxon coins, a view of a castle, Henry II and Becket from a manuscript in the Cotton Library, gentlemen and ladies of rank of the fifteenth century, and other similar examples.[109] Some illustrations, like those of the fifteenth-century rustics

---

[103] This was not George Scharf (1788–1860), best known now as a London topographical artist, but his eldest son, who shared the same name and profession. See P. Jackson, *George Scharf's London: Sketches and Watercolours of a Changing City, 1820–50* (1987), 1–18, for details of both.

[104] E. Penrose ('Mrs Markham'), *A History of England*, ed. anon. (1853), title-page and facing 9, 317, 96. Many of these illustrations were architectural. Scharf's letters to Murray in the early 1850s show that the artist was working on illustrations for a work relating to English architecture, an assignment of which the publisher apparently relieved him, on the grounds that his methods made the illustrations too expensive. Perhaps Murray was here making good use of some of these costly images. JMA: Scharf MSS, G. Scharf to J. Murray, 2 Oct. 1851, 1 Sept. 1852, 19 Oct. 1854.

[105] Penrose, *History* (1853), 46, 227; Planché, *History*, 110, 199.

[106] Penrose, *History* (1865), 3, 18, 214, 276; Planché, *History*, 3, 28, 207, 253.

[107] Taylor, *England*, 3, 18, 82, 102, 315; Planché, *History*, 12, 39, 86, 125, 321.

[108] Taylor, *England*, 102; Planché, *History*, 115.

[109] T. Birkby, *The History of England* (1870), 1, 23, 26, 70.

and Mabuse's portrait of Henry VII and his queen, were almost certainly derived from the original edition of Markham's *History*,[110] an indication of the influence of this work in establishing the use of metanymic images as textbook illustrations.

The evolution of the textbook in this period is placed in sharp relief when the text of a rogue work such as Dickens's *A Child's History of England* (1851–3) is examined. Here is a work in which the author—with a novelist's preference for a good story over factual concerns—refused to revise the traditional form of the history textbook. Derek Hudson has pointed out that Dickens 'undertook no original research', relying largely for his facts on Thomas Keightley's *History of England* (1839), and not resisting 'the temptation to briskly elaborate' on 'promising material'.[111] The traditional tales of Arthur and Canute were repeated,[112] and the tale of Blondel's rescue of Richard I was included with the comment that 'you may believe it if you like'.[113] The story of Edward, Eleanor, and the poisoned dagger, meanwhile, was one 'which I am very willing to believe'.[114] The vivid and impressionistic description of the death of Prince Arthur, one of the many purple passages of the work, explains why the author was unwilling to neglect such promising material.[115]

Dickens rose to anger when confronted with revisionist research which endangered the traditional narrative. He resisted adamantly new interpretations of Mary I's reign: 'The stake and fire were the fruits of this reign and you will judge this Queen by nothing else.'[116] Dickens maintained, with the anecdotes, the moral approach of the early nineteenth-century textbook, with an emphasis on family values and virtues interpreted in a form applicable to children. He criticized William II for erecting a splendid tomb for his father, commenting that it would have been 'more dutiful in him to have attended the sick conqueror when he was dying'.[117] He deplored Henry I's acts, which, he said, were often described as policy or diplomacy, commenting that 'nothing that is not true can possibly be good'.[118] In Dickens's rather ironic example of the traditional textbook, the illustrations matched the text. In the frontispiece for the first edition of 1852, which was drawn by F. W. Topham, four standard anecdotes were featured: Alfred in the neatherd's hut, Canute rebuking his courtiers, Edwy and Elgiva, and Queen Eleanor and the Fair Rosamund. Marcus Stone's later illustrations to the main text were of traditional anecdotal subjects too, such as Prince Arthur and his keeper Hubert and Lady Jane Grey in the Tower.[119]

The revision of the textbook away from the story-tale format gave rise to a large number of works which continued the historical narrative tradition, while making no claim to be serious textbooks. Such works were, of course, produced in the earlier period—including, for instance, Emily Taylor's *Stories from History* (1833)—but most works of this genre written after 1850 took more liberties with

---

[110] Penrose, *History* (1846), 168, 231; Birkby, *History*, 67, 88.
[111] C. Dickens, *The New Oxford Illustrated Dickens*, 21 vols. (1958), xx, p. xi.
[112] Ibid. xx. 145–6, 162.   [113] Ibid. xx. 230.   [114] Ibid. xx. 256.
[115] Ibid, xx. 234–35.   [116] Ibid. xx. 411.   [117] Ibid. xx. 182.
[118] Ibid. xx. 198.   [119] Ibid. xx. facing 120, 233, 404.

history than this most instructive volume. *Tales and Stories from History* (1870) by Agnes Strickland is a typical example. In the Advertisement for this work, the author announced that: 'Each of the stories is either founded upon, or connected with, some important event in History and furnishes useful information as the Manners and Customs of the particular era to which it relates.'[120] The intention to illustrate 'Manners and Customs'—now neglected by textbooks in favour of political and national history—was common to such works, as was the recognition that this genre was a mere complement to textbook history: 'the Tales are by no means intended to supply the place of History'.[121] A similar work was May Beverley's *Romantic Passages in English History* (1863). It included, for instance, the tales of Prior Rahere, the founder of St Bartholomew's Hospital, and of Catherine of Aragon's first marriage. All the tales had a factual basis, but they exercised much poetic licence. Catherine of Aragon, for instance, is represented as being in love with her husband of a few months and is kidnapped by Welsh rebels.[122] The development of a scientific and factual style for the history textbook began to force metaphoric illustration—particularly the traditional anecdotal style—out into the pages of historical novels and such pseudo-historical works as these. May Beverley's *Romantic Passages in English History* was illustrated very suitably by Robert Barnes, in a manner more suggestive of a contemporary novel than an instructive historical work. Popular Victorian genre subjects —such a deathbed attended by a devoted wife, and a loving bride gazing up at a fine but flawed husband—appeared in pseudo-historical guise: Catherine of Aragon attends the dying Prince Arthur, and Queen Anne of Bohemia admires King Richard II.[123] Arthur's curtained bed has the high-piled pillows of a Victorian bed, and Richard II sports the centre parting and oiled locks of a Victorian dandy. Strickland's *Tales and Stories* capitalized more fully on the anecdotal tradition: several favourite subjects appeared as illustrations in this work, including Alfred the Great as a harper, and Queen Margaret and her son encountering the robber of Hexham (who wears an eighteenth-century three-cornered hat like a highwayman's).[124]

Some writers went to quite another extreme. The increasing emphasis on serious and factual history seems to have led many writers and publishers to feel that, in the age of examinations, illustrations were a frivolous distraction from the

---

[120] A. Strickland, *Tales and Stories from History* (1870), advertisement. This retrieval of the traditional form of textbook history by a leading woman historian, whose arguments for her own biographies of royal women are justified on similar grounds to the ones she gives here, suggests that much of the difference between the 'traditional' and 'progressive' models analysed here depended on the largely female and amateur authorship of the former, and the professional and male authorship of the latter (see ch. 6 for further exploration of the distinctive nature of women's history-writing). It would be unwise to over-emphasize this possibility, however, as there are examples of male writers continuing this story-tale tradition of history to greater extremes than Strickland: William Collier in his *Pictures of the Periods: A Sketch-Book of Old England* (1865), for instance.

[121] Strickland, *Tales*, advertisement.

[122] M. Beverley, *Romantic Passages from English History* (1863), 143-245.

[123] Ibid., facing 244, 89.   [124] Strickland, *Tales*, 72, 297.

serious purpose of a textbook. As early as C. M. Yonge's 1852 work, *The Kings of England*, there were signs of the development of this attitude: both illustrations, and the 'manners and morals' approach to history characteristic of Markham's conversations were dismissed. The author commented that no space 'has been bestowed on manners, costumes, etc, since these may best be learnt from the numerous prints within the reach of any one, and they are more suited to amuse the play-hours of an intelligent child and form an agreeable supplement to historical studies, than to be regarded as a part of history itself'.[125] The vast majority of textbooks published in the 1860s and 1870s, particularly those designed for senior pupils and examination entrants, were unillustrated. Examples include H. Ince's and J. Gilbert's *Outlines of English History* (1865), J. S. Laurie's *Outlines of English History* (1876), S. Grimaldi's *A Synopsis of English History* (1871), and G. R. Greig's *A School History of England* (1872), among many others. The very titles of these works suggested their stream-lined, fact-based, and businesslike approach. The lack of interest in textbook illustration was revealed by the late editions of Markham's *A History of England*. The 1869 and 1875 editions, issued by Murray, drew on the illustrations of the 1853 edition, but did not use all of them. Scharf's full-page illustration of Stonehenge disappeared, for instance, and only one of the many Bayeux Tapestry illustrations was retained.[126]

TELLING STORIES: THE PICTURESQUE TRADITION

The early nineteenth-century philosophical history textbook—in some ways rather belying the historiographical period to which it belonged—was a collection of historical anecdotes from traditional sources, accompanied by metaphoric illustrations which showed little interest in historical reconstruction; it was intended to inculcate moral virtues by example, pertaining particularly to the domestic and social environment of the child. This anecdotal narrative of 'true stories' remained at the heart of the picturesque history textbook, although the quest for authenticity led to the exploitation of antiquarian research to enhance both text and image. From the 1850s on, the textbook assumed a more scientific and examination-orientated form, in which political and national history predominated and the young citizen was encouraged to practise more public virtues which would benefit the Empire. As the textbook was a naturally conservative form, this process was a slow one and clear signs of change are most evident after 1870, with the increasing state provision of education. The illustrations of the textbook also evolved in this period, as imaginative reconstructions, however carefully researched, were replaced by 'authentic' metanymic images— or were simply not replaced at all.

The writers of historical tales and their illustrators, however, continued to practise their art in another form: the complementary historical tale which

125 Yonge, *Kings*, p. iii.   126 Penrose, *History* (1853), 8, 58–9.

illustrated manners and customs, and retained the traditional style of illustrations. Picturesque history may have gone underground but it was not extinguished. Imaginative reconstruction of history, for both children and adults was (and is) a necessary function of the civilized society, even when that society holds by historical standards which emphasize strict factual accuracy and scientific methodologies. Scientific history was written to train the nation's citizens, but the Empire was still to find a need for rousing historical sagas, from the pens of writers such as G. A. Henty, to animate the past for its young children.

4

The Picturesque Face of the Past: The 1840s Novels of William Harrison Ainsworth

Among all the objects of art [*wrote the eighteenth-century theorist of the picturesque, William Gilpin*], the picturesque eye is perhaps most inquisitive after the elegant relics of ancient architecture; the ruined tower, the Gothic arch, the remains of castles and abbeys . . . They are consecrated by time, and almost deserve the veneration we pay to works of nature itself.[1]

The nineteenth-century picturesque historian shared Gilpin's fascination with the tangible remains of the national past, architectural, artistic, and textual. Heralding the rise of the heritage industry, picturesque historiography was both derived from and fuelled early nineteenth-century nationalism, feeding on and encouraging the exploration of the English—rather than the classical—past. The 1830s and 1840s, in particular, saw attempts by promoters of the historical picturesque to focus attention on and to reconfigure the architectural remains of the English past as national monuments and shrines. The participants in this nascent heritage culture produced travel books, guide books, history books, landscape paintings, and prints of antiquities, among other forms of art and literature. Pioneered by such individuals as Walter Scott, the historical picturesque was an open arena for both the antiquary and the amateur, the pedant and the popularizer. Indeed, it must be recognized that some participants in the movement, such as the creators of the Eglinton Tournament and Queen Victoria's costume ball, were not at all serious-minded and showed but little interest in engaging fully with the national narrative: like the present-day proponents of 'living history', they favoured reconstructions of the national past which dwelt on its drama, pageantry, and colour, rather than interpreting and expounding its meaning.

In Chapter 3, the importance of the 'true story'—the marriage of fact and fiction, historical detail and stirring narrative—in early and mid-nineteenth-century history-writing was emphasized: it is therefore no surprise to find writers of fiction among the leading proponents of the historical picturesque.

[1] A. M. Ross, *The Imprint of the Picturesque in Nineteenth Century British Fiction* (Ontario, 1986), 9. Ainsworth had a copy in his library, at his death, of Gilpin's *Remarks on Forest Scenery and Five Essays on Picturesque Subjects* (1808). See [Anon.], *Catalogue of the Library of the Late Celebrated Novelist, William Harrison Ainsworth . . . which will be sold by auction* (1882), 8.

As Scott's novels had demonstrated, historical romances were, perhaps, the natural medium for a mode of history which emphasized narrative and accumulation of descriptive detail rather than source criticism and analysis. This chapter will examine three novels—*The Tower of London* (1840), *Old Saint Paul's* (1841), and *Windsor Castle* (1843)—by William Harrison Ainsworth, the most important of the historical novelists of the 1830s and 1840s who attempted to capitalize on the popularity of the Waverley novels. They are typical of the contemporary 'footnote novel', a work full of historical details, which merged history and fiction, sometimes with a manifestedly didactic intention. This emphasis on the inclusion of authentic details to create a sense of historical immediacy and presence—reminiscent of Barthes's 'reality effect'—was a technique derived from the novels of Scott and a prominent characteristic of the picturesque history text.

However, Ainsworth's novels are unique in their intensive mobilization of both text and image to produce works of picturesque history: the author relied on the close collaboration of illustrators such as George Cruikshank.[2] In these novels, ancient architectural remains and their imagined occupants were composed into tableaux vivants, detailed historical reconstructions replete with authentic details both textual and visual. But despite Ainsworth's brilliant manipulation of Scott's reconstructive techniques, deployed in a most favourable publishing context (he and Cruikshank enjoying almost total control over their productions), his portrayals of English history are curiously hollow. A Gothic and essentially ahistorical view of the past is at the empty centre of a elaborate textual and visual presentation of stirring scenes from the national past. Ainsworth's fictions are, therefore, at once a triumph for the picturesque historical vision and an indication of its limitations when carried to extremes.

PICTURESQUE PRECURSORS: THE GOTHIC NOVEL
AND THE WAVERLEY NOVEL

Ainsworth's perception of the meaning of the past and its relics owed much to the Gothic novel, a forerunner of the historical novel which was in itself 'a mode of history, a way of perceiving an obscure past and interpreting it'.[3] However, the Gothic perception of the past was distinctly different from that of Walter Scott, the most important early nineteenth-century historical novelist: it suggested a

---

[2] Cruikshank (1792–1878), the illustrator of Dickens and Ainsworth, needs little introduction. Besides many novels, he also illustrated political satires such as *The Political House which Jack built* (1819), and works of non-fiction such as W. H. Maxwell's *The History of the Irish Rebellion* (1845). A good outline of his career can be found in R. McLean, *George Cruikshank: His Life and Work as a Book-Illustrator* (1948), but the authoritative biography is R. L. Patten's recent *George Cruikshank's Life, Times and Art*, 2 vols. (Cambridge, 1992 and 1996).

[3] D. Punter, *The Literature of Terror* (London and New York, 1980), 59. See also P. W. Day, *In the Circles of Fear and Desire: A Study of Gothic Fantasy* (Chicago and London, 1985), 31–34, where the past is described as a 'function of the literary dreamscape' of the Gothic (p. 33).

past which was terrifying, violent, and essentially irrational, ordered by fatalistic and supernatural means, legends, and events. Critics have commented on the incoherence of the forms of the Gothic novel and its preoccupation with the fragmentary and the incomplete, and it has been seen as an exploration of bourgeois fears of and fascination with the feudal past, and anxieties aroused by the French Revolution, radical English politics, and the development of a new industrial and capitalist society.[4] Clearly, then, Gothic vision was (and is) not concerned with perceiving the past accurately in a historical sense,[5] but with emotional responses to it.[6] Ainsworth's historical vision was related to the approach of these novels, to their attempt to realize and resolve fear, and thus a tension was created with the methods of realist historical fiction which he employed.

Ainsworth's intense use of detailed illustrations, closely related to the text, created a related tension with the Gothic visual tradition. The illustrations of Gothic novels show little interest in realistic detail, historical or otherwise: they were intended to project images of mystery or horror, frequently murky ones where either technical incompetence or good artistic perception left a great deal to the imagination.[7] It is tempting to see reference to the work of late eighteenth-century artists of the fantastic, such as Piranesi and Henry Fuseli, whose art was more concerned with states of mind than visual clarity or technical accuracies. Scott himself made a perceptive comment on Ann Radcliffe's description of the castle of Udolpho in her immensely popular Gothic novel, *The Mysteries of Udolpho* (1794): 'it affords a noble subject for the pencil but were six artists to attempt to embody it upon canvas, they would probably produce drawings essentially dissimilar to each other, yet all of them equally authorized by the printed description'.[8] It was the emotional impact, not the architectural order, of the castle which preoccupied the author and links can be made between Piranesi's *Imaginary Prisons* and Radcliffe's novels.[9] The Gothic is, perhaps, an essentially anti-pictorial genre where illustrations are best provided by the reader's imagination.[10]

While his vision derived from the Gothic novel, Ainsworth, like his fellow historical novelists, owed his reconstructive methods to the historical fiction of Walter Scott. Scott's contribution to the development of the historical novel was

    [4] See D. H. Richter, *The Progress of Romance: Literary Historiography and the Gothic Novel* (Columbus, Ohio, 1996), 53–83, for a recent neo-Marxist consideration of the social, cultural, and political origins of the Gothic novel. A. Bhalla, *The Cartographers of Hell: Essays on the Gothic Novel and the Social History of England* (New Delhi, 1991) offers a less sophisticated perspective, while M. Kilgour, *The Rise of the Gothic Novel* (1995), 10–15, dwells (rather unconvincingly) on the genre as a manifestation of nostalgia for medieval communality and Anglo-Saxon liberties.

    [5] Punter, *Literature*, 53, 128, 404–6.

    [6] G. E. Haggerty, *Gothic Fiction/Gothic Form* (Philadelphia, 1989), 1–35.

    [7] See, for typical examples, F. S. Frank, *The First Gothics: A Critical Guide to the English Gothic Novel* (1987), facing 120, 300.

    [8] W. Scott, *The Lives of the Novelists* (1827), quoted in *Sir Walter Scott: On Novelists and Fiction*, ed. I. Williams (1968), 119.

    [9] M. Levy, *Le Roman 'gothique' anglais* (Toulouse, 1968), 270–4.

    [10] B. Hennessy, *The Gothic Novel* (Harlow, 1978), 45.

long ago declared by Georg Lukas to be the use of a genuine historicist perspective, the development of a form of historical realism.[11] Many critics have remained in basic agreement with this thesis, seeing Scott's novels essentially as a confrontation or a debate between an old feudal social structure, heroic but barbaric, and a new bourgeois and progressive society, comfortable if dull.[12] This sociological approach to the past was derived from Scottish Enlightenment philosophers such as Dugald Stewart and John Bruce, and thus links Scott with the world of the eighteenth-century philosophical historian.[13] But it was not as a successor to the philosophical historian that Scott's immediate successors imitated him: Ainsworth and others looked instead to his antiquarian approach, to the wealth of historical detail which he amassed.[14]

As a pioneer of picturesque history, Scott was extraordinarily well-read in the literature, poetry, and documents of the past—and particularly the Scottish past.[15] His antiquarian enthusiasms were part of the Romantic national revivals of the Celtic fringes; however, Scott's achievement in the Waverley novels was to defuse the threat to the English national narrative offered by this picturesque historiography of the margins and make it available to an English audience as well. As convinced as David Hume that union with England and the adoption of an Anglo-British identity was the way forward for Scotland, Scott reined in his Romantic attraction to the Scottish past by representing it as indeed past: from this perspective, he can be and has been seen as a betrayer of Scottish Romantic nationalism.[16] Accordingly, some modern commentators point to Scott's historical realism as the instrument of a particular historical ideology, in which the

[11] G. Lukas, *The Historical Novel*, trans. H. and S. Mitchell (Harmondsworth, 1962), 29–69.

[12] See for instance D. Daiches, 'Sir Walter Scott and History', *Études anglaises*, 24 (1971), 458–77, and D. Brown, *Walter Scott and the Historical Imagination* (1989). F. R. Hart presents a more sophisticated version of the same theory in *Scott's Novels: The Plotting of Historic Survival* (Charlottesville, 1966). For an interpretation which contradicts most modern criticism of Scott, see J. Anderson, *Sir Walter Scott and Society* (Edinburgh, 1971).

[13] P. D. Garside, 'Scott and the Philosophical Historians', *Journal of the History of Ideas*, 36 (1975), 497–512.

[14] Edward Bulwer Lytton, who made his characters represent social groups and historical movements, was one of the few historical novelists of the period who appeared to be influenced by a philosophical interpretation of history, although he shared the common concern for a very visual reconstruction of the past in his novels. Lytton felt that he was in a class apart, as his condemnation of his contemporaries for 'crowding the page with quotations, and the margins with notes' indicated. Lytton's approach to history was more evidently related to immediate contemporary concerns than those of many of his contemporaries. J. C. Simmons, *The Novelist as Historian* (The Hague and Paris, 1973), 35–48; E. B. Lytton, *The Last Days of Pompeii* (1834; 2 vols., 1850 edn.), i, pp. viii–ix; C. Dahl, 'History on the Hustings: Bulwer Lytton's Historical Novels of Politics', in R. C. Rathburn and M. Steinmann (eds.), *From Jane Austen to Joseph Conrad* (Minneapolis, 1958), 60–71. See also A. C. Christensen, *Edward Bulwer Lytton: The Fiction of New Regions* (Athens, G., 1976), 112–35.

[15] See, for an instance of Scott's debt to his reading, J. Mitchell, *Scott, Chaucer, and Medieval Romance: A Study in Scott's Indebtedness to the Literature of the Middle Ages* (Lexington, K., 1987).

[16] See K. Trumpener, *Bardic Nationalism* (Princeton, 1997), 128–57, and C. Kidd, *Subverting Scotland's Past* (Cambridge, 1993), 256–67.

picturesque past was at once celebrated, and contained and depoliticized.[17] As a result, Scott achieved a degree of popularity unimaginable to his fellow proponents of the Celtic 'national tale', and was able to bequeath his reconstructive techniques—though not his historical perceptions—to the historical romancers of the 1830s and 1840s. Ainsworth's methods, by which he created a historical tableau from a mass of antiquarian details, were distinctly Scott's, applied to narratives woven around monuments at the heart of the English historical consciousness.

PIECING TOGETHER THE PICTURESQUE PAST

A Gothic vision of the past and Scott's realist reconstructive methods were welded together by Ainsworth's particular use of the concept of the picturesque. The definition of Gilpin and other writers of the picturesque established that it was a category apart from beauty: it was an assembly of landscape features which would make a good picture.[18] As a picturesque author, Ainsworth wrote to appeal first to the eye, rather than the mind, like other romancers after Scott.[19] This reconstruction of the visual impact of the national past, rather than exploration of the historical process, was common to many historical works of the 1830s and 1840s:[20] it was condemned by a critic in *The Edinburgh Review*, who felt it indicated an undue emphasis on appearance rather than substance:

In seeking with exclusive earnestness to realize past ages to our imagination, we run the risk of losing sight of those general characteristics common to men in all circumstances, in our attention to those which are distinctive. Substantial reality no longer suffices us— we must have outward verisimilitude also; and we become apt to mistake the show for the substance. We withdraw our eyes from the man himself, to fix them on his coat-of-mail, trunk hose, or periwig; and history becomes a gallery of pictures rather than a series of examples.[21]

Wedded to the now threatened neo-classical approach to history as a source of moral exempla, the critic blamed this reconstructive treatment of history on Scott, who had 'substituted the picturesque for the philosophical style'.[22]

In his concentration on Scott's desire for detailed historical reconstructions, the critic had missed the novelist's theoretical grasp of historical change. The

---

[17]　e.g. I. Duncan, *Modern Romance and the Transformation of the Novel: The Gothic, Scott, and Dickens* (Cambridge, 1982); J. Kerr, *Fiction against History: Scott as Storyteller* (Cambridge, 1989).

[18]　Ross, *Imprint*, 6.　　　[19]　Simmons, *Novelist*, 14–18.

[20]　G. P. R. James was the other leading historical novelist of the period whose work was similar to Ainsworth's in its visual recreation of the past, although his works have no such impressive illustrations. See S. M. Ellis, *The Solitary Horseman, or The Life and Adventures of G. P. R. James* (1927). The critic Horne recognized the essentially pictorial quality of his works when he described them as 'capital illuminations, worthy of being let into the margin of history' (R. H. Horne, *A New Spirit of the Age* (1844; Oxford, 1907 edn.), 161).

[21]　[H. Merivale], 'The Pictorial History of England', *ER* 74 (1842), 433.　　　[22]　Ibid. 434.

young Scott had been very attracted to 'what was striking and picturesque' in historical narrative, but the mature author felt that his education in the 'philosophy of history' had trained him to exploit such colourful details as 'examples in illustration' of general principles.[23] His use of the picturesque in his novels suggested at once his attraction to this approach, and his recognition of its inadequacy as a means of grasping the meaning of historical events. In *Waverley* (1814), for instance, the young hero's picturesque vision of the places and events is continually eroded by Scott's mature grasp of the grim historical realities behind the attractive images. Picturesque vision for him was only viable as a pleasant form of harmless nostalgia, harnessed by prudent reason.[24] Scott felt that the barbaric past was picturesque only in decline, and in contrast with a civilized present— when, in fact, it had ceased to be dangerous.[25] Unhindered by any such profound theories concerning the historical process, Ainsworth was free to use the picturesque to structure his fictions more fully than Scott could.[26]

This was true, too, in the case of the illustrations to the historical novel. Those to Ainsworth's novels of the 1840s were strictly controlled by the constant aim of picturesque historical reconstruction and based on a close collaboration of author and illustrator. But illustrators of Scott were working with an author who relied very little, if at all, on their visualizations of his novels. In 1809, Scott wrote to a friend that 'nothing is more difficult than for a painter to adapt the author's ideas of any imaginary character',[27] and when the Cadell Magnum Opus edition of the novels was being published in 1829–33, he felt that the production of the illustrations caused unnecessary delays.[28] Although Scott had shown sufficient concern for historical detail to send John James Masquerier some information concerning costume and period accessories to aid him in his illustration of *The Last Lay of the Minstrel* (1805),[29] this seems to have been unusual. Scott did, too, suggest subjects for the Magnum Opus illustrations, some of which were adopted,[30] but the choice of subjects must have lain more with the artists or the publisher, as they were frequently related to the illustrator's usual specialism: Abraham Cooper, for instance, who was a battle-artist, illustrated Burley and

---

[23] J. G. Lockhart, *Narrative of the Life of Sir Walter Scott* (1836–8; 1906 edn.), 29.

[24] Ross, *Imprint*, 46–72. This interpretation is challenged, however, by Jane Millgate in *Walter Scott: The Making of a Novelist* (Edinburgh, 1984), 35–57, who claims that Scott perceived romance and the picturesque as educative. Wolfgang Iser's contention that Waverley's imagination and picturesque vision is used to 'combine the various aspects together in a unified picture', to draw together the multiplied individual viewpoints which Scott used to create historical reality, is, perhaps, more persuasive. W. Iser, *The Implied Reader: Patterns of Communication in Prose Fiction from Bunyan to Beckett* (Baltimore and London, 1974), 89, 99.

[25] Ross, *Imprint*, 58–9.

[26] Duncan, *Modern Romance* presents Dickens and other mid-19th-cent. writers of realist fiction, rather than Ainsworth and his ilk, as the true successors of Scott's historicized analysis of the role of the individual in the modern nation-state.

[27] C. Gordon, 'The Illustration of Sir Walter Scott: Nineteenth Century Enthusiasm and Adaption', *JWCI* 34 (1971), 301. W. Scott to G. Ellis, 21 Aug. 1804.

[28] J. Millgate, *Scott's Last Edition: A Study in Publishing History* (Edinburgh, 1987), 17.

[29] Gordon, 'Illustration of Walter Scott', 300.   [30] Millgate, *Edition*, 122 n. 5.

Bothwell in combat for *Old Mortality* (1816), and Clarkson Stanfield, an artist of
sea-scapes, portrayed Oldbuck consoling Mucklebackit, on a beach by a boat,
from *The Antiquary* (1816).[31]

The artists whose work was really within the picturesque tradition were not
courted for appropriate collaboration with Scott, as Ainsworth's illustrators were
to be. The work of these artists was to provide a precedent for the illustrations of
Ainsworth's 1840s novels: the 1820s and 1830s saw the development of a minor
school of the picturesque, among artists responding to a topographical and antiquarian movement to record architecture and localities which seemed under
threat. It was particularly encouraged by the expansion of lithography as a
medium: artists such as George Perfect Harding, the Lewis family, and Joseph
Nash produced many lithographs of picturesque views, and it was the main
medium for the French *Voyages pittoresques dans l'ancienne France*.[32] Other
artists, such as Samuel Prout and George Cattermole produced their views of
scenery and ancient architecture in steel-engravings.[33] Specific works which can
be seen as precursors in the picturesque tradition for Ainsworth's novels include
Thomas Hosmer Shepherd's *London and its Environs in the Nineteenth Century*
(1829), illustrated by James Elmes, William Henry Pyne's *The History of the
Royal Residences* (1819), illustrated by Charles Wild and others, John Thomas
Smith's *Antiquities of Westminster* (1807), and Prout's *Facsimiles of Sketches
Made in Flanders and Germany* (1833).[34] Before the Abbotsford edition of 1842,
no publisher tapped the potential exhibited by artists of the picturesque school to
produce an illustrated edition of Scott's novels which would reflect that aspect
of his historical vision.

Nevertheless, in one aspect Ainsworth's use of Scott's techniques for historical reconstruction could draw on a visual precedent. The concept of the picturesque was related to eighteenth-century interest in the theory of association:
Uvedale Price, for instance, felt that ruins made an effective addition to a landscape 'by the impression they make on the senses, and by the reflection they suggest to the mind'.[35] Gothic writers exploited this technique of impressionistic
association frequently: lacking any sense of a process of historical change and
evolution, they presented instead a stark contrast of past and present, and the
term picturesque quickly acquired an association with the relics of the past
and signs of ageing.[36] Scott himself had added to this rudimentary method a

    [31] W. Scott, *The Waverley Novels*, 48 vols. (Edinburgh, 1829–33), x, frontispiece; v,
frontispiece.
    [32] M. Twymman, *Lithography 1800–1850* (Oxford, 1970), 167–253.
    [33] B. Hunnisett, *Steel-Engraved Book Illustration in England* (1980), 106–34.
    [34] G. N. Ray, *The Illustrator and the Book in England* (Oxford, 1976), 21–2, 31, 52–5.
    [35] Ross, *Imprint*, 17.
    [36] Ruskin noted that the marks of age had become 'the subject of especial choice among certain
schools of art, and . . . have impressed upon those schools the character usually and loosely
expressed by the term "picturesque" '. J. Ruskin, *The Seven Lamps of Architecture* (1849; 1905
edn.), 192–3.

more sophisticated technique of historical association of place, characteristic of picturesque history: he described the neighbourhood of Kelso, for instance, as presenting 'objects not only grand in themselves, but venerable from their association'.[37] He considered such an approach as a form of 'picturesque in action', rather than in landscape, disclaiming any proficiency in picturesque art—'But shew me an old castle or a field of battle, and I was at home at once, filled it with its combatants in their proper costume, and overwhelmed my hearers with the enthusiasm of my description.'[38] Scott was fortunate in one illustrator whose Romantic vision made him a fellow proponent of historical association of place: William Turner. The illustrations to Scott's poetry by this artist in the Cadell edition show a use of the past/present contrast. Turner's illustrations, it has been shown, included ancient buildings and ruins, but also modern figures: Scott as a boy, or the elderly Scott with Turner and others, on tour as the illustrations were drawn.[39] The similarity of Ainsworth's association of place and historical reconstructive narrative will become apparent.

The progression of reconstruction, from the present place to the past events and people associated with it, was paralleled by Scott's progression from part to whole, a process described by Stephen Bann in relation to Abbotsford, Scott's reconstructed baronial hall. Bann notes Scott's penchant for appropriating fragments of the past, and incorporating them into a unified and reconstructed presentation of the past: a technique which contrasts with the Gothic author's attraction to the incomplete precisely because it was fragmentary and incomprehensible. Bann defines this process, in the terms of literary criticism, as synecdochic (using a part, by virtue of a quality associated with it, to describe a whole), and argues that it was extended to Abbotsford, for which Scott possessed himself of parts of the ruined abbey of Melrose.[40] Scott had earlier learnt to use a historical fragment to generate and validate a whole by means of associations. When visiting historic sites, he cut pieces of wood from trees, and

intended to have a set of chessmen made out of them, each one having reference to the place where it was cut—as the kings from Falkland and Holy-Rood; the queens from Queen Mary's yew-tree at Crockston; the bishops from abbeys or episcopal palaces; the knights from baronial residences; the rooks from royal fortresses and the pawns generally from places of historical note . . .[41]

Ainsworth, too, used historical fragments—from buildings, chronicles, costumes, pictures—to generate a reconstructed whole, and invest it with some kind of authenticity.

---

[37] Lockhart, *Scott*, 30.   [38] Ibid. 40.

[39] A. M. Holcomb, 'Turner and Scott', *JWCI* 34 (1971), 393–4. This point has been recently highlighted too in G. Finlay, *Landscapes of Memory: Turner as Illustrator to Scott* (1980), 158–60. See also J. Reed, *Sir Walter Scott: Landscape and Locality* (1980) for further information on Scott's historical association of place.

[40] S. Bann, *The Clothing of Clio* (Cambridge, 1984), 100–2.   [41] Lockhart, *Scott*, 39–40.

'LET US ATTEMPT TO PRESERVE WHAT REMAINS': THE PAST,
THE PRESENT, AND THE PICTURESQUE

'Little of the old town, however, is left. The lover of antiquity . . . will search in
vain for those picturesque black and white timber habitations, that were common
sixty years ago . . . there is scarcely a house left which has the slightest historical
association belonging to it.'[42] In a late novel, *The Good Old Times: The
Manchester Rebels of the Fatal '45* (1873), Ainsworth meditated thus on the
changes which had taken place in his native Manchester in the previous hundred
years. Born and bred in a city experiencing rapid industrial change, he was visually aware at an early age of the destructive potential of time.[43] The novelist had
an urgent sense of the dangers threatening the physical structures which were
the country's heritage, which he attempted to convey to his readers.[44] Nostalgia—
the sense that the present is in some way deficient—was an emotion to which
Ainsworth and other fellow picturesque romancers of the 1830s and 1840s were
particularly prone.[45] In the second chapter of *The Manchester Rebels*, he
described the Manchester of 1745: 'it formed an agreeable mixture of old and new.
The rivers that washed its walls were clear and abounded in fish. Above all, the
atmosphere was pure and wholesome, unpolluted by the smoke of a thousand
factory chimneys. In some respects, therefore, the old town was preferable to the
mighty modern city.'[46] Only the qualification of the last sentence interrupts the
elegiac mood.

These were not just the reflections of a septuagenarian in nostalgic mood, for
the novels which Ainsworth wrote thirty years before—while living in the midst
of the rapidly changing and expanding English capital—show the same consciousness of the destructive passage of time. Here, for instance, is his description of sixteenth-century London in *The Tower of London* (1840):

Then, gardens and stately palaces adorned its [the Thames's] banks; then, the spires and
towers of the churches shot into an atmosphere unpolluted by smoke; then, the houses,
with their fanciful gables, and vanes, invited and enchained the eye; then the streets . . .
were narrow and intricate; then, there was Baynard's Castle; the ancient tavern of the
Three Cranes; the still-yard; and, above all, the Bridge, even then old, with its gateways,
towers, drawbridges, houses, mill and chapel, enshrined like a hidden and cherished
faith within its inmost heart. All this has passed away.[47]

[42] W. H. Ainsworth, *The Good Old Times: The Manchester Rebels of the Fatal '45* (n.d.; all other
references to the 1 edn., 3 vols., 1873), p. iv.

[43] S. M. Ellis, *William Harrison Ainsworth and his Friends*, 2 vols. (London and New York,
1911) i. 1–48.

[44] G. J. Worth, *William Harrison Ainsworth* (New York, 1972), 73. Worth, however, makes
little attempt to analyse this aspect of Ainsworth in any depth.

[45] See M. Chase and C. Shaw, 'The Dimensions of Nostalgia', in C. Shaw and M. Chase. (eds.),
The Imagined Past: History and Nostalgia (Manchester and New York, 1989), 3.

[46] Ainsworth, *Rebels*, i. 17–18.

[47] W. H. Ainsworth, *The Tower of London: An Historical Romance* (1840), 15–16.

In *Old Saint Paul's* (1841), too, the panorama of old London is recalled. The hero, Leonard Holt, views the cityscape from the roof of the cathedral:

Then, every house was picturesque . . . Then, that which was objectionable in itself and contributed to the insalubrity of the city, namely the extreme narrowness of the streets, and overhanging stories of the houses, was the main source of their beauty. Then, the huge projecting signs with fantastical ironwork—the conduits—the crosses . . . the maypoles—all were picturesque; and as superior to what can now be seen; as the attire of Charles the Second's age is to the ugly and disfiguring costume of our own day.[48]

In this passage, a brief recognition of the discomfort of a past age is almost completely obscured by an intense appreciation of the visual attractiveness of old London: Ainsworth maintained the necessary distance from objects of contemplation which the picturesque mode required. In both passages, the contrast of past and present is highlighted by the repetition of 'then'. However, it is in *Old Saint Paul's* that the consciousness of the destructiveness of the passage of time is most emphatic as this novel is focused on a building which had totally vanished. Many of the plates of the novel, which were by John Franklin,[49] attempted to recreate the cathedral from every angle, and the figures of the actors of the story were always inconspicuous, showing a subordination of fictional to topographical and antiquarian interest. The viewer is reminded of such 1840s publications as Charles Knight's *Old England* (1845), which was full of illustrations of the national monuments of the past: a fascination with the visual appearance, past and present, of ancient buildings was abroad.

It is perhaps not surprising, then, that the destructiveness of time on the architecture of former ages is one of the central themes of *Old Saint Paul's*. Even before the fire of 1666, the climax of the novel, the old cathedral is in decline; the verger tells Leonard Holt that it has 'known better days' and 'seen sad changes'.[50] Its destruction in the fire evokes this elegiac description from Ainsworth: 'Not a vestige of the reverend structure was left untouched . . . its mighty pillars—its galleries—its chapels—all, all were destroyed. The fire . . . rendered the venerable cathedral . . . a heap of ruin and ashes.[51] Despite the construction of the new cathedral, Leonard Holt—a fellow Mancunian and thus a projection of Ainsworth himself—continues to experience a sense of loss, for though he visits it with 'feelings of admiration', he never feels 'the same sentiments of veneration and awe' which the old cathedral had aroused in him.[52] This tallies with the authorial comment made earlier with reference to the city as a whole: 'though it was rebuilt, and in many respects improved, its original and picturesque character was entirely destroyed'.[53] Clearly the improvements did not compensate for the loss of the picturesque. When Ainsworth deplored the decay of the Tower of

---

[48] W. H. Ainsworth, *Old Saint Paul's: A Tale of the Plague and the Fire*, 3 vols. (1841), i. 301–2.

[49] Franklin was a London-based painter of genre, portraits, and literary subjects, who flourished in 1830–68. Wood, *Dictionary*, 164.

[50] Ainsworth, *Paul's*, i. 53.   [51] Ibid. iii. 299.   [52] Ibid. iii. 327.   [53] Ibid. i. 301.

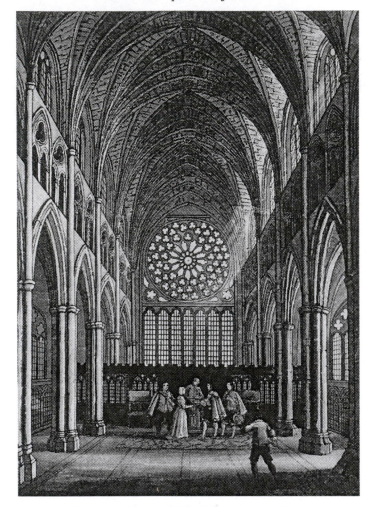

Fig. 12. J. Franklin, *Leonard Holt Preventing the Marriage of the Earl of Rochester with Amabel in the Choir of St Paul's*, from W. H. Ainsworth, *Old St Paul's: A Tale of the Plague and the Fire*, 3 vols. (1841), i, facing 308

London, he was able to adopt a tone of warning rather than just simple regret, for this national monument still remained partially intact:

It is piteous to see what havoc has already been made by alterations and repairs. The palace is gone—so are many of the towers—and unless the progress of destruction is arrested, the demolition of others will follow . . . It is not possible to restore the Tower to its pristine grandeur. But it *is* possible to prevent further mutilation and desecration . . .[54]

---

[54] Ainsworth, *Tower*, p. v.

When creating his historical tableaux, Ainsworth experienced 'a kind of double vision', characteristic of both the Gothic and picturesque modes: he saw his subjects as they were at some period in the past and simultaneously contrasted them with their present, usually debased, appearance.[55] This duality of vision is reflected in the 1836 scheme for an unrealized work, in which both *The Tower of London* and *Old Saint Paul's* originated. *The Lions of London* was to be a sort of story-tale guide book to old and new London, illustrated by John Leech and George Cruikshank. Ainsworth described the proposed format to Macrone: 'Each number will embrace old and new London. Let Leech undertake the old—the romantic—the picturesque; George the modern comedy and manners.'[56] This duality of vision dominated the illustration of *The Tower of London*. Whereas Franklin's illustrations to *Old Saint Paul's* aimed simply at displaying the old cathedral from as many angles as possible (Fig. 12),[57] Cruikshank's illustrations to *The Tower of London* were intended to provoke a dialogue of comparison. Their form is reminiscent of A. W. N. Pugin's *Contrasts* (1836) in which the architect attempted, by way of contrasting plates, to show the inferiority of modern architecture and manners and morals to medieval Gothic architecture and the age of faith and chivalry which he believed it to embody. In book 2 of *The Tower*, for instance, the villain, the Duke of Northumberland, recants and is reconciled to the Catholic Church. Ainsworth introduces the reader to St John's chapel, where the ceremony takes place, with a rich description of its Roman Catholic ornaments.[58] At this point, the text breaks to show the chapel as it is now, bare and neglected (Fig. 13). The contrast is reinforced by the steel-engraving for the chapter, which details the ornamentation of the chapel (Fig. 14).[59] Ainsworth had already expressed concern for the restoration of the chapel in the Preface: 'It *is* possible to clear the reverend and massive columns of St John's Chapel, like the giants of departed days, from the thick coat of white-wash with which they are crusted—to sweep away the presses with which its floors are encumbered, and to find some equally secure, but less interesting depository for the Chancery Rolls.'[60] A similar juxtaposition is presented in the two illustrations for book 2, chapter 2, when Lady Jane Grey is imprisoned in the Brick Tower. The steel-engraving shows the Gothic windows and fine tapestries, which, in the wood-cuts, have been bricked over and removed.[61]

Clearly, these two types of illustrations fit easily into Bann's categories of metaphoric and metanymic. The interplay between each pair contrasts with the more loosely conceived illustrative patterns of textbooks or editions of Hume or some of Charles Knight's publications, which use both varieties of illustration, but rarely corresponding ones such as these. Ainsworth's almost total control

[55] Worth, *Ainsworth*, 72.

[56] Ellis, *Ainsworth*, i. 312. W. H. Ainsworth to J. Macrone, Nov.? 1836. See Patten, *Cruikshank*, ii. 35–6. Cruikshank produced a monthly wrapper designer, a wood-engraving of St Paul's; it was later adapted for *Old St Paul's*.

[57] Ainsworth, *Paul's*, i, facing 308.   [58] Ainsworth, *Tower*, 151–2.

[59] Ibid., facing 153.   [60] Ibid., p. v.   [61] Ibid. 126 and facing.

Fig. 13. G. Cruikshank, *Interior of Saint John's Chapel in the White Tower*, from W. H. Ainsworth, *The Tower of London: An Historical Romance* (1840), 152

over his illustrations allows his message to emerge easily from the images: the viewer is in no doubt that a picturesque past is contrasted with a less satisfying present, and that (more mundanely) preservation of the national architectural heritage is called for.

'THE GOOD OLD TIMES!—ALL TIMES ARE GOOD WHEN OLD!': AINSWORTH'S INTERPRETATION OF THE PAST AND THE NECESSITY OF PRESERVATION

In the face of Ainsworth's picturesque awareness of the passage of time and its ravages, it is natural to ask if he inherited any more theoretical debts from Scott.

Fig. 14. G. Cruikshank, *The Duke of Northumberland Renouncing the Protestant Religion*, from Ainsworth, *Tower*, facing 153

As his use of the past and present contrast did not suggest an attempt like Scott's to balance loss and gain—Ainsworth lamented the aesthetic aspects of the lost past without much qualification—did he favour the beliefs and lifestyle of the English past as well as its appearance? Did his conservationism imply conservatism? Or was Ainsworth's engagement with the national narrative limited to a vague sense of the value of modern improvements, coupled with a fascination with the picturesque aspects of the English past?

Ainsworth had no illusions about the conditions of life in the past: as George Worth has pointed out, his fictional world is 'a singularly violent one that was marked by turmoil, cruelty and intrigue'.[62] In *The Tower of London*, we are informed that the history of the building is 'dark and bloody'.[63] In *Old Saint Paul's*, the triumph of middle-class values, represented by Leonard Holt and his employer, Stephen Bloundel, over the violence and immorality of the declining world of aristocrats such as the Earl of Rochester, suggests relief, as well as regret, at the collapse of feudal society.[64] But Ainsworth does not dwell on this theme,

---

[62] Worth, *Ainsworth*, 76.   [63] Ainsworth, *Tower*, 128.

[64] R. Maxwell, 'City Life and the Novel: Hugo, Ainsworth and Dickens', *Comparative Literature*, 30 (1978), 158.

and his response to declining feudalism is clearly allied to the Gothic writers' repelled yet attracted sense of the frightening barbarity of past ages rather than to Scott's sociological perspective.

On the other hand, there are occasional signs of Ainsworth's sense of loss, in terms of beliefs and customs which were valuable, which suggest initially that his interpretation of the national past might have more analytic depth and objectivity than the fantasies of a Gothic romancer: here, perhaps, is a denunciation of the Whiggish narrative of national progress. His 1854 novel, *The Flitch of Bacon*, which was centred round the old Dunmow custom of presenting a large pork joint to a couple who had lived in perfect harmony for a year, led to a revival of the custom which Ainsworth was glad to sponsor.[65] More allusively, the presentation of Northumberland's recantation in *The Tower of London*, with its Puginesque undertones, suggests a lurking fondness for the Old Faith.[66] This conclusion seems borne out by Ainsworth's sympathetic treatment of some of the Catholic characters in *Guy Fawkes, or, The Gunpowder Treason* (1841), notably Fawkes himself and the heroine, Viviana Radcliffe (later, his praise of the Penderels in *Boscobel, A Tale of the Year 1651* led to rumours that he was a Catholic[67]).

But these *aperçus* never amount to more than a passing enthusiasm: at no point in his novel did Ainsworth voice a comprehensive protest against modern social, religious, or political values in the manner of other nineteenth-century writers such as Thomas Carlyle and William Morris. The root of his nostalgia for the English past was not a painful sense of loss of political, spiritual, or social values, so much as a feeling that the past was simply more picturesque than the present. Ainsworth and other popular historical novelists of his kind looked to the past, not for a perspective on contemporary issues, nor out of a deep-seated interest in historical movements, but as a source of drama and pageantry, of display.[68]

Simply preserving the national past was for Ainsworth a form of moral righteousness: it needed no further ideological justification. In *The Miser's Daughter* (1844), a tale of the eighteenth century, Ainsworth achieved something close to the structural format of Scott's novels, in an attempt to defend this belief. The miser, a mercantile money-maker in the process of ruining the gentry and aristocracy, does not care for the past and is eventually destroyed by it. Scarve neglects his old house, which is consequently in 'a ruinous condition': the young hero, Randolph Crewe, is shown into a room where the windows, which bear armorial bearings of the former owners, are repaired with rags and paper.[69] Meanwhile the virtuous characters, such as Randolph's uncle, Abel, respect the past and preserve it. Abel lives in an old house, with 'a frescoed ceiling, from the time of Charles II' and keeps 'plenty of old china; and old japanned cabinets; a good

---

[65] Ellis, *Ainsworth*, ii. 197–217.   [66] Ainsworth, *Tower*, 151–3.
[67] Ellis, *Ainsworth*, ii. 279–80.
[68] H. Shaw, *The Forms of Historical Fiction* (Ithaca, NY, and London, 1983), 26–7, 83. Shaw points out that Ainsworth's fiction does show a recognition of the 'past as past', although in a debased form.
[69] W. H. Ainsworth, *The Miser's Daughter* (1844; 1848 edn.) 1, 13–14.

library in which the old poets, old dramatists and the old chroniclers found a place, and above all, a good store of old wine'.[70] Scarve's neglect of the past—he fails to keep a promise to marry his daughter Hilda to Randolph—is one of the causes of his downfall, while Abel's preservation of the memory of the deceased wife of Scarve, whom he once loved, encourages him to help Hilda, and, eventually, through her marriage to Randolph and the birth of her children, to receive consolation for her loss.

What makes this plea for appreciation and preservation of the past so different from a novel by Scott or Morris is the total absence of political, social, or spiritual elements in Ainsworth's interpretation. The past is not to be preserved as the repository of any particular values: the Jacobite characters, for instance, who do represent particular historical values, are marginalized. Ainsworth did not consider whether the past could intelligently inform present concerns; he valued it simply because it was old and picturesque and, therefore, deserved preservation. Preserving the picturesque face of the past was a central theme for the novel written just before *The Miser's Daughter*: that novel was *Windsor Castle*.

'THE RESTORATION OF THE STRUCTURE': PICTURESQUE PRESERVATIONS

This fortification, one of the oldest of the Castle . . . is now in a state of grievous neglect and ruin. Unroofed, unfloored, filled with rubbish . . . with one side entirely pulled down . . . Still, notwithstanding its dilapidated condition . . . its appearance is highly picturesque . . . Amid the rubbish choking its lower chamber, grows a young tree, green and flourishing—a type, it is hoped of the restoration of the structure . . .[71]

The symbol of hope is repeated in the vignette by William Delamotte,[72] illustrating this description of the Garter Tower in *Windsor Castle*.[73] Themes of the decay and destruction of the national heritage are very muted in this novel; preservation and reconstructive endeavours are its keynotes. Unlike most Victorian writers, Ainsworth has something to advance in favour of George IV, who 'accomplished the restoration of the Castle to more than its original grandeur . . . Sir Jeffry Wyattville was to him what William of Wykeham had been to Edward the Third. All the incongruities of successive reigns were removed; all, or nearly all the injuries inflicted by time were repaired . . .'[74] He instructs the sceptic to view the effects of Wyattville's alterations from the north, the Eton Playing Field, and in the Upper Quadrangle, and to discover thus 'the triumph of the whole'.[75]

[70] W. H. Ainsworth, *The Miser's Daughter* (1844; 1848 edn.) 23.

[71] W. H. Ainsworth, *Windsor Castle* (1843; 1891? edn.), 124.

[72] William Alfred Delamotte was a landscape painter, watercolourist, and lithographer, who had studied under the historical painter, Benjamin West. He produced views of Wales, Oxford, the Thames, and France, and illustrated topographical works (Wood, *Dictionary*, 124). He was thus associated with the 'picturesque' topographical movement of the 1820s and 1830s, represented by artists such as the Pethers, and partially inspired by the illustrated tours of Gilpin.

[73] Ainsworth, *Castle*, 125.   [74] Ibid. 164–5.   [75] Ibid. 165–6.

Delamotte neatly punctuates the text at the appropriate points with illustrations of the admired views.[76] Here, then, is a celebration of the synecdochic technique of Scott's Abbotsford—the generation of whole from part—as presented by the reconstruction of a great national monument, Windsor Castle.

For Ainsworth, reconstruction must subsume and embody preservation: he admires 'the judgement which with [Wyattville] has preserved the castle of Edward the Third. Some additions have been made . . . but the architect has yielded to no temptation to substitute his own design for that of William of Wykeham and no small difficulties have been combatted and overcome for the sake of preserving the outline of the edifice . . .'[77] Thus Ainsworth balances a concern for preservation with a desire for reconstruction: the castle is not to be left in its ruined state, but reconstructed according to its original design, as a coherent whole which incorporates and depends on the authentic remains. His attitude is reminiscent of that of many nineteenth-century architects of the Gothic Revival and members of the Ecclesiological Society, who, when working on medieval buildings, aimed to reconstruct them as they would have been (or should have been), in the critically approved 'decorated gothic' style.[78] Influenced by the reconstructive methods of Scott's fictions, Ainsworth's slant on the picturesque is a decidedly nineteenth-century one: although not immune to the visual appeal of ruins in a state of pleasing decay, he prefers restoration to rumination.

Nevertheless, he still signals his adherence to aesthetic rather than historical imperatives by his desire to see ugly or unsuitable extensions to buildings destroyed, even when of considerable age themselves. In *The Tower of London*, he calls for the removal of the Grand Storehouse, an 'ugly Dutch toy', which conceals 'a stern old Norman dongon, fraught with a hundred historical associations and recollections'.[79] The removal of unsightly incrustations informs the Preface, as Ainsworth calls upon the public to 'stop further mutilation and desecration'.[80] A similar note is struck in Ainsworth's final comments on Wyattville's work at Windsor, in which he suggests that the removal of houses obscuring the view of St George's chapel and of other 'old incongruous buildings' would render the castle 'indeed complete'. Preservation, removal, and reconstruction are all to be directed by a sense of the picturesque, a desire to create a unified and meaningful whole, to compose a picture. Ainsworth's urgency here is conveyed by image as well as text: Delamotte's wood-cut shows the Curfew Tower and adjacent buildings, not as they were in the 1840s, but as they would have been if Wyattville's design had been completed (Fig. 15).[81]

Ainsworth did not only intend to preach preservation and reconstruction to others; he meant to attempt it himself, employing the reconstructive methods of

---

[76] Ainsworth, *Castle*, 165–7.   [77] Ibid. 167–8.

[78] See C. Miele, ' "Their Interest and Habit': Professionalism and the Restoration of Medieval Churches, 1837–77', in C. Brooks and A. Saint (eds.), *The Victorian Church: Architecture and Society* (Cambridge and New York, 1995), 151–72.

[79] Ainsworth, *Tower*, 137.   [80] Ibid., p. v.   [81] Ibid. 168–9.

Fig. 15. [W. A. Delamotte], *Curfew Tower and Other Buildings as Proposed to be Altered by Wyatville*, from W. H. Ainsworth, *Windsor Castle* (1891?), 168

Scott to create a picturesque whole. He was, indeed, active on the practical side of preservation: he served on the British Archaeological Society's Deputation for the preservation of the Tower of London, and also on the parish committee for the preservation of Willesden church, an important location in his early novel, *Jack Sheppard* (1839).[82] But Ainsworth's real preservation and reconstruction work was contained within his fictions. In the 1849 Preface to his early novel, *Rookwood* (1834), a work inspired by a visit to 'an old hall with which I was acquainted', he declared his intention to renovate the old Gothic romance with the hand of a 'skilful architect'.[83]

Clearly, the novelist already had experienced a sense of constructing a work from imperfect fragments to produce a whole, which he rendered in an architectural metaphor. To proceed from a fragment of the past to a reconstruction was as natural to Ainsworth as to Scott. In a very early work, 'The Churchyard', from *December Tales* (1822), Ainsworth referred to a 'piece of oak', a relic cut from an old school tree, and, as he mentioned it, he started to recall in detail the tree's destruction and the bonfire which followed.[84] While text is a form of architecture, architecture became, by virtue of its historical associations, a form of text which narrated the national past. This is evident in the dialogue between Winwike, the

---

[82] Ellis, *Ainsworth*, ii. 43 n.
[83] W. H. Ainsworth, *Rookwood: A Romance* (1834; 1878 edn.), p. xxvii.
[84] Ellis, *Ainsworth*, i. 107–8.

Tower Warder, and the villainous Spanish ambassador, Simon Renard, on the roof of the Tower:

'There you behold the Tower of London', said Winwike, pointing downward.
'And there I read the history of England', replied Renard.
'If it is written in those walls, it is a dark and bloody history', replied the warder, 'and yet your excellency says truly. The buildings on which we stand and those around us, are the best chroniclers of our country.'[85]

Some buildings were, quite literally, texts of the past, since they carried inscriptions which riveted Ainsworth's attention. In the Preface to *The Tower of London*, he described the prison chamber in the Beauchamp Tower, as 'like a mystic scroll . . . covered with inscriptions—each one a tragic story in itself'.[86]

   As in the case of Scott, Ainsworth's conception of the picturesque was influenced by specific associations with historical events in the national past, which his novels were to embody in a detailed reconstruction. He called for the preservation of buildings such as the old council-chamber in the Tower, which he described as 'teeming with historical recollections':[87] fragments of the past which could invest both architectural and textual reconstructions with a sort of associative authenticity. Like Scott, his imagination moved from the historic site before him, to the generation of an imaginary reconstruction of historical events. This is apparent in a passage from *The Tower of London*:

Viewed from the summit of the White Tower, especially on the west, the fortress still offers a striking picture. In the middle of the sixteenth century, when the outer ramparts were strongly fortified—when the gleam of corslet and pike was reflected upon the dark waters of its moat—when the inner ballium walls were entire and unbroken, and its thirteen towers reared their embattled fronts—when its drawbridges were constantly raised, and its gates closed—when its palace still lodged a sovereign—when councils were held within its chambers—when its secret dungeons were crowded—when Tower Hill boasted a scaffold, and its soil was dyed with the best and richest blood of the land . . . — when the steps of Traitor's Gate were worn by the feet of those who ascended them . . . —when every structure had dark secrets to conceal—*then*, indeed, it presented a striking picture to the eye and mind.[88]

A more detailed analysis of Ainsworth's reconstructions will now examine closely how he recreated the picturesque face of the past.

'A STRIKING PICTURE TO THE EYE AND MIND':
AINSWORTH'S PICTURESQUE RECONSTRUCTIONS

The process of informing the mouldering walls with life, as Ainsworth expressed it in the Preface of *The Tower of London*,[89] involved a collaboration of author and artist in the novels of the 1840s of a kind never envisaged in the case of the Scott

---

[85] Ainsworth, *Tower*, 128.   [86] Ibid., p. v.   [87] Ibid., p. iv.
[88] Ibid. 140–1.   [89] Ibid., p. iv.

novels. *Windsor Castle* has been described by one modern critic as 'the most extraordinary collaboration between author and illustrator in the Victorian period'.[90] At least one contemporary reviewer agreed: in *The New Monthly Magazine*, he described the work as 'superb', commending the illustrations for surpassing 'both in spirit and number, the embellishments of any romance in our literature'.[91]

This collaboration was at its fullest with Cruikshank, who worked with Ainsworth on many of his most popular works, including *Jack Sheppard*, *The Tower of London*, *Windsor Castle*, and *The Miser's Daughter*. It gave some credibility to Cruikshank's later claim that he was the real author of some of Ainsworth's novels, as he 'used to send him tracings or outlines of the sketches and drawings from which I was making the etchings in order that he might write up to them'.[92] Whether Cruikshank suggested more than details to Ainsworth is still a matter of debate: it is, however, certain that the two acted in the closest collaboration when creating *The Tower of London*, of which they were joint owners, with Bentley their publisher merely acting on commission.[93] They paid joint visits to the Tower, during which they examined closely those areas which were to be highlighted in the next number.[94] Nor was the association with the other illustrators involved in work on these principal novels much less close: in replying to Cruikshank's accusations in 1872, Ainsworth revealed how he had visited the French artist, Tony Johannot,[95] in Paris, to give him the subjects for his four plates for *Windsor Castle*. He passed 'several pleasant days in his society', during which, no doubt the proposed illustrations were discussed thoroughly.[96] To Delamotte, Ainsworth wrote the following:

I shall be glad to see you to a family dinner at half-past three tomorrow . . . bring your sketch books with you . . . Remind Mr [Dudley] Costello, when you see him, to get the order from Lady Mary Fox, for her apartments in Windsor. You had better go to Hampton Court and sketch Will Sommers and some of the other figures in the old pictures of Henry VIII's time, carefully.[97]

---

[90] J. A. Sutherland, *The Longman Companion to Victorian Fiction* (Harlow, 1988), 675.

[91] [P. G. Patmore], 'Ainsworth's *Windsor Castle*', *The New Monthly Magazine*, 67 (1843), 268.

[92] Ellis, *Ainsworth*, ii. 92. Ellis dismisses Cruikshank's claims completely, but J. R. Harvey has suggested that the statement made by the artist was 'no more than the simple truth'; R. L. Patten has recently given further endorsement to Cruikshank's claims, especially in his analysis of the creation of *The Tower of London*. Certainly there is evidence of Cruikshank's descriptions of the plates which he was drawing being simply paraphased by Ainsworth in the text of his novels. See J. R. Harvey, *Victorian Novelists and their Illustrators* (1970), 39–42, and Patten, *Cruikshank*, ii. 132–41, 483–6.

[93] Patten, *Cruikshank*, ii. 128–31.

[94] Ellis, *Ainsworth*, i. 412; Patten, *Cruikshank*, ii. 138–9.

[95] With his brother Alfred, Tony Johannot was responsible for the illustration of many historical novels, including the works of Scott and Hugo. See A. Marie, *Alfred et Tony Johannot: Peintres, graveurs et vignettistes* (Paris, 1925).

[96] Ellis, *Ainsworth*, ii. 103.

[97] Ibid. ii. 57–8. W. H. Ainsworth to W. A. Delamotte, 1843?

Ainsworth and his artists, especially Cruikshank, shared a concern for authentic detail in their reconstructions of the past. Ainsworth was very conscious of his historical sources; more often than not, these sources were the original inspiration for his novels. Access to these was facilitated by his lifelong friendship with James Crossley, a Manchester lawyer who became President of the Chetham Society, a historical body dedicated to the publication of local source materials.[98] While writing *Jack Sheppard* in 1837, Ainsworth wrote to his friend, inquiring about sources, both textual and visual:

I want to consult you about my new romance, which is a tale of the reign of George the First; and as that monarch cuts a conspicious figure in the story [*in the event, he did not*], I shall really be thankful if you can lend me any memoirs, or other matter, relating to him . . . It is my intention to introduce Jack Sheppard. Have you any history of old Newgate? or pictures of that old prison . . .[99]

When publishing the first number of *Old Saint Paul's*, he asked Crossley for 'any hints', and looked forward to discussing his work with his friend.[100] It was Crossley who suggested to Ainsworth the use of Pott's *Discoverie of Witches*, a Chetham Society publication, as the basis for *The Lancashire Witches* (1849).[101] Other erudite friends no doubt helped the novelist, and Ainsworth read voraciously to provide himself with further information. His library contained many works obviously instrumental in the writing of his novels: John Bayley's *History and Antiquities of the Tower* (1821-5), James Hakewell's *History of Windsor and its Neighbourhood* (1813), Daniel Defoe's *City Remembrancer* and his *Journal of the Plague Year*, as well as an anonymous work, *Due Preparations against the Plague*, attributed by Crossley to Defoe, clearly contributed to the three principal novels discussed here.[102] In the face of such research it is no surprise to find, in such a novel as *The Tower of London*, that the wholly fictitious elements could be described by one reviewer as 'very slight', for 'well-authenticated incidents . . . constitute the fabric of Mr Ainsworth's romance'.[103]

Ainsworth expected his artists to research their sources too, and the illustrations show that they did. In *Jack Sheppard* (1837), Cruikshank's reliance on Hogarth's 'Industry and Idleness' series—the basis for the novel itself—was clearly visible in the illustrations.[104] Franklin's illustrations owed much to the seventeenth-century pictures of old St Paul's by the seventeenth-century engraver, Wensclaus Hollar, possibly in the versions shown in Charles Knight's *London*, published opportunely in the same year as the novel. Franklin appears

---

[98] Ellis, *Ainsworth*, i. 50.
[99] Manchester, Central Reference Library (MCL): MS 928. 23. A8: ii, fo. 54ʳ·ᵛ. W. H. Ainsworth to J. Crossley, 29 May 1837.
[100] MCL MS: iii, fos. 16ᵛ, 27ᵛ. W. H. Ainsworth to J. Crossley, 22 Jan., 17 Nov. 1841.
[101] Ellis, *Ainsworth*, ii. 145.
[102] *Ainsworth Catalogue*, 33, 21; Ellis, *Ainsworth*, i. 425.
[103] [Anon.], 'The Tower of London', *Fraser's Town and Country Magazine*, 23 (1841), 171.
[104] Harvey, *Novelists*, 45-9; Patten, *Cruikshank*, ii. 97-8.

frequently to have derived the architectural elements from one of these two sources, simply adding the figures of the characters to the scene.

Ainsworth and his artists achieved this form of historical reconstruction by the use of textual and pictorial fragments intended to invest the whole with historical authenticity. The fragments were exploited in three different ways, which could be characterized in the phraseology of grammar as synomic, syndetic, and synthetic. Into the first category falls Ainsworth's use of archaic substitutes, synonyms, for the names of various foods and items of clothing, for instance. In this example from *The Tower of London*, the author is describing a supper, which consists of 'a cold chine of beef . . . a goodly provision of forcemeat balls . . . a soused gurnet floating in claret . . . a skirrett pasty . . . an apple tansy . . . a nine-hooped pot of mead'.[105] 'Tansy' and 'mead' are anachronistic words 'lifted' from his reading of sixteenth-century sources. They are too minimal to qualify as quotations or to be traced to particular sources. The same technique is evident in the illustrations. A good example is Cruikshank's plate, *The Quarrel between Will Somers and Patch in the Great Kitchen of the Castle*,[106] an illustration for *Windsor Castle*: the various garments and headdresses of the crowd depicted could not be traced, except in the case of Somers, to specific visual sources, since they are very generalized. But they do identify the period as sixteenth-century, just as the garments worn in Franklin's *The Grocer's Family at Prayer* indicate the late seventeenth century.[107] Such plates probably owed much to the study of costume books, such as Strutt's *Complete View of the Dress and Habits of the People of England* (1796–9), a copy of which Ainsworth possessed and probably studied with his illustrators.[108]

Ainsworth also employed a technique for incorporating fragments which could be called syndetic (literally, the joining of clauses by conjugations). Whole phrases, sentences, and even paragraphs are quoted overtly in the middle of the text, with quotation marks, and often a reference to the source, included. These fragments lend historical authority; for a moment, the novelist assumes the mantle of the historian, to an extent that Scott, who confined such material to notes and appendices, never did.[109] As Edward Bulwer Lytton in his 'serious' historical novels attempted to produce genuine interpretative revisions, so Ainsworth aimed to rehabilitate Mary I in *The Tower of London*: in the Preface, he claimed, with all the dignity of a real historian, that her only fault was bigotry and it was time that 'the cloud which prejudice has cast over her should be dispersed'.[110] Her appearance in the novel leads him to quote very substantially from two contemporary sources, the Venetian ambassador Michele and Bishop Francis Godwin, to back his interpretation.[111] But quotations are not used just to add testimony in controversial areas, but as a matter of course in his novels. When John Booker, an astrologist, makes his first appearance in *Old Saint Paul's*,

[105] Ainsworth, *Tower*, 81–2.   [106] Ainsworth, *Castle*, facing 195.
[107] Ainsworth, *Paul's*, i, facing 4.   [108] *Ainsworth Catalogue*, 34.
[109] Simmons, *Novelist*, 16–17.   [110] Ainsworth, *Tower*, p. vi.   [111] Ibid. 116–17.

Ainsworth describes him as 'a native of Manchester . . . born in 1601, of a good family. "His excellent verses upon the twelve months", says Lilly, in his autobiography, ". . . procured him much reputation all over England . . ."'.[112]

Ainsworth's third method of incorporating the fragments—the synthetic— involved the use of a substantial piece of source material, usually a speech, which remained unacknowledged, as no division was made between the quotation and Ainsworth's text. It was absorbed wholesale into the narrative, with only slight alterations. An excellent example can be found in the last chapter of *The Tower of London*, where Lady Jane Grey makes her last speech from the scaffold. This was lifted almost entirely from contemporary sources—the chronicle *Queen Jane and Queen Mary*, and Raphael Holinshed's *Chronicle*—with only the alteration of a few obscure conjugations, and the addition of three words.[113] At such junctures as this, Ainsworth assumes the mantle not of a historian so much as a contemporary chronicler: indeed, he does refer to himself as a chronicler, and in the Preface to *The Tower of London*, he quotes the sixteenth-century chronicler, John Stow, with the dedication of a neophyte.[114]

Ainsworth's illustrators followed this example. Their work, too, employed quotations, some of them easily recognizable, and intended to be so. The obvious example occurs in Cruikshank's illustrations to *Windsor Castle*: in this work, Henry VIII's appearance shows a clear debt to Hans Holbein's portraits, which could be seen at Hampton Court and Windsor—for instance, in the plate *Henry's Reconciliation to Anne Boleyn*.[115] Other examples abound. In the Cruikshank plate *The Dismissal of Cardinal Wolsey*, the image of the Cardinal is clearly derived from the well-known anonymous portrait, now in the National Portrait Gallery: the Cardinal is viewed in profile, as in this portrait.[116] The figure of Anne in Johannot's *The Meeting of Henry and Anne* is close to the Hever portrait, then believed to be by Holbein, and reproduced in Lodge's *Portraits of Illustrious Personages*.[117] *The Tower of London*, too, abounds with artistic quotations: in Cruikshank's plate *Queen Jane Interposing between Northumberland and Simon Renard*,[118] the figure of Jane was probably derived from the *Herwologia* (1620), a source for other nineteenth-century versions of her appearance,[119] while Northumberland bears a close resemblance to the Penshurst portrait—note particularly the cap cast upon the ground. The plate, *Queen Mary Surprising Courtenay and the Princess Elizabeth* (Fig. 16)[120] shows study of at least one of Hans Eworth's 1554 portraits of Mary I—probably the one held by the Society of Antiquaries in London, and mentioned in Sir Frederick Madden's *The Privy*

---

[112] Ainsworth, *Paul's*, i. 151–2.

[113] H. Chapman, *Lady Jane Grey* (1962), 205; Ainsworth, *Tower*, 422.

[114] Ibid., pp. vii–viii.   [115] Ainsworth, *Castle*, facing 72.   [116] Ibid. facing 239.

[117] Ibid., facing 29; E. Lodge, *Portraits of Illustrious Personages of Great Britain*, 12 vols. (1821–34), i, plate 3.

[118] Ainsworth, *Tower*, facing 75.   [119] Strong, *Painter*, 125.

[120] Ainsworth, *Tower*, facing 215.

Fig. 16. G. Cruikshank, *Queen Mary Surprising Courtenay and the Princess Elizabeth*, from Ainsworth, *Tower*, facing 215

Purse Expenses of the Princess Mary (1831), one of Ainsworth's sources.[121] These metaphoric illustrations are similar to the anecdotal tradition of textbook illustration in the first half of the nineteenth century: governing both is the same emphasis on dramatic and personal anecdotes and the telling of a tale, with the additional impulse towards 'authentic' reconstruction by visual quotations.

Unlike Ainsworth, his illustrators present their quotations almost always synthetically rather than syndetically. Although we may recognize them, they are not identified—by, say, a caption—as an authentic reproduced image. They are incorporated in the whole picture with no artistic quotation marks. The nearest Cruikshank comes to using artistic quotation marks occurs in the plate *Queen*

---

[121] R. Strong, *The National Portrait Gallery: Tudor and Jacobean Portraits*, 2 vols. (1969), i. 212–13; Ainsworth, *Tower*, p. vi.

Mary surprising Courtenay and the Princess Elizabeth (Fig. 16): in the background are portraits of Henry VIII and his first two wives. Henry is instantly recognizable from the Holbein portraits; Anne Boleyn appears to derive from the Hever portrait. Ainsworth aids Cruikshank in drawing attention to these quotations which demand recognition, by making Sir Henry Bedingfeld remark to Queen Mary that her parents 'would almost seem—from their pictures on that wall—to be present now'.[122] Clearly, they provide the backing of a historical example, of a rivalry for the love of one man between the mothers, to authenticate that postulated by Ainsworth between the daughters. J. R. Harvey has noted this tendency of early nineteenth-century illustrators to use pictures—often well-known ones—within their plates to draw parallels, to elucidate parts of the plot where delicacy prevented clarity, or to justify actions by their protagonists.[123]

In their attempts to reconstruct history, both Ainsworth and his illustrators share an obsession with the face of the past. Above all, they wanted to show not what the past meant, but what it looked like. Jonathan E. Hill has argued that Cruikshank's style changed after he had seen his illustrations for *Oliver Twist* used to create theatrical tableaux vivants; instead of a vignette style of illustration, full of action, he developed a static tableau vivant method with 'a far closer matching of illustration and text'. This theory seems plausible, but his argument that Cruikshank created the illustrations not for the novel, 'but rather to be resurrected on the stage' and 'mysteriously made to breathe',[124] underestimates the commitment which Cruikshank—and, indeed, the other illustrators—made to their joint enterprise with Ainsworth. 'Let nothing turn you aside from the Tower! the Tower!', the excited Cruikshank wrote to the author;[125] these do not sound like the words of a man whose enthusiasm for the novel was limited to its stage adaptations. The past could made to breathe mysteriously in book-form by the perfect agreement of text and image. Ainsworth—who had also seen the success of the tableaux vivants in many adaptations of *Jack Sheppard*[126]—willingly continued the use of these methods in his novels, creating (for instance) just the right textual accompaniment to Cruikshank's plate for book 1, chapter 1, of *The Tower of London* (Fig. 17).[127] Jane has just entered the Tower and has been offered a crown as the symbol of her new status:

At that proud moment, all Jane's fears were forgotten, and she felt herself in reality a queen. At this moment, also, her enemies, Simon Renard and Noailles, resolved upon her destruction. At this moment Cuthbert Cholmondeley, who was placed a little to the right of the queen, discovered, amid the spectators behind one of the warders, a face so exquisitely beautiful, and a pair of eyes of such witchery, that his heart was instantly captivated; and at that moment, also, another pair of very jealous-looking eyes, peering out of a window in a tower adjoining the gateway, detected what was passing between

---

[122] Ainsworth, *Tower*, 217.   [123] Harvey, *Novelists*, 147–8.

[124] J. E. Hill, 'Cruikshank, Ainsworth and Tableau Illustration', *VS* 3 (1980), 425–59.

[125] Ellis, *Ainsworth*, i. 411. G. Cruikshank to W. H. Ainsworth, 1840?

[126] Ibid. i. 362–70.   [127] Ainsworth, *Tower*, facing 16.

Fig. 17. G. Cruikshank, *Queen Jane's Entrance into the Tower*, from Ainsworth, *Tower*, facing 16

the youthful couple below, and inflamed their owner with a fierce and burning desire of revenge.[128]

A cursory examination of the plate reveals a careful inclusion of all the simultaneous events described here. A similar example occurs at the end of *Windsor Castle*: as a cannon fires, signalling the death of Anne, Herne the Hunter appears to Henry to urge him off to marry Jane Seymour.[129] While the essential element of Scott's novels is the active conflict of different social groups and ideals, and the evolution towards civilized society, in Ainsworth's novels, such static, fully visualized tableaux of frozen moments in the past are the peak of the novelist's achievement.

THE FACE BECOMES A MASK? THE DECLINE OF PICTURESQUE RECONSTRUCTION

The attempt to reconstruct the face of the past in all its authentic detail could have its drawbacks. The greater the number of images employed, the more detached

---

[128] Ainsworth, *Tower*, 17. [129] Ainsworth, *Castle*, 314–15.

they become from the reality which they are intended to represent; they indicate the 'obvious danger that we become indifferent to the significance of the past and hypersensitive to its look'[130]—precisely the complaint reviewers made of the works of both Scott and Ainsworth in the 1830s and 1840s. R. H. Horne, for instance, condemned Ainsworth as 'a reviver of old clothes' and a manufacturer of 'good-tempered portraits'; his prefatory quotations from the *Memoirs of Mme Tussaud* suggest a perception of Ainsworth's novels as close relatives of the wax-work spectacle.[131]

The type of picturesque reconstruction practised by Ainsworth and his illustrators became increasingly obsolete after 1860. The continuing demands of authenticity gave rise to a new historiographical phase, in which Romantic, antiquarian, and picturesque approaches to the national past gave way to an emphasis on 'scientific' and 'factual' modes of history-writing. With the development of history as a professional discipline came increasing doubt about the viability of historical reconstructions by novelists such as Ainsworth. Also symptomatic of the new climate was the establishment of Society for the Protection of Ancient Buildings, which advocated the preservation of architectural remains as they were, rather than attempts to reconstruct them to meet some standard of architectural purity or picturesque unity. Such developments reflected a sense that the past was not easily resurrected, even in the most superficial form.

Under the influence of contemporary realist fiction, the reading public lost interest in the Ainsworthian historical novel, where behind the elaborate reconstructions of text and image, history served primarily as spectacle and entertainment. Historical fiction—a good vehicle for picturesque historiography—was in many ways unsuitable for the national narrative of the scientific historian. Some later nineteenth-century historical novels, explored in Chapter 9, suggest a crisis in the post-1850 period, during which the genre of historical fiction was severely tested. In this new climate, Ainsworth struggled hopelessly with the structure of the picturesque historical novel which he had written in the 1840s: the collapse of his career is the subject of the last chapter of this book. Imaginative historical reconstruction and picturesque history were to survive the later nineteenth-century crisis of historical fiction—but not without adaptation and transformation.

---

[130] Shaw and Chase, 'Nostalgia', 10.   [131] Horne, *Spirit*, 400–1, 405.

5

'A United People': Charles Knight and the Making of a Picturesque History of England

As the 1840s novels of W. H. Ainsworth show, the growth of picturesque historiography fostered an new interest in the history of the everyday lives, customs, and habits of the British people, and the physical remains of the national past. For much of the eighteenth century, these subjects were the preserve of antiquaries and were passed over by most philosophical historians. By the early nineteenth century, under the aegis of Romantic nationalism and picturesque historiography, they had assumed a new significance and writers of history wished to incorporate them into the dominant national narrative. In their efforts to do so can be found the origins of the disciplines of British social, economic, and cultural history—and, on a more populist front, the beginnings of the heritage industry. While Ainsworth had engaged only tangentially with the national narrative, concentrating on the reconstruction of the face of the English past, others had different ambitions. But the adaptation of the traditional political narrative to include the social, economic, and cultural history of the British people was no easy task and no mid-nineteenth-century historian truly achieved it.

This chapter is an analysis of the solution attempted by one historian, Charles Knight, a publisher with a reputation for the use of copious illustration, in his *Popular History of England* (1855–62). Based on the concept of nationhood, his perspective was similar to that of many other nineteenth-century historians. Unoriginal though Knight was in that respect, his prolific use of illustrations renders him outstanding among writers of picturesque history. His Whig Constitutionalist interpretation, touched with nostalgia for the more community-based society of the past, was typical of his age; but his mid-century publications, filled with antiquarian and metanymic illustrations of a type rarely seen before in history books, were fundamental in changing the illustration of works such as those examined in the last two chapters. Despite its present obscurity, his *History* may well be the one of the most important models for, and precursors of, the illustrated twentieth-century textbook history of the English people.

PICTURESQUE HISTORY: A PROBLEM FOR TEXT AND IMAGE

With the Enlightenment came the desire to deal with the whole man and the first real manifestation of interest in English social, cultural, and economic history. The materials essential for a history of English 'manners and morals' were to be found largely in the works of sixteenth-, seventeenth-, and eighteenth-century antiquaries. The contribution of antiquaries and county historians to the accumulation of facts relevant to picturesque historiography—and thus the new historical disciplines of the later nineteenth century—has long been recognized.[1] The illustrations of antiquarian works had an equal, if not greater, impact on the development of picturesque historiography. For the creator of picturesque reconstructions, the most important of the antiquaries was probably Joseph Strutt, whose collection of images from original manuscripts became a mine for images and information for historians, novelists, and artists alike.[2] However, as we have already seen, in the early nineteenth century most multi-volumed English history books for adults—even those which took account of 'manners and morals' such as those of Sharon Turner—remained unillustrated, or followed the conventions of the Bowyer edition of Hume's *History*.[3] Devoted to the particular and the provincial, the antiquarian approach did not seem a suitable textual model for a national narrative: it took time for even its images to claim their place on the pages of national histories, replacing the metaphorical illustrations characteristic of both philosophical and the earliest picturesque histories.

Eighteenth-century conjectural or philosophical history seemed to offer the means to fuse the fruits of antiquarian research with a broader and more sociological theory of history. Leaders of the Scottish Enlightenment, such as Dugald Stewart and Adam Ferguson, were interested in tracing the development of mankind from barbarism to civilization through a series of social and economic evolutions. This approach is apparent in a variety of works such as J. Logan's *Elements of the Philosophy of History* (1781).[4] However, historians of English history—as opposed to philosophers of history—did not respond to this Enlightenment challenge: the universalist perspective of Enlightenment thought could militate against intensive research into the history of a particular society, favouring instead comparative and general approaches. Somewhat disappointingly, the typical philosophical history of the late eighteenth century—including much of Hume's *History of England*—was a primarily political narrative promoting civic values rather than a history of an evolving society. Indeed, many late eighteenth-century historians did no more than append separately a few facts concerning dress and customs. Interpretative links were neither stated nor

    [1] J. Simmons, 'The Writing of English County Histories', in J. Simmons (ed.), *English County Histories* (Wakefield, 1978), 1.

    [2] See Ch. 3 for the use of Strutt's illustrations in textbooks.   [3] See Ch. 2.

    [4] T. P. Peardon, *The Transition in English Historical Writing 1760–1830* (New York, 1933), 52–4.

inferred: an example of this compartmentalized approach—which became characteristic of early nineteenth-century textbooks—is R. Henry's *History of Great Britain on a New Plan* (1771–93).[5] Nor did the advent of Utilitarianism and political economy in the early nineteenth century produce any more adaptations in the average historical work. The most strenuous attempts to broaden the scope of politically orientated history were made by historians with modest ambitions, who concentrated upon the history of a variety of governmental institutions: the works of this school included J. Reeve's *History of English Law* (1783–4), and institutional histories such as this paved the way for Henry Hallam's history of the English constitution.[6]

Antiquarian curiosity and philosophical ideas achieved a real synthesis in the work of the historical novelist, Walter Scott, whose Waverley novels provided the greatest impetus to the development of social history in the early nineteenth century. As has been argued in Chapter 4, Scott subsumed facts which had formerly been deemed fit only for the antiquary into a historical theory of social change derived from the Scottish philosophical school and expressed through the flexible medium of fictional narrative.[7] Although the status of historical novels as a highly effective and influential vehicle of picturesque historiography was thus established, illustrations to Scott's novels remained principally metaphoric until the Abbotsford edition of 1842–4. This edition was the first to carry substantial numbers of 'real', as well as 'ideal' illustrations—that is, metanymic illustrations, such as views of locations from the novel, as well as metaphoric ones of scenes from the story.[8] Thus the historical novel was no visual model for the illustration of the new historical disciplines of the later nineteenth century until the 1840s novels of Ainsworth were published. Moreover, it was destined to be only a temporary vehicle of the social-history text: the picturesque historical novel lost its prestige in the later nineteenth century, as analysis of the works of Ainsworth shows.[9]

Even while picturesque historiography was dominant, historians were attempting to wrest social history from historical novelists and to incorporate it into national and political narratives. When T. B. Macaulay wrote that 'a truly great historian would reclaim those materials which the novelist has appropriated' so that 'the history of the government, and the history of the people, would be exhibited justly, in inseparable conjunction',[10] he forecast his own efforts to retrieve the field of picturesque history from the novelist. Nevertheless, despite its famous third chapter, Macaulay's *History of England* (1848–55) was a predominantly political account; and—as with previous multi-volumed histories—it was

[5] T. P. Peardon, *The Transition in English Historical Writing 1760–1830* (New York, 1933), 34–7.

[6] Ibid. 40–2; G. P. Gooch, *History and Historians in the Nineteenth Century* (1952), 274–6.

[7] See Ch. 4 for recent interpretations of Scott.

[8] [Eastlake], 'Illustrated Books', *QR* 74 (1844), 196. See Ch. 4 for fuller treatment of the illustrations to Scott's novels.

[9] See Chs. 4 and 10.

[10] Macaulay, 'History', in *Miscellaneous Essays and the Lays of Ancient Rome* (1926), 37.

unillustrated.[11] The struggle apparent in Henry's *History of Great Britain* still continued: reconciling the history of the government and the history of the people was one of the greatest problems for the budding social historian in the nineteenth century. Thomas Carlyle's attempt to achieve such a fusion in *The French Revolution* (1837) was subordinated both to his desire to paint vivid word-pictures of the past (picturesque reconstructions *par excellence*) coupled with his concern to make radical political statements:[12] thus this textual epitome of the picturesque approach to history could be no true precursor for the social, cultural, and economic historiographies of the future.

Thus, in the early nineteenth century, institutional history appeared to offer the only potential framework—however restrictive—for a picturesque narrative of national history in other than a fictional form. Legal and constitutional history thrived in works such as Francis Palgrave's *The Rise and Progress of the English Constitution* (1832), which derived information from writs and charters, and J. M. Kemble's *The Saxons in England* (1849), which relied on research completed by himself and Benjamin Thorpe on early English laws, which (they believed) were derived from ancient Germanic social organization.[13] All these historians were preoccupied, like Macaulay, with the issues of governmental power and the liberties of the people. As J. W. Burrow has shown, most English historians shared an optimistic belief in the ultimate social progress of the nation, inspired by or connected with constitutional government: political progress was figured as the sign of social change.[14] A history of the English people, as developed in the later nineteenth century, was to be ordered by this principle: within this tradition worked J. R. Green, William Stubbs, Freeman, and even Frederic Maitland.

It is against this background that Charles Knight and his *Popular History* must be viewed. When he wrote the *History*, Knight was already the popularizing publisher and editor of a wide variety of educational works, with a highly developed political and social perspective. He had experience in the production of integrated texts and images, and a deep interest in historical and antiquarian literature. Few mid-century authors were as well equipped as Knight to embark upon the creation of a picturesque history of England which would rival the historical novel. The *Popular History*, written late in his life, was described by his granddaughter as 'perhaps the most arduous work of his life, and in some respects the most successful'.[15] His success—and his failure—can be gauged by an analysis of both his life and his *History*.

SOCIAL VIEWS: PEOPLE AND PRINT

The social, economic, and political views of Charles Knight's maturity were informed by both Enlightenment and Utilitarian philosophy. The elderly writer

---

[11] See Ch. 2.   [12] A. L. Le Quesne, *Carlyle* (Oxford, 1982), 46–7.
[13] Gooch, *History*, 268–72.   [14] J. W. Burrow, *A Liberal Descent* (Cambridge, 1981).
[15] A. A. Clowes, *Charles Knight, A Sketch* (1892), 84.

of the autobiographical *Passages of a Working Life* recalled his youthful concern with the state of society, and, particularly, of the lower classes. He remembered his 'chronic state of suspicion as to the general excellence of our political and social system', adding, 'I was a sort of communist in 1808'.[16] Certainly he originally distrusted mechanical progress, but his rather Luddite humour[17] faltered as he grew older and did not survive a trip to the industrial towns of the North in 1828, which he undertook on business for the Society for the Diffusion of Useful Knowledge (SDUK), for which he was to become publisher.[18] Not only was he converted to wholesale admiration for new machinery, but—perceiving the wider implications of technological advance—he revised his social and economic views. The advocate of the working classes now praised the Gregs, Manchester manufacturers, for their excellent relations with their staff: in their factory, he believed that he saw capitalists and labourers working in harmony.[19] Furthermore, he 'learnt to estimate the benefits of [the] relaxation of the system of Protection' for British industry.[20] These two themes—the relationship of the classes and the free operation of economic laws—were to remain the central concerns of his social vision for the rest of his life.

His new vision for society, fully established by the 1830s, the decade of Whig reformism, owed much to the work of Adam Smith and to the Utilitarian school.[21] His revised opinions were apparent in 1830, when he wrote *Capital and Labour*, as a response to the agricultural riots of that year, a work 'especially addressed to working men', intended to prove that 'the interests of every member of society . . . are one in the same'.[22] Knight was convinced that 'Capital and Labour are . . . destined to perform a journey together to the end of time.'[23] Clearly, capital had the advantage, but it also had 'equalities of duties'.[24] Here Knight clearly drew on Adam Smith's depiction of the interdependence of capital and labour, established by the division of labour. Imitating Smith, Knight saw the worker's right in his own labour as inviolable, a right with which governments and individuals must not meddle.[25] While the social condition of the workers was important to society as a whole, co-operation between the classes was, for Knight, the best means of social improvement.[26] He followed Smith in denying that violent action on the part of the workers would achieve anything to their benefit: trade unions, by turning violent, loosened the bonds of 'mutual regard' between capitalists and labourers. The interests of capital and labour were too

---

[16] C. Knight, *Passages of a Working Life During Half a Century*, 3 vols. (1864) i. 73, 75.

[17] Ibid. i. 182–3. See also A. C. Cherry, 'A Life of Charles Knight (1791–1873) with Special Reference to his Political and Educational Activities' (MA thesis, University of London, 1943), 38–134, which gives an analysis of Knight's editorials in *The Windsor and Eton Express*, of which he was the editor, 1812–26: this shows the gradual evolution of his opinions in the face of the post-war economic depression and popular disturbances.

[18] Knight, *Passages*, ii. 76–109.   [19] Ibid. ii. 85.   [20] Ibid. ii. 87.

[21] See Cherry, 'Charles Knight', 243–81, for a full analysis of Knight's mature social, political, and economic views.

[22] Knight, *Passages*, ii. 168.   [23] C. Knight, *Capital and Labour* (1830; 1845 edn.), 43.

[24] Ibid. 44.   [25] Ibid. 58.   [26] Ibid. 233.

closely interdependent: 'All men are united in one bond of interests, and rights and duties.'[27] Nevertheless, nostalgic communitarianism continued to be apparent in his historical thinking, forming a sometimes uneasy relationship with the individualism of aspects of political economy as it was popularized in the early nineteenth century. Both analytical approaches were evident in the narrative of constitutional and economic progress which he later wrote.

Knight's writing and publishing activities were inspired by a wish to educate the lower classes in their own true interests—interpreted through the tenets of liberal Utilitarianism—as a means of consolidating the national community. Early on, he aspired 'to become a Popular Educator', and he planned a cheap miscellany of 'wholesome literature for the people'.[28] It was his plan for a National Library which brought him into contact with Henry Brougham, and through him with the SDUK.[29] Throughout the half-century, his publishing work was dominated by his desire to provide cheap, good, illustrated literature for the masses. With John Murray, he published the *Library of Entertaining Knowledge*; in 1832, he established *The Penny Magazine*, 'a landmark in popular education'; from 1833, he published *The Penny Cyclopaedia*.[30] Social reforms were his concerns: he was publisher for the Poor Law Commission in the 1830s;[31] in 1849, he published material for the General Board of Health during the cholera epidemic of that year, and also wrote *Plain Advice* on matters of hygiene for the lower classes.[32] He published works aimed at improving public knowledge of economics and its laws, such as Charles Babbage's *On Currency* (1833) and G. Dodd's *British Manufactures*.[33] Whether Knight's publications were read by any but the labour aristocracy among the working classes may be doubted; there can be no doubt, though, that they reflected and refuelled the dominant political, social, and economic preconceptions of the early Victorian middle classes.[34]

---

[27] C. Knight, *Capital and Labour* (1830; 1845 edn.), 246.

[28] Knight, *Passages*, i. 225–7.

[29] Ibid. ii. 37–8, 44–9. See Cherry, 'Charles Knight', 282–389, for a full history of Knight's work with and for the SDUK.

[30] Knight, *Passages*, ii. 117–33, 200–4; C. C. Morbey, *Charles Knight: An Appreciation and Bibliography of a Great Victorian Publisher* (Birmingham, 1979), 3. The *Penny Magazine* (1832–45) is perhaps his best known and most debated contribution to popular education. Recent debate has centred on the issue of the extent of its ideological content—whether or not it preached a particular political message and/or a bourgeois ethic. See C. A. Fox, 'Graphic Journalism in England during the 1830s and 1840s', 2 vols. (D.Phil. thesis, University of Oxford, 1975), i. 145; P. Anderson, *The Printed Image and the Transformation of Popular Culture* (Oxford, 1991), 54, 60; S. Bennett, 'The Editorial Character and Readership of *The Penny Magazine*: An Analysis', *VPR* 17 4 (1984), 127–41.

[31] Knight, *Passages*, ii. 241–6.   [32] Ibid. iii. 100–3.

[33] Morbey, *Knight*, nos. 5, 84–8.

[34] Knight's publications often appear in contemporary fiction and biography as the reading of middle-class adolescents: see, for instance, Edmund Gosse's *Father and Son* (1907; 1983 edn.), 50–1, 88, where the author describes the lasting impact the *Penny Cyclopaedia* had on his early education.

'TRUE EYE-KNOWLEDGE': KNIGHT'S PRINCIPLES OF
AUTHENTIC ILLUSTRATION

Knight's second keen interest was in the provision of copious, effective, and correct illustrations in the works which he wrote and published: of all publishers, he was most the deeply attracted to the visual aspect of Romantic picturesque historiography. A childhood acquaintance with the artist and antiquary, John Britton, author of *The Beauties of England and Wales* (1801), which Knight described as wedding 'archaeology to a high style of illustrative art',[35] must have been an early inspiration. Knight's works certainly exhibit a 'sense of place', a topographical tendency typical of English Romantic nationalism, which clearly owed much to the powerful landscape movement of the early nineteenth century. Always visually aware, he observed the pictures in the castle at Windsor, his native town;[36] later, in London, while living next to the printseller Colnaghi, he received 'some lessons in taste' and, no doubt, realized the popular appeal of graphic art.[37] He attributed the failure of the *Weekly Penny Sheet*, an early journalistic endeavour, to the financial impossibility of providing it with illustrations.[38] The illustrations for the *Menageries* (1819), written and published by Knight for the SDUK, proved a trial, too; wood-engravings were either expensive or of poor quality.[39] Eventually, Edward Cowper, the printer-inventor,[40] helped the publisher to improve his printing plant to produce more illustrations by stereotype castings and steam printing. Knight sent casts of his best cuts all over the world for insertion in popular publications.[41] After the improvements had been adopted, great paintings were reproduced for *The Penny Magazine* (1832–45), and a *Gallery of Portraits* (1832–4), similar to Lodge's but including men of intellectual distinction, was published. A whole series of major 'pictorial' works followed: *The Pictorial Bible* (1835–7), *The Pictorial Shakspere* (1837), *London* (1841), and *The Pictorial History of England* (1837–50). The Orbis Pictus series of 'lavishly illustrated books' came next; they are described by Charles Morbey as 'perhaps the finest example of Knight's belief in the power of illustration in education'.[42] Knight was much of the same opinion, alluding to these works with justifiable pride as 'the largest body of eye-knowledge that has ever been brought together'.[43] His concern for art and illustration pervaded his whole publishing career: his publications included Anna Jameson's *Memoirs of the Early Italian Painters* (1845), *Pictorial Half-Hours, or Miscellanies of Art* (1851), and, significantly, W. A. Chatto's seminal *Treatise on Wood-Engraving, Historical and Practical* (1839), illustrated with engravings by one of a prominent family of illustrator-engravers, John Jackson.[44]

---

[35] Knight, *Passages*, i. 31.   [36] Ibid. i. 53.   [37] Ibid. ii. 6.

[38] Ibid. i. 244.   [39] Ibid. ii. 114–15.

[40] *DNB*, xii. 385–6. Cowper ran a printing firm with his brother, which was taken over in the 1820s by William Clowes the elder, Knight's main printer.

[41] Knight, *Passages*, ii. 222–4.   [42] Morbey, *Knight*, 4.

[43] Knight, *Passages*, iii. 19.   [44] Morbey, *Knight*, nos. 139, 228, 46.

Jackson was one of the many wood draughtsmen and engravers that Knight drew about him in the 1830s and 1840s. They included Thomas Williams, William Harvey, John Orrin Smith, Ebenezer Landells, the Dalziel brothers, the Whympers, and Edmund Evans.[45] Knight did not need to create this circle of artists, as they were already linked together in many respects, and they formed a basis for the development of graphic journalism in these years. Celina Fox, examining the living and working conditions of London wood-engravers and popular journalists, emphasizes the close-knit community which they formed and the 'cross-fertilization of personnel and ideas', which physical proximity and common financial insecurity produced.[46] Of the circle associated with Knight, many were pupils of Thomas Bewick, the father of nineteenth-century wood-engraving (Harvey, Jackson and Landells, for example), and others were pupils of other members of the circle (Orrin Smith was a pupil of Harvey, and Evans of Landells). Many had collaborated before: Harvey had designed the illustrations for Whittingham's 'Pocket Novels', which were engraved by Williams. Many continued to work together: Stephen Sly, another member of the circle, for instance, introduced into it his friend F. W. Fairholt, the antiquary and engraver.[47] From the letters of the circle, we can gain a clear idea of their working practices in the years in which they produced illustrations for Knight's works. William Harvey, whom Knight admired very much and described as the only man in London who understood wood-engraving properly,[48] was probably the principal designer and foreman of the group.[49] In a letter arranging the illustration of a treatise on pyrametrics for the SDUK, Sly revealed the initial stage in the collaboration of author and illustrator: 'If you have any more treatises, I should be glad if you would let me have them for perusal, after which I will see Mr Baldwin [the author] and confer with him on the sizes and styles of the embellishments.'[50] After this, Jackson explained the next stage: 'After the *drawings* had been made on the wood, they were submitted to you [*a SDUK supervisor, but in many other cases, this figure would have been Knight*], by me; by you, to the authors, who returned together with their remarks, in writing, which you handed to me, with your writing also.'[51] After this, the wood blocks would be corrected and dispatched to the printer. The whole process was dependent on a close-knit community of artists, established by Knight as publisher for the SDUK.

Authenticity was the guiding principle in Knight's choice of illustrations, a principle dictated by his desire to provide 'true eye-knowledge'. Knight's obsession with 'authentic' images is important, not only within the context of his own

[45] Engen, *Wood-Engravers*, 146.   [46] Fox, 'Graphic Journalism', i. 120–71.

[47] Engen, *Wood-Engravers*, 115–17, 133–4, 149–50, 241, 81–4, 290, 239–40, 85–6, for biographies of these artists as mentioned.

[48] London, University College: SDUK Papers, Knight 36. Scribbled on a letter of *c.*20 Jan. 1839 to H. Waymouth to C. Knight.

[49] SDUK Papers, Harvey 41. W. Harvey to S. M. Knevett, 14 Mar. 1844. In this letter, Harvey describes his self-effacing mediation between author and engraver.

[50] Ibid. Sly 25. S. Sly to T. Coates, 29 May 1828.

[51] Ibid. John Jackson 38. J. Jackson to T. Coates, 20 July 1841.

work, but as an expression of the concerns of historical illustration, picturesque historiography, and graphic journalism at this time.[52] Knight himself, while commenting on *London*, revealed some of the defining characteristics of authentic illustration: 'The Bible, the History of England were books of universal interest in which I could carry out my plan of rendering wood-cuts real illustrations of the text, instead of fanciful devices—true eye-knowledge, sometimes more instructive than words'.[53] Thus for Knight, authentic illustrations were almost always metanymic, and roughly contemporary with the person, scene, or building they purported to portray. The balance of metaphoric and metanymic illustrations—a combination of both was characteristic of picturesque historiography—was definitely tilted in favour of the latter in Knight's publications. He reiterated his conditions in several of his most important illustrated publications. In *The Pictorial History*, the Preface announced that the wood-cuts 'have in general been taken from drawings, sculptures, coins, or other works of the period which they are employed to illustrate; but . . . it has not been possible to adhere to this rule in every instance with perfect strictness'. In such cases, illustrations were sometimes given from later periods but only when an image was 'sufficiently accurate'.

A clear distinction was drawn between such illustrations and metaphoric ones from modern history paintings, which were given for 'other reasons altogether than their fidelity in regard to costume and other characteristics'.[54] In *London*, these illustrative principles were restated: abstract subjects were avoided, Knight wrote, in favour of those appealing to 'the reader's eye'; the illustrations were drawn with the intention of 'uniting to the imaginative power the strictest fidelity in every detail of Architecture and Costume'.[55] If we credit the *Passages*, he was from an early age suspicious of the veracity of history paintings: even while visiting Windsor Castle as a boy, he found himself doubting the historicity of the Baroque allegories—abstract subjects indeed—with which it was decorated: 'I was not quite content to believe that the Roman Triumph which Verrio painted in St George's Hall—in which Edward, the Black Prince and his royal prisoner were the principal personages—was a faithful representation of the costumes and manners of the fourteenth century.'[56] As an adult, he was no more tolerant of the history paintings of the later eighteenth-century English school. While selecting illustrations for the *Pictorial Shakspere*, he was disheartened to find that, at first, no pictures seemed available except for theatrical prints and the paintings of the Bowyer's Shakespeare Gallery, which he described as 'little more than vehicles for the display of false costumes'.[57]

---

[52] See C. Fox, 'The Development of Social Reportage in English Periodicals during the 1840s and Early 1850s', *Past and Present*, 74 (1977), 90–111, for some of the problems and questions of 'authentic' presentation of the social life of the city in illustrated journals of the mid-century.

[53] Knight, *Passages*, ii. 262.

[54] G. L. Craik and C. Macfarlane, *The Pictorial History of England*, 4 vols. (1837–50), i, p. viii. As the publisher providing the illustrations, it seems very likely that Knight suggested the terms of the preface.

[55] C. Knight *et al.*, *London*, 6 vols. (1841), i, p. ii.

[56] Knight, *Passages*, i. 53.   [57] Ibid. ii. 284.

The efforts of Knight to gather portraits for the *Gallery of Portraits* are a manifestation of his zeal in the cause of 'authenticity'; he found the influence of the SDUK and its members was 'most valuable [for] securing the admission of copyists to Royal Galleries and private collections'.[58] He even travelled about with his artists, no doubt to supervise the accuracy of their work: he went to Stratford-upon-Avon with Harvey, who was completing some sketches of Shakespeare's native town for the *Pictorial Shakspere*.[59] He wrote to Sir Henry Ellis, the principal librarian at the British Museum and editor of *Illustrative Letters* (1825–46), discussing illustrations, including one of a tomb at St Mary's church in Warwick, and asking about the availability of views of sixteenth-century Calais, Guisne, and Ardres for this publication.[60] Knight's principles for assessing authenticity appear to have been appreciated and accepted by his contemporaries: Lady Eastlake praised the illustrations of his *Pictorial History* as 'accurate representations of persons, and things'.[61]

The relationship created by Knight between text and image, in publications before the *Popular History*, repays attention, for he often achieved an intensive integration of text and image which ideally characterized works of picturesque historiography. Knight himself was certainly conscious of the increased appeal and importance of illustrations if presented in a real association with the text. He commented that an edition of *The Arabian Tales*, which he published with illustrations by William Harvey was 'almost without rival', as the artist had worked 'with the assistance of the author's mind'.[62] This process was, perhaps, more prosaic than Knight made it sound: it appears that Lane, the translator, provided oriental accessories for Harvey's designs.[63] *The Penny Magazine* was Knight's training ground in the use of text and image. Here his use of images was carefully tied—or, as Knight described it, 'annexed'—to the text. In spite of the intoxi-cation of being able to reproduce huge numbers of images, he included few superfluous examples and practically no 'fillers' at the bottom of pages.[64] A com-ment in an anonymous review of the National Gallery may have expressed his opinion of the significance of integral, rather than ornamental, illustration: 'Pictures . . . must be studied as attentively as books, before they can be thor-oughly understood.'[65] Patricia Anderson has shown how early issues of the *Magazine*, although containing much purely factual information, also included reproductions of, for example, works of art with commentaries which interpreted them in terms of their power to transmit civilizing virtues: hard work, economy, and self-improvement. She examines examples such as the image of the Dying Gladiator and scenes from William Hogarth's engravings to substantiate her argument, showing how sometimes details of the originals were subtly altered to

[58] Knight, *Passages*, ii. 247–8.   [59] Ibid. ii. 303.

[60] Clowes, *Knight*, 198–200. H. Ellis to C. Knight, 5 Nov. 1838.

[61] [Eastlake], 'Illustrated Books', 194.   [62] Knight, *Passages*, ii. 258–9.

[63] Engen, *Wood-Engravers*, 116.

[64] These observations derive from an examination of *The Penny Magazine* (*PM*), 1832–5.

[65] *PM* 1 (1832), 67.

add strength to the textual interpretation.[66] Independent observation suggests that Anderson's approach is substantially correct, and reveals the essentials of Knight's usual approach to relating text and image. However, several works of the 1840s, such as *Old England*, do seem dominated by a drive simply to reproduce as many illustrations as possible. In that work, text and image appear on separate pages, and a page of illustrations contains any number of diverse images, metanymic and metaphoric—portraits, landscapes, imaginary scenes from books and emblematic vignettes—in a pattern like that of a picture-essay. Why Knight chose to experiment with this alternative form is unknown (although sheer exhilaration with the increased availability of cheap illustrations may be one explanation); certainly, he did not continue with it, as the *Popular History* is illustrated in the *Penny Magazine* style.

It is easy to be critical of Knight's techniques. As William Vaughan has indicated, Knight's publications are simply not in the same class as highly ornamental 'illuminated' volumes of the 1840s, such as S. C. Hall's *Book of British Ballads* (1841).[67] However, his works seem to have been put together with a concern for text and image informed more by an intellectual than a purely aesthetic objective. If a pleasing page layout was not a great concern, Knight was eager to ensure that related text and images appeared on the same page. It is important to bear in mind the constraints of Knight's publishing circumstances: perhaps a more visually integrated pattern than this was unobtainable, as (unlike the publishers of the works which Vaughan describes), Knight was not always dealing with original illustrations designed for a particular work. In fact, he appears to have been notorious for the recycling of illustrations: in the *Punch* of 1847, a reviewer noted, in a list of (imaginary) literary curiosities, a work of Knight's, 'in which you have not some recollection of having seen the woodcuts five or six times before'.[68] As a popularizing publisher, Knight must have felt that the production of new images was an uncalled-for expense. Of course, many of his publications, such as the *Pictorial History*, were out of the range of the working-class purchaser, so this would be not be such an important factor, but if Knight already possessed a suitable illustration, he seems not to have bothered with the production of an alternative.

APPROACHING THE NATIONAL PAST: SOURCES AND PERSPECTIVES FOR *A POPULAR HISTORY*

A third great interest of Knight's was the history of his country, and he was familiar with contemporary antiquarian and historical works and their writers. A

[66] Anderson, *Image*, 50–83.

[67] W. Vaughan, *German Romanticism and English Art* (New Haven, Conn., and London, 1979), 166.

[68] [Anon.], 'New Curiosities of Literature', *Punch*, 13 (1847), 132. Quoted in Fox, 'Graphic Journalism', i. 242.

childhood at Windsor fostered his taste for history, and he early became a keen reader of history books.[69] The committee for his *Library of Entertaining Knowledge* included historians such as Henry Hallam and James Mill, the historian of British India; Henry Ellis of *Original Letters* was 'my old and valued friend'.[70] In the 1830s and 1840s, he was the publisher of many historical works which showed a growing interest in antiquarian and picturesque approaches to the English past. Among them were J. R. Planché's *History of British Costume* (1834), J. Brand's *Observations on Popular Antiquities* (1841), and *The Paston Letters* (1841–2), edited by A. Ramsay.[71] These publications were often his sources for preliminary forays into picturesque history, as is shown by a series of essays published as *Once Upon a Time* (1850), and described as 'Glimpses of the Past': here, in an essay on the letters of the Pastons, he commented that they were 'the only people of the old time who have allowed me to know them thoroughly', and to grow 'intimate with all their domestic concerns'.[72] Before *The Popular History*, though, his most relevant and important historical projects were works such as *The Pictorial History*, written by G. L. Craik and C. Macfarlane, and *Old England*. Knight supervised the writing and illustrating of *Old England* exceptionally closely: visits to historical localities were made 'for the purpose of superintending this pictorial and descriptive work on our antiquities' which were 'an important preparation for writing the history of England'.[73] These works were sources for both the text and images of *A Popular History*. The illustration of Gaulish huts from the Antonine Column, for example, appeared in both *The Pictorial History* and *Old England* before it surfaced in volume i of *A Popular History*.[74] Alfred's Jewel appears in both *The Pictorial History* and *A Popular History*.[75] A print of Henry VIII and his Council from Hall's *Chronicle* appeared in *Old England* before resurfacing in the later work.[76] Illustrations of *Playing at Bucklers* and *Maids Dancing for Garlands* appeared in both *London* and *A Popular History*, as did an image of the Old Academy in St Martin's Lane.[77] A Roman Victory and a portrait of Anne Boleyn had appeared in *The Pictorial Shakspere*, before they were used in the *Popular History*.[78] Some of the illustrations can even be traced back to *The Penny Magazine*: a series of Hogarth's engravings was reproduced in this paper between February 1834 and May 1835 and formed the visual basis for a chapter on Hogarth and society in *A Popular History*.[79] Thus the illustrations for the *Popular History* were substantially

[69] Knight, *Passages*, i. 52, 81, 103.   [70] Ibid. ii. 119–20, 259.

[71] Morbey, *Knight*, nos. 46, 139, 263.

[72] C. Knight, *Once Upon a Time*, 2 vols. (1850), i. 1.   [73] Knight, *Passages*, iii. 20.

[74] Craik and Macfarlane, *Pictorial History*, i. 98; C. Knight (ed.), *Old England: A Pictorial Museum*, 2 vols. (1845), i. 17, no. 50; Knight, *History*, i. 10.

[75] Craik and Macfarlane, *Pictorial History*, i. 161; Knight, *History*, i. 105.

[76] Knight, *Old England*, ii. 8, no. 1413; Knight, *History*, i. 273.

[77] Knight, *London*, i. 184, iii. 209; Knight, *History*, ii. 293, vii. 65.

[78] C. Knight (ed.), *The Pictorial Shakspere*, 8 vols. (1837), *Tragedies*, ii. 178, *Histories*, ii. 344; Knight, *History*, i. 16, ii. 336.

[79] *PM* 3 (1834), 121–8, 209–16, 249–56, 287–8, 329–30, 377–84, 401–2, 481–2; 3 (1835), 12–13, 29–30, 81–8, 113–14, 145–6, 172–5, 193–5, 209–16; Knight, *History*, v. 465–74.

recycled ones: some deriving originally from manuscripts, paintings, and anti-quarian publications, some being views of monuments and places commis-sioned by Knight for earlier publications.

Thus was the author of a picturesque history of England formed. It was but natural that a man with Knight's concern for social conditions and popular education should be bent upon producing a work which was for and about the people. His opinion of other historians reflected this concern: in the *Passages*, he praised the historian of Greece and prominent Utilitarian, George Grote, for his adherence to the 'democratic principle', while he condemned J. A. Froude as the apologist of Henrician autocracy.[80] T. B. Macaulay—at once a Whiggish historian, a social historian, and, moreover, a contributor to some of his earlier periodical publications[81]—was Knight's ideal of a historian. In the eighth vol-ume of his *Popular History*, Knight praised Macaulay for writing an anti-Jacobite history to put in 'the place of that sugar-candy of History which sees nothing but the misfortunes of the great and forgets the wrongs and the sufferings of the lowly . . . a diet fitter for a great people'.[82]

His intention to create a history of the people *and* for the people was clear: in the 'Advertisement' of *Old England*, he announced that the work was intended to open national antiquities to all ranks, an aim which clearly links the picturesque vision of the past with the development of the heritage industry.[83] *Old England* attempted to display the national past through a vast collection of illustrations; Knight now wished to produce a more intellectually demanding history. *The Pictorial History* had been modelled on Henry's *History* and broken into div-isions, but Knight was subsequently critical of this arrangement, believing that the intervals were too long, and repetition too frequent. In the *Passages*, he recalled his determination to 'endeavour to trace . . . the essential connection between our political and our social condition. To accomplish this, I would not keep the People in the background, as in many histories . . .'[84] He traced the course of the history of the English people and their improvements, as Norman despotism was contained by the tenacity of Anglo-Saxon freedoms.[85] The people gradually, in Knight's interpretation, became more and more central even to political history, as the 'influence of Public Opinion' grew 'with the material as well as the moral development of our country'. Good government and the improvement of the social state of the people were irrevocably linked; his *Popular History* was to be the fullest of national histories, tracing 'the connection between the progress of good government' and that of 'industry, art, and letters'.[86]

Besides the difficulties of composing his *History*, Knight faced the problems of selecting illustrations for his work. His concern for authentic images was seen once again in the *Popular History*: he felt that contemporary portraits of the

[80] Knight, *Passages*, iii. 192. [81] Ibid. i. 280–95, 315–21.

[82] Knight, *History*, viii. 471–2. [83] Knight, *Old England*, i. Advertisement.

[84] Knight, *Passages*, iii. 277. [85] Ibid. iii. 278.

[86] Ibid. iii. 283–4. Three chapters of the *Popular History*, dealing with the fine arts, were not written by Knight, but it is likely that he would have monitored their contents to ensure a uniformity of interpretation: I have therefore treated them as an integral part of his text.

Fig. 18. After J. L. David, engraved J. Jackson, *Bonaparte Crossing the Alps*, from C. Knights' *The Popular History: An Illustrated History of Society and Government*, 8 vols. (1856–62), vii. 394

sixteenth century would give 'images more durable than words can convey, of some of the leading personages of this period'.[87] William Hogarth, interpreted in *The Penny Magazine* as a teacher of moral values, was received here as a most valuable source of illustrations for a social history: Knight described his works as 'the best materials for the history of manners in the transition time from Anne to George III'. He included a whole chapter on 'Hogarth and Society', profusely illustrated with prints from the *Marriage à la Mode* and other engravings.[88] He was as quick as ever to denounce inauthenticities and anachronisms.[89] *A Popular History* contained only a small number of modern English history paintings and those included were exceptional in some way. Benjamin West, a mediocre artist in Knight's eyes, was worth some attention as he 'put an end to the more outrageous anomalies previously tolerated, and the historical painter was thenceforth in this country understood to be to some extent amenable to the law which governs the historical writer'.[90] Rather surprisingly, Knight also included the French history painter J. L. David's famous and grandiose portrait of Napoleon crossing the Alps (Fig. 18), but with the critical comment that it represented 'the hero of a melo-drama in the grandest of "poses"'.[91] Authenticity was not only a matter of truth to the historical facts, but an efficient deflator of the pretensions of traditional 'heroic' history.

[87] Knight, *History*, ii. 499.   [88] Ibid. v. 465–74.   [89] e.g. ibid. vii. 99.
[90] Ibid. vii. 74–5.   [91] Ibid. vii. 394.

PROBLEMS FOR THE PICTURESQUE HISTORIAN

A Popular History followed the example of many of its predecessors—in both its material and its sources—in its inclusion of the details of daily life as a part of history. The account of Alfred's reign was supplemented with a description of society and rural industry, illustrated from a Saxon calendar which had been engraved for Strutt's *Manners*,[92] a predictable source, typical of textbook histories of the period. Knight gave much attention to the Domesday Book, exploiting it for information on such diverse subjects as ranks in society, hunting, mills, cities and burghs, and the building of castles.[93] Illustrations were copiously provided: one, for instance, shows a hunting scene of the period, originally drawn from Royal Manuscript 2B vii.[94] Knight justified his inclusion of material from the Domesday Book on the grounds that its social statistics are 'as truly a matter of history as the events of this beginning of the Norman period'.[95]

However, despite his declared aim of integrating analysis of social conditions with the history of the government, many of Knight's attempts at social description appear in separate chapters devoted to that purpose alone. Chapter 26 of volume i, for instance, contains the 'Domestic History' of medieval England, written as a commentary on the Household Rolls of Swinfield, a thirteenth-century Bishop of Hereford, which had recently been published by the Camden Society.[96] Volume ii contains another general survey of society, this time of the sixteenth century, in chapter 29: inns, holydays, and the decay of towns are among the topics discussed, and illustrations include wood-cuts of the old parsonage at Lynton and a chained Bible,[97] while volume v contains no less than four consecutive chapters devoted to the beginnings of the Industrial Revolution.[98]

But clearly Knight could not rest satisfied with presenting a few chapters of social facts, essentially unconnected to the main political text; like Macaulay, he postulated a link between political progress and social improvement to create coherence in his text. He attempted to connect the social and political narratives which were separated by chapter divisions: when for instance describing eighteenth-century England as a developing commercial and manufacturing country, he announced that this constituted 'the most important feature of her advancing political condition' and was essential to an understanding of 'our present place among the nations'.[99] But this thesis could not rest on repeated assertion alone, and Knight soon found that the materials available were inadequate for the creation of a history of social improvement. Although he had to hand the theories of social change and causation developed by Enlightenment and Utilitarian thinkers, he had little else to draw on in the way of critical and interpretative apparatus. The development of historical criticism of documents, and of statistics for social and economic studies, were still at a rudimentary stage

---

[92] Knight, *History*, i. 87–92.   [93] Ibid. i. 203–14.   [94] Ibid. i. 206.
[95] Ibid. i. 213.   [96] Ibid. i. 391–410.   [97] Ibid. ii. 475–99.
[98] Ibid. v. 1–63.   [99] Ibid. v. 1.

in mid-nineteenth-century Britain. Moreover, there was the weight of precedent to contend with: traditional approaches to national history—political, philosophical, didactic, anecdotal, antiquarian—were inevitably bound to influence his text and illustrations.

No doubt aware of the problems which he faced, Knight reached a solution which was common to his more prestigious contemporaries: he decided to focus his narrative on the development of the Anglo-Saxon constitution and the liberties of the subject. This provided a link between the social condition and the political history of the country, but was not without its drawbacks. Anglo-Saxon liberties had long been the subject of much attention, and, for the liberal apostle of slow but steady progress, could be problematic: many 'conservative radical' writers, bemoaning the passing of a golden age of liberty and lamenting present sufferings under 'the Norman yoke', had exploited the same body of arguments.[100] Naturally, it was not easy for Knight to avoid the implications of their thesis. He was forced to insist, for instance, that the Norman Conquest had no deep effect on the English people—an argument which, ironically, results in just that separation of the social from the political which he was trying to avoid. He attempted to retrieve his position: 'Such is the course of most political revolutions. If the spirit of a people be not wholly trodden down . . . tyranny is only a passing storm which purifies while it destroys.'[101]

Knight more than once created a division between the political structure of the country and the social condition of the people, in order to support his thesis of slow but constant national progress. He reconciled his account of late fourteenth-century prosperity and social progress with the continued presence of a feudal social structure by dismissing the latter as a mere political and legal excrescence, which did not really interfere with the steady increase of prosperity.[102] Other apparent signs of something less than steady progress were countered as well as Knight could manage. The pessimism of Hogarth's social vision is moderated by the comment that he lived in an age when 'some very signal changes in morals and manners were strongly developing themselves'.[103] Thus the artist's portrayal of eighteenth-century society was presented as a rather prejudiced one, despite Knight's original reliance on Hogarth's work as a picture of manners, and his presentation of the artist as 'the steady asserter of truth and matter-of-fact in painting'.[104] Here we see the problems of a social historian confronted by visual material which he has no critical means of interpreting in relation to the society which created it, except those of contemporary Ruskinian art criticism: the categories of 'truth', 'nature', and high moral meaning which this offered him were clearly inappropriate for his purpose. But minor discrepancies were overlooked by Knight, who maintained his theory of continuous and interdependent

---

[100] See C. Hill, 'The Norman Yoke', in *Puritanism and Revolution: Studies in the Interpretation of the English Revolution of the Seventeenth Century* (1958), 50–152.

[101] Knight, *History*, i. 197–8.   [102] Ibid. ii. 17.

[103] Ibid. v. 473.   [104] Ibid. v. 463.

progress, in the social and political life of England, into the last two volumes of *The Popular History*, where it was not so hard to support.[105]

But the problem posed by Knight's adherence to a theory of continuous progress was not the real heart of the problem of maintaining a link between the social and political narratives. The Anglo-Saxon liberties gave Knight an interpretative framework in which the subjects' lives and freedoms would be equal in value to the prerogatives and acts of the government, thus connecting the history of politics and the history of the people. But this did not remedy the real problems of inappropriate information and inadequate techniques of criticism and analysis. Knight wrote not so much a social, cultural, and economic history of the English people as a redefinition of the traditional political narrative to make it a populist constitutional history. The struggles with the political text which this involved are clear in both text and image in the *Popular History*.

Knight was well aware that most of the original sources available to him, the chroniclers traditionally consulted by the English historian, offered materials more suitable for a history of kings and statesmen than of the common people. The extensive publication and exploitation of public and private records was only just beginning; as his published sources went, primary source materials such as the Paston Letters were still the exception rather than the rule. He remarked despairingly that the only portion of history with an 'abiding human interest' before Alfred was the establishment of Christianity.[106] He refused, however, to accept the judgement of the chroniclers whom he was forced to use as to what constituted an important historical event. As he considered the reign of Richard II, he remarked contemptuously,

Rymer . . . describes the reign of Richard II as 'a reign which affords but little matter that may shine in history . . .'. To us who regard battles, and sieges, and processions, and Te Deums, as less important matter for history than the progress of the people, the reign of Richard II is one of the most interesting of our annals.[107]

For Knight, it was not only the chroniclers who were at fault—modern historians had failed to employ the right perspective in interpreting their sources. David Hume was criticized by Knight for failing to realize that the minor events of Henry III's reign detailed by 'the monk of St Albans' might be 'a mirror of the state of society' and 'as instructive' as the writings of the court chroniclers Matthew Paris and Jean Froissart.[108]

At times, Knight seemed almost to exult at the absence from a source of what would normally be considered as important historical events: he recorded Robert Walpole's years of peaceful government, when there were few 'stirring events', with the comment: 'Happy is the nation which has little to offer to the historian . . . but its provision of the funds for sustaining labour; its general contentment . . . its leisure to examine into social evils, which chiefly affected those

---

[105] Knight, *History*, vii, p. v.   [106] Ibid. i. 71.   [107] Ibid. ii. 1.   [108] Ibid. i. 359.

masses of the people'.[109] But while eighteenth-century sources might be fruitful for the historian of social progress, most sources were less useful. Knight was apologetic in his comments on Henry I's reign: 'The transition period of Henry I is, in many respects, one of the most interesting of our history. It is not marked by any very great events.'[110] Knight was here stranded between a sense of important changes and the absence of supportive evidence in the sources. There is almost a suggestion that the absence of important political events is a warrant for believing great social development is in progress.

But the history of often obscure social progress which has 'little to offer the historian' would not provide substance to fill the *Popular History*. This Knight knew full well, and sometimes he betrayed his concern lest he become little more than the despised chroniclers, reminding himself that the historian who wished to be more than a mere annalist must look for a 'more artistical connexion' than the 'junxtaposition [sic] of dates'.[111] Occasionally, he pulled himself up with a start: an account of Stephen's reign is prefaced with the comment: 'this narrative is a picture of the entire social state—the monarchy, the church, the aristocracy, the people, and it appears to us, therefore, to demand a more careful examination than if the historical interest were chiefly centred in the battles and adventures belonging to a disputed succession'.[112] It seemed as if the reminder was indeed needed, as the text was surrounded by images bound to centre attention on the political struggle of Matilda and Stephen: a portrait of Stephen, his seal, his coat of arms, and coins from his reign. Successive pages restored the balance pictorially with illustrations of Durham Cathedral, an imaginary reconstruction of the excommunication of a baron, and a baron's seal.[113] The inclusion of the reconstruction, however, suggests that 'authentic' visual material for his history of the people could be as difficult for Knight to find as textual sources.

Steering clear of the Scylla of bald political narrative, however, Knight feared a fall towards the Charybdis of historical romance. The paucity of sources which yielded up materials suitable for social history might lead the historian into the realm of historical romance. The historian had an uneasy suspicion that the novels of Walter Scott, after all, were perhaps the nearest the nineteenth century had approached to the writing of a real history of the people. While describing the Porteous Riots of 1736, Knight, conscious of the shadow of *The Heart of Midlothian* (1818), remarked that these events were 'the property of romance' and that a factual account would seem dull, but 'an impartial review . . . is as much to be aimed at as a picturesque narrative'.[114] Here he temporarily abandoned the role of picturesque historiographer, apparently identifying with a view which was to be adopted by his scientific successors in their determined separation of history from fiction. It is, therefore, significant that no illustrations of the Riots were given, as if to contain them within a prosaic narrative. The ghost of *Waverley* (1815) was exorcised more firmly when Knight came to deal with the events of 1745: the reader was reminded that

---

[109] Knight, *History*, vi. 60.   [110] Ibid. i. 249.   [111] Ibid. vii, p. iv.
[112] Ibid. i. 249.   [113] Ibid. i. 249–50, 258, 269.   [114] Ibid. vi. 79.

the welfare of the governed is of far higher importance than the personal successes or misfortunes of those who govern them . . . This is not the romantic view of public affairs . . . But . . . let us never forget that the real fight was on one side for constitutional government, on the other side for irresponsible power; on the one side for progress, on the other side for retrogression.[115]

Identifying historical romance (rather unjustly in the case of Scott) as the vehicle of anti-populist and Tory sentiment allowed Knight to obscure its contribution to social history and to justify his redefined political narrative as a real history of the people.

REDEFINING POLITICAL HISTORY AS SOCIAL HISTORY

How was Knight to extract from his politically orientated sources, from the details of the affairs of kings and councils, a history of and for the people? In these texts, Knight felt he could see the potential for redefinition. In the first volume, he declared firmly that from 'the very earliest times, [we read] not only of kings, and priests, and mighty warriors, but of a people with strong passions and generous impulses . . . the beginnings of a great nation'.[116] Knight was determined to employ a new perspective on the often restricted material available to him. Commenting on the tendency of accounts of the eleventh century to include too much of the affairs of Normandy, Knight reflected on the errors of history which centres on the affairs of courts:

This arises from the habit of too commonly looking at the history of a king as the history of a nation . . . as a general principle, that personal history must be regarded as a very imperfect, and a very unimportant chronicle [of the people] . . . We shall endeavour to avoid this error, and principally to regard the acts of the Norman kings merely as illustrations of the course of events, and progress of society in England.[117]

Knight here appeared to vacillate—and not surprisingly, as the details of the lives of kings and great political figures occupied more time and space in his *History* than he might have wished. Frequently, Knight justified these inclusions by relying on the very argument that he apparently intended to reject: that the history of the king was, in some way, the history of the nation. Here stands political history redefined as an 'illustration' of the wider history of the people. This is clear in the account given of the reign of Alfred, whom no Victorian historian would dare to marginalize. Knight defended his concentration on the deeds of the king by describing Alfred as 'not only the great warrior and statesman, but the most practical improver of the people' who was 'well acquainted with the condition of the population over which he was to rule'.[118] Thus Alfred's actions could be seen as shedding an accurate light on the state of the country. Knight's narrative of the events of William I's reign was neatly excused for its concentration on the king and political events, by the assertion that 'from 1068 to 1072, the history of the

---

[115] Knight, *History*, vi. 115.   [116] Ibid. i. 2.
[117] Ibid. i. 201.   [118] Ibid. i. 85–6.

king is the history of the country'.[119] The adjacent illustration reflects the tensions of Knight's text. Despite Knight's inclusion of many illustrations from original manuscripts, often copied from the works of Strutt or other antiquaries, his use of images remained very eclectic—and essentially picturesque. A whole series of engravings by T. A. Prior, apparently based on the traditional pattern of portraits of the kings of England produced by Vertue, appear in the *Popular History*. Prior's work sometimes even included illustrative vignettes of the type Vertue used, and the pattern is only slightly disturbed when Prior arrived at the early modern period, and included notable statesmen, writers, and painters absent from Vertue's series. This rather feeble attempt at the remodelling of a very traditional style of illustration echoes Knight's attempt to redefine the political text.[120]

Other great political figures proved more susceptible than Norman kings to the attempt to merge their lives with that of the nation, as they could be portrayed as the mouthpieces of popular and national opinion. According to Knight, Earl Godwin, for instance, was the representative of the national sentiment of the people, oppressed by the Norman favourites of the court of Edward the Confessor, where 'the great idea of nationality had but little place'.[121] Such figures were exploited by Knight to rescue popular opinion from the obscurity to which, he felt, history had consigned it. In Earl Godwin's case, the reader is justly dubious of this interpretation of the ambitious earl, but Knight was on safer ground when he described Robin Hood as 'the representative of the never-ending protest of the people against misrule,—a practical protest which set up a rude kind of democratic justice'.[122] Indeed, modern historians faced with the same dearth of knowledge of popular opinion in the Middle Ages, have similarly (though with greater sophistication) analysed the Robin Hood legends as the expression of popular grievances.[123] It is a pity that Knight's illustrations could not match this intelligent perception—he was forced to fall back on the metaphoric style, popularized by such novels as *Ivanhoe* (Fig. 19) (his fear of the influence of historical romance on the writing of social history was not always misplaced).

To merge king and/or leader and people thus, however, was not the summit of Knight's achievement. He adopted a more dynamic approach when, while presenting the same historical events as a traditional political narrative, he encouraged the reader to reinterpret these events by viewing them from a different perspective. Unfortunately, his insights were often transmitted with moralistic reflections reminiscent of Mrs Markham and her philosophical distaste for medieval barbarisms. He commented upon the fact that the 'martial spirit' and chivalry of Edward III's reign was emphasized in 'the usual historical relations', to the exclusion of any recognition of the 'savage disregard of life' and its effect on the condition of the 'general people'.[124] This critical attitude to England's

---

[119] Knight, *History*, i. 185.   [120] e.g. ibid. i, facing 185; viii, facing 480.
[121] Ibid. i. 161–2.   [122] Ibid. i. 325.   [123] See J. C. Holt, *Robin Hood* (1982).
[124] Knight, *History*, i. 449.

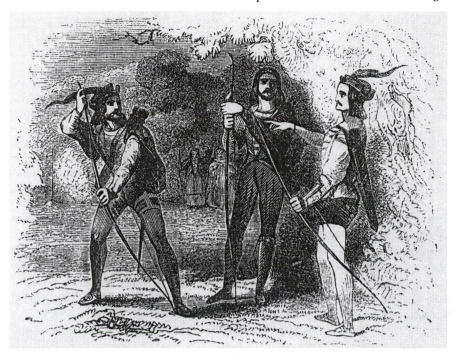

Fig. 19. *The Sherwood Outlaws*, from Knight, *History*, i. 324

military glories was reaffirmed in his remarks on Agincourt: a victory of which 'a people may be justly proud', but 'a fearful sacrifice of human life to a false ambition'.[125] Other efforts were more successful in their review of events from a populist angle. The disputes of the barons and King John, and the signing of the Magna Carta were interpreted as events of great importance, because they concerned not just those directly involved, but—through their long-term consequences—the entire nation.[126] This was not a substantially original line of argument, but some reinterpretations of traditionally important political events from a social and economic perspective reflect more credit on the picturesque historian. Resting firmly on the evidence of the Paston Letters, Knight treated the Wars of the Roses dismissively, feeling that they were not so important as had often been assumed. The internal administration of England proceeded, he wrote, 'with the same regularity as if the struggle for supremacy were raging on the banks of the Seine instead of the banks of the Thames . . . they [the people] were really prospering in an increase of material wealth'.[127] He refused to execrate Richard III in the traditional manner, showing more interest in his social and economic policy than whether or not he murdered his nephews. Considerable space was devoted to a description of his encouragement of the printing trade, which

---

[125] Knight, *History*, ii. 64.   [126] Ibid. i. 347.   [127] Ibid. ii. 98.

could be expected to have endeared him to Knight.[128] The historian also emphasized the significance of social and cultural events: when he described the affair of the South Sea Bubble, he directed the reader to view it as an event upon which 'we may still look with greater interest than upon the Treaties and the Wars'.[129] Social events, Knight insisted, were as important to the course of history as political ones: the eighteenth-century revolution in the arts and sciences was as important as political events.[130]

THE IDEA OF THE NATION: ECONOMIC FREEDOM
AND THE PRINCIPLE OF CO-OPERATION

Through these endeavours to redefine the political text, Knight arrived at a theme which created a link between the political narrative which he was forced to produce, and the picturesque history which he had hoped to create. It was an essentially predictable one: the history of the people was written as the history of the nation. Thus the political narrative—the emergence of a nation—became a history of the people. But although his solution to the problem of writing a social history of the people was largely unoriginal, Knight brought to the hackneyed tale of constitutional and institutional progress a broader social, economic, and cultural perspective characteristic of the spirit of Romantic nationalism. Liberty and fraternity—if not equality—informed a narrative in which the growth of political and economic freedom and the co-operation of all ranks and classes within the national community guaranteed the progress, peace, and prosperity of the English people. More muted in Knight's text is his recognition of the place of the state in this national project: as he dwells on the importance of a free economy and the abolition of all forms of protection, the reader may miss the few but significant indications of the role of the national state in promoting the progress of the people. Such touches exhibit Knight's position on the cusp of change, as Romantic nationalism of the early nineteenth century moved towards the state-centred nationalism which was to characterize later Victorian Britain.

Naturally, Knight's idea of nation showed through most clearly when he came to discuss recent European history in volumes vii and viii. Both the increased availability of suitable source materials and the emergence of nation-states allowed him to evade the limitations that the medieval period had imposed upon him: he was no longer dependent on the works of a small band of chroniclers, whose narrow focus on court events had forced him to fall back fall back on an unconvincing identification of the lives of monarchs with the history of their people. With much more credibility could the defeat of Napoleon by Britain and her allies, for instance, be attributed to the 'People', the 'nations' of Europe.[131] Knight warmed to his theme: hope for Britain in the long years of the war came,

---

[128] Knight, *History*, ii. 198–9.   [129] Ibid. vi. 39.
[130] Ibid. vii. 40.   [131] Ibid. vii. 472.

he argued, with the emergence of the peoples of Europe as the arbiters of history: when England has not 'kings for allies' but 'Nations for her friends'.[132]

If Knight was to redefine his political narrative as social history, however, he needed to develop an idea of nationhood which would surmount the difficulties presented by the earlier periods. This he found in a particular interpretation of 'the people'. By defining 'the people' as the totality of the community—rather than just the lower classes—the opposition of the history of kings and councils to that of the people could be presented as to be a false dichotomy. Thus the political historian's view of the past was less a false one than an incomplete one, which needed to be judiciously revised and supplemented. Progress towards a unified political and social community, where all classes lived in harmony, guaranteed in the free exercise of their natural economic and political rights by an enlightened government, was the central idea of Knight's *History*. The skeleton of this theory, which was based on Adam Smith's economics, was clear in his *Capital and Labour*. Here, Knight had described the society in its medieval state, where Crown seizures, slavery, and the 'monstrous regulations' of town merchants, had hindered growth.[133] It had progressed from this state to its present happy condition, where the abolition of economic restrictions, the accumulation of large capital, the development of the division of labour, and the advances in knowledge and machinery, were the basis of progress.[134] But all these beneficial results were dependent on the co-operation of labour and capital: 'society has always acted on the principles of co-operation'.[135]

These ideas pervade the *Popular History*, where the progress of economic freedom was carefully documented by Knight. He reflected on the lessons to be drawn from an examination of the medieval economy: 'an amelioration of the condition of the poor, through raising them in the scale of self-respect by kindly intercourse; and by summoning all the powers of scientific administration to sweep away the habits of economical ignorance which we have inherited—this is the lesson which we must draw from the contemplation of that state of low civilization'.[136] Here is a declaration in favour of a free economy (combined with a due recognition of the necessity of 'scientific administration' as well as 'kindly intercourse' to further the progress of the nation). By the sixteenth century, Knight argued, the economic restrictions of feudal society were decaying: 'The commercial spirit had penetrated into the whole system . . . and the iron bond of feudal protection and dependence was changed for lighter link of mutual interest'.[137] But the age of restriction was still not passed: the Settlement Law was introduced which, Knight believed, destroyed lower class 'habits of self-dependence'.[138] The Combination Laws of 1749, intended to prevent workers forming trade unions, also met with Knight's criticism, as another example of economic restriction. Their repeal in 1824 led him to reflect that conflicts between

---

[132] Knight, *History*, vii. 492–3.   [133] Knight, *Capital*, 54–5.   [134] Ibid. 232.
[135] Ibid. 233.   [136] Knight, *History*, i. 397–8.   [137] Ibid. ii. 465.
[138] Ibid. iv. 276.

employers and workers could only be remedied by the 'real and solid instruction of all classes' in the 'great natural laws' which inevitably regulate their relations.[139] Nevertheless, the lifting of oppressive economic laws was an essential step forward. The Poor Law Amendment Act of 1834 was, for Knight, the repeal of a 'systematic slavery'.[140] However, much education was needed before 'friendly intercourse between man and man' would replace 'that proud reserve and that suppressed insolence' which were 'the remaining badges of feudality'.[141]

For Knight, economic freedom for all classes was but a part of a larger scheme of co-operative enterprise between the classes, secured by mutual understanding and respect and fostered by good government. Although medieval society had been subject to destructive economic restrictions, it had seen the beginnings of the spirit of co-operation. This spirit was, for Knight, a growth of the Anglo-Saxon social system: like Ruskin, he translated the titles of 'lord' and 'lady' as 'loaf-giver', a translation to which he gives visual substance by the inclusion of an illustration showing a distribution of bread to the poor, from an Anglo-Saxon manuscript of 'undoubted authenticity'.[142] Guilds formed for the prosecution of felons represented for him the co-operative 'principle of association for public objects' in its infancy. Governments which worked with and for the people, which unified the nation rather than divided it, which put into practice the co-operative principle, were thus to be commended. Athelstan, buried at Malmesbury in the midst of the people whom he sheltered and aided, almost seems to merge with the community where his memory lingers: 'The people have extensive common-rights; and as the peasant-boy drives his herds to the rich pastures watered by the Avon, he thinks of king Athelstan who granted these rights to his towns; in whose school he learnt to read'.[143] Illustrations of the abbey and his tomb reinforced this impression, as Knight clearly views these as part of a popular heritage (Fig. 20). Knight added that, despite antiquarian assertions that the abbey was Norman, 'popular belief' dated it to Athelstan's day.

Meanwhile, governments which promoted division by separating themselves from the people, or one social group from another, met with Knight's criticism. He argued that, during the despotic reign of Edgar, 'the principle of nationality was destroyed which had been growing up since the days of Alfred'.[144] Knight used an illustration of the Pledge from Strutt's *Manners* to suggest the decline of mutual trust and the onset of social collapse, arguing that such a drinking custom portrayed deep social dissension. The King's chief adviser, Archbishop Dunstan, was one of the main agents of this undesirable change. His promotion of monasticism, on the grounds of the immorality of the secular clergy, created a clerical class separated from the people: married clergy, friends of the people whom they lived among, possessed of 'domestic virtues' and 'national feelings' were contrasted with the monks, fond of 'ascetic seclusion' and foreign disciplines, who have 'no country but the church'.[145] But Dunstan was not solely

---

[139] Knight, *History*, vi. 186.   [140] Ibid. viii. 339.   [141] Ibid. viii. 397.
[142] Ibid. i. 91–2.   [143] Ibid. i. 128.   [144] Ibid. i. 146–7.   [145] Ibid. i. 140.

Fig. 20. *Tomb in Malmsbury Abbey*, from Knight, *History*, i. 129

responsible for the decline of the English nation: the increase of a foreign—
Norman—influence in England before the Conquest produced, too, a dimin-
ution in social cohesion: 'The time was fast approaching when no earl would
defend a burgher against injustice.'[146] The intrusion of Norman interest was
represented visually by an illustration of Conisburgh Castle: Knight argued that
it was impossible to tell whether it was built before or after the Conquest.
But he believed the 'Saxon practice of social co-operation for public objects'
endured through the age of Norman rule to go forth centuries later 'to banish
from the civilized world the despotism which asserts the empire of the few over
the many'.[147] The Magna Carta carried on the ideal of social co-operation,[148] and

[146] Knight, *History*, i. 167.   [147] Ibid. i. 184.   [148] Ibid. i. 375.

in late medieval society, there were other signs of the survival of the co-operative spirit of a united people. English success in the Hundred Years War is attributed by Knight to the mutual trust between classes in England, which was absent in France.[149] Chaucer's fellowship of pilgrims in *The Canterbury Tales* was seen as a reflection of medieval society at its best, displaying a union of all ranks with mutual respect:

Surely in this fellowship . . . we may recognize a state of society where class distinctions were so marked that haughtiness and reserve were not thought necessary for the assertion of individual dignity; but in which there was a natural respect of man for his fellows,—the spirit which had made England great, and which may yet survive the modern tendency of grovelling prostration before rank and riches.[150]

This hint of 'Young England' or 'Tory Radical' nostalgia for the medieval age, despite his belief in progress, was not infrequent in Knight's *Popular History*.

According to Knight, however, the real age of social co-operation and union arrived in the second half of the sixteenth century—in the reign of Elizabeth—at a time of increased economic freedom and expansion. The Duke of Somerset, as the Protector of Edward VI, was the first Tudor statesman to perceive that 'the state was something more than a king, a nobility, a church, an army'.[151] But while Somerset merely succeeded in conciliating the poorer class at the expense of his favour with his own,[152] Elizabeth I was able to unite herself to the entire people, as classes were reconciling themselves with each other with the decline of feudalism. According to Knight, she 'threw herself upon her people' and 'governed a community' dominated by the strength of the emerging middle classes.[153] The Elizabethan age was indeed a golden one for Knight. The rebuilding of St Paul's, illustrated by a print of the cathedral, was a symbol of the principle of social co-operation to the historian, a symbol of the creation and preservation of a national popular heritage, which Knight himself was attempting to create and preserve in his illustrations:

Public spirit at this time . . . manifested itself in . . . the union of high and humble, the sovereign and the burghers, the noble and the priest, to carry through . . . the restoration of St Pauls. That principle has formed one of the foundations of a generous and confiding nationality, in which the inequality of ranks, is lost in a concurrence of duties.[154]

The response of the people to the Armada threat also won his applause: they displayed the 'national spirit' of 'a really free population': 'There was inequality of rank amongst them, but equality of duties and interests.'[155] England was saved in that hour by the co-operation of all classes in the national effort, 'in a brotherhood made closer by a common danger and a mutual dependence'.[156] Imperfect as the social structure was, this was an age of true and free co-operation, when feudal military force had been replaced by 'an organisation of the people amongst themselves equally effective, and far more inspiriting'.[157]

---

[149] Knight, *History*, i. 455.   [150] Ibid. i. 482.   [151] Ibid. iii. 19.
[152] Ibid. iii. 31.   [153] Ibid. ii. 127–8.   [154] Ibid. iii. 130.   [155] Ibid. iii. 219.
[156] Ibid. iii. 227.   [157] Ibid. iii. 214.

Fig. 21. [F. Fairholt], *Plough Monday. Dance of Bessy and the Clown*, from Knight, *History*, iii. 254

This merrie olde England was a society cemented by communal customs, which Knight recalled with some regret:

'the use of Wakes was recognized as promoting neighbourhood and freedom . . . 'that old hearty spirit of social intercourse . . .'. The object of the church-ale was thoroughly practical, and in complete accordance with one great national characteristic—that of voluntary contributions for public objects . . . All these indications of a kindly spirit, not chilled by distinctions of rank, are gone. Let us strive to revive the spirit in all forms fitting to our own age.[158]

Metaphoric illustrations of reconstructions of these communal customs, such as the Plough Monday dance (Fig. 21, probably by Fairholt, the artist who of all Knight's circle was most accustomed to antiquarian illustration) were lavish and, by Knight's usual standards, inauthentic. Their inclusion is therefore a measure of the strength of Knight's desire to impress them, his argument, and the whole dream of 'Old England' on the reader's mind. Mutual participation in sports formed an essential element of this social intercourse: 'It was this frank and rough fellowship in their field sports . . . which united the squire, and the yeoman and

<hr />

[158] Knight, *History*, iii. 254.

the ploughman, the merchant, the artificer and the sturdy apprentice'.[159] The English spirit of co-operation had made a people fit for self-government: local association was 'the familiar condition of an Englishman's existence'.[160]

But the seventeenth century saw the renewal of divisions as Puritan strove against Cavalier, separating society 'into two great classes of the pious and the profane'.[161] At one extreme, Charles I held himself totally separate from his people, believing his 'sovereignty to be an inherent possession, and not a sacred trust'.[162] At other extreme, anarchy—the division of all social groups, the loss of all social organization and co-operation—threatened England. Knight remarked significantly that the Levellers of 1649 were 'in a small way, the precursors of the "socialists" of 1849'.[163] Neither the Commonwealth nor the Restoration brought unity: for Knight, the failure of the latter was symbolized in the loss of the chance, from the 'want of co-operative action, to rebuild London to a better plan after the Fire of 1666'.[164] He included Wren's plans as a sort of map of Utopia. It was only after the events of 1688, when 'the compact between the king and the people was recognized', that improvement came.[165] The illustration here showed the obverse side of a medal, where Britannia is attended by the symbols of justice and plenty. At last, the constitution bound sovereign and people together. The events of 1715 and 1745 and the Atterbury Trial, however, show that old Jacobite preju-dices and the theory of divine rule still linger on, a theory which degraded a 'nation', a 'people' into 'but men born to obey'.[166] But the cohesion of society and the community of classes is never again really lost. This is made evident, Knight believed, by the contrast with the state of France, undergoing revolution. Knight attributed the Revolution to the separation of class from class, and people from government: 'the French monarchy . . . sought to govern its subjects by dividing them. The separate parts of the social fabric had no coherence. The whole fell to pieces when it was attempted to repair the rotten edifice.'[167]

The theory of gradual progress towards class co-operation and social improvement was evident in Knight's interpretation of the events of his own cen-tury. Although he believed that the Reform Act of 1832 was a necessary measure of parliamentary reform to bring the people and government into unity, Knight was not inclined to sympathize with the Chartists of 1848. Reasonable men of all classes were joined against the anarchistic Chartists, who found that 'they alone were not the People'. A force of special constables assembled to control them, 'a band where a real equality of rights and duties placed the peer side by side with the shopkeeper'.[168] Since this successful venture, co-operation and concord had triumphed, and the nation, Knight concluded, had entered upon a new era 'unimpeded by class prejudices and unembittered by class animosities. We were becoming a united people.'[169]

[159] Knight, *History*, iii. 255.   [160] Ibid. iii. 408.   [161] Ibid. iii. 414.
[162] Ibid. iv. 58.   [163] Ibid. iv. 117.   [164] Ibid. iv. 290.
[165] Ibid. iv. 449.   [166] Ibid. iv. 47.   [167] Ibid. vii. 160–1.
[168] Ibid. viii. 559.   [169] Ibid. viii. 562–3.

FROM PICTURESQUE TO SOCIAL HISTORY

Knight's *Popular History* was intended to be the history of a society becoming ever more united in the pursuit of progress and improved social conditions, in an atmosphere of increasing economic and political freedom. It was an ambitious attempt at the history of the making of a national community and a nation-state. As a work of picturesque history, it was not entirely successful: the high tidemark of Romantic and picturesque historiography was reached not in the history book but in the historical novel, a genre which offered a narrative freedom to the writer bent on the historical reconstruction of the lived experience of the past that the author of a multi-volumed history could not expect. Nor is it social, cultural, or economic history as the twentieth-century reader would perceive it: it is essentially a traditional political text redefined. Its mixed success as a history of the people was no doubt reflected in its restricted readership: the bulky volumes of the *Popular History* were beyond a working man's pocket and Knight's attempt to introduce the working classes, as well as the middle classes, both into and to his narrative of Romantic nationalism must have gone unnoticed by substantial parts of the community he was addressing.

Nevertheless, the *Popular History*'s emphasis on the importance of including the entire community in the historical narrative, and its attention to social, cultural, and economic factors—as in other 'social histories' of the period—made it a precursor of the new historical disciplines of the twentieth century, especially social history. Many of the textual sources and 'authentic' illustrations which Knight helped to popularize still appear in both contemporary history books and heritage publications. Who does not hear of the Pastons when studying fifteenth-century history? Who has not seen photographs of the Alfred Jewel in a history textbook, or a print of Hogarth's? Knight was, perhaps, as much the maker of our modern social history—if in a rather different way—as the more famous historians, Macaulay and Green. His text may be forgotten: but his promotion of the use of copious numbers of metanymic illustrations (which allowed a popular audience among the middle classes to take visual possession of its national heritage, transferring it from the pages of gentlemanly antiquarians) was of profound significance, not only for the illustration of history in the nineteenth but also the twentieth centuries. Our visualization of our national past owes more to Charles Knight than has yet been acknowledged.

6

Separate Spheres and Early Women's History

'. . . history, real solemn history, I cannot be interested in . . . The quarrels of popes and kings, with wars or pestilences, in every page; the men all so good for nothing, and hardly any women at all'.[1] Catherine Morland's well-known opinion of 'real solemn history' might well serve to summarize those of many other women in the late eighteenth century. While gentlemen were perusing David Hume's *History of England*, Catherine read the only form of historical literature which focused on the lives and experiences of women: the Gothic novel.[2] Like the 'common people' whose everyday lives Knight had attempted to explore and integrate into the national narrative, or Roman Catholics whose role in English history was championed by John Lingard (as discussed in the next chapter), women were a culturally marginalized group who could appear to have no place in the dominant national narrative. But during the late eighteenth and early nineteenth centuries, women had been attempting to find a space for themselves in both the politics and history of their nation.[3] As the biological reproducers and guarantors of the nation—the mothers of the race, the womenfolk in need of protection from the foreign foe—they had always been accorded a passive role; but it hardly needs to be said that women were rarely active or leading participants in national politics and events. Nevertheless, they could negotiate an intermediate role as carriers of the British values and ways, promoters and preservers of the cultural and historical traditions of their country.[4]

Women could attempt to enter into the history of the nation, and feature more frequently in its historiography and history books. Although Christina Crosby argues that women were still perceived in the mid-nineteenth century as 'outside history, above, below, or beyond properly historical and political life . . . the

[1] J. Austen, *Northanger Abbey* (1818; Harmondsworth, 1982 edn.), 123.
[2] See J. Spencer, *The Rise of the Woman Novelist from Aphra Behn to Jane Austen* (Oxford, 1986), 198–200, where she discusses how the very absence of women from history was explored in Sophia Lee's Gothic novel, *The Recess* (1783–5), which she describes as 'romance's revenge on recorded history'.
[3] L. Colley, *Britons: Forging the Nation 1707–1837* (New Haven, Conn., 1992), 237–81: here Colley explores how women negotiated a role in the national opposition to Napoleon and other significant political occasions of the era.
[4] These roles for women within the nation-state are explored in F. Anthias and N. Yuval-Davis, *Women–Nation–State* (1989), introduction, 6–11.

unhistorical other of history',[5] there was in fact a considerable change by the 1830s and 1840s, when Romantic and picturesque historiography—with its mission to create a narrative of the nation which dealt with more than high politics—was at its height. The opportunities offered by picturesque historiography to write the history of marginalized constituencies into the national narrative and simultaneously to challenge that narrative were seized by women writers. By the midnineteenth century, a number of women had taken up the pen to write about women in the national past, mainly in the form of biographies of prominent, usually royal, women.[6] The most significant women to do so in the 1830s and 1840s were Agnes and Elizabeth Strickland,[7] Mary Anne Everett Green, Hannah Lawrance, Mrs Matthew Hall, and Anna Brownell Jameson. This chapter will focus on the works of these women hisorians, and the illustrations accompanying their works, with particular reference to the most seminal of all these histories, the Stricklands' *The Lives of the Queens of England* (1840–8) and *The Lives of the Queens of Scotland* (1850–8).

WOMEN HISTORIANS

The decision of a woman to write history was not an uncomplicated one, as it involved a challenge to the gender role assigned to the nineteenth-century woman. Writers of women's history have argued for over twenty years that the late eighteenth and early nineteenth centuries saw the increasing compartmentalization of the public and private spheres of middle-class life, and the growing restriction of women to the domestic arena of the home.[8] The impact of separate spheres ideology on the lives of nineteenth-century women and its theoretical dominance of women's history is now under review.[9] However, while it is clear that nineteenth-century women's lives are too complex and varied to be explained in terms of separate spheres, it is undeniable that the ideology itself was immensely influential. Within the context of the domestic ideal of womanhood, writing—if it led to publication and a career, rather than remaining a strictly

[5] C. Crosby, *The Ends of History: Victorians and 'the Woman Question'* (New York and London, 1991), 1.

[6] See R. Maitzen, ' "This Feminine Preserve": Historical Biographies by Victorian Women', *Victorian Studies*, 38 (1995), 371–93, for further discussion of this phenomenon. For earlier women writers of history, see N. Z. Davies, 'Gender and Genre, Women as Historical Writers, 1400–1820', in P. Labalme (ed.), *Beyond their Sex: Learned Women of the European Past* (New York and London, 1980), 153–82, and D. R. Woolf, 'A Feminine Past? Gender, Genre, and Historical Knowledge in England, 1500–1800', *American Historical Review*, 102 (1997), 645–79.

[7] See M. Delorme, ' "Facts not Opinions": Agnes Strickland', *History Today*, 38 (1988), 45–50, for an introductory but rather simplistic outline of the sisters' career and work.

[8] Even recent women historians such as Leonore Davidoff, Catherine Hall, and Jane Rendall work within this framework. See L. Davidoff and C. Hall, *Family Fortunes* (1987); J. Rendall, *The Origins of Modern Feminism: Women in Britain, France, and the United States, 1780–1860* (1985).

[9] See A. Vickery, 'Golden Age to Separate Spheres: A Review of the Categories and Chronology of English Women's History', *Historical Journal*, 36 (1993), 383–414.

amateur accomplishment—could be seen as an unfeminine intrusion into the public sphere.[10] Many women were afraid to put their names to what they published. A woman, therefore, who wrote serious, multi-volumed national histories, could be a suspect individual.[11] Some women historians retreated from writing 'public' political history, by writing textbooks. Mrs Markham's *History of England* (1823) presented itself as an amateur work aimed at a domestic audience.[12] If the female historian intended to write history for adults, the most effective solution appeared to be to disclaim any ambition to be seen as a philosophical historian and to exploit the freedom of historical expression offered by picturesque historiography. In particular, retreat into the private and domestic sphere of female biography was a safe option: although women were not the only biographers of prominent, and especially royal and noble, women, they were by far the most frequent.[13]

But this apparent submission to the male-dominated character of the national narrative could have radical implications. Just as Lingard's conciliatory attempt to write Catholics into the national past was linked to a subversive reinterpretation of Protestant historiography, so women historians found that a focus on the history of women could produce a critique of the traditional narrative. The ambiguity of a public highlighting of women's role and place in a domestic sphere is indicated by historians such as Jane Rendall and Linda Colley. There was a potential in the domestic ideal for an emerging public role for women: offering support for public campaigns and acting as cultural carriers for national values. More radically, however, women could adopt a female perspective on events in the public arena and become missionaries of distinctly female values in the male public world. The elasticity of the ideology of the separate spheres is apparent in both the lives and the texts of women historians.

Many women historians selected women in powerful positions—queens, princesses, aristocrats—as their subjects. The reason for this choice was probably not only the availability of historical evidence of such women, but also the appealing ambiguity of their situation, at once public (by virtue of their rank) and private (by virtue of their gender). Their circumstances reflected the paradox inherent in those of their biographers—women who appeared to affirm the private nature of female experience by the public acts of writing and publishing. But the paradox ran deeper than the mere subject material. Ambiguous elements lace historical accounts which initially appear supportive of the Victorian ideal of

[10] S. M. Gilbert and S. Gubar, *The Madwoman in the Attic: The Woman Writer and the Nineteenth Century Literary Imagination* (New Haven, Conn., and London, 1984), 132.

[11] Among the few women who did so, in the late 18th–mid-19th cents., were Catherine Macaulay (*History of England from the Accession of James I to that of the Brunswick Line*, 1763–83) and Harriet Martineau (*History of England during the Thirty Years Peace*, 1849). See, among many other studies, B. Hill, *The Republican Virago* (Oxford, 1992), and R. K. Webb, *Harriet Martineau: A Radical Victorian* (New York, 1960).

[12] See Ch. 3.

[13] Male hack writers, such as John Doran and Jesse Heneage, also produced royal female biographies, exploiting the popularity of this historical genre.

womanhood. The essentially transitional—and essentially picturesque—nature of these biographies of great women is recognized by Bonnie G. Smith. She views them as an important stage before women historians turned to the writing of works on the universal condition of women in the past—women's history, in other words—and social history.[14] A formal recognition of women's presence and importance, in both the national community and the nation's historical record, was essential before new ideas on their role could evolve, or old ones be challenged.

The mixture of submissive and subversive in these historical biographies is often confusing and even contradictory. The potentially radical nature of the women historians' work was disguised: texts could appear to be dedicated to maintaining the male view of what constituted female virtue—a virtue which was too delicate to stand exposure to the rough realities of the public sphere. The employment of these methods in women's literature of the period has been recognized: Sandra Gilbert and Susan Gubar have pinpointed the way in which women writers working within male-devised genres created submerged meanings beneath the public message of their texts, 'simultaneously conforming to and subverting patriarchal literary standards'.[15] However, most of the women historians here discussed were more conservative individuals than the writers discussed by Gilbert and Gubar: their consciousness was of a 'womanist' rather than a feminist complexion,[16] and the degree to which they were aware of the appearance of contradictory submissive and subversive elements in their texts is by no means clear. The combination varied, of course, from one woman's work to another, and a brief glance at the different backgrounds from which they emerged alerts the reader to the different nuances of their texts.

The women historians considered here range from professional writers such as Hannah Lawrance, a contributor of more than fifty articles to the *British Quarterly Review* from 1847 to 1870, including articles on female education and employment,[17] to the obscure and clearly conservative Mrs Matthew Hall. Mary Anne Everett Green became a professional historian, publishing an edition of the diary of the seventeenth-century figure John Rous in 1856 and helping to edit the Calendar of State Papers in the 1870s.[18] Best known as an art historian, Anna Jameson epitomizes the dichotomy which could develop between the life of a woman writer and her written opinions: separated from her husband, she was for

<hr/>

[14] B. G. Smith, 'The Contribution of Women to Modern Historiography in Great Britain, France and the United States, 1750–1940', *American Historical Review*, 89 (1984), 714–18. Smith recognizes how the choice of subject created a tension between public and private when she describes the works as 'political alter-histories', which, nevertheless, had to be conceived in terms of 'moral standards for the behaviour of womankind'.

[15] Gilbert and Gubar, *Madwoman*, 72–3.

[16] This terminology was used by Clarissa Campbell Orr in her paper 'Agnes Strickland, Historian of Women, and the Langham Place Group', delivered at the Age of Equipoise Conference, Trinity and All Saints College, Leeds, 15–16 July 1996.

[17] *WI* v. 452–3.   [18] *DNB* lxii. 369–70.

many years the family breadwinner and became an authority on female labour—yet she deplored the existence of female absolute monarchs.[19] Her texts often seem to attempt to compensate for her unwomanly lifestyle.

The complexity revealed here is echoed in the joint authorship of the Strickland sisters, which is a paradigm of the problems of the female historian. It was Agnes's name alone which appeared on the title-page,[20] it was she who was the subject of a biography by a third sister, Jane Margaret Strickland, in 1887. The biography described a feminine and self-effacing spinster, a lover of needlework and weddings.[21] Agnes was a much more ambitious character than Jane would allow—there are hints to be found even in the *Life*[22]—but the real omission of the book was the almost absent Elizabeth, who had died in 1875 and thus could no longer have influenced the treatment of her life and opinions. Elizabeth was memorialized in a very short appendix at the end of the *Life*, which did not succeed in disguising the reason why Agnes had served as the public figurehead of their joint work. In the tone of a rather resentful younger sister, Jane described Elizabeth as 'well-skilled in business of every kind . . . possessing the governing powers, in no ordinary degree, and perhaps exercising them not always to the liking of the governed'. Her style was perceived as 'more masculine and nervous [than Agnes's]'.[23] Jane appears to have separated the submissive and subversive elements of the Stricklands' works, and to have placed the full burden of the disturbing and unacceptable elements on Elizabeth,[24] whose domineering character and lack of public connection with the works made her the ideal scapegoat. The apparently retiring paragon of domestic virtue, Agnes, was the public figure,

[19] See G. Macpherson, *Memoirs of the Life of Anna Jameson* (1878) and C. Thomas, *Love and Work Enough: The Life of Anna Jameson* (Toronto, 1967) for Jameson's life. In A. Jameson, *Memoirs of Celebrated Female Sovereigns* (1869), p. ix, she gives her opinion of female sovereignty. Art history, with its connotations of graceful accomplishment, was one form of history open to women in the 19th century: witness the considerable contributions of women such as Emilia, Lady Dilke and Elizabeth, Lady Eastlake.

[20] A. (and E.) Strickland, *The Lives of The Queens of England* (1840–8; 12 vols., 1845–8 edn.), i, p. xiv. Agnes wrote that her sister had 'forbidden her name to be united (with mine) on the title-page'. Despite this intimation of Elizabeth's collaborative role, the public continued in apparent ignorance of her existence: see the standard modern biography, U. Pope-Hennessy, *Agnes Strickland, Biographer of the Queens of England, 1796–1874* (1940), 238.

[21] J. M. Strickland, *Life of Agnes Strickland* (Edinburgh and London, 1886), 40.

[22] Ibid. 167–9.   [23] Ibid. 384, 387.

[24] Letters dated 1872–3 between Elizabeth Strickland and Bell and Daldy, the publishers of the 'concentrated' reprinted edns. of *The Lives of the Queens of England*, and the life of Mary, Queen of Scots, from *The Queens of Scotland* reveal the context behind Jane's remarks. While Agnes was ill, Elizabeth managed the revision of these works and upset both Agnes and Jane. She showed, for instance, a not unjustly critical attitude to the length of Agnes's life of Mary, Queen of Scots, telling Bell that the revised version was 'superior to the original which to my taste was diffused too much only Capt Blackwood seemed to desire its extension as much as possible' (Reading University Library: The Bell Archives, MSS 308/55, 308/56, 308/57, 308/116. E. Strickland to Bell and Daldy, 11 Dec. 1872, 17 and 18 Jan., 3 May 1873. Hereafter, Bell MSS. These letters are not properly foliated).

while Elizabeth, who seemed to be designed to brave the male-dominated out-side world, was the private character. The reason for this inversion is obvious: the more feminine Agnes was the acceptable face of women's history-writing, as she appeared less challenging.

The authorship of the sisters symbolizes the contending elements within the texts of women historians. Moreover, the lively letters of Elizabeth—when com-pared with the rather vapid epistles of Agnes—suggest that she experienced the struggle of the submissive and the subversive to a degree which Agnes did not. Elizabeth was the originator of the scheme of the *Lives*, which evolved from some sketches of the queens of France which she wrote for *The Court Journal*.[25] Clearly the dominant character, she dealt with problems with the publisher, Colburn.[26] She was also the author of most of the more overtly radical parts of their joint publications.[27] Awareness of her subversive impulses seems to have led Elizabeth to disguise herself and Agnes as obscure gentlewomen, 'not the least blue', devotees of 'the needle and the pencil' and 'always at home with our own sex'.[28] In a letter to Thomas Phillipps, one of their antiquarian advisers, she repu-diated the status of a writer: 'there is an intriguing spirit among many women who are professedly literary, which makes me shrink back on my own natural station of a country gentlewoman rather than be classed among them (and now you have my true reason for keeping my name from a titlepage)'.[29] Thus Elizabeth—as well as Jane—put forward the more conventionally feminine Agnes as the public figure-head of their venture, obscuring the ambiguous implications of her own text.

THE PUBLISHER AND THE ILLUSTRATIONS: THE SHAPING OF THE ILLUSTRATED WOMEN'S HISTORY BOOK

The problems and characters of the women historians were not the only factors shaping the production of illustrated women's history in the mid-nineteenth century. The influence of the publisher was a very important factor—still more important than in the case of male writers, as the publisher, almost always a man, usually had the added weight of his sex and business experience to exploit. The

[25] MSS. Phillips-Robinson, c. 476, fo. 252ᵛ. E. Strickland to T. Phillips, n.d. Elizabeth was the editor of this publication, which was the property of Colburn, for several years. Pope-Hennessy, *Strickland*, 33–6.

[26] Pope-Hennessy argues that Agnes, as the public figure of their enterprise, dealt with the pub-lisher. However, Elizabeth, who had more personal experience of Colburn, seems to have stepped in when any crisis arose, a not infrequent event. Ibid. 63–6.

[27] I have followed the attributions of authorship given in Strickland, *Life*, 384–6. Jane Strickland appears to have ignored the joint nature of the research: Elizabeth's involvement in the research for (and possibly the writing of) the lives of Elizabeth I and Mary, Queen of Scots, is made clear in the Bell and Daldy correspondence (Bell MSS 308/118, 308/172. E. Strickland to Bell and Daldy, 3 Sept. 1872, 9 Jan. 1873).

[28] MSS Phillipps-Robinson, d. 128, fos. 215ʳ–216ʳ. E. Strickland to T. Phillipps, 24 July 1840.

[29] Ibid., d. 128, fo. 232ᵛ. E. Strickland to T. Phillipps, 5 Nov. 1840.

publisher responsible for many of the works here discussed was Henry Colburn, a man with a reputation for ruthless dealing and extravagant 'puffing' of his works. Colburn catered for the middle-class library reader, concentrating on fiction, memoirs, and travel books, often with an aristocratic or royal connection.[30] After publishing the Stricklands' *Lives of the Queens of England* in the 1840s, 'a success for its publisher, critically and financially',[31] he published M. A. E. Green's *Lives of the Princesses of England* (1849–55), and probably arranged for his successors, Hurst and Blackett, to publish Mrs Hall's *Queens Before the Conquest* (1854). His relationship with the Stricklands illustrates the balance of power between such women historians and their publishers.

Right from the start, the sisters were 'unsettled about the Colburn business'.[32] In a letter of November 1840, Agnes revealed that he had offered them a mere £100 for the copyright of the *Lives*, but they would take nothing less than £2,000.[33] A month later, Elizabeth complained that Colburn's staff 'watch to wrong us out of a great deal of money': 'if they had to deal with gentlemen the whole matter would come to a dead stop'.[34] Colburn did finally pay the requested sum (due probably to the sisters' employment of a male friend, Dr Blundell, to negotiate for them[35]), which was still well below the value of the work: at the publisher's death in 1855, it was valued at £6,900.[36] Later, Elizabeth claimed to be withholding the revised fourth volume of the *Lives* until Colburn paid for it, adding that ladies 'cannot tell such gents their minds . . . but they can be passively and quietly obstinate'.[37] This was the sole means of manipulating the publisher, and, given their desire for publication, it could be a blunt weapon.

In view of the weak situation in which women historians found themselves, it is natural to assume that their power to select illustrations was much curtailed. In reality, their position was rather uncertain. The inclusion of illustrations in itself might be indicative of some influence on the part of women historians: as has already been seen, most multi-volumed histories did not have illustrations. Artistic interests and modest artistic talents being considered pleasing in women, it is probable that they themselves promoted the inclusion of illustrations as a means of emphasizing the difference between their (apparently) minor and feminine histories and the more serious volumes of male scholars: it identified them as histories of a picturesque rather a philosophical cast. It is worth remembering that novels and textbooks, which women wrote with general male approval, were also highly illustrated genres.[38] In the case of the Stricklands' *Lives of the Queens*

---

[30] J. Sutherland, 'Henry Colburn, Publisher', *PH* 19 (1986), 59–84.   [31] Ibid. 77.

[32] MSS Phillipps-Robinson, c. 476, fo. 234[r]. A. Strickland to T. Phillipps, 25 June 1841.

[33] Ibid., d. 128, fo. 198[v]. A. Strickland to T. Phillipps, 22 Nov. 1840.

[34] Ibid., d. 128, fo. 242[v]. E. Strickland to T. Phillipps, 19 Dec. 1840.

[35] Ibid., d. 128, fo. 231[r]. E. Strickland to T. Phillipps, 5 Nov. 1840.

[36] Sutherland, 'Colburn', 76–7.

[37] MSS Phillipps-Robinson, c. 476, fo. 251[r]. E. Strickland to T. Phillipps, n.d.

[38] See Ch. 3 for further analysis of gender distinctions influencing illustration. Among the women historians, there is one special case: Mary Anne Everett Green's husband was a painter and may, perhaps, have copied likenesses for inclusion in her *Lives of the Princesses*.

of England, it seems probable that Colburn, the publisher, was very little inter-ested in the illustrations (and thus that the sisters were the enthusiasts for their inclusion): they are limited in number (frontispiece and title-page only), and the artists involved were insignificant. The illustrators and copyists are difficult to trace in most cases: those for the *Lives* were apparently August Hervieu and one W. Read. Hervieu was a painter of portraits, and mythological and literary subjects: one of the many works which he exhibited was a portrait of Agnes Strickland,[39] which suggests that he was fairly well acquainted with the sisters, who may have recommended him to Colburn in the first place. The other artist was probably an obscure aquatint engraver of marine scenes.[40] By the time *The Lives of the Queens of Scotland* was published by the more respectable firm of Blackwoods of Edinburgh, the Stricklands enjoyed a considerable literary repu-tation: this is reflected in the employment of a more distinguished illustrator, the Scottish animal-painter, Gourlay Steell.[41] The engraver was probably Charles Armytage, a London painter of figures and historical subjects.[42]

The illustrations themselves were frequently metanymic—simple copies of portraits, effigies, and paintings. However, some were not, and it is highly probable that the Stricklands had the choice of subjects. It is clear, too, from the internal evidence of the text and surviving letters, that both Colburn and Blackwood relied on the sisters to suggest portraits and other artefacts to be copied. Thus there is considerable reason to believe that, in this and other cases, women historians were able to achieve a matching of the meaning of text and image characteristic of a picturesque work of history. The Strickland sisters were always looking out for appropriate portraits, paintings, and effigies, espe-cially when they toured country houses to see manuscripts or visit friends. While visiting Sizergh Castle in 1840, in search of relics of Catherine Parr, they 'superin-tended the copying of a beautiful portrait of Mary of Modena—the artist came to take directions last night but he cannot work it in watercolours. I must try what I can do. The artist's copy is for our 5th volume'.[43] This quotation suggests that the sisters sometimes took copies themselves, perhaps to be copied again by an artist back in London. In 1845, Agnes wrote to Thomas Phillipps that: 'We are engraving a portrait of Catherine of Braganza, from the Hampton Court gallery, for vol. 8 of The Queens, a Lely.'[44] The reference within the text of Catherine's life to the portrait 'in which Lely has depicted her among the Hampton Court gallery of beauties . . . from which the frontispiece of this volume is taken'[45] shows the importance of illustrations to the Stricklands.

---

[39] Wood, *Dictionary*, 221.   [40] Engen, *Wood-Engravers*, 161.

[41] Wood, *Dictionary*, 449.   [42] Ibid. 26.

[43] MSS Phillipps-Robinson, d. 128, fo. 220ᵛ. E. Strickland to T. Phillipps, 27 July 1840. Pope-Hennessy suggests, probably rightly, that Elizabeth was the sister who made the final selections of illustrations: certainly this was the case with the 1852 illustrated edn. of *The Queens of England*. Colburn did produce possible illustrations, but these were frequently rejected by Elizabeth on the grounds of inauthenticity or poor quality. Pope-Hennessy, *Strickland*, 193–6.

[44] MSS Phillipps-Robinson, c. 493, fos. 201ᵛ–202ʳ. A. Strickland to T. Phillipps, 17 Feb. 1845.

[45] Strickland, *Queens*, viii, frontispiece, 311–12.

In the sisters' correspondence with the publishers Bell and Daldy, in the early 1870s, discussion of illustrations is frequent and very revealing, since the illustrations from the original Blackwood edition of *The Queens of Scotland* were a source for the revised life of Mary, Queen of Scots, which was then being negotiated. Elizabeth owned to having 'rather disliked' two of the illustrations for Mary's life in the Blackwood edition,[46] but it seems unlikely that these were imposed upon the sisters by the Scottish publisher, as it is clear that he relied on them to supply suitable illustrations. It was Elizabeth who had arranged for an engraving of Darnley's portrait, from a print by George Vertue of which she was the owner: she complained that 'Blackwood's artist never returned' it, although she was pleased to see 'so fine a copy'.[47] The significance which illustration had assumed for the sisters is shown by Elizabeth's anxiety in the 1870s about the appropriate positioning of images in the text: she asked for the portraits of Mary and Darnley as a young couple to appear in the same volume which 'records their doings', for as they looked then, 'so we present them to the reader'.[48] A different facet of their concern is revealed by Agnes's dismissal of Bell's offer of a reproduction of the portrait of Mary, Queen of Scots, which was shown in Lodge's *Portraits of Illustrious Personages*: telling him bluntly that it 'will not do', she sent him a likeness which she believed to be more authentic from the Blackwood edition, 'an original portrait'.[49]

The sisters' adherence to the ideal of authentic illustration, as Charles Knight would have defined it—in preference to the imaginary vignettes of metaphoric illustration—was a constant of their career. It was earlier manifested when Colburn proposed a revised eight-volumed edition of *The Queens of England* with illustrations. In a letter to Mr Gerrard of Bristol, Agnes asked for an impression of the seal of Marguerite of France: 'We cannot find any historical representations either in carvings, or painted glass, or illuminated chronicle; therefore we are anxious to obtain a drawing of her seal.[50] The use of pre-existing illustrations did not limit the Stricklands' ability to exploit the images within the text to reiterate their interpretations of events and persons. Despite their apparent objectivity, such images were interpreted, or 'connoted', by the text, which, in a sense, illustrated the images, infusing a strong message.

Clearly, many of the women historians conformed to and yet subverted the historical illustrations used, in the same way as they did the texts. Their illustrators were men; and, although the women probably chose the subjects themselves, illustrations of the metaphoric kind remained within the structural confines of established patterns of images of women. Nineteenth-century art portrayed women fulfilling their domestic ideal role—as in George Elgar Hicks's *Woman's Mission* (1863), which showed woman as the guide to youth, companion to man,

---

46 Bell MSS 308/56. E. Strickland to Bell (and Daldy), 17 Jan. 1873.
47 Ibid. 308/119. E. Strickland to Bell (and Daldy), 21 Dec. 1872.
48 Ibid. 308/54. E. Strickland to Bell (and Daldy), 8 Jan. 1873.
49 Ibid. 308/180. A. Strickland to Bell (and Daldy), 25 June 1872.
50 Strickland, *Life*, 184.

and guardian of old age—and also as missionaries to other less fortunate woman. The only visual alternatives to these conventional roles were those of fallen women, prostitutes, and adulteresses: in other words, those who had singularly failed to achieve the domestic ideal.[51]

This was as true for historical paintings as for those of genre: even women artists, such as Henrietta Ward, a painter of historical genre, worked within these confines, producing works such as *Queen Mary Quitting Stirling Castle* (1863), a celebration of the Queen's maternal instincts.[52] The case of Ward—an artist who frequently drew her subjects from the Stricklands's works—offers an artistic parallel to the sisters' experience. For women artists, producing history paintings was as fraught a project as the writing of serious multi-volumed histories was for women historians: many, including Ward, participated in the newly developed hybrid category of historical genre. A product of picturesque history, this offered a more domesticized view of history, concentrating on scenes from the private lives of public figures, authentic reconstructions of the national (rather than the classical) past. The painters of historical genre were by no means exclusively female: Ward's husband too painted many works of this kind, although he experimented more widely than she did in other genres. But—like picturesque history-writing—historical genre offered the chance for women to represent history, to portray the national past, without provoking criticism for unwomanly ambitions.

Like women historians, the approach of a woman artist to feminist concerns (if any) had to be oblique and disguised: indeed, it has been recently argued that to see any such criticism of the domestic ideal in the works of such nineteenth-century women artists as Ward is anachronistic.[53] Whatever the judgement in this case (and Ward's use of such ambiguous texts as the works of the Stricklands as acknowledged sources deserves further consideration), it is clear that women historians could—through their texts—infuse the stereotyped images with which they were presented by (male) illustrators with new and forceful meaning. It is to these texts and illustrations that we now turn.

OBSCURITY AND THE ART OF OBLIQUE WRITING

Conscious of the male opinion that the chief glory of a woman is not to be talked of, women historians seemed to defer to it, apparently applauding the absence of women from the history of the nation. When Anna Jameson recorded the lives of

---

[51] H. E. Roberts, 'Marriage, Reduncancy and Sin: The Painter's View of Women in the First Twenty-Five Years of Victoria's Reign', in M. Vicinus (ed.), *Suffer and be Silent: Women in the Victorian Age* (Bloomington, Ind., and London, 1973), 45–76; L. Nead, *Myths of Sexuality: Representations of Women in Victorian Britain* (Oxford, 1988).

[52] P. G. Nunn, *Victorian Women Artists* (1987), 132–46.

[53] P. G. Nunn, *Problem Pictures: Women and Men in Victorian Painting* (Aldershot, 1995), 95–113.

aristocratic women of the late seventeenth century in *The Beauties of The Court of Charles the Second* (1831), a commentary attached to a series of engravings of Peter Lely's *Windsor Beauties* executed by her father, her subjects often seem on the point of vanishing. The life of Henrietta Boyle, Countess of Rochester, provokes the comment that it was 'the highest eulogium that could be pronounced' that, while her husband held public offices of great importance, 'we do not even hear of her'.[54] Her portrait is just as unobtrusive: 'a delicate and pleasing, but not a striking picture'.[55] Jameson speculated that female virtue might be 'far too delicate' a thing to be blazoned abroad by the trumpet of Fame.[56]

But women historians were also provoked by the absence of women in the histories written by men. Hannah Lawrance, in *The Historical Memoirs of the Queens of England* (1838), wrote that the English queens 'remain almost unknown' and that, anxious to rescue 'the memory of these illustrious women from oblivion', she had been forced to turn to 'contemporary sources', finding no information about them anywhere else.[57] In the Preface to *The History of Woman* (1843), which Lawrance wrote after the research for the *Memoirs* had revealed to her much unexploited material relating to her own sex, she reiterated that it was still only 'a faint and shadowy view' that her readers had of the foremothers of the nation.[58] Lawrance was not alone in her reaction to the absence of women from most historical texts; Mary Ann Everett Green, the author of *The Lives of the Princesses of England* (1849–55), described her field of study as 'an untrodden one'.[59]

Most of these women historians perceived themselves—or affected to do so— as the writers of a private, female, sort of history, and deprecated their own scholarship. It was an established practice for women writers to produce lighter reading matter, and this consideration shaped the comments of a reviewer of Lawrance's *Memoirs*. Lawrance's scholarship was above average and, unusually, uncomplicated by any claim of female inferiority. The reviewer was quick to perceive that Lawrance had chosen 'a walk not common to literary ladies': 'The historical memoirs which we have been accustomed to receive from female pens, are generally compilations from sources neither recondite nor difficult of access. She [has] . . . dug deeper in the tumulus of antiquity, than many accredited excavators of the other sex.'[60] Despite this candid praise, the reviewer firmly categorized her work as a picturesque rather than a philosophical history: there was

[54] A. Jameson, *The Beauties of the Court of Charles the Second*, 5 parts (1831), iv. 122.

[55] Ibid. iii, plate iii; iv. 127.   [56] Ibid. iv. 135.

[57] H. Lawrance, *The Historical Memoirs of the Queens of England from the Commencement of the Twelfth Century to the End of the Fifteenth Century*, 2 vols. (1838), i, pp. iii–iv.

[58] H. Lawrance, *The History of Woman in England and her Influence on Society and Literature from the Earliest Period to the Year 1200* (1843), iii.

[59] M. A. E. Green, *The Lives of the Princesses of England from the Norman Conquest*, 6 vols. (1849–55), i, p. v.

[60] [C. Johnstone], 'Hannah Lawrance's *Historical Memoirs of the Queens of England*', *Tait's Edinburgh Magazine*, NS 5 (1833), 257. Johnstone was, in fact, a woman, which may partially explain the generosity of the review.

applause for Lawrance's 'skill in picturesque narrative' and her work was recommended her work as a 'graceful fragment of early history' to those 'appalled by the
dry and repulsive facts of general history'.[61]

Many women historians frequently claimed to be writing for women only (just
as women textbook writers stressed that their audience was purely juvenile). This
exclusivity, they hoped, would excuse them from male criticism, as they were laying claim only to the acceptable, intermediate role of cultural carriers of national
values—and only to members of their own sex. Mary Hays's *Female Biography*
(1803) and many late eighteenth-century historical works by women had established the pattern here: in *Female Biography* the author claimed that her work was
intended to excite 'a worthier emulation' among 'the rising generation'.[62] She
excused herself for any deficiencies which might be detected by the serious male
historian, claiming no originality, for 'my book is intended for women, and not
for scholars', and was not expected to 'astonish by profound research'.[63] The
Stricklands, though they did not orientate their work towards their own sex
solely, clearly perceived their history as likely to be read in a domestic setting,
rather than an academic one—perhaps read aloud while women sewed. In the
Preface to volume xii of *The Lives of the Queens of England*, they offered their
gratitude to readers who have 'brought our Queens into their domestic circles,
[and] associated them with the sacred joys of home'.[64] In C. M. Yonge's novel
Heartsease, or The Brother's Wife (1854), her heroine Violet and her sister-in-law,
Theodora, cement their friendship by finishing off 'the volume of Miss
Strickland's *Queens*, which they were reading together' on their last evening
alone together before Theodora leaves for the Continent.[65]

Female historians frequently disclaimed any ambition to write 'real solemn
history', the public history of the nation which men produced. When describing
the Battle of Flodden, for instance, the Stricklands took cover under a convenient
male text, Walter Scott's *Marmion*, which could be utilized to deal with that male
preserve, war: 'The recital of battles from a woman's pen is almost as impertinent
and out of place as disquisitions on theology: both have been sedulously avoided
in these royal biographies.'[66] The sisters denied any intention to appropriate the
audience of the public, male historian; they were catering to the taste of readers
who would otherwise neglect history, the reader 'who would yawn over the prosaic sameness of battles, sieges and political dissertations'.[67] Details of dress were

---

[61] [C. Johnstone], 'Hannah Lawrance's *Historical Memoirs of the Queens of England*', *Tait's
Edinburgh Magazine*, NS 5 (1833), 263.

[62] M. Hays, *Female Biography; or, Memoirs of Illustrious and Celebrated Women of All Ages and
Countries*, 6 vols. (1803), i, pp. v–vi. Mary Hays, the earliest woman historian considered, was a late
18th-cent. feminist in the Wollstonecraft tradition, an advocate of equal rights for women, in particular in education.

[63] Ibid. i, p. x.   [64] Strickland, *Queens*, xii, p. xv.

[65] C. M. Yonge, *Heartsease; or, The Brother's Wife* (1854; 1877 edn.), 328.

[66] A. (and E. Strickland), *The Lives of the Queens of Scotland and Princesses Connected to the
Royal Succession*, 8 vols. (Edinburgh, 1850–8), i. 92.

[67] Ibid. i. 117.

often included, either as of interest to women readers, or as items to be classified under some other heading than that of 'History'. A description of the costume of Mary, Queen of Scots, concluded with an apology for such details which are 'deemed beneath the dignity of history', yet 'possess biographical and antiquarian value'.[68] At least one reviewer of the Stricklands' work accepted these statements at face value, commenting that information was conveyed 'in an easy and familiar style which reduces the labour of the historical student to a mere pastime ... Miss Strickland does not pretend to be very profound'.[69]

However, this distinction between men's and women's history-writing could be given a different edge. In *The Queens of England*, Elizabeth Strickland became overtly critical, and we find this emphasis on the impossibility of history without biography, philosophical without picturesque history: 'history, separated from the companionship of her sister biography, is an inexplicable riddle; for in the individual characters of rulers and princes ... can alone be traced the springs of an outward and visible action which history records'.[70] Criticism of the male text, of 'real solemn history', is evident in other women historians. Green sharply deplored the lack of detail on William I's daughters in the histories of Orderic Vitalis: 'had he devoted a little more space to these royal ladies, he would have done a greater service to an inquisitive posterity than by long eulogiums of antiquated abbots, or the quarrels of obscure monks'.[71] It is true that this is an attack on a 'monkish chronicler', often a popular nineteenth-century target, yet here, surely, is the voice of another discontent.

INFLUENCE: THE FEMALE FORM OF POWER

Women historians obscured their exposure of female lives and experiences in the public sphere by emphasizing the private virtues—filial affection, conjugal devotion, maternal love—which their subjects possessed and exemplified. The assertion of their influence was mitigated by the restriction of its exercise and effects to domestic or 'feminine' areas: primarily the home and family, but also—and more ambiguously—the semi-public spheres of moral and religious issues, and social and cultural developments. Significantly, they almost invariably used the word 'influence', with its implications of unobtrusive persuasion, rather than 'power'. Without exception, they stressed the domestic virtues and benign social influence of their subjects. Lawrance, in the Preface to *The Historical Memoirs*, emphasized that 'wide and important sphere' over which woman's influence extended, 'maternal counsels' being particularly important.[72] Lawrance also

---

[68] A. (and E. Strickland), *The Lives of the Queens of Scotland and Princesses Connected to the Royal Succession*, 8 vols. (Edinburgh, 1850–8), vi. 36.

[69] [J. Hosack?], 'Miss Strickland's *Lives of the Queens of Scotland*', *Tait's Edinburgh Magazine*, NS 18 (1851), 238.

[70] Strickland, *Queens*, v. 246.   [71] Green, *Princesses*, ii. 3.

[72] Lawrance, *Memoirs*, i, p. iii.

usually gave priority to women's contribution to the advance of national culture and literature, as the Preface of *The Historical Memoirs* shows.[73] In her subsequent work, *The History of Woman*, Lawrance was still more concerned with this aspect of woman's influence: it was written, she said '[to] trace the progress of female society from the earliest period of her history, and to illustrate the influence of woman on our civilization and literature. Important has been that influence'.[74] The Stricklands struck similar chords: in *The Queens of England*, they argued that 'the influence of the wife and companion of a sovereign must always be considerable', adding that it had generally been exerted for 'worthy purposes' and that the queens had been 'instruments in the hand of God, for the advancement of civilization and religious influence'.[75]

The fullest scope of women's social influence often remains discreetly undefined, yet there is a hint of ambition. Anna Jameson was explicit on the subject of female political power: accepting that women were confined to private life, she pointed out that

in that privacy . . . are inculcated and directed the principles and opinions of those men who are to legislate for the happiness and welfare of nations . . . If a woman could once be taught . . . to appreciate the great stake she has in the political institutions of her country . . . she would no longer mix up with these considerations . . . prejudices and personal feelings which have rendered at all times the political interference and influence of the sex a fertile source of evil, and a never-ending topic of reproach and regret . . .[76]

This passionate outburst tackled the issue of women's political influence on the legislators of the country, and claimed for them a stake in the political institutions of the nation. This influence, was, however, to be channelled through women's (primary) domestic role as mothers. Jameson later wrote *The Communion of Labour* (1856), which argued for extending maternal influence into society: here we can see her teetering on the borderline between the feminine and the feminist, converting women's biological role into a social and cultural mission.

How were the domestic virtues of women and their legitimate influence in society, ideals apparently adopted by the women historians, explored in the actual texts of these histories? Their allegiance to these ideals of womanhood was not just a placatory gesture reserved for the prefaces. Before the reader parade devoted, faithful, tender daughters, wives, sisters, and mothers: themes which illustrations to the biographies frequently reiterate. Green claimed that Henry the Lion of Saxony found his English wife, Matilda, 'the ready and sympathising solacer of his troubles'.[77] Is it a coincidence that the marriage portrait of Matilda and Henry is the illustration for volume i of *The Lives of the Princesses*?[78] The virtue of a good mother was the theme of Mrs Matthew Hall, when she praised St Helena, mother of Constantine the Great: 'It is an acknowledged fact that in

---

[73] Lawrance, *Memoirs*, i, p. iv.
[74] Lawrance, *History*, pp. v–vi.
[75] Strickland, *Queens*, xii, p. ix.
[76] Jameson, *Beauties*, v. 176–8.
[77] Green, *Princesses*, i. 246.
[78] Ibid. i, title-page.

the history of nearly all those individuals who have attained an eminent distinction in good or great qualities, the hand of a mother may be traced as implanting
the first seeds which riper years have matured'.[79] These themes were still more
evident in the works of the Strickland sisters. Berengaria of Navarre, wife of
Richard I 'little deserves to be forgotten by any admirer of feminine and conjugal virtue'. This perfect wife was commemorated in the portrait for volume ii
of *The Queens of England*; this was taken from her effigy in the abbey of Espan,
where she retired after Richard's death, and it shows her in her 'bridal costume'—
as Agnes Strickland was careful to point out, since it enhanced her depiction
of the queen, as 'faithful to his memory unto death'.[80]

The perfect wife was most fully embodied in Agnes Strickland's biography of
Mary of Modena, the second wife of James II. In 1688, he is forced to send her
abroad with their new-born son, the Prince of Wales. The scene as she waits for a
carriage at Lambeth church, after crossing the river from Whitehall, was shown in
an illustration to volume ix (Fig. 22). This encapsulated for Strickland the loving
wife and mother. She stands 'with her infant son fondly clasped to her bosom',
looking 'with streaming eyes towards the royal home where her beloved consort
remained, lonely and surrounded by perils'.[81] In exile abroad, her domestic
virtues further blossom, as she is

assuredly much happier in her shadowy court at St Germains than she had been as a
childless and neglected wife, amidst the joyless splendour of Whitehall. She was now
blessed with two of the loveliest and most promising children in the world, and possessed
of the undivided affections of a husband who was only the dearer to her for his misfortunes. Like the faithful ivy, she appeared to cling more fondly to the tempest-scathed oak,
in its leafless state than when in its majestic prime.[82]

Like Mary of Modena, Mary II and Anne—James's disobedient daughters—are
judged by domestic standards, and act as foils to their stepmother. Elizabeth
Strickland's account of Mary's arrival in England as queen abounded with references to her unfilial conduct.[83] The vignette for volume xi explicitly drew attention to Mary's poor conduct as a daughter: it illustrates a tale in which Mary, while
walking in St George's Gallery at Windsor, was confronted by Lady Catherine
Graham, the 9-year-old daughter of the Jacobite Lord Preston, who had come to
plead for the life of her father: 'how hard it is that my father should die for loving
yours', the child was reported to have said. The Queen, 'pricked in conscience',
was said to have relented. Strickland punctured this pleasant picture by suggesting that Lord Preston—who was indeed pardoned—was spared only to reveal the
names of other Jacobites.[84] The lives of the last three Stuart queens, in fact,
offered the Strickland sisters an ideal opportunity to turn the documentation of
private virtues into a political statement, in a celebration of femininity laced with
the sentimental Toryism which characterized their political stance.

[79] Mrs M. Hall, *The Lives of the Queens before the Conquest*, 2 vols. (1854), i. 117, 174.
[80] Strickland, *Queens*, ii, frontispiece, 11, 36.
[81] Ibid. ix, title-page, 258. In the illustration, however, she appears to be looking at the child.
[82] Ibid. ix. 326–7.   [83] Ibid. xi. 5–7, 66–9.   [84] Ibid. xi, title-page, 178–9.

Fig. 22. *Escape of the Queen and the Prince of Wales,* from A. (and E.)
Strickland, *The Lives of the Queens of England* (1845–8), ix, title-page

Not only wifely but maternal devotion too was given a very high profile in the
works of women historians. Elizabeth I was a problem for Agnes and Elizabeth
Strickland and their fellow biographers—her virtues and her faults alike were distinctly 'unfeminine'. Agnes, who deplored the Queen's callous application of
torture to prisoners and found her oaths 'revolting when used in parlance by a
female',[85] tried to establish some feminine quality, to which Elizabeth might plausibly lay claim, by emphasizing her love of children. She was associated with them
on the title-page to volume vi, which illustrated the traditional tale of children
presenting the imprisoned Princess Elizabeth with flowers while she was in the
Tower: 'Elizabeth was all her life remarkable for her love of children, and her natural affection for them, was doubtless increased by the artless traits of generous
feeling and sympathy, which she experienced in her time of trouble, from her
infant partisans in the Tower.'[86] Elizabeth was not a very convincing figure as an

---

[85] Strickland, *Queens,* vi. 369, 477.   [86] Ibid. vi. title-page, 104.

Mary of Lorraine shews the infant Queen her Daughter, in the Royal Nursery to Sir Ralph Sadler.

Fig. 23. G. Steell, engraved J. C. Armitage, *Mary of Lorraine Shews the Infant Queen*, in A. (and E.) Strickland, *The Lives of the Queens of Scotland and Princesses connected to the Royal Succession*, 8 vols. (1850–8), ii, title-page

ideal mother, especially given the absence of offspring. The emotion which in her was a redeeming trait is seen as the guiding principle of Mary of Lorraine, whose biography is Agnes Strickland's paean to maternal affection. When Mary, on her second marriage, to James V of Scotland, was forced to part with the son of her first marriage, Agnes grew positively rhapsodic about 'the divine instinct which pervades the feminine portion of the creation'.[87] Volume ii of *The Queens of Scotland* shows Mary of Lorraine, the proud mother, exhibiting the infant Mary, Queen of Scots, to the English ambassador, Sir Ralph Sadler (Fig. 23). This event took place after the Governor of Scotland, Arran, had denigrated the baby's health and beauty. The Queen Dowager led the ambassador, 'in the genuine spirit of fond and proud maternity' to the nursery 'where her darling was and exaltingly displayed her to him'.[88]

---

[87] Strickland, *Queens of Scotland*, i. 370.   [88] Ibid. ii, title-page, 30.

Mary of Lorraine's regency is seen as the direct result of her maternal instincts: she retained the reins of government, despite many difficulties, 'for the sake of her child';[89] when she resigned power, it was again at the call of domestic affection.[90] If she was glad to return to the domestic and affective sphere deemed natural for women, she was not unusual among the queens and princesses whose biographies the women historians wrote. There was always praise for those who retired from the public stage with relief, or what was seen as relief. Mary Tudor was much favoured by Green for her love-match to Charles Brandon, Duke of Suffolk, after the death of the King of France, her first husband. She retired into 'domestic life', as Green put it, living contentedly in the country with her husband.[91] Green compared her favourably to her sister, the ever-scheming Queen Dowager of Scotland: while Mary rightly sought the private life of family life and love as soon as she was able, Margaret remained in the public sphere, meddling in politics: 'In the gentler graces of the female character, and above all in the un-wavering steadfastness of her attachments, Mary Tudor bore as strong a resemblance to Elizabeth of York, as in her more turbulent irritability and vengefulness did the more talented but wilful Margaret to her brother Henry VIII.'[92] While Mary was seen as the true daughter of her mother, Margaret was identified with her brother. The illustration to volume iv is the well-known portrait of Margaret and her two brothers as children, while that to volume v is the marriage portrait of Mary and Suffolk—*Cloth of Gold, Cloth of Frieze*: this appears to be a reiteration of the comparison.[93]

The role of women as keepers of the domestic flame had, however, a social dimension which made them the carriers of national, cultural, religious, and moral values. All the women historians displayed their subjects as the protectors and patrons of the nation's cultural progress. A preoccupation with this aspect of their social mission was most apparent in the prefaces of Hannah Lawrance, as we have seen earlier. In *The History of Woman*, for instance, Lawrance identified Saxon women as the guardians of learning: 'not only were the most illustrious of these schools of learning found and presided over by women, but these women were themselves, pre-eminently lights in a dark age'.[94] This is an unusual assertion of the role of women as the makers as well as the carriers of culture. More typical of such texts is the presentation of Editha, the wife of Edward the Confessor, who, although she 'distinguished herself by learning', is shown as the patron of Ingulphus the historian, who records how she would question him, while still a boy, in literature, poetry, and logic, and reward his proficiency with money.[95] This paradigm of the role of women as the protectors and carriers of culture is shown in an illustration for *The History of Woman*, with her protégé.[96] It symbolized clearly the ambiguity of the role of women in the world of culture, as the

[89] Strickland, *Queens of Scotland*, ii. 218.   [90] Ibid. ii. 248–9.
[91] Green, *Princesses*, v. 126.   [92] Ibid. v. 113.
[93] Ibid. iv, frontispiece; v, frontispiece.   [94] Lawrance, *History*, 72.
[95] Ibid. 173–5.   [96] Ibid. title-page.

women historians saw it. They generally coupled a claim to importance with a graceful acknowledgement of their still subordinate role to male creativity.

However, most women historians laid their primary emphasis on the religious and moral aspects of women's wider mission. In the nineteenth century, religion and things spiritual and moral were frequently seen as distinctly 'feminine'. National heroines of the faith were particularly prominent in Mrs Matthew Hall's *Queens before the Conquest* (1854). The frontispiece of volume i captured one of the main themes of the book: it shows the Empress Helena carrying a large cross. Hall was enthusiastic in her praise for the Empress, who was 'the patroness of Christianity, the discoverer of the true Cross, the builder of churches, the mother of the oppressed, the glorious career of whose influence has, in a thousand ways, directly and indirectly, descended from her own day with her name and history'.[97] But many of the other queens described by Hall are equally prominent for their religious influence: in fact, Mercia, Kent, and Northumbria were all 'indebted for conversion [to Christianity] to the influence of the female sex'.[98] Other women historians, too, had their religious heroines. Everett Green, for instance, portrayed Elizabeth of Bohemia as the Protestant Princess *par excellence*,[99] while Agnes Strickland shared Hall's view of the Saxon queens. She described them, in a phrase that indicates how closely a woman's legitimate influence was seen as an extension of her domestic role, as 'the nursing mothers of the Christian faith in this island'.[100]

The more diffuse effects of women's moral mission are also much discussed. Elizabeth Strickland noted the fact that, after his wife's death, 'the happiness, the good fortune and the respectability of Edward III departed'.[101] The virtuous behaviour of Henry VIII in his youth was ascribed by Elizabeth to the moral influence of Catherine of Aragon, as the conduct of a man is 'almost invariably influenced by the moral qualities of the woman who has his heart in keeping'.[102] For all the women historians, peace-making constituted a large part of women's moral mission, and they often portrayed their subjects as peace-makers. For Green, Joanna, daughter of King John and wife to Alexander of Scotland, exercised ideal moral influence, only meddling in politics 'in a manner true to her amiable character', which meant mediating between her brother, Henry III, and her husband.[103] The peace-maker *par excellence*, is, however, Catherine Parr. Agnes Strickland presented her as perfectly fitted 'to reconcile the rival interests, and to render herself a bond of union between the disjointed links of the royal family' of Henry VIII. She won the 'affection and respect of her grateful step-children'.[104] Moreover—and here her peace-making becomes a force for political change—she also procured the restoration of Mary and Elizabeth 'to their proper rank at court, and recognition in the order of succession'.[105] The vignette to the volume shows

[97] Hall, *Queens*, i, frontispiece, p. iv.   [98] Ibid. ii. 15.
[99] Green, *Princesses*, v. 186, 542–7.   [100] Strickland, *Queens*, i, p. xxi.
[101] Ibid. ii. 360.   [102] Ibid. iv. 108–9.   [103] Green, *Princesses*, i. 392.
[104] Strickland, *Queens*, v. 31.   [105] Ibid. v. 36.

Henry 8th and his Family

Fig. 24. *Henry 8th and his Family*, from Strickland, *Queens*, v, title-page

the Hampton Court painting of the family of Henry VIII (Fig. 24)—the perfect accompaniment to the portrait of Catherine, which is the other illustration to the volume, since it is the visual assertion of her success as a peace-maker. Playing down the nakedly dynastic nature of this propagandist group portrait, Agnes interpreted it as the private memorial of a happy family: the design of the picture, she wrote, seemed to have been 'to introduce all the members of the royal house of Tudor, as a united family'. In the portrait, Edward leans in 'a caressing attitude' upon his father, while Henry 'embraces his son'. Mary and Elizabeth appear 'as if to offer filial homage to the royal pair' (to whom they are in much greater proximity than in the original, where their placement outside the canopy of state blatantly affirms their illegitimacy and their lower ranking in the order of succession[106]). The Queen beside Henry is Jane Seymour, but this is but another sign of Catherine's almost superhuman tactfulness, since she refused to take offence at her husband's determination to exclude her from the portrait in favour of the dead mother of his son.[107]

[106] Strickland, *Queens*, v, title-page, 50.   [107] Ibid. v. 52.

A HISTORY FOR WOMEN?

Women historians excused away their history as a special, inferior kind, but the development of a sense of women's historical identity led them, in many cases, to the beginnings of a critique of the traditional national narrative, and its values and judgements. Though many of the antiquarian details of costume, domestic life, and personal history were produced by women historians with an apology for their being beneath 'the dignity of history', there was frequently a note of dissatisfaction with male public history. Elizabeth Strickland, for instance (more overtly critical than her sister), began a description of late seventeenth-century London and its life with the comment that, for anyone seeking a description of London in the 1690s: 'vain would it be to search among the folios which it has pleased the policy of modern writers to call history; in truth, filled up as they are with dry details of foreign battles, and the mere outward movements of cabinet diplomacy, such narrative is the, history of any country rather than our own'.[108] Of course, such protests against the 'dry details' of political history were prevalent also among other, male historians such as Macaulay: the existence of such criticism no doubt encouraged women historians to voice their own particular complaints, conscious that only when everyday life in the past became the subject of serious historical investigation would the historical experience of women be fully explored. The fact that traditional history was more often the record of the destruction, than the progress, of civilization also irritated Elizabeth, who noted the insignificant amount donated to Sebastian Cabot for the discovery of Newfoundland in the Privy Purse Expenses of Henry VIII. 'Scanty is the reward of the benefactor of the human race, dim are their records' and few people find them, 'while those of the destroyers are blazoned forth'.[109] For her, the bias given to human affairs by an emphasis on leading political events led to a distorted version of national history.

But the documentation of domestic life of the nation could become not just a supplement but a threat to male public history: like other picturesque historians, some women writers questioned the values as well as the content of traditional multi-volumed histories. If Thomas Carlyle saw history as the biographies of great men, the Stricklands 'believed it to be the story of eminent women',[110] but they did not share his interpretation of greatness, envisaging a private, domestic heroism, achieved by women, but impossible for men:

'Few great men are heroes in the eyes of their valet de chambre' says a proverb universally allowed to be founded on an accurate appreciation of the masculine temper; at the same time its application does not extend to women, for owing to daily and hourly habits of self-control and self-government, practised by well-educated females in domestic

---

[108] Strickland, *Queens*, xi. 248. [109] Ibid. iv. 103.
[110] Pope-Hennessy, *Strickland*, 3.

life, from their infancy, many an illustrious woman has been a heroine in the eyes of her handmaiden.[111]

Mary of Modena, for one, meets up to these high standards: her 'personal attendants' left glowing records of her.[112]

The values of private life—of which women were the primary carriers—were seen by some of the women historians as deserving protection from the political actions of men. Women were perceived as the victims of male public historical values. This was clear when Green described the marriage of Isabella, second daughter of King John, to the Emperor of Germany: 'the splendour of the alliance' meant not a thought was given by her father and his nobles to her chances for happiness.[113] There was a challenge to male historical values in the determination of the women historians to extend their judgement on the basis of domestic qualities to men as well as women: the personal turned political with a vengeance. James II and the crisis of 1688 were reinterpreted with a Tory slant, by means of these domestic standards.[114] The disloyalty of two daughters to a model father, rather than the (Whig) questions of national civil and religious liberties, formed the central focus of the narrative: though male relations have constantly provoked civil wars, Elizabeth Strickland noted that 'history produces only two other instances of warfare between daughters and fathers'.[115] Shakespeare's *King Lear*, not Henry Hallam's *Constitutional History*, was the literary model here. James II's ideal fatherhood was asserted in the vignette to volume x (Fig. 25): it is an illustration of an incident recorded in the text, when Pepys visited James, then Duke of York, and described in his diary how the prince played with his child 'like any ordinary private father'.[116] Picturesque history had promoted a natural interest in the private lives and virtues of great men, but women historians were among the few to turn the domesticization of history into a political statement.

If woman's role as domestic angel could be used to issue judgements from a domestic angle on great men in the national narrative, so too with great issues. Often women historians can be detected taking the values of the only areas of human experience where they were entirely free to pass judgement, and turning them against men and their world-historical visions. If they were to be at once dismissed and praised for the ability to see events only from a woman's point of view, this could become an asset, a means of historical reinterpretation. This could be a light-hearted matter: Agnes Strickland switched round the tale of Henry VIII and Anne of Cleves, and imagined how Anne would have felt—something the male-orientated historical record could not be expected to reveal. Describing

---

[111] A. (and E.) Strickland, *The Lives of the Tudor Princesses including Lady Jane Grey and her Sisters* (1868), 387.

[112] Strickland, *Queens*, x. 204.   [113] Green, *Princesses*, ii. 10.

[114] Interestingly, the Strickland sisters first became Jacobite in their historical sympathies in reaction to their father's admiration for William III. In 1847, Macaulay, another 'Whig' male, attacked the sisters' Stuart volumes in *The Edinburgh Review* for lack of 'masculine gravity and impartiality'. Pope-Hennessy, *Strickland*, 6, 180–2.

[115] Strickland, *Queens*, x. 404.   [116] Ibid. x, title-page, 241.

Fig. 25. *Mary II and her Father*, from Strickland, *Queens*, x, title-page

their meeting at Rochester and Henry's disenchantment, she commented ironically that it was 'possible that Anne was not a whit more charmed'.[117] She added
that 'Anne had the most reasonable cause for dissatisfaction of the two.'[118]

Reinterpretations from a woman's point of view could be less frivolous.
Elizabeth Strickland reassessed Mary I and portrayed her bad reputation as the
results of men's actions, and men's interpretations of the role of woman. She is
the victim of male destructiveness. Elizabeth indicated that 'Bloody Mary' herself
was merciful in disposition by pointing to her leniency to Suffolk and other prisoners on her accession, when she was still 'uncontrolled by council or husband'.[119] At Wyatt's Rebellion, she was 'far more merciful than her ministers'[120]
and 'several instances are to be found of the queen's interference to save persons
from the cruelty of her privy council'.[121] The effects of the male destructiveness,
which marred Mary's reign and reputation, were sarcastically indicated in a
description of the procedure for her coronation:

neither the Saxons nor the Normans owned a sovereign-regina . . . The Norman nobility and their descendants, through evident distaste to female authority had refused to

---

[117] Strickland, *Queens*, iv. 321.   [118] Ibid. iv. 329.   [119] Ibid. v. 288.
[120] Ibid. v. 345.   [121] Ibid. v. 291.

recognize the rightful heiress, Matilda the Empress, Eleanora of Brittany, and Elizabeth of York, as sovereign ladies. The effects of ferocity . . . had destroyed the promising heirs-male from every branch of the great stem Plantagenet . . . the throne was surrounded by female claimants . . . Thus our combative forefathers . . . had no alternative but to submit to the domination of a female. This they did with the worst grace in the world; and . . . they insisted on her being encumbered with spurs and girded with swords, and other implements of the destructiveness in which their souls delighted.[122]

The merciful nature of Mary was contrasted with this image of an aggressive, destructive aristocracy, who overturned their own rules of inheritance to avoid the succession of a woman, and, having themselves reduced the candidates for the nation's government to the only persons who were not involved in their warfare, forced upon their chosen ruler the emblems (and methods) of their own suicidal conduct.[123]

Such comments implied not only disgust with male public values as expressed in senseless wars, but also a doubt as to male ability to govern ably without the tempering influence of women. The women historians frequently suggested discontent with the unrivalled primacy of the male, by hinting that many kings' wise measures were attributable to their female relatives. Women shored up the thrones of kings: Mrs Matthew Hall, for instance, praised Ethelfleda, daughter of Alfred, the chief minister and support of her brother, Edward the Elder, who devoted herself to 'a life of heroism and care of her country's good', throwing off 'all the weakness of her sex' and appearing 'in history rather as a general than a mother or a wife'.[124] Green, too, frankly displayed women shoring up male power. Philippa, daughter of Henry IV, was married to the weak Scandanavian monarch, Eric: 'it was only through the energy of her private character that Eric was so long enabled to maintain his exalted character'.[125] The single word 'private' obviated criticism of Philippa as a wife publicly domineering over her husband, though it is clear that Green saw her as the real sovereign: she remedied debasement of the coinage, dauntlessly combated Holstein at war, and saved Copenhagen from ruin. After her death, he soon lost the throne.[126]

Sometimes the women historians' indignation at the losses in social, political, and religious status, which they believed the women of their century to have experienced, breaks forth. Mrs Hall's praise for Boadicea's heroic patriotism was embellished with the claim that she was not alone: thousands of women enlisted under her, enjoying the right to fight for their country and having 'no less courage than the men'.[127] Agnes Strickland took up the cause of women's education: Catherine Parr and Lady Jane Grey, praised by the scholars of their own day, 'would inevitably have been stigmatised as blue-stockings if they had lived in the nineteenth instead of the sixteenth century'.[128] Even women's employment was

---

[122] Strickland, *Queens*, v. 305–6.
[123] The life of Mary I was one of the most frequently attacked parts of *The Queens of England*. Pope-Hennessy, *Strickland*, 105–6, 237–8.
[124] Hall, *Queens*, ii. 165.   [125] Green, *Princesses*, iii. 365.   [126] Ibid. iii. 374–88.
[127] Hall, *Queens*, i. 63.   [128] Strickland, *Queens*, v. 59.

considered: Elizabeth Strickland used Queen Anne's decision to employ a woman, rather than a recommended male servant, as a confectioner, as an opportunity to make a plea for the nineteenth-century lady to employ women in any household position which they could sustain, sparing them poverty and the 'temptation to weakness'.[129]

A CASE STUDY: MARY, QUEEN OF SCOTS

The combination of conventional and subversive elements is neatly illustrated in Agnes Strickland's presentation of that uniquely controversial figure, Mary, Queen of Scots. Debate over her character and conduct was often politically or religiously motivated—Scottish by birth, French by upbringing, Catholic, and an apparent plotter against the English crown, she was a natural choice for the role of *femme fatale* in the national narrative. But, in the nineteenth century, the debate over Mary was still more a matter of gender.[130] Historical opinion at the time was generally unfavourable towards her: the Romantic movement may have revived an sympathetic interest, but it did not produce much serious historical reinterpretation of the Scottish queen. Mary Hays, writing at the turn of the century, had given a rather diffident account of Mary in her *Female Biography*, remarking that it was 'difficult to form a just opinion of the character of Mary'.[131] But Agnes Strickland's mid-century account was a firm defence of Mary, a defence seen as typically feminine by William Makepeace Thackeray:

Mary of Scotland . . . finds adherents ready to conspire for her even in history . . . How devotedly Miss Strickland has stood by Mary's innocence! Are there not scores of ladies in this audience who persist in it too? Innocent! So was Helen of Greece . . . Madame Laffarge never poisoned her husband; and Mary of Scotland never blew hers up . . . and Eve never took the apple—it was a cowardly fabrication of the serpent's.[132]

For women writers, as Thackeray failed to detect, Mary, Queen of Scots was the archetype of femininity, the classic Romantic heroine victimized by men. Only women could rightly judge such a figure and the 'cowardly fabrication' was the work of someone other than the serpent. 'The woman gave it to me, and I did eat'.

Strickland had no doubt of the identity of the fabricators: in the Preface to *The Queens of Scotland*, she opened her attack on the male historical view of Mary, but with caution, since the principal protagonist was the much admired John Knox, a doyen of Scottish Protestantism and patriotism. She asserted that his zeal made him view the daughter of his old enemy, Mary of Lorraine, through 'a distorted lens'. She concluded that his harsh words 'have no real effect as matter of

---

[129] Strickland, *Queens*, xii. 86–7.

[130] Roy Strong writes that the double image of Mary, as potentially a perfect lady or a murderous adulteress 'may have considerably increased her potency as a symbol of the suppressed womanhood of mid-Victorian England'. Strong, *And When Did You Last See Your Father? The Victorian Painter and British History* (1978), 134.

[131] Hays, *Biography*, v. 273.

[132] W. M. Thackeray, *The Oxford Thackeray*, ed. G. Saintsbury, 17 vols. (1908), xii. 714–15.

evidence'.[133] The vignette to volume iii indicates her awareness of the problems of religious controversy, represented by Knox, for the historian favourable to Mary: it shows Knox lecturing Mary at a hawking. Strickland aimed to discredit this most dangerous of historical opponents, asserting that Knox was 'a woman-hater by nature, and a defier of female authority from principle'.[134] She accused him of recording rumour rather than fact, of listening to the 'malignant tale-bearers' of 'coarse scandals'.[135] This contrasted with Carlyle's defence of Knox as a national hero, the mighty deliverer of his country: this role excused his harshness and rudeness to the Queen, which was necessary to a servant of 'the Nation and Cause of Scotland'.[136] One of the Stricklands' reviewers realized what Agnes would be facing, in the way of established (male) historical opinion, when she challenged Knox's interpretation of Mary: he warned her that she must expect the 'wildest imputations' if she proposed to meet 'prejudice and bigotry' with nothing stronger than 'historical evidence'.[137]

Knox (and most male historians) were not, in the opinion of Strickland, fair judges of Mary. How could opinions be corrected? Earlier, Mary Hays had suggested that all that was needed was an equal standard of judgement, as impartial an assessment of a female, as of a male sovereign. Historians should perceive that the role of monarch required other qualities than those of a wife, whose 'aimable weaknesses' arose out of 'a state of subjection and dependence'.[138] This sensible argument that the female ruler should be assessed as a monarch, and not a woman, was not employed by Strickland, who indeed based her defence of Mary as monarch on Mary as woman: unlike Hays—a feminist in the tradition of Mary Wollstonecraft—Strickland based her argument not on a call for equality, but an assertion of difference, of femininity. Already perceived as essentially feminine, Mary was an excellent paradigm for a defence of women which exploited their womanliness—the qualities men instructed women to cultivate—as the irrefutable core of the argument. Strickland was, indeed, only able to defend Mary because 'in the wide range of female royalty, there is not a princess whose conduct has afforded a more touching exemplification of the tender characteristics of her sex'.[139]

Accordingly, Mary's private and public lives were both presented in terms of the Victorian ideal woman, for, within the separate and domestic sphere, women historians could claim a right to make judgements of their own. She was shown as domestic in habit, tender in personal relationships, socially influential as a carrier of religious and cultural enlightenment, and a peace-maker to boot. Mary was the perfect wife—she exhibited the 'utmost deference' to her first husband, François II of France, and was 'unremitting in her tender attention' in his last illness. She was 'the angel of his life', 'the only true mourner'.[140] She bore with the uncouth

[133] Strickland, *Queens of Scotland*, i, p. xii.
[134] Ibid. iii, title-page, 337.   [135] Ibid. iii. 345.
[136] T. Carlyle, *On Heroes and Hero-Worship, and the Heroic in History*, 2 vols. (1837–9; Oxford, 1927 edn.), ii. 42–3.
[137] [Hosack?], '*Queens*', 238.   [138] Hays, *Biography*, iv. 292.
[139] Strickland, *Queens of Scotland*, v. 140–1.   [140] Ibid. iii. 103, 133, 135.

Darnley, her second husband: with 'wifely patience and feminine delicacy', she refused to complain of neglect, infidelity, and intemperance.[141] An illustration to volume iv, which shows her presenting her new-born son to Darnley, asserted her role as a loving mother. Strickland perceived her as motivated by 'the purest feelings of maternal love, and solicitude for the safety, health, and weal of the babe' when she left him in the care of the Earl of Mar at Stirling.[142]

The problem of the incompatibility of feminine virtues with the demands of sovereign rule, emphasized by Hays, was side-stepped by Strickland: Mary ruled through female influence, not the exercise of sovereign rule, reigning 'as a woman . . . by her feminine charms and graceful manners'.[143] She ruled as a woman ought, with tolerance, peace-making, and mercy. Her mercy was 'benevolence and feminine compassion';[144] her care for the poor was 'maternal';[145] she reconciled feuds; legal reforms, and the arts and industry were promoted under her 'wise and maternal jurisdiction'.[146] But Strickland's apparent avoidance of the contradictions inherent in the concept of female rule was highly ambiguous. It may have originated as an attempt to disguise her power as a feminine property, but it involved the carrying of 'feminine' values, such as religious toleration, pacifism, concern with social and economic issues like poverty, into the public sphere.

The perfect femininity of Mary was a defence, not only because it overtly mollified male opinion, but because it carried implications which quietly subverted male assumptions. The charges against Mary were refuted by the establishment of a clear male/female divide, which forced men out of the category of those capable of judging the evidence relating to Mary. The Casket Letters were condemned as a forgery because they were clearly not the work of the perfect lady which Mary represented so well.[147] Equally, Strickland argued, it was clear that the Bothwell match was a forced one: only those who know nothing of 'the female heart' (i.e. men) could suggest 'a paradox so absurd'.[148] This assertion of a clear division between male and female feelings and experiences was the inevitable outcome of the concept of 'natural spheres' for the sexes. Now it was being used by women to affirm their individuality and right to judge matters which fell within their sphere. Strickland claimed that the guilt or innocence of Mary, Queen of Scots, was such a matter, and applied the test of female opinions of the evidence, the judgement of Mary's contemporaries, and, ultimately, women historians and readers. This approach was evident from the beginning:

If the favourable opinions of her own sex could be allowed to decide the question, then we may say that a verdict of not guilty has been pronounced by an overpowering majority of female readers of all nations, irrespective of creed and party . . . with the notorious exceptions of Queen Elizabeth, Catherine de Medecis and the Countess of Shrewsbury, Mary had no female enemies.[149]

---

[141] Strickland, *Queens of Scotland*, iv. 272.   [142] Ibid. iv, title-page; v. 221.
[143] Ibid. iv. 44, 201.   [144] Ibid. iv. 212.   [145] Ibid. iii. 253.
[146] Ibid. v. 359–60.   [147] Ibid. v. 4.   [148] Ibid. v. 293.   [149] Ibid. iii. 3.

Fig. 26. G. Steell, engraved J. C. Armitage, *Queen Mary's Forced Abdication*, from Strickland, *Queens of Scotland*, v, title-page

Mary's own sex not only refused to condemn her; they stood by her. The account of her escape from Lochleven was dominated by the loving heroism of women in her cause. There was the laundress who was the go-between for the Queen and George Douglas, 'a true-hearted Scotchwoman, kind, compassionate and courageous'; there was brave Mary Seton, who remained at the castle to impersonate the Queen; there was Jane Kennedy, who swam the lake to join her.[150] The chivalry of Douglas himself pales beside this devotion. In disgrace and prison, her ladies remained 'fondly and faithfully' loyal.[151] Mary's innocence of Darnley's death was evidenced, for Strickland, by Lady Atholl's wish to join Mary in her prison in England, bringing her daughter.[152] The account of her trial and execution is full of references to 'her faithful ladies' who 'with devoted love, kept tearful vigils'.[153] The vignette to volume vii emphasizes the allegiance to death of the women: it shows Mary blessing them, just before she mounts the scaffold.[154]

In Strickland's account of Mary's life, it was men who were the villains of the piece, the instigators of her downfall: she was the victim of male cruelty and ambition. The vignette to volume v (Fig. 26), for instance, highlights Strickland's

---

[150] Strickland, *Queens of Scotland*, vi. 58–71.   [151] Ibid. vi. 289.
[152] Ibid. v. 15–16.   [153] Ibid. vii. 64.   [154] Ibid. vii, title-page.

indignation at the victimization of Mary by men, epitomized in her forced abdication. While Robert Melville tried to persuade the Queen, Lindsay—'that brutal ruffian' whom Mary had generously pardoned for his part in Rizzio's death—threatened 'the defenceless woman' at his mercy, and seized her arm 'so rudely as to leave the prints of his mail clad fingers visibly impressed'. It is this moment which the vignette depicts. A weeping female attendant looms in the background, signalling the appropriate response of sympathy; the mail gauntlet on the ground symbolizes the cruel brute force of men. During Mary's imprisonment in England, the rule of her (male) usurpers was associated with continued cruelty to women.[155] Suitably, her usurping half-brother Moray was murdered by one Bothwellhaugh, whose house had been given by Moray to John Bellendon; this henchman had turned out his predecessor's wife, just after childbirth, into the cold of mid-winter, thus causing her death.[156] When Mary's death came, it was again the work of men: Strickland revised her early interpretation of the signing of the death warrant by Elizabeth to exonerate the English queen and place the blame firmly on her ministers.[157]

DOMESTIC POLITICS: WOMEN'S HISTORY AND NATIONAL HISTORY

The theory of the separate spheres located women in the ahistorical realm of the private and the domestic, outside the worlds of business and politics where the history of the nation was made. Women historians exploited the idea of separate spheres to establish a distinct female identity and role, but they also used it to attempt to write women into national history and even to mount a criticism of male historical views and values. In these texts and images, women were able simultaneously to conform to and to subvert both the domestic ideal of womanhood and the traditional historical narrative, in which women played only a marginal role. Picturesque history—with its broadening of the perimeters of history to include subjects and sources once considered beneath the dignity of history—offered the Strickland sisters and other women historians the same authorization to challenge the national historical consciousness which it presented to the Roman Catholic historian, John Lingard, the subject of the next chapter. Until the early twentieth century, such works as these here discussed and their successors were to remain the major arena for the development of women's history (and indeed social history): the professionalization of history as an academic discipline tended to exclude women from the pursuit of scientific history in the later nineteenth century.[158]

---

[155] Strickland, *Queens of Scotland*, v, title-page, 367–8.
[156] Ibid. vii. 56–8.   [157] Strickland, *Life*, ix. 69–70.
[158] B. G. Smith, 'Gender and the Practices of Scientific History: The Seminar and Archival Research in the Nineteenth Century', *American Historical Review*, 100 (1995), 1150–76, addresses the language in which the scientific history enterprise was described and shows how—both physically and ideologically—women were at least initially excluded as the active participants. It is

This manipulation of separate spheres theory was, however, common among the contemporaries of these women historians, figures advancing into the public limelight in other more practical spheres: local government, school teaching, and nursing, among others.[159] Whether or not the separate spheres had ever really existed, the theory was a powerful instrument which women started to turn to their own benefit. The strategies of the women historians were echoed in many areas in the nineteenth century as some women began to make the transition from the feminine to the feminist, from the private to the public, to write themselves into the history of the nation.

appropriate that one of the few women to write history of this kind—Kate Norgate—was a protégée of J. R. Green, the advocate of a more democratic form of national history and himself something of an outsider of the historical establishment.

[159] P. Hollis, 'Women in Council: Separate Spheres, Public Space', in J. Rendall (ed.), *Equal or Different? Women's Politics, 1800-1914* (Oxford, 1987), 192–213; C. Steadman, ' "The Mother Made Conscious": The Historical Development of a Primary School Pedagogy', *HWJ* 26 (1985), 149–63; stet *sub voce* A. M. Rafferty, 'Nursing History as Women's History: The Case of Education' (Social Studies Dept., Oxford, 1 May 1991).

7

John Lingard's *History of England*:
A Catholic History

Nineteenth-century Catholic writers of history faced an audience potentially more hostile than that met by women historians; like women historians, they aimed to subvert, adapt, and revise the dominant historical discourse. In this narrative, however, Protestantism had been enshrined since at least the seventeenth century as an important element in the formation and expression of English national identity. Thus the most significant nineteenth-century Catholic history of England, John Lingard's *History of England* (1819–30) was a discreet and carefully written text, in which impartiality of opinion and the unvarnished presentation of facts were proclaimed as the historian's guiding principles.[1] So restrained was its narrative that it was initially published by a Protestant publisher, Joseph Mawman, and was probably aimed more at scholars than the general public: for this reason, no doubt, it was unillustrated.

But Lingard could not exercise fully the philosophical detachment of the eighteenth-century rationalist. He and his *History* were part of a revival of confidence within the Catholic Church, which claimed a place in national life while defining itself more determinedly as Catholic; both were also part of an evolution towards a more Romantic, a more populist, and picturesque approach to history. Lingard's revisions of his text grew bolder with each successive edition and, in 1837–9, the first illustrated edition of the *History* appeared, intended for a wider readership. Published by another Protestant firm, Baldwin and Cradock, it carried frontispiece illustrations by the well-known graphic designer, William Harvey. Most of the subjects chosen, such as *Henry VI and Margaret Meeting after the Battle of St Albans*, would not suggest to the reader that the *History* was written by a Catholic.[2] Only a few, such as *Lord Stafford Led out to Execution* and *The Marriage of Mary and Philip II at Winchester* would have alerted a Protestant reader.[3] Lingard was probably responsible for choosing the subjects: *The Marriage of Mary and Philip*, for instance, would be a natural choice for

---

[1] E. Jones, *The English Nation* (Stroud, 1998), 173–7, offers a parallel discussion of Lingard's response to the hostile audience anticipated for his *History*.

[2] J. Lingard, *The History of England* (1819–30; 13 vols., 1837–9 edn.), p. v, frontispiece.

[3] Lingard, *History* (1837–9), p. vii, frontispiece; p. xii, frontispiece.

a historian born in Winchester, who, contrary to popular historical opinion, believed the marriage to have been a happy and satisfactory one.[4]

The contrast between this careful avoidance of heavy Catholic polemic— typical of the text of Lingard's *History*, as well as his selection of the illustrations —and the more aggressively Catholic pattern of illustration in the 1854-5 edition, published by the Catholic firm of Dolman after the historian's death, catches the eye. Charles Dolman was younger and, naturally, more attuned to the world of popular publication than the retiring Lingard had ever been: in his bolder edition, the illustrations highlight the Catholic tendencies of the text far more frequently and obviously, and the use of familiar images with a potential Catholic interpretation is far more loaded. Yet they do not present an incongruous effect, since Lingard and Dolman were both participants in the Catholic Revival and shared a common historical perspective, although they differed on how to express it. An examination of the Dolman edition of Lingard's *History* shows how a publisher could shift the emphasis of a text by control of illustration, exposing or exaggerating aspects which the writer had partially concealed. *The History* oscillated between conciliatory attempts to write Catholics into the national narrative as unsung patriots, and subversive and partisan attacks on Protestant historiography as inaccurate and biased. Dolman's choice of illustration high-lighted both aspects, rendering *The History* more openly controversial and making it more entirely the product of early Victorian Romantic historiography.[5]

CATHOLICISM, CRITICISM, AND CHANGE IN NINETEENTH-CENTURY BRITAIN

An examination of the 1854-5 edition of Lingard's *History of England* must begin with a sketch of the historical and the historiographical contexts.[6] The writer of a Catholic history of England in the nineteenth century faced many difficulties. English Protestants were indoctrinated from infancy with a most unfavourable interpretation of the past deeds of the Church of Rome and its English adherents, both through the channels of popular historical consciousness (in the form of November the Fifth celebrations) and through educational and recreational literature. History textbooks informed the English people of Mary I's 'natural sourness of . . . temper' and the 'most violent and sanguinary measures' she resorted to in her treatment of Protestants such as Latimer and Ridley:[7] it is no wonder that it was the habit of schoolboys to stick pins through the eyes of Queen

---

[4] J. Lingard, *The History of England* (10 vols., 1854-5), v. 248-9.

[5] See S. Gilley, 'John Lingard and the Catholic Revival', in D. Baker (ed.), *Renaissance and Renewal in Christian History* (Oxford, 1977), 313-27, for the best recent analysis of Lingard as a Romantic historian.

[6] The latter is covered in far greater detail in Jones, *The English Nation*, which examines in a book-length study the growth of the Protestant interpretation of English history.

[7] E. Penrose [Mrs Markham], *History* (1846), 274, 277.

Mary in the illustrations of their history books.[8] A remarkable number of Victorians also recalled the impact made upon them in childhood by the illustrations to John Foxe's *Book of Martyrs*, which depicted in terrifying detail the deaths of Protestant martyrs during the Marian persecutions. Naturally, therefore, an event such as the establishment of Roman Catholic dioceses in England and Wales—popularly known as the 'Papal Aggression'—which occurred in 1850 (a mere four years before Dolman began publishing his edition), provoked sermons which reiterated the Protestant interpretation of the past, charging the congregation to remember the fires of Smithfield and Oxford and the Gunpowder Plot.[9]

Nevertheless, there were some signs of change in nineteenth-century Britain. The Romantic movement, particularly the Gothic Revival, led to a more sympathetic perception of the medieval Catholic Church: a link between faith and works was made explicit in the life and work of Catholic converts such as the architect, A. W. N. Pugin, and Kenelm Digby, author of *The Broadstone of Honour* (1823).[10] Such nostalgic perceptions of medieval society and the Catholic Church could fuel historical reinterpretation, by encouraging the study of architectural remains and documentary sources which rationalist contemporaries of Hume had considered too barbaric and recondite to repay attention. However, the first historical reinterpretations of the Protestant interpretation of English history by Protestants tended to be the work of enthusiasts rather than scholars and antiquaries. William Cobbett's polemical *History of the Protestant Reformation* (1824–6) was such a virulent attack on the Reformed faith that Pope Leo XII reputedly exclaimed 'Surely such a man cannot be a Protestant'.[11] Cobbett's repugnance towards the English Protestant Church was shared by some Romantics in the early Oxford Movement, such as Hurrell Froude, who would have rejected his radical political opinions.[12]

By the 1850s, therefore, more sympathetic (if idealized) perceptions of the medieval Catholic Church, and a loosening of the links of Church and State, brought about changes in the intellectual climate. Much of the political debate surrounding the issue of the 'double allegiance' of Catholics to the British government and the Pope, which had dogged late eighteenth- and early nineteenth-century emancipation campaigns, was now rendered obsolete. The Catholic

---

[8] L. Madigan (ed.), *The Devil is a Jackass* (Leominster and Stratton on the Fosse, 1995), 13.

[9] e.g. W. Bennett, *Popery Set Forth in Scripture: Its Guilt and its Doom* (1850), quoted in E. R. Norman, *Anti-Catholicism in Victorian England* (1967), 172. Preached at St Mary's, Walthamstow, on 5 Nov. 1850. D. Cressy, The Fifth of November Remembered', in R. Porter (ed.), *Myths of the English* (Cambridge, Mass., 1992), 68–90 explores the commemoration of the Gunpowder Plot from the 17th to the 20th cent.

[10] For Pugin, see P. Stanton, *Pugin* (1971); M. Aldrich, *A. W. N. Pugin: Master of Gothic Revival* (New Haven, Conn., 1995); P. Atterbury and C. Wainwright, *Pugin: A Gothic Passion* (New Haven, Conn., and London, 1994); for Digby, see K. L. Morris, 'Kenelm Henry Digby and English Catholicism', *RH* 20 (1991), 361–70.

[11] E. R. Norman, *The English Catholic Church in the Nineteenth Century* (Oxford, 1984), 11–12.

[12] I. Ker, *John Henry Newman* (Oxford, 1988), 112–13.

Emancipation Act of 1829 had admitted Catholics into national politics at the highest level, and, later, the Maynooth Grant (1845) and the disestablishment of the Church of Ireland (1869) were indications that the state had come to accept the presence of a significant Catholic minority. But it is dangerous to over-estimate these changes. English converts to Catholicism were, despite the Anglo-Catholic movement and the prestige of converts such as John Henry Newman, very few; Romantic sympathy for the medieval Catholic Church did not always breed toleration of the modern Catholic Church.[13] The anti-Catholic furores of the nineteenth century were firmly rooted in an atmosphere of popular suspicion, reinforced by antagonistic pronouncements of such high-profile figures as Lord John Russell and Charles Kingsley,[14] in which national identity and Protestantism, Church and King, remained almost as firmly linked as in the days of the Gordon Riots.

While opinions of the Catholic Church held in nineteenth-century society remained mixed and ambiguous, the Church itself was experiencing a period of revival and apparent expansion. Traditionally, historians have identified this revival as a 'Second Spring', either boosted by the release of Catholics from civil and religious disabilities, or else imposed by a triumph of the Ultramontane party, identified with Cardinal Nicholas Wiseman and some of the Oxford con-verts. Both these interpretations rested on certain presuppositions: one was that the eighteenth-century English Catholics were a deprived, isolated, and uninfluential minority. The other was that the mid-nineteenth-century Church was divided into two parties, a division that even a recent historian, Edward Norman, accepts without much qualification: the flamboyant Ultramontanes, attached to Rome and a centralized papal authority, and the Old Catholics, the maintainers of an eighteenth-century tradition of unostentatious and very English piety, which incorporated the national ideals of liberty and loyalty to the Crown.[15]

These presuppositions have now been rightly challenged: John Bossy and others have exposed the falsity of the traditional interpretation of the late eighteenth-century Catholic body, emphasizing its participation in English economic, social, and even political life, and the vitality and deep piety of its

---

[13] This was evidenced in Robert Southey's *The Book of the Church* (1824), a Romantic and High Church polemic in defence of the Church of England apparently published as a response to Lingard's *History of England*: while admiring the social structure of late medieval England and advocating the establishment of Anglican sisterhoods, Southey supported the existing State and Church establishment, opposing Catholic emancipation and exhibiting a rationalist horror of Catholic 'priestcraft' and 'superstition' reminiscent of his youthful radical opinions. Such a work signalled the revival of providentialist interpretations of history from partisan religious viewpoints. See S. Gilley, 'Nationality and Liberty, Protestant and Catholic: Robert Southey's Book of the Church', in S. Mews (ed.), *Religion and National Identity* (Oxford, 1982), 409–32.

[14] See K. L. Morris, 'John Bull and the Scarlet Woman: Charles Kingsley and Anti-Catholicism in Victorian Literature', *RH* 23 (1996), 190–218.

[15] Norman, *Church*, 3–4.

religious life.[16] Meanwhile, the traditional interpretation of the Catholic revival is disputed by students of nineteenth-century Catholicism, who identify it less as a matter of actual conversion and growth, and more as a matter of bringing nominal Catholics into active observance and creating a distinctly Catholic lifestyle, based not on new 'Roman' beliefs and devotions, but ones already accepted in English Catholic tradition.[17] Such a revision was indeed overdue: the 1854-5 publication of Lingard's *The History of England* can now be pictured within the context of a native Catholic revival, rooted in the experiences of eighteenth-century Catholicism, influenced by the Romantic movement, and preceding (although increasingly overshadowed by) the rise of Ultramontanism. Historian, publisher, and illustrator must all be examined against this background before an analysis of the text and images.

LINGARD: A HISTORIAN IN TRANSITION

John Lingard was born of Catholic parents in 1771 in Winchester; educated and ordained at Douai College in France, he returned to England in 1793 and became a tutor at Crook Hall, afterwards Ushaw College, a Catholic seminary. Later, he became vicar of Hornby, Lancashire, where he remained for the remainder of his life.[18] His *The Antiquities of the Anglo-Saxon Church* was published in 1806; the first edition of *The History* appeared between 1819 and 1830. A revised edition of the *Antiquities* (under the title of *The History and Antiquities of the Anglo-Saxon Church*) appeared in 1845;[19] *The History of England* was revised and republished on a more regular basis before Lingard's death in 1851.

Many of the alterations of his text and shifts of emphasis in his arguments can be attributed to the events of the half-century during which Lingard was an author. The polemical tone of *The Antiquities*, for instance, may reflect the disappointment of the English Catholic body at the failure of the government to follow the 1800 Act of Union with Ireland with Catholic Emancipation, as was expected.[20] By the 1820s, Catholic hopes were raised once again by the

[16] J. Bossy, *The English Catholic Community 1570-1850* (1975), 295-322; M. Rowlands, 'The Education and Piety of Catholics in Staffordshire in the Eighteenth Century', *RH* 10 (1969), 67-78; R. W. Linker, 'The English Roman Catholics and Emancipation: The Politics of Persuasion', *Journal of Ecclesiastical History* 27 (1976), 151-80.

[17] e.g. G. Connolly, 'The Transubstantiation of Myth: Towards a New Popular History of Nineteenth Century Catholicism in England', *Journal of Ecclesiastical History*, 35 (1984), 78-104; M. Heimann, *Catholic Devotion in Victorian England* (Oxford, 1995).

[18] M. Haile and E. Bonney, *The Life and Letters of John Lingard 1771-1851* (1912), 7, 19, 33-7, 61-6, 112.

[19] See P. Phillips, 'John Lingard and *The Anglo-Saxon Church*', *RH* 23 (1996), 178-89, for a recent analysis of this work. Phillips suggests that Lingard's reasons for the revising this work in the early 1840s were advances in Anglo-Saxon studies in general and the publications of Tractarian clergy on the early British Church seem to have provided the impetus for the aged historian.

[20] Haile and Bonney, *Life*, 79-99.

successful passage of the 1821 and 1825 emancipation bills through the Commons: so Lingard was more restrained in his commentary on religious events in *The History*, even through his simple factual narrative (as he presented it) remained very controversial. By 1847, when revising his text, he felt less anxious about the introduction of material 'respecting the penal laws which I had withheld in the former [editions]',[21] possibly encouraged by the higher profile of Catholics and their concerns.

It is, however, unlikely that Lingard's historical opinions changed radically in the course of writing and revising *The History*. In 1819, he commented to a fellow Catholic historian and priest, John Kirk, that 'whatever I had said or purposely omitted has been through a motive of serving religion'.[22] Different shades of opinion, therefore, appear to have been largely matters of style, occasioned by external pressures of the political climate. Lingard could be persuasive or polemical according to necessity. It is the fundamental presence of both defensive and offensive approaches, both tones of Olympian detachment and passages of partisan rhetoric, in all his work which signals his status as a transitional figure, both in the nineteenth-century Catholic Revival and in the evolution from the philosophical histories of the rationalist school to the picturesque narratives of Romantic historiography.

LINGARD: LIBERTY, LOYALTY, AND THE ENGLISH CATHOLIC

Much of Lingard's intellectual and religious outlook seems to identify him as an archetypical Old Catholic. He was, in fact, a late associate of the Cisalpine group, whose reformist views have been seen as an extreme version of the principles of the eighteenth-century Catholic body. The Cisalpines—who included Joseph Berington, Charles Butler, and John Kirk—were rationalist theologians and philosophical historians, products of the Enlightenment: their emphasis was on the development of a rational faith, based on the scriptures and Church tradition, which expressed itself in more comprehensible and accessible worship and in deep personal and private devotion. They advocated rule by councils within the Church, the election of bishops by clergy, and the limitation of overall authority in non-essentials by local customs and wishes, viewing the Pope as the first of bishops rather than as an ultimate authority. In addition to these proto-democratic views, they held ecumenical and conciliatory views, believing that Catholics should integrate themselves into English society, placing less emphasis on customs and institutions peculiar to Catholics. In politics, they expressed their support of the English constitution as loyal subjects and advocates of liberty: they believed that Catholics should co-operate with the state and should offer substantial concessions, if it was necessary to allay Protestant fears in order to gain the vote. Theirs were the politics of persuasion rather than coercion:

---

[21] Haile and Bonney, *Life*, 347.   [22] Ibid. 167. J. Lingard to J. Kirk, 18 Dec. 1819.

they emphasized the separateness of politics and religion, of the State and the Churches.[23]

Lingard's own views seem to correspond to these opinions very closely. He disliked flaunting Catholicism, and frequently appeared to feel that discretion was the better part of valour. He wished, for instance, that the 1850 restoration of English bishoprics had been made with less display.[24] Repelled by aspects of his Church usually associated with the Ultramontanes, he was impatient of the new 'Romish' practices of clergy such as Nicholas Wiseman and some of the Oxford converts, and suspicious of the conversions of J. H. Newman and W. G. Ward.[25] His personal relations with Protestants of all shades were unusually amicable: C. J. Blomfield, later Archbishop of London, whom Mawman suggested to Lingard as a reader for *The History*, became a good friend.[26] In an ecumenical spirit, Lingard published a work called *Catechical Instructions* (1841), designed to be used by Protestants as well as Catholics.[27] Of course, his links with Pro-testants were often strongest in the case of those Nonconformists who shared with Catholics a common interest in emancipation and related issues. Like them, he was anxious for the state to assume a secular or at least non-denominational identity, distancing herself from the Established Church: he favoured state secular education, leaving religious instruction to the clergy and ministers of each denomination.[28] For Lingard, the separation of religious from political issues was essential in order to refute the Protestant argument of the unpatriotic 'double alle-giance' of the English Catholic. His writings throughout his career stressed that it was possible to be Catholic and English, loyal to the Church and the Crown.

Nevertheless, however loyal English Catholics pronounced themselves to be, the early nineteenth-century Protestant interpretation of history always appeared to subvert their claims. Recognizing this problem, Cisalpine historians such as Berington and Charles Butler had developed a 'definitely Cisalpine interpreta-tion of Catholic history in England', which portrayed loyal English Catholics resisting the Ultramontane demands of a self-seeking papacy and the religious orders. This led them down antiquarian paths rarely frequented by the philo-sophical historian, for their endeavours rested on the Continental monastic tradition of source-based research, pioneered by the Maurists and Bollandists.[29]

---

[23] J. P. Chinnici, *The English Catholic Enlightenment: John Lingard and the Cisalpine Movement 1780–1850* (Shepherdstown, West Virginia 1980), 39–106.

[24] Haile and Bonney, *Life*, 360–1.   [25] Ibid. 304–10, 321–6.

[26] Ibid. 178.   [27] Ibid. 283–5.

[28] Shepherd Letters, i, fo. 69. J. Lingard to H. Joyce, 6 Dec. 1842.

[29] E. Duffy, 'Ecclesiastical Democracy Detected, II: 1787–1796', *RH* 10 (1970), 318–19; Chinnici, *Lingard*, 107–33; Phillips, 'Lingard and *The Anglo-Saxon Church*', 180–1. Phillips speculates convincingly on the possibility that Lingard became familiar with the works of Mabillon and the Bollandists as early as 1790s during his education at Douai. It is but fair to mention at this point D. F. Shea, *The English Ranke: John Lingard* (New York, 1969), which stresses the similarity of German source criticism and Lingard's methods. However, Shea ignores the influence of the Low Countries and French schools on the historian and is, moreover, extraordinarily inaccurate. For the Maurists and Bollandists, see D. Knowles, *Great Historical Enterprises and Problems in Monastic History* (Edinburgh, 1963), 3–62.

Such an approach offered the means of subverting the dominant national narrative of Protestant historians, which was based largely on the texts of their sixteenth-, seventeen-, and early eighteenth-century predecessors, rather than on any original research. Berington and Butler—the pioneers of this historiography of Catholic nationalism—were friends to, and models for, the younger Lingard: many of their views are apparent in his interpretations of English history, and their diligent use of sources was perfected by their disciple.

Lingard's appreciation of the necessity of reinterpreting the English past, to emphasize the loyalty of Catholics and the beneficial and important role they had played in the history of the nation, was long-standing. At the request of Bishop William Poynter, a moderate open to the possibility of concessions in return for the vote, he defended their Catholic ancestors from the charge of disloyalty to the Crown through the allegiance to the Pope in his publication of 1812, *Documents to Ascertain the Sentiments of British Catholics in Former Ages respecting the Power of the Pope*. In his first major work of history, *The Antiquities of the Anglo-Saxon Church* (1806),[30] polemical though it essentially was, Lingard in places pursued a conciliatory line of argument, stressing the fundamental role of Catholicism in the emergence and growth of English civilization. In the Preface, he pointed to the transformation worked by the Christian missionaries sent from Rome, who raised the ferocious Anglo-Saxons to 'a degree of civilization, which . . . excited the wonder of the other nations of Europe'.[31] Lingard painted a glowing picture of Catholicism as the basis of the moral and constitutional development of the nation, symbolized by the harmonious co-operation of Church and State, and concluded that 'the progress of civilization kept equal pace with the progress of religion'.[32]

LINGARD'S 'WANT OF CANDOUR': TRUTH, SOURCES, AND CONCEALMENT

Lingard's desire to prove the loyalty of Catholics to the state, and to stress the principles which Catholics held in common with their countrymen led him, in *The History*, to adopt a style of argument which appeared to be more conciliatory than confrontational: he stressed his impartial examination of original sources, rather than indulging in polemical rhetoric.[33] He aimed to rest his case on the facts which he had gathered, and to avoid drawing out the full implications. Hostile reviewers criticized this tendency. In *The Edinburgh Review* of 1825, John Allen—a prominent Whig historian, atheist, and intimate of Holland House as well as a critic for the *Review*—set out to argue that Lingard was 'a decided

---

[30] Phillips, 'Lingard and *The Anglo-Saxon Church*', offers a more extensive analysis of this work than can be given here.

[31] J. Lingard, *The Antiquities of the Anglo-Saxon Church* (1806; Newcastle, 1810 edn.), pp. iv–v.

[32] Ibid. 32.

[33] Jones, *The English Nation*, 177–84, examines Lingard's use of original source materials in greater depth than is appropriate here.

partisan of the Church of Rome', an opponent of civil liberty, but he found it difficult to discover points upon which to focus his criticism.[34] Lingard's sins of omission were the subject of H. J. Todd's criticism, in his 1827 *Reply to Lingard's Vindication*, where he accused the historian of partial statements and evasions of the truth, 'artfully clothed with the captivating exterior of much excellent writing and great apparent candour'.[35] Reviewing *The History* in *The Edinburgh Review* of 1831, the historian Henry Hallam also accused Lingard of deceptive candour, attacking Lingard's apparently dispassionate account of the Reformation, 'in which [an] almost affected indifference to the whole subject seems to guide his pen' and 'the conclusions are always left to the reader'.[36]

Naturally, supporters of Lingard saw him as concerned with factual accuracy rather than cunningly reticent in his commentary. *The Dublin Review* in 1842 argued that Lingard's *History* was so different from the traditional Protestant interpretation of history that its 'very impartiality [became] a source of imputation'.[37] Lingard defended his text from criticism by assertions of his own truth to his authorities—his works were always introduced with a preface indicating his careful attention to his sources. He was always highly critical of the failure of other historians to consult their evidence: he described the seventeenth-century historian, Lord Clarendon, as a writer who 'could never have looked at the documents which he pretends to quote',[38] and the inaccuracies of T. B. Macaulay led him to conclude that his work was essentially 'factless'.[39]

LINGARD: THE CATHOLIC CONTROVERSIALIST

Nevertheless, Lingard's opponents were not entirely mistaken in their criticisms: Lingard's 'truth', however impartially conveyed, was undoubtedly intended to overturn the traditional Protestant interpretation of the national past. While the historian attempted to write Catholics into the national narrative on the grounds of their patriotism, Lingard could not be unaware that this narrative—in which Protestantism and national progress were portrayed as providentially linked— was not one to which he could simply attach a Catholic appendix. If the style of his *History* was unobtrusive, the carefully arranged content of the often subversive text was not. Thus to identify Lingard too fully with the Cisalpines, as J. P. Chinnici has done, limits understanding of the more aggressive aspect of

---

[34] [J. Allen], 'Lingard's *History of England*', *ER* 42 (1825), 6–7; *DNB* i. 309–10.

[35] H. J. Todd, *A Reply to Dr Lingard's Vindication of his History of England as far as respects Archbishop Cranmer* (1827), 134. Henry Todd, an editor of Milton and author of many other works, was a fast-stream Anglican clergyman, chaplain in turn to several earls, sometime Keeper of Manuscripts at Lambeth Palace, and a royal chaplain in ordinary. From 1820, he was rector of the valuable Yorkshire parish of Settringham. *DNB* lvi. 428–30.

[36] H. Hallam, 'Lingard's *History of England*', *ER* 53 (1831), 18–19.

[37] [MC Mahon], 'Lingard's *History*, 316.

[38] Shepherd Letters, i, fos. 57, 59. J. Lingard to H. Joyce, 3 Sept. 1842.

[39] Haile and Bonney, *Life*, 345.

his Catholicism: he was a late-comer to the movement, which was partially exhausted by 1800. Eamon Duffy rightly indicates the vast difference between Berington's attitude to the papacy and its prerogative, particularly in the Middle Ages, and Lingard's. Rather than disowning papal interventions as both unlawful and unhelpful, the younger historian—touched, however gently, by the Romantic preoccupation with the medieval Church—saw them as legitimate and beneficial exercises.[40] While Chinnici's portrayal of Lingard links him too closely to the Cisalpine movement, Edwin Jones's over-emphasizes Lingard's alleged impartiality and his critical use of original sources, presenting him as an isolated figure, the sole prophet and precursor of scientific history and its methodologies.[41] While it is undeniable that Lingard's approach to original sources was uniquely critical, judicious, and exhaustive, he was by no means unique among historians in his attention to such sources: 'authentic sources' were the watchword of the picturesque historian. Moreover, his pursuit of historical sources was inspired by as keen a passion for argument as any contemporary Romantic historian: he did not consider himself, nor should he be considered, as removed from the historical and religious debates of his day. There was a rampantly Catholic side to Lingard's character, which gave him no wish to avoid controversies with Protestant historians: Sheridan Gilley rightly describes him as 'the hammer of the anglican hierarchy' and highlights his role in ushering a new age of religious controversy in early nineteenth-century England.[42]

In these years, Lingard was, in fact, a leading polemicist for his Church. In the *Observations on the Laws and Ordinances* of 1812, although much of Lingard's argument was aimed at allaying Protestant fears of Catholic 'double allegiance', he nevertheless attacked the whole concept of the necessity of Catholic concessions, pointing out trenchantly that Catholic states never made their Protestant subjects 'purchase the extension of their civil rights with additional restrictions on the exercise of their religion'.[43] Frequently, Lingard's reassuring picture of loyal and sensible Catholics could give way to attacks on Protestant heroes and terse accounts of the injustices received by his co-religionists. *The Antiquities* was frequently polemical, being more 'obviously biased in both purpose and content'[44] than *The History*. He attempted openly to undermine the Protestant claim to reproduce the purity of the Early Church, by portraying the early English Church, essentially approved of by Protestant historians, as wholly Catholic in doctrine and practice. The Anglo-Saxons, he claimed, accepted

[40] E. Duffy, 'Ecclesiastical Democracy Detected, III: 1796–1800', *RH* 13 (1975), 143.

[41] Jones, *The English Nation*, 168–217. This analysis of Lingard's contribution to English historiography is particularly valuable for the consideration given to the Catholic historian's attempt to place English history within a European context.

[42] Gilley, 'Lingard and the Catholic Revival', 315–16.

[43] J. Lingard, *Observations on the Laws and Ordinances which Exist in Foreign States Relative to the Religious Concerns of their Roman Catholic Subjects* (1817), in *A Collection of Tracts on Several Subjects, Connected to the Civil and Religious Principles of Catholics* (1826), 479.

[44] Chinnici, *Lingard*, 112.

without question the Roman Catholic form of church government, looking up to the Pope 'with awe and reverence'.[45] But it was the issue of clerical celibacy which displayed Lingard at his most argumentative: he stated firmly that it was biblically based, accepted and practised in the Anglo-Saxon Church, and beneficial in its effects.[46] Lingard affirmed not only the structure, but the doctrines and customs of his Church, by revealing them as part of the life of the Anglo-Saxon Church. Pilgrimages, for instance, were defended by a polemical comparison with the Protestant Englishman's Grand Tour visits to classical sites.[47] Individuals were defended, too: Lingard sternly rejected Sharon Turner's unfavourable interpretation of the character of the tenth-century archbishop and saint, Dunstan, ruthlessly exposing the historian's failure to assess his sources critically.[48]

The controversy with John Allen and H. J. Todd over issues in *The History*, however, exhibited Lingard at his argumentative best: the one opponent represented the school of rationalist philosophical history, scornful of the religious enthusiasms of all faiths and denominations, while the other represented the long-lived tradition of Protestant nationalist historiography. Allen attacked Lingard in *The Edinburgh Review* in two articles in April 1825 and June 1826, accusing him of having 'no generous sympathy in the cause of freedom'.[49] More specifically, he attacked Lingard's interpretation of Anglo-Saxon history in both *The Antiquities* and *The History*: in describing the events of the reign of Edwy, Lingard had 'of course sided with his own church'.[50] At the beginning of the second article, he commented on Lingard's 'talents for ecclesiastical controversy';[51] he then launched an attack upon Lingard's representation in *The History* of the Massacre of St Bartholomew's Day—which, he claimed, showed 'inexcusable indifference to historical accuracy'.[52] Allen presented his own version of the events of the Massacre, insisting that it was a premeditated Catholic conspiracy—a theory which Lingard had refuted. Todd's attack on Lingard was presented in his 1826 *Vindication*, which was mainly a defence of Archbishop Thomas Cranmer, of whom the historian had given an unfavourable account in the fourth volume of his *History*. He assailed Lingard's narrative of Cranmer's career at twelve different points, including his representation of Cranmer's protest at his consecration against the authority of the Pope as a private one, and his account of Cranmer's death.[53]

Lingard's *Vindication* of 1826 retracted none of his original arguments and attacked the facts produced by his opponents. It opened with the sarcastic

---

[45] Lingard, *Antiquities*, 150, 159.   [46] Ibid. 68, 72, 76–7.   [47] Ibid. 305.

[48] Ibid. 397; Phillips, 'Lingard and *The Anglo-Saxon Church*', 186–7.

[49] [Allen], 'Lingard's *History*' (1825), 6.   [50] Ibid. 9.

[51] [J. Allen], 'Lingard's *History of England*: The Massacre of St Bartholomew', *ER* 44 (1826), 94.

[52] Ibid. 95.

[53] H. J. Todd, *A Vindication of the Most Reverend Thomas Cranmer . . . and therewith of the Reformation in England* (1826), 38–49, 116–34.

reflection that the focus of Allen's second article was on a mere note on an event of French history, despite his claim to be expressing his opinion on the whole of a work on English history.[54] He pointed out a number of weak links in Allen's argument, keenly pinpointing the weakest when he argued that it was unlikely that a planned massacre would open with an attempt to assassinate a single man, whose death would alert others to their danger.[55] Lingard's defence of his interpretation of Cranmer's character and actions was similarly trenchant. He argued, for instance, that there was no evidence that Cranmer's protest against the Pope's authority was either public or reiterated.[56] Such was the force of his argument that Todd replied with a *Vindication* of his own in 1827.

Thus Lingard the pamphleteer; it was, however, exploitation of his restrained text by other polemicists which revealed the controversial potential of *The History of England*. Cobbett's *History of the Protestant Reformation in England and Ireland* was based on facts culled from Lingard's *History* (which he sometimes distorted).[57] The radical plagiarist exaggerated and exposed the framework of Lingard's historical interpretation: the Reformation, he claimed, was produced by lust, hypocrisy, and perfidy, fed by plunder and innocent blood, and resulted in misery, beggary, and hunger for the common people.[58] Polemic could descend into abuse: while Lingard was merely critical of Cranmer's cowardice, Cobbett described him as a 'cold-blooded, most perfidious, most impious, most blasphemous caitiff'.[59] The extremism of his work showed how controversial the carefully presented content of Lingard's *History* could be, and it comes as no surprise to learn that *The History* served satisfactorily as the basis for Catholic history textbooks even during the late nineteenth-century age of Ultramontanism.[60]

LINGARD AND DOLMAN: A HISTORIAN AND HIS PUBLISHER

The mutations of Lingard's approach from defensive to offensive, and back again, are further complicated in the 1854–5 edition of *The History* by the attitude of the Catholic publisher, Charles Dolman. Born in 1807, Dolman had entered publishing through his mother's family, the Bookers; he devoted his early career to the publication of Roman Catholic periodicals. From 1838 to 1844 he was publisher of the *Catholic Magazine*, which was intended to promote goodwill between Catholic and Protestant and to explain Catholicism to a wider audience. Simultaneously, he was the publisher and proprietor of the less eirenic *The*

---

[54] J. Lingard, *A Vindication of Certain Passages in the Fourth and Fifth Volumes of the History of England* (1826), 7.

[55] Ibid. 16–17, 63–6.   [56] Ibid. 74–9.

[57] W. Sambrook, *William Cobbett* (1973), 136.

[58] W. Cobbett, *A History of the Protestant Reformation in England and Ireland* (1824–26; 2 vols., 1857 edn.), i. 3.

[59] Ibid. i. 32.   [60] Gilley, 'Lingard and the Catholic Revival', 316–17.

Dublin Review, the voice of intelligent and militant Catholicism.[61] In 1845, he founded his own periodical, *Dolman's Magazine and Monthly Miscellany of Criticism*, later united with another Catholic journal to form *The Weekly Register*: the *Magazine* was a moderate publication, which—unlike the *Dublin Review*—avoided the controversial issues of Irish politics. A flamboyant figure in the Catholic Revival, with links to the Ultamontane party, Dolman nevertheless turned his popularizing skills to use outside the sphere of the periodical: in 1850, he began the publication of de luxe editions of Catholic classics, such as Lingard's *History*.[62]

Lingard—whose *History* had been rejected by two Catholic publishers before Mawman had accepted it, and who was no great admirer of Catholic publishers—had a high opinion of Dolman as 'the only one among us that a gentleman can trade with'.[63] However, the author and the publisher did not seem to favour similar approaches. By the 1840s, Lingard was something of an anachronism in the Catholic world, and Dolman's more populist and propagandist style alarmed him. In 1848, he wrote to Edward Price: 'I shall disappoint Mr Dolman. He is too fond of puffing . . . I think such things disadvantageous in the long run. People are too discerning now not to see the object, and on that account think contemptuously of the work.'[64] A year later, he described the struggle of the two temperaments to Hannah Joyce, the adopted daughter of an old Nonconformist ally of the emancipation struggle, the Unitarian minister William Shepherd:

You will probably have heard that I am giving a new library edition of my history . . . Two years ago, Dolman, the proprietor, told me that he wished to do so . . . I consented [to make revisions], and now and then worked on it as my ailments allowed . . . We . . . had got to the reign of James II when he published a prospectus promising I should refute many statements in Macaulay. This was silly in him. He expected the preface to be written immediately . . . I was too ill to write a preface, and had no intention of mentioning Macaulay . . . Well, three months passed—no preface was ready, his subscribers began to complain . . . I had him now at my mercy, and compelled him to consent to a very short preface . . . so I am at last freed from a plague.[65]

On this occasion, Lingard succeeded in restraining the enthusiasm of the publisher.[66]

The historian's attitude to his publisher—a mixture of respect and fear for his impetuosity in the Catholic cause—suggest more subtle differences between the two than the labels of Old Catholic and Ultramontane can really explain: neither

---

[61] In *WI* ii. 19, he is listed as publisher, rather than a proprietor, 1838–44. MSS relating to *The Dublin Review* suggest that he was, in fact, at times the proprietor or part-owner of the magazine, which had an unstable financial status in its early days. London, Westminster Diocesan Archives: Bagshawe MSS, box 1, packet 2, box 4, packet 2. These papers are not adequately catalogued.

[62] See R. A. Mitchell, 'Charles Dolman', *New DNB*, for a full account of Dolman's life and career.

[63] Haile and Bonney, *Life*, 327. J. Lingard to J. Walker, early 1846?

[64] Ibid. 348. J. Lingard to E. Price, Feb. 1848.

[65] Shepherd Letters, i, fo. 97. J. Lingard to Mrs H. Ridyard [née Joyce], 21 Dec. 1849.

[66] Haile and Bonney, *Life*, 349.

belonged entirely to either party. It cannot be denied that Dolman was the representative of a more confident and propagandist phase of the Catholic Revival than Lingard ever inhabited, since he produced the more militant and Ultramontane *Dublin Review*.[67] The contributors to this publication, men such as Wiseman and C. W. Russell, were from a generation influenced by the Romantic movement's glamorization of the medieval Catholic Church and its society: J. Warren has analysed, for instance, the *Review*'s consistent opposition to 'Protestant' philosophical systems, such as J. S. Mill's, and its support for medieval scholasticism and its leading light, Thomas Aquinas.[68] It is, therefore, not surprising that in 1842, a reviewer in *The Dublin Review*, while praising Lingard's *History*, tacitly found fault with Lingard's 'want of candour', as an almost excessive self-restraint, adding that many Catholics thought him 'too impartial'.[69]

In the 'puffing' Advertisement for his edition of *The History*, Dolman also commented on Lingard's restrained style, which he interpreted very perceptively, no doubt to the author's discomfort:

Dr Lingard has done [his account of the Reformation] with exquisite tact. The superficial reader may think him cold when narrating the sufferings of Catholics during the long continuance of the penal laws; the acute thinker will rise from the perusal of Dr Lingard's pages with a much stronger abhorrence of those hateful penal laws, of that wasting series of persecutions, than if the author had coloured his narrative with even the most indignant and burning eloquence . . . Few would ever suspect him of being a Catholic.[70]

These comments suggest, however, that Lingard's intention was far closer to Dolman's than the historian liked to admit: the difference was more of style. Lingard's fear of Dolman's 'puffing' seems provoked at least partially by Dolman's wish to expose openly the polemical content of his text, which the historian had attempted to disguise. Dolman was happy to support at least one publication which exploited Lingard's *History* for its controversial content. *A True Account . . . of the Gunpowder Plot* was published in 1851 by Dolman in reply to the anti-Catholic furore provoked by the 'Papal Aggression'. Its author, the 'Vindicator', focused on past Catholic misdeeds such as the Plot, giving extracts of Lingard's *History* and Charles Dodd's *Church History* (1737–42) to justify his arguments. The 'Vindicator' pointed out the irrelevance of the arguments employed by the critics of the Roman Catholic Church in press and pulpit, in denouncing the Plot, which had nothing to do with the present crisis.[71] To counter 'distorted accounts', the 'Vindicator' reprinted two other narratives, written objectively in 'a calm and dispassionate tone', which showed that the Pope and the ecclesiastical authorities had made every possible attempt to restrain the conspirators.[72]

[67] Lingard himself found *The Dublin Review* often 'controversial', and complained of 'German research' and 'German mysticism', which were 'not at all to the taste of the English reader'. Bagshawe MSS, box 1, packet 2.

[68] J. Warren, '*The Dublin Review* (1836–75), its Reviewers and a "Philosophy of Knowledge"', *RH* 21 (1992), 86–98. Charles William Russell (1812–80) was the president of Maynooth College.

[69] [MC Mahon], 'Lingard's *History*', 322–3.

[70] Advertisement in [Anon.], *A True Account of the Gunpowder Plot* (1851).

[71] Ibid., pp. vi–ix.   [72] Ibid., pp. ix–x.

Unlike Cobbett, this anonymous author retained the moderate narrative of the historian, while setting it in a framework of polemic which highlighted its controversial content: the 'Vindicator' and Dolman refused to accept the restrained style of *The History* at face value.[73] While Lingard was alive, he had restrained the enthusiasm of the publisher, but after his death, when Dolman selected the illustrations for the edition of 1854–5, reprinted from the revised edition Lingard referred to in his letter to Miss Joyce, he was free to express his more militant brand of Catholicism. The illustrations used by Dolman are related to Lingard's themes and arguments, but score points for the Catholic cause in a much less subtle way than the text of *The History*.

ILLUSTRATING A POINT: DOLMAN AND THE ILLUSTRATORS

In the task of exposing the polemical content of Lingard's text, Dolman was probably much aided by at least one like-minded Catholic, as determined as he to break the dominance of a Protestant historical iconography. He used the work of three artists—one a fellow Catholic, one probably a Quaker, and one not yet identified. The first was James Doyle, brother of the better known Richard Doyle. Born in 1822 of Catholic parents,[74] he early showed an interest in history and genealogy, hanging painted shields and swords around the family home. In 1840, he collaborated in a subversion of traditional historiography, writing the narrative for a series of historical pictures planned by Richard and later published as *English Comic Histories*.[75] In 1845, he exhibited a successful painting of *A Literary Party at Sir Joshua Reynolds's*, and a series of his designs after Walter Scott was accepted by the Queen and Prince Albert for the Summer House at Buckingham Palace.[76] In 1849, he exhibited *The Black Prince on the Eve of the Battle of Poitiers*, parleying with Cardinal Talleyrand of Perigord; in 1851, he showed another successful work, *Caxton and his Press*.[77] Such works—with their

[73] Dolman wanted Lingard to review a new edn. of Dodd's *Church History* for *The Dublin Review*, but the historian refused, claiming that he was 'now desirous of quiet, how much soever I may formerly have rejoiced in the excitement of controversy'. He added that it might prove 'prejudicial to Mr Dolman', a view with which the publisher 'quite disagree[d]'. Bagshawe MSS, box 3, packet 1.

[74] R. Engen, *Richard Doyle* (Stroud, 1983), 11–12. The information concerning the illustrators is taken from the Advertisement in *A True Account of the Gunpowder Plot*, but the Christian name of Doyle is not mentioned. However, the Doyle concerned is almost certainly James. The signature on the relevant illustrations in Lingard's *History* is closest to that of James; and the style of illustration is almost identical with that of illustrations known to be his in *The Lover's Stratagem* (1849) and his own *A Chronicle of England BC 55–AD 1485* (1864). It is possible that he was aided by his brother Charles, who had much useful experience in architectural drawing. Engen, *Doyle*, 86.

[75] Engen, *Doyle*, 15, 28–30. See Ch. 8 for the further analysis of potential subversiveness of comic histories and their illustrations.

[76] Ibid. 102.

[77] Ibid. 126; [Anon.], *Richard Doyle and his Family* (Victoria and Albert Museum Exhibition catalogue, 1983–4), 23.

Fig. 27. [J. E. Doyle], *The Barons at St Edmondsbury Swearing to Obtain the Great Charter*, in J. Lingard, *The History of England*, 10 vols. (1854–5), ii, frontispiece

medieval and 'manners and morals' subject-matter—indicate that Doyle was under the influence of the Romantic movement, and its picturesque and anti-quarian approach to the past.

In the 1840s, Doyle began work on a book entitled *A Chronicle of England, B.C. 55–A.D. 1485*, which he both wrote and illustrated, and which was not published until 1864. Doyle showed a picturesque historian's fascination for historical documentation—he substantially revised the original draft of the *Chronicle*, prior to the long-awaited publication, 'drawing his facts in all cases from the original sources'. As an artist, he exhibited a concern to achieve the 1840s standards of picturesque reconstruction and authenticity, studying 'whatever might contribute to the truthfulness of the representation' in the way of costume, architecture, local scenery, and portraiture, 'so far as authorities existed'.[78] Some of the illustrations for this work clearly served as the prototypes for, or were drawn from, those of *The History*. A comparison, for instance, of *The Oath at Edmondsbury* in the *Chronicle* and the same event portrayed in *The History* (Fig. 27) shows the same basic layout, simply reversed: one baron takes the oath, Langton stands beside him, others wait their turn, a monk watches.[79]

[78] Doyle, *Chronicle of England*, pp. iii–iv.
[79] Ibid. 222; Lingard, *History*, (1854–5), p. ii, frontispiece.

Doyle's style of illustration in both works suggests an attraction to the 'German manner' of line-drawing. He would certainly have seen many illustrated books in the 1840s which imitated the line styles of German illustrators such as Neuteuther and Rethel—S. C. Hall's *Book of British Ballads* (1842), for example—even if he did not see specimens by the German artists themselves. In addition, the art of the German Catholic Revival school, the Nazarenes, and their successors, was enjoying some influence in English history-painting circles in the 1840s and 1850s, most particularly in the monumental works prepared for the Westminster Hall competition. The work of a 'Germanist' such as William Cave Thomas, who had visited Munich to study under Hess, and who was associated with the Pre-Raphaelite brotherhood, might well have influenced Doyle: his competition composition, *St Augustine Preaching* (1842), shows a style of line-drawing very similar to Doyle's. For Doyle and other Catholics of his generation, the adoption of his distinctive German style of illustration carried a spiritual significance. Clearly, medievalizing styles did not imply Catholic sympathies for all artists— the Pre-Raphaelites included only one Catholic convert—but for many, they could. William Dyce's German style was connected with his fervent Anglo-Catholicism, and J. R. Herbert, another Germanist influenced strongly by the Nazarenes, was a convert to Catholicism, whose canvases such as *Sir Thomas More and his Daughter* (1844) were clearly propagandist.[80] Doyle's style linked him with Dolman, as one of a generation committed to a more Romantic and confident expression of their Catholic faith.

One of the other two illustrators was Howard Dudley, born in 1820 in London, the son of an Irishman from Tipperary. At an early age, he moved to Sussex: he determined at the age of 14 to illustrate works of local history and antiquities. Setting up a printing press of his own, he published *Juvenile Researches; or a Description of some of the Principal Towns in the Western Part of Sussex and the Borders of Hants* (1835), which was followed by *The History and Antiquities of Horsham* (1836). After a period spent in Edinburgh, from 1852 he lived in London, where he died in 1864.[81] Dudley's parents were Quakers, a denominational allegiance which he probably shared:[82] his participation in the illustration of Lingard's *History* would no doubt have pleased the author, who had fostered the co-operation of Catholics with other Nonconformist religious denominations. Dudley's style appears rather versatile, and—as one of his illustrations was a definite plagiarism from Harvey's designs for the 1837–8 edition of Lingard's *History* (Fig. 28)[83]—it is tempting to speculate that he was very much a hack

    [80] W. Vaughan, *German Romanticism and English Art* (New Haven, Conn., and London, 1979), 155–246; Wood, *Dictionary*, 219, 470; M. Pointon, *William Dyce, 1806–1864: A Critical Biography* (Oxford, 1979).
    [81] Engen, *Wood-Engravers*, 77.
    [82] J. Glover, 'Juvenile Researches, or the Diligent Dudleys', *Sussex County Magazine*, 22 (1948), 50. I am grateful to Timothy J. McCann of the West Sussex County Record Office for this reference.
    [83] Lingard, *History* (1837–8), vi, frontispiece; Lingard, *History* (1854–5), iv, facing 264.

Fig. 28. [H. Dudley], *The Arrival of Cardinal Wolsey at the Abbey of Leicester*, from Lingard, *History*, iv, facing 264

draughtsman and engraver, like Dolman a popularizer at heart. Certainly the melodramatic style of some of his plates (*The Burial of Lady Arabella Stuart*,[84] for instance) would not have been out of place in a popular magazine such as *Lloyd's Weekly Gazette*. It is possible that the last of the three illustrators, 'Hervey' was a relative (son or brother?) of Thomas Kibble Hervey, who wrote for *The Dublin Review* in its early days and also for the *Art Journal*.[85]

Two precedents influenced the illustration of the 1854–5 edition. One was the 1837 edition: illustrations common to both include such subjects as *Cardinal Wolsey's Arrival at the Abbey of Leicester*, *Lord Stafford Led out to Execution*, and *The Marriage of Mary and Philip*.[86] Dolman seems to have accepted many of the more Catholic subjects from the 1837 edition. The other influence was the more polemical pattern of illustration in Doyle's *Chronicle*: this is most clearly seen in the illustration to the Magna Carta events. In the 1837 edition, the illustration—like practically all representations of John's reign in other historical works—showed the king with the barons, signing the Charter.[87] The *Chronicle* and the 1854–5 edition, however, show *The Oath at Edmondsbury* (Fig. 27).[88] This

[84] Lingard, *History* (1854–5), vii, facing 63.   [85] *DNB* ix. 472.
[86] Lingard, *History* (1837–9), vi, frontispiece, vii, frontispiece, xii, frontispiece; Lingard, *History* (1854–5), iv, facing 65, 264, ix, facing 248.
[87] Lingard, *History* (1837–9), iii, frontispiece.
[88] Doyle, *Chronicle*, 222; Lingard, *History* (1854–5), iii, frontispiece.

choice of subject stressed the involvement of the Church, and its support—in the person of Stephen Langton, Archbishop of Canterbury—for English liberties: Dolman would naturally have preferred this subject to the signing of the Magna Carta. Doyle's technique of selecting a popular subject for illustration—not the usual scene, but a related one open to a more blatantly Catholic interpretation— can be seen in Dolman's edition of Lingard's *History*.

THE HISTORY OF ENGLAND: THE BENEFIT OF CLERGY

Lingard opened his *History of England* with an attempt to establish his own impartiality and the character of his work as the result of research into primary sources. In the Advertisement to volume i of the first edition, he claimed to have consulted the 'most ancient authorities' and 'authentic documents'.[89] Leaving the reader (apparently) to draw his own conclusions from the facts supplied was a frequent trick of Lingard's in the restrained text of the *History*.[90] It is a contrast with the *Antiquities*, although in both works Lingard's underlying intention was the same. In the *History*, as in the *Antiquities*, he sought to write the Catholics into the national narrative, portraying them as loyal subjects, and, in particular, very active supporters and forwarders of the English constitution, laws, liberties, and civilization.

Lingard began his apologetic in his depiction of Anglo-Saxon England. The first Roman Catholic missionaries, St Augustine and his priests, were shown as supporters of King Ethelbert's laws.[91] Lingard exploited the universal applause for Alfred to the benefit of the Catholic Church, by indicating that this ideal king was a devout Catholic 'deeply impressed with religious sentiments, which influenced him throughout life'.[92] This aspect of Alfred's character is stressed in the accompanying illustration (Fig. 29): rather than Alfred as a harpist in the camp of Guthram, or as the patron of learning and law, Alfred is portrayed as the sponsor of Guthram as the Dane is baptized into the Church of Rome.[93] The clerics are standing, while the laity kneel; Alfred and the officiating cleric stand facing each other on a raised dias, as the King gently bows, introducing his convert. The scene suggests sacred and secular powers acting in harmony, with a faint emphasis on the deep respect of the temporal powers for the Catholic Church. When the King was less virtuous than Alfred, Lingard argued, the Church was a channel for justice for wronged subjects. When William I was buried at Caen, he told his readers, the funeral was interrupted by Asceline Fitz-Arthur 'who had often fruitlessly sought reparation from the justice of William':[94] it was the prelates who paid him and promised him the full value of the land which the King had stolen from him. This example of the superior justice of the spiritual power was selected for illustration: the corpse occupies a central

[89] J. Lingard, *The History of England* (1819–30), i, p. iii.
[90] e.g. Lingard, *History* (1854–5), v, 70.   [91] Ibid. i. 54–6.   [92] Ibid. i. 102.
[93] Ibid. i. facing 108.   [94] Ibid. i. 255.

Fig. 29. [J. E. Doyle], *Alfred Presenting Gothrun for Baptism, AD 678*, from Lingard, *History*, i, facing 108

position, dominating the doorway of the abbey, but above it is held the crucifix of the Church. While Asceline points downward, towards the corpse and the stolen land, a supporter gestures melodramatically at the heavens, and in the direction of the crucifix.[95]

Lingard also showed the clergy as the supporters of the constitution. Even Becket was seen as the protector of liberties: the historian pointed out that many of the conditions of the Constitutions of Clarence, which Becket resisted, were not ancient customs at all but recently introduced by the Norman usurper, William I.[96] This was a clever exploitation of the English constitutional tradition, which emphasized the antiquity of its freedoms (and thus the role of precedent). Another Catholic Archbishop of Canterbury, Stephen Langton, was also praised for his 'zeal in the cause of freedom',[97] and Archbishop Robert de Winchelsea was shown as as staunch an opponent of the unjust exactions of Edward I as the Earls of Hereford and Norfolk.[98] However, Archbishop Scrope of York—the leading figure in a rebellion against Henry IV—needed more attention. Lingard argued that he haboured no evil intent against the King; his judge, Gascoigne, refused to sentence him on the grounds that he was a prelate, and even the Lords

---

[95] e.g. Lingard, *History* (1854–5), i. facing 255.   [96] Ibid. ii. 68–9.
[97] Ibid. ii. 247.   [98] Ibid. ii. 300.

avoided declaring him treasonous. These details add a new dimension to the illustration of Gascoigne refusing to pass sentence on Scrope, which, instead of simply stressing Gascoigne's adherence to English law, also suggests Scrope's essential heroism and innocence, further enhanced by details of a blameless life.[99]

Even unappealing cardinals such as Henry Beaufort—usually seen as a scheming and avaricious cleric, too much under the influence of the Pope—and Thomas Wolsey were seen as public-minded in Lingard's interpretation. Despite his ostentation and wealth, Wolsey was described as generous with money, interested in the reform of the Church and of the legal system for the benefit of the poor, as well as a patron of learning and the universities.[100] After his fall from power, Lingard portrayed him as little less than a saint: exiled to his bishopric at York, his behaviour was exemplary, The more he was known, the more he was beloved'.[101] The historian presented him as the only man capable of dealing with Henry VIII: 'The best eulogy on his character is to be found in the contrast between the conduct of Henry before and after the Cardinal's fall. As long as Wolsey continued in favour, the royal passions were confined within certain bounds; the moment his influence was extinguished, they burst through every restraint'[102] An illustration of Wolsey's arrival at the abbey of Leicester (Fig. 28), on the point of death, reinforces the image of a public hero—Benjamin West's extremely popular painting, *The Death of Wolfe*, springs to mind momentarily, as the Cardinal sinks amid a crowd of monks and crucifixes, which remind the viewer that this is a hero of the Church. The image is decidedly ambiguous: it drew on a tradition of similar illustrations of Wolsey's last moments, both in textbooks and history books, such as Robert Smirke's version for the Bowyer edition of Hume, and therefore does not seem an unusual subject.[103] But the presentation of this dramatic arrival, rather than the deathbed itself, allowed Harvey in his 1837 design to construct a pleasing Gothic ceiling. Dudley used this precedent, but 'panned in' on the actors to make a more specific point about Wolsey as a national Catholic hero.[104]

THE HISTORY OF ENGLAND: PEACE-MAKING POPES
AND LOYAL CATHOLICS

After the mid-sixteenth century, Catholics as the active supporters and protectors of English liberties were difficult to find, and the other central strand of Lingard's defensive argument may now be examined. This dealt with the problem of papal supremacy, affirming that this authority, exercised by the popes with wise moderation, was beneficial for the English, and did not create

[99] e.g. Lingard, *History* (1854–5), iii. 217–18.   [100] Ibid. iv. 191–4.
[101] Ibid. iv. 263.   [102] Ibid. iv. 264.
[103] R. Bowyer, *A Series of One Hundred and Ninety-One Engravings . . . Illustrative of 'The History of England'* (1812), plate 93.
[104] Lingard, *History* (1837–9), vi, frontispiece; Lingard, *History*, (1854–5), iv, facing 264.

a conflict of loyalties with an Englishman's allegiance to his king and country. In his narrative of the Middle Ages, Lingard departed from the Cisalpine interpretation of history in his attempt to establish a favourable picture of the papal supremacy as a benefit to the country, an external spiritual power upholding justice and liberty.

Lingard argued that Englishmen in the past had found no difficulty in accepting papal authority and portrayed interventions by the popes as uniformly to the benefit of the nation: Pope Celestine, for instance, gave a 'severe but merited reproof' to Philip of Beauvais for taking up arms and fighting Richard I.[105] In narrating the dispute between the Pope and King John over the appointment of Langton as Archbishop of Canterbury, the historian emphasized Pope Innocent's moderation: before issuing an edict of excommunication, Innocent 'proceeded with deliberation and allowed his disobedient son time to repent'.[106] Lingard ably argued that John's submission to the Pope—usually viewed as undermining to English national sovereignty—was not disgraceful, as vassalage was common in that age. Indeed, the barons consented to it because 'it offered a protector, to whom, as superior lord, they might appeal from the despotic government of his vassal'.[107] So much for this famous affront to English independence. The suppression of this traditionally anti-Catholic subject as an illustration is not, therefore, surprising: Lingard's sensible analysis of the historical context of the submission carried uncomfortable implications for those readers who wished to find the roots of nationhood in the English Middle Ages.

The popes supported Henry III in the crisis with Simon de Montfort, which might have appeared, to the nineteenth-century reader, to put them on the opposite side from liberty. But Lingard reminded the reader of how Clement IV implored the victorious king to remember that 'clemency was the firmest pillar of the throne'; meanwhile, the papal envoy Ottoboni, 'by diffusing a spirit of moderation, greatly contributed to the restoration of tranquillity'.[108] Papal peacemaking was a favourite theme of Lingard's. He protested:

Writers have not always sufficiently appreciated the benefits which mankind derived from the pacific influence of the Roman pontiffs . . . Europe would have been plunged in perpetual wars had not pope after pope laboured incessantly for the preservation, or restoration of peace . . . their legates spared neither journey nor fatigues to reconcile the jarring interests of the courts, and interpose the olive of peace between the swords of contending armies.[109]

At the Battle of Poitiers, for instance, Cardinal Talleyrand was 'indefatigable in his endeavours' to make peace.[110] Papal advice was portrayed by Lingard as always wise and beneficial to the English nation, rather than interfering and divisive. When the young Edward III asked for advice from Pope John XXII, the

---

[105] Lingard, *History* (1854–5), ii. 143.   [106] Ibid. ii. 161.
[107] Ibid. ii. 166.   [108] Ibid. ii. 234.   [109] Ibid. iii. 75–6.
[110] Ibid. iii. 84. Given Doyle's earlier painting of this subject, it is surprising that it was not chosen for illustration.

pontiff sensibly told him to shun favouritism and to govern by 'the united advice of barons, prelates and commons assembled in parliament'.[111]

The good effects (in the main) of papal intervention were but one side of Lingard's argument concerning the supremacy: the other was the proof of Catholic loyalty. Lingard was determined to show that Catholic subjects in the past denied any temporal supremacy to the Pope, and were true English patriots, loyal to the Crown and/or constitution. During the reign of Edward III, the Pope laid claim to the first fruits of benefices and to temporal authority over England; the English replied that they would only accept the spiritual authority of the Pope. Lingard commented: 'This is an important occurrence in our history as it proves beyond contradiction that the distinction between the spiritual and temporal power of the pope, which is maintained by the Catholics of the present day, was a principle fully recognised and asserted by Catholic ancestors many centuries ago.'[112]

Under Protestant governments, Lingard argued, Catholics were always loyal. He emphasized the allegiance of Edmund Campion, an English missionary priest arrested by the authorities, who, when asked if he admitted Elizabeth I's title to the throne, replied that he took her 'not only for queen, but his lawful queen'. Campion and two others were later executed, 'praying with their last breath for the queen as their legitimate sovereign'.[113] Lingard stressed that all Catholic missionary priests came to England with 'the sole view of exercising the spiritual functions of the priesthood'. If Elizabeth I feared the deposing power of the pontiff, Lingard argued, she should have offered 'liberty of conscience' to Catholics who would abjure 'the temporal pretensions of the pontiff'.[114] Lingard was indignant at the execution of innocent Catholics after the Armada in 1588: at their trials, 'nothing was objected against them but the practice of their faith'.[115] The loyalty of Catholics was again emphasized by the historian in the case of the Penderells, who helped the young Charles II to escape after the Battle of Worcester. Lingard allowed himself a touch of irony as he described them as 'men of tried fidelity, who, born in the domain, and bred in the principles of a loyal Catholic family, had been successfully employed in screening priests and Cavaliers from the searches of the civil magistrates and officers'. According to Lingard, one of their sisters commented to the suspicious king 'I would die sooner than betray you', and their mother visited Charles and blessed 'God that he had chosen her sons to preserve . . . the life of their sovereign'.[116] Dolman enthusiastically completed Lingard's apotheosis of this ideal loyalist Catholic family by adding an illustration of Charles hiding in the famed oak tree. This image carefully includes not only Charles II, but two of the Penderell brothers, one attending him and one keeping watch, while a sister approaches with food for the King.[117]

[111] Lingard, *History* (1854–5), iii. 23–9.
[112] Ibid. iii. 132.   [113] Ibid. vi. 167–8.   [114] Ibid. vi. 169.
[115] Ibid. vi. 255.   [116] Ibid. viii. 157.   [117] Ibid. viii. facing 156.

THE HISTORY OF ENGLAND: CHARGING IT ON THE INNOCENT?

Lingard was not uncontroversial in the *History*, although his commentary lacked the expansive sarcasm of the *Antiquities*. Even his claims to have carefully researched his narrative—true though they are—are not to be accepted at face value. Edwin Jones has shown that Lingard's brilliantly pioneering use of the practically inaccessible Simancas archives—years before G. A. Begenroth made the supposed first British examination of them, resulting in the publication of *The Calendar of State Papers from Spanish Sources* (1862)—was directed by specific, overtly Catholic objectives, such as clearing the character of Philip II of Spain from several charges, including that of suborning Lopez, a Spanish agent, to kill Elizabeth I. He achieved his objectives in most cases.[118] Much of this offensive approach is immediately obvious in the text: he reinterpreted Catholic characters favourably, and Protestant ones unfavourably, in an attempt to break the traditional Protestant interpretation of English history. He revised the interpretation of Thomas à Becket, a traditional Protestant bugbear, by an apparently dispassionate appeal to the evidence, claiming that if Becket's devotion had been a 'mere affectation of piety', his hypocrisy was unlikely to have deceived the keen eyes of his contemporary adversaries.[119] His most radical reinterpretations concerned the characters and events of the Reformation. He redeemed the character of Mary I, for instance, by portraying her as a merciful sovereign, who executed only three people after the crisis of her accession—'an instance of clemency perhaps unparalleled in the history of those ages'.[120] He excused the executions of heretics which took place in her reign, by pointing out that 'the extirpation of erroneous doctrine was inculcated as a duty by the leader of every religious party' and Mary 'only practised what *they* taught'.[121]

However, one of the Catholic historian's most concentrated efforts at vindication involved Mary, Queen of Scots, who has already been seen as the icon of that other outsider of Victorian historiography, the woman historian. Lingard avoided making open statements in her favour, but his narrative of her career implied a sympathetic reappraisal. He denied that Mary was a member of a Catholic League to exterminate Protestants, claiming that it was intended merely to secure freedom of worship for Catholics.[122] In discussion of the murder of Darnley, he aimed to appear moderate in his judgement, but was clearly inclined to support Mary, holding that there was 'no credible evidence' that she even knew of the plot to kill him.[123] He interpreted the Babington Plot as two plots, 'one by Morgan against the life of Elizabeth, and . . . an underplot against the life

---

[118] E. Jones, 'John Lingard and the Simancas Archives', *The Historical Journal*, 10 (1967), 57–76.

[119] Lingard, *History* (1854–5), ii. 60.   [120] Ibid. v. 211.   [121] Ibid. v. 259.

[122] Ibid. vi. 61 n. 1.   [123] Ibid. vi. 70.

Fig. 30. [J. E. Doyle], *Death Warrant Read to Mary, Queen of Scots*, from Lingard, *History*, vi, frontispiece

of Mary'.[124] There was pity, too, for Anthony Babington and his friends, none of whom, but for Walsingham's spies, 'would ever have thought of the offence for which they suffered'.[125] At Mary's trial, Lingard argued, the failure of the prosecutors to produce the originals of the letters on which they based their case 'suggests a strong presumption in her favour'.[126] He described how, when her death warrant was read aloud to Mary, she swore her innocence of any plotting against the life of Elizabeth, on a Catholic Testament, adding that she was being executed for her faith.[127] This presentation of Mary as not just a martyr, but a Catholic martyr, is heightened by the choice of this scene for an illustration (Fig. 30).[128] There is perhaps, in the image, a suggestion of Jesus before the High Priest or Pilate: the choice of this scene, rather than the immensely more familiar execution, suggests a deliberate decision by Doyle or Dolman to break with the traditional iconography, which allowed both Protestant and Catholic to meet on the grounds of sentimental sympathy for a beautiful victim. Since Lingard was reluctant to state outright his sympathy for Mary's predicament and his conviction of the illegality of her treatment, he voiced it by way of comment on the similar fate of a Protestant princess, Arabella Stuart, cousin of James I.

[124] Lingard, *History* (1854–5), vi. 199.   [125] Ibid. vi. 210.
[126] Ibid. vi. 211.   [127] Ibid. vi. 225.   [128] Ibid. vi. frontispiece.

Describing her death, he remarked: 'she expired, the victim of an unfeeling policy, which, to guard against an uncertain and imaginary danger, scrupled not to rob a female relative of her liberty and life. She was interred privately in the night at Westminster, in the same vaults to which the remains of the unfortunate Mary queen of Scots had been removed.'[129] An illustration of her funeral reinforced these points: Dolman appeared to be working the text for all it was worth. It is perhaps worth bearing in mind that, until the nineteenth century, Catholics were interred at night, for fear of interruption by Protestant authorities: the image of Arabella's funeral, which features many smoking torches, appears to be reinforcing the theme of persecution.

Lingard also exonerated Henrietta Maria, the French Catholic wife of Charles I, who was frequently accused by Protestant historians of inciting the king to tyrannical and divisive acts against the English nation. Commenting that her influence was 'considerably exaggerated', he added robustly: 'On most questions she coincided in opinion with secretary Nicholas; nor will it be rash to conclude that the unfortunate monarch would have fared better, had he sometimes followed their advice.'[130] James, Duke of York, a Catholic and the future King James II, was compared favourably with his brother Charles II: Lingard described him as prudent, attentive to his duties at the Admiralty, decisive, and affable to subjects.[131] While describing the Great Fire of 1666, Lingard indignantly refuted the tale of the seventeenth-century Protestant bishop, Gilbert Burnet, who accused a Catholic artisan, Grant, of turning off the water of the New River, to prevent the putting out of the fire. He added that, against all those accused of starting the fire at the time, 'no vestige of proof could ever be discovered'. The monument attributing it to the Catholics, therefore, infuriated him: 'Next to the guilt of him who perpetuated an atrocious crime, is the guilt of those who charge it on the innocent.'[132]

Lingard was rather guarded in his account of James II's reign, obviously a very controversial subject, but he managed to exonerate James from several of the charges levelled against him by Whig historians. He described his aims at the opening of his reign as reaching no further than religious and civil toleration for Catholics, and argued that, given his own beliefs, this was essential to his security as a monarch.[133] With this argument, he neatly avoided making any unrealistic claims concerning James's progressive views, while presenting the Anglican opponents of toleration as almost rebellious. Lingard refused to view James's admission of the Protestant hero, Monmouth, to a last interview after his rebellion as cruel, pointing out that this occurred at the Duke's request and that a refusal 'might, with greater reason, been adduced a proof of cruelty'.[134] He was restrained in his narrative of Jeffrey's 'Bloody Assizes', but he commented that

---

[129] Lingard, *History* (1854–5), vii. 63.   [130] Ibid. ix. 95.
[131] Ibid. ix. 48.   [132] Ibid. ix. 64–6.
[133] Ibid. x. 63.   [134] Ibid. x. 84.

the claim of Alice Lisle—a much lamented victim of the trials—to be unaware of the guilt of those rebels whom she sheltered in her house was 'a mere pretence [which] must be evident to anyone who attends to the unwilling testimony of the witnesses'.[135]

THE HISTORY OF ENGLAND: THE RUTHLESSNESS OF REFORMERS AND ROUNDHEADS

Lingard did not limit his onslaught on the traditional Protestant narrative of national history to the rehabilitation of Catholic figures and their actions: he also directly attacked Protestant heroes and their actions. The Reformation, while rousing Lingard to a cold fury, offered him the opportunity to sever the traditional link between national progress and the adoption and maintenance of the Protestant faith by the English people. Lingard opened his attack on a Continental front: although he accepted that the conduct of the German Catholic clergy was very lax, he was highly critical of Martin Luther. He described the great reformer as 'vain of his talents for disputation', and accused him of breaking his promise to accept the Pope's edict on the indulgences.[136] Then English Reformation figures came under fire. Anne Boleyn, whom the Protestant historians viewed as a proto-evangelical, was dismissed by Lingard as 'no more a Protestant than Henry'; he claimed that she and the King had co-habited and even asserted that a son was born to them before their marriage.[137] Nor did the criticisms by Todd make Lingard revise his opinion of Cranmer.[138] He recorded with horror how the sentences against the Friars Observant and the Carthusians, who refused to take the Oath of Supremacy, were 'executed with a barbarous exactitude'.[139] The pretexts for the dissolution of the monasteries were farcical, Lingard argued: it was welcomed by the King, 'whose thirst for money was not exceeded by his love of power',[140] while the evidence against the monks was collected by 'clerical adventurers of very equivocal character'.[141] The reign of Edward VI was treated equally critically by the Catholic historian: Lingard commented that the zeal of Duke of Somerset and the rest of the governing Council was really stimulated by 'the prospect of reward', rather than Protestant fervour.[142] The executions of Protestant extremists under Edward VI permitted Lingard to remark sarcastically: 'It might indeed have been hoped that the men who had writhed under the lash of persecution would have learnt to respect the rights of conscience.'[143]

Not only the Protestant figures of the Reformation were condemned, but even the general results of the change were deplored in a manner which savours of

[135] Lingard, *History* (1854–5), x. 89.   [136] Ibid. iv. 222–4.
[137] Ibid. v. 1–2.   [138] Ibid. v. 3–4.   [139] Ibid. v. 19.
[140] Ibid. v. 27.   [141] Ibid. v. 28, 48.   [142] Ibid. v. 123.   [143] Ibid. v. 158.

Cobbett's social comment. With a rare digression from the narration of political and ecclesiastical affairs, Lingard briefly shows a picturesque historian's interest in the everyday life of the English people, to which he refers to shame Protestant opponents: 'Within the realm poverty and discontent generally prevailed . . . the poor began to resort to the more populous towns in search of that relief which had formerly been distributed at the gates of the monasteries.' Morals, Lingard argued, did not improve, as spiritual courts lost their authority, opening 'a wider scope to the indulgence of criminal passion'.[144] The executions for heresy in Mary's reign, Lingard remarked, teach the mind 'to bless the legislation of a more tolerant age',[145] but he attempted to excuse the Catholic persecutors by indicating that the Protestant victims were not without responsibility for their deaths. After John Rogers and several other Protestants had been burnt, Philip II's chaplain, Alphonso di Castro, preached against the death penalty for heresy. There was a lull in the executions, Lingard argued, until the excesses of Protestant fanatics provoked renewed prosecution.[146]

The Catholic historian was determined to shatter the link between true patriotism and Protestantism characteristic of the dominant historical narrative. The early Protestants, Lingard argued, despite their claim to wish for nothing more than religious freedom, were disloyal and tyrannical: the doyen of the Scottish Reformation, John Knox, preached doctrines which were 'the parents of sedition and civil war',[147] and the Scottish Lords of the Congregation, in their peace negotiations with the Crown, sought 'religious domination' rather than 'religious freedom'.[148] Lingard was irritated by the tendency of Protestant monarchs, such as Elizabeth I, to denounce their Catholic subjects as disloyal, while encouraging rebellion for religious motives by aiding Protestant rebels in France and the Netherlands: the Armadas were, for him, the deserved punishment for such 'perpetual interference'.[149] In fact, Lingard disputed the Protestant interpretation of Elizabeth's reign as a national Golden Age: he described Sir Francis Drake and his men, traditionally regarded as imperialistic heroes of the period, as 'no better than public robbers and assassins'.[150] To glowing accounts of Elizabeth's reign by Protestant historians he opposed 'the dismal picture of national misery drawn by Catholic writers', commenting that neither Elizabeth nor her ministers 'understood the benefits of civil and religious liberty'.[151]

The theme of Protestants as no champions of true religious freedom (and thereby, of civil and national progress) continued in Lingard's narrative of the events of the seventeenth century: the Gunpowder Plot merely increased the impetus of Protestant injustice and intolerance, instead of teaching the values of tolerance.[152] The Puritans of the seventeenth century were, for Lingard, poor protectors of freedom: they used the attainder beloved of Henry VIII, 'the most

---

[144] Lingard, *History* (1854–5), v. 180.   [145] Ibid. v. 239.
[146] Ibid. v. 231, 239.   [147] Ibid. vi. 16.   [148] Ibid. vi. 27.
[149] Ibid. vi. 116.   [150] Ibid. vi. 235.   [151] Ibid. vi. 324.   [152] Ibid. vii. 45.

arbitrary of our monarchs', against Thomas Wentworth, Earl of Strafford and Charles I's chief minister.[153] He commented with an air of impartiality that the trial and execution of Archbishop Laud was the result of 'religious, and not political rancour', adding with disdain that he and his Puritan persecutors were 'equally obstinate, equally infallible, equally intolerant'.[154] But the Puritans were the real targets of his attack. The religious intolerance of the Commonwealth's Act against Catholics led him to reflect that these 'champions of religious liberty' had 'very confined' ideas of toleration: 'they refused to extend it either to prelacy or the church of Rome'. Catholics, he complained, were 'still the victims of persecuting statutes': he gave the example of an orphan Catholic serving maid, whose twenty years' savings of £20 were reduced to £6.14s.4d. on the suspicion of her faith.[155] The Protestant hero, Oliver Cromwell, was regarded by Lingard very critically. The historian pointed out that Cromwell saw himself as the instrument of God, which 'enabled him to persevere in habits of the most fervent devotion, even when he was plainly following the unholy suggestions of cruelty, duplicity and ambition'.[156] Lingard's exposure of Cromwell's character allowed Dolman to force a reinterpretation of a traditional Protestant subject of illustration: Cromwell refusing the crown. The illustration alone would have appeared to be simply a straightforward presentation of an event which was often used by Protestant historians to prove Cromwell's moral integrity and care for the national good; in conjunction with Lingard's textual narrative of this 'mighty farce', the image appeared as a reinforcement of the historian's exposure of Cromwell's ambition and hypocrisy.[157]

But it was the Popish Plot, of all seventeenth-century events, which roused Lingard's animus against Protestant extremism most fully: he described it as 'an imposture . . . supported by the arts and declamations of a numerous party'.[158] On the fact of a routine triennial meeting of the Jesuit order in London, Titus Oates and his associate Tonge raised 'a huge superstructure of malice and fiction',[159] supported by forged letters. When Oates told his tale before the Council, 'the members of the Council gasped in astonishment at each other. The facts appeared so incredible, the means by which they had come to the know-ledge of the informer were so devoid of probability, and the character which he gave of himself exhibited such baseness and dishonesty, that his hearers were bewildered and amazed.'[160] The King, questioning Oates, easily proved the factual inaccuracies of his story.[161] This scene, which stressed the fraudu-lence of Oates and, therefore, the gullibility and bigotry of anyone who seriously believed his tales and the cowardice and cruelty of those who did not, was ap-propriately selected for illustration.[162] In the image, the King and his councillors look on with apparent scepticism and disapproval, as the sharp-chinned and

[153] Lingard, *History* (1854–5), vii. 238.   [154] Ibid. viii. 42.
[155] Ibid. viii. 194–5.   [156] Ibid. viii. 14.   [157] Ibid. viii. 250.
[158] Ibid. ix. 172.   [159] Ibid. ix. 173.   [160] Ibid. ix. 176.
[161] Ibid. ix. 176–7.   [162] Ibid. ix. frontispiece.

unappealing Oates delivers his testimony. Lingard described the subsequent trials and executions of innocent Catholics as 'judicial murders'.[163] To create a real sense of the Protestant injustice and cruelty exhibited during the Popish Plot, Lingard focused on the trial and execution of the Catholic Lord Stafford, which was, for the Protestant leaders in Parliament, a victory which 'covered them in disgrace'.[164] This elderly man was accused by Oates and other informers, whose 'very characters were a sufficient condemnation of the cause which they appeared to support'.[165] He confessed only to aiding those bent on gaining toleration for Catholic worship. Lingard commented: 'The spirit with which he defended himself at his trial surpassed the expectations of his friends, and confounded the hopes of his enemies; and his Christian piety and fearless deportment on the scaffold confirmed the growing opinion of his innocence.'[166] Naturally, he is shown in an illustration, being led to execution.[167]

The victims of the rampantly pro-Protestant Rye House Plot were, however, guilty, argued the Catholic historian: he was unsparing in his treatment of the Protestant heroes, William, Lord Russell, and Algernon Sydney. He undermined the credibility of Sydney as a patriot anxious for the good of his country by exposing him as 'the hireling of the French ambassador', paid for his opposition to the King.[168] At his trial, Russell made, in Lingard's opinion, 'but a feeble defence': he pointed out that, although Russell had not technically broken the statute of treason by levying war against the King, he had clearly planned to do so. With a malicious recollection of the Popish Plot, Lingard told his reader that there was some hope that Russell might have been pardoned—but that it was unlikely that the King would have offered that mercy to those he thought treasonous, which they had 'by intimidation prevented him from extending to so many victims whom he believed to be innocent'.[169]

Although Lingard was reserved in his defence of the Catholic James II, he was less restrained in his criticism of the Protestant heroes, James, Duke of Monmouth, and William of Orange, later William III. While William of Orange was denounced as an ambitious schemer rather than a defender of English liberties,[170] Monmouth was still more heavily criticized. Lingard denounced his 'intemperate' proclamation on his landing in England to raise a rebellion,[171] and portrayed the captured Monmouth as a mean-spirited coward who was willing 'to accept life on any terms'.[172] Another unpleasant facet of Monmouth's character was revealed by his treatment of his wife. In prison, the reader was informed, he received her first visit 'coldly'; at her last visit, he was civil but unconcerned when her distress resulted in a fainting fit. This scene was chosen for illustration (Fig. 31): the indifferent Monmouth stands aside while his wife collapses artistically, supported by two gentlemen, a guard, two maids, and a couple of watching

[163] Lingard, *History* (1854–5), ix. 189.   [164] Ibid. ix. 241.
[165] Ibid. ix. 241.   [166] Ibid. ix. 248.   [167] Ibid. ix. facing 248.
[168] Ibid. x. 39–44.   [169] Ibid. x. 34–5.   [170] Ibid. x. 187.
[171] Ibid. x. 79.   [172] Ibid. x. 84.

Fig. 31. [H. Dudley], *Last Interview between the Duke of Monmouth and his Wife*, from Lingard, *History*, x, facing 85

children. The attention and the pity of the viewer is focused thus on the wronged but loving woman, and Monmouth's dismal prospects do not intrude sufficiently to transfer any sympathy to him. In the text, the reader is reminded that, to his death, he remained unrepentant of both his long extra-marital affair and his treasons:[173] his lack of loyalty to his country and king is thus linked to his unfaithfulness to his wife.

THE HISTORY OF ENGLAND: ACCEPTED AND SUSPECTED

In writing his *History*, Lingard's aim was to produce a history of England which could and would be read by Protestants, to write English Catholics into the dominant narrative of the history of the nation. To some extent, he achieved this: his impartiality of tone and meticulous research won him the qualified approval of even his most strident critics and foreshadowed the critical techniques of the scientific historian. But his critique of the traditional Protestant interpretation of English history, supported by a pioneering analysis of his sources which has largely stood the test of time, led him also towards the creation of a rival Catholic history of England. For Lingard was not simply a philosophical historian in the

[173] Lingard, *History* (1854–5), x. 85–7.

Cisalpine tradition; he was also a picturesque historian influenced by Romantic enthusiasm for the Old Faith, a Catholic who shared with other younger and more militant Catholics—men such as Dolman and Doyle—a desire for the defence and revival of the Catholic Church. Controversy as well as apologetic was present in his *History*. At the time of his death, the University of Oxford still demurred at commending his work to the student of medieval history,[174] and when a student such as then evangelical William Gladstone took even the most cursory of notes on his *History*, he could not help passing criticisms.[175] The 1854-5 edition of Lingard's *History* was used by Dolman and his illustrators, not only to infuse traditional subjects with new meaning, but as a suitable setting for even more forthright visual statements of Catholic sentiments. The *History* was at once accepted and suspected; all Lingard's restraint could not obscure what the more pugnacious Dolman, and the artists he employed, displayed by way of pointed illustrations.

[174] P. Slee, *Learning and a Liberal Education* (Manchester, 1986), 48.

[175] London, British Library: Additional MSS: 44727, fos. 141–8; 44792, fos. 77–9. These notes appear to date from 1837 to the early 1840s.

8

Thackeray, A'Beckett, and Leech:
'The Dignity of History'

The dignity of history sadly diminishes as we grow better acquainted with the materials which compose it. In our orthodox history-books the characters move on as a gaudy playhouse procession, a glittering pageant of kings and warriors, and stately ladies . . . Only he who sits very near to the stage can discover of what stuff the spectacle is made. The kings are poor creatures, taken from the dregs of the company; the noble knights are dirty dwarfs in tin foil; the fair ladies are painted hags with cracked feathers and soiled trains. One wonders how gas and distance could ever have rendered them so enchanting . . .[1]

Thus William Makepeace Thackeray, in a review of the newly published correspondence of Sarah Churchill, first Duchess of Marlborough and favourite of Queen Anne. The future writer of *Vanity Fair* (1847-8), the novel which took as its text the cry of the Old Testament preacher, 'Vanity of vanities', already sounds the note of disillusionment, this time with the historical representations and reconstructions of his period, in both their textual and their visual forms. For Thackeray, the picturesque portrayals of national history characteristic of the early nineteenth century—despite all their attempts to achieve authentic reconstructions of personalities and events—were inaccurate, inflated, and romanticizing. The falsification and inaccuracy of historical novelists such as W. H. Ainsworth and of their artistic counterparts, the painters of historical genre pictures, provoked his criticism. He was equally intolerant of the philosophical historiography still apparent in multi-volume histories and history textbooks and their illustrations, where history was presented in the form of edifying anecdotes, intended to teach by exempla and to support traditional values and views.

Thackeray was not alone in his satirical attacks on the historiographical errors of his age. He was simply the most talented of a group of writers and artists who, under the editorship of Douglas Jerrold, created the comic journal *Punch*.[2] Thackeray and his companions aimed their shots at a plethora of the nation's

---

[1] W. M. Thackeray, *The Oxford Thackeray*, ed. G. Saintsbury, 17 vols. (1908), i. 79.

[2] G. N. Ray, *Thackeray: The Uses of Adversity, 1811–1846* (1955), 348–83.

political, social, and cultural shibboleths, employing a complex interplay of text and image in satirical parodies and pastiches.[3] Gilbert A'Beckett, a fellow *Punch* writer, produced *The Comic History of England*, illustrated by John Leech, between 1846 and 1848; this work exhibited the same comic and ironic approach to national history as Thackeray adopted, although A'Beckett's underlying philosophy was essentially cruder. In the 1850s, Thackeray's fictions were to explore, in both text and image, the nature of historical representation, resulting in the author's loss of faith in the mission of national history.

The use of irony and the comic presentation of Thackeray's early works and *The Comic History of England* does not disguise their seriousness of purpose, and fits well into the theoretical framework postulated by Hayden White in his seminal work, *Metahistory*.[4] White argues that there are four basic modes of emplotment, which are used to transform chronicles into stories, or histories (he chooses not to distinguish between fictional and non-fictional texts). These are romance, comedy, tragedy, and irony, or satire. The last of these forms is concerned, he explains, with frustrating the normal expectations set up in the other three modes.[5] As such, it presupposes exploitation of the other modes, and expresses disillusionment with them:

the advent of the satirical mode of representation signals a conviction that the world has grown old. Like philosophy itself, Satire 'paints its gray on gray' in the awareness of its *own* inadequacy as an image of reality. It therefore prepares consciousness for its repudiation of all sophisticated conceptualizations of the world [i.e. other emplotments] and anticipates a return to a mythic apprehension of the world and its processes.[6]

Thackeray and his fellows can be perceived as the ironic voices of the mid-century crisis of national history, the satirical attackers of the picturesque reconstructions of historical novelists and the didactic 'true stories' of the textbooks. Their ironic play on the image of the theatre (an obvious metaphor for the staging of the other emplotments, romance, comedy, and tragedy) was intended to express the flimsy artificiality which they perceived as inherent in these picturesque reconstructions. The metaphor was natural in an age which encouraged narrative, pictorial, and theatrical arts to become interchangeable: theatre gave rise to literary paintings, textual scenes were frequently illustrated, tableaux vivants appeared on stage, and art criticism used the language of the theatre.[7]

---

[3] For the history of *Punch*, see M. H. Spielmann, *The History of 'Punch'* (1895). R. D. Altick's *Punch 1841–51: The Lively Youth of a British Institution* (Columbus, Ohio, 1997) offers analysis of the content of the early issues of the journal: for 'pictorial jokes', see pp. 150–84.

[4] S. Bann, *Romanticism and the Rise of History* (New York, 1995), 45–59, offers a similar analysis, reading *The Comic History of England* as an example of the ironic mode described by White, affording an independent confirmation of the conclusions arrived at in this chapter.

[5] H. White, *Metahistory* (Baltimore and London, 1973), 7–8.   [6] Ibid. 10.

[7] See M. Meisel, *Realizations: Narrative, Pictorial and Theatrical Arts in Nineteenth Century England* (Princeton, 1983), for discussion of the interactions of these art forms.

'THE SCENES OF WHICH THE SPECTACLE IS COMPOSED'

Thackeray attacked contemporary historical novelists in an early historical novel of his own, *The Memoirs of Barry Lyndon* (which was originally published in 1844, under the title *The Luck of Barry Lyndon*).[8] In this novel about an eighteenth-century Irish adventurer—an anti-hero whose nationality rendered him a partial outsider in terms of English national identity and, therefore, a detached (though not always a reliable) observer—Thackeray accused novelists of purveying versions of history in which great historical figures assume undue and unrealistic importance, and are rarely shown for what they are. Lyndon, an accomplished liar (a fact which makes Thackeray's irony double-edged), assures his readers that:

Were these memoirs not characterized by truth, I might easily make myself the hero of some strange and popular adventures, and, after the fashion of novel-writers introduce my readers to the great characters of this remarkable time. These persons . . . if they take a drummer or a dustman for a hero, somehow manage to bring him into contact with the greatest lords and the most notorious personages of the empire.[9]

Lyndon describes his experiences as a soldier on the day on which the Battle of Minden took place, when he himself saw no one of higher rank on his side than a couple of orderly officers. What Lyndon and the reader both remember are not the great issues or people involved in the battle, but how he

finished off a poor little ensign . . . and in the poor ensign's pocket found a purse of fourteen louis-d'or, and a silver box of sugar plums, of which the former present was very agreeable to me. If people would tell their stories of battle in this simple way, I think the cause of truth would not suffer by it.[10]

Lyndon makes no attempt to hide the brutality of war and its participants, even himself. He adds: 'while . . . we are the present moment admiring the "Great Frederick" as we call him, and his philosophy and liberality, and his military genius, I, who have served him, and been, as it were, behind the scenes of which the spectacle is composed, can look at it only with horror'.[11]

Thackeray did not always attack historical novelists so obliquely. In *Punch*, in July 1847, the errors and pretensions of the well-known historical novelist, G. P. R. James (Ainsworth's chief rival) became the burden of his comic complaint in the parodic *Barbazure* by G. P. Jeames. Thackeray mocked James's tendency to superimpose misunderstood medieval paraphernalia on a clearly contemporary framework of characters and sensibilities. The hero, whose name, Romane de Clos-Vougeot, is more evocative of nineteenth-century champagne than medieval romance, is accompanied by a warrior described as

---

[8] A good introduction to Thackeray's attitude to contemporary historical literature and art can be found in D. Douglas, 'Thackeray and the Uses of History', *The Yearbook of English Studies*, 5 (1975), 164–73.
[9] *Oxford Thackeray*, vi. 69–70.   [10] Ibid. vi. 70.   [11] Ibid. vi. 71.

complete with 'campron and catapault, with ban and arriere-ban, monon and tumbril, battle-axe and riff-lard, and other appurtenances of ancient chivalry'.[12] The youth opens a conversation with his well-armoured companion: 'But Fatima, Fatima, how fares she? . . . Since Lammas was a twelvemonth . . . my letters are unanswered . . . The postman hath transversed our camp every day and never brought me a *billet* . . .'.[13] Thackeray targeted here James's lack of historical sense, and his inability to achieve a realistic understanding of the circumstances and emotions of medieval life. He was not afraid to aim his shots at higher game either: in *Rebecca and Rowena* (1850), a continuation of Walter Scott's *Ivanhoe*, similar anachronisms occur, and Thackeray ironically used them to achieve an ending which he felt was more satisfactory. Rowena, for instance—a feeble figure in the original novel—gains character and realism when transformed into a nagging and jealous wife, more like Mrs Caudle than a medieval chatelaine. *The Legend of the Rhine* (1845) is a similar attempt to turn on its head a serious but defective original, this time by Alexander Dumas.

But novelists are not the only objects of Thackeray's critique. In *Miss Tickletoby's Lectures on English History* (1842), the writers of inaccurate and simplistic textbooks come under fire. Thackeray exposed their lack of research and their Romantic credulity: Miss Tickletoby refers her auditors to 'the veracious history of one Tasso'—an Italian poet—for true accounts of the Crusades, and to 'so good an authority' as *Ivanhoe* for information on the misconduct of King John.[14] The tendency of textbook writers to draw morals for the present day from tales of the past—which thus becomes a series of anecdotal exempla to be learnt, rather than experiences to be explored and understood—was also satirized by Thackeray. The tale of Henry II, Rosamund, and the jealous Queen Eleanor elicits this original, and by no means disinterested, precept from the female lecturer: 'Take care, then, my dear young friends, if you are called upon to govern kingdoms, or simply, as is more probable, to go into genteel businesses and keep thriving shops, take care to *never offend your wives*.'[15]

With these works for *Punch*, Thackeray included illustrations which complement the messages of the text. In *The Legend of the Rhine* (illustrated by Cruikshank), we are early introduced to the knight, Ludwig of Hombourg: an illustration of this character as he travels towards Nuremberg shows him sheltering under an umbrella and carrying a watch and a very nineteenth-century travelling bag, thus reinforcing the humorous anachronisms of the text.[16] The tale of Rosamund and Queen Eleanor in *Miss Tickletoby's Lectures* is complemented by a parody of the common textbook illustration of this subject, which turns the sublime romance into ridiculous comedy, just as Miss Tickletoby's moral did.[17] Rosamund appears as a fat young lady, sitting knitting, and the Queen is a hatchet-faced old woman. Similar illustrations are included in *Rebecca and Rowena* and *Barbazure*.

[12] *Oxford Thackeray*, viii. 128.   [13] Ibid. viii. 129.   [14] Ibid. vii. 282, 296.
[15] Ibid. viii. 289.   [16] Ibid. ix. 5.   [17] Ibid. vii. 288.

The illustrations to Thackeray's works (both by the author himself and other artists) should not be dismissed as an amusing but essentially dispensable accompaniment to the text.[18] Just as in Ainsworth's best-selling novels of the 1840s, neither the text nor the illustrations of Thackeray's *jeux d'esprit* can claim an obvious primacy. As has been repeatedly pointed out by commentators, the illustrations are almost always integral to the text: they not only portray the action of the plot and illuminate character, but also make comic and ironic asides, broaden the implications of the events of the text, and even—in certain cases—offer information only hinted at in the text.[19] In the discussion here, it will be seen that they are intended to reiterate and extend points made about early Victorian reconstructions of the national past in Thackeray's text. It may seem ironic that the works of Thackeray—the satirist of the historical reconstructions of the 1830s and 1840s—should be such classic exempla of the close interaction of text and image characteristic of picturesque historiography. But this paradox is explained by a consideration of his early life and career.

Thackeray had originally intended to pursue a career as a painter, and was thus well placed to consider Victorian visual portrayals of the past, in the form of both the academic and classically based history painting and of the picturesque reconstruction characteristic of historical genre. He trained briefly in the studio of the academic painter Henry Sass, the Gandish of *The Newcomes* (1853–5), whose pupils included John Millais and W. P. Frith; his friends included many artists, such as the historical genre painter, Daniel Maclise, and the illustrator, George Cruikshank.[20] Anxious to combine his literary and artistic talents, Thackeray generally attempted to illustrate his own works: all the *Punch* pieces mentioned above were illustrated by him, with the exceptions of *The Legend of the Rhine* and *Rebecca and Rowena* which owed their images to Cruikshank and Richard Doyle respectively. When other illustrators were employed, Thackeray worked closely with them, in a collaboration characteristic of many mid-nineteenth-century authors and illustrators, such as Ainsworth and Cruikshank. Doyle, whom Thackeray affectionately portrayed as J. J. In *The Newcomes*, worked in close collaboration with the writer on his parody of Scott's novel. He shared Thackeray's irreverent attitude to Victorian medievalism, being the illustrator both of that famous flop, the Eglinton Tournament, and of *Scenes from English History* (1840), the text of which was written by his brother, James Doyle, the serious historian and historical illustrator of the family.[21] Richard himself had early began to doubt the truth of many historical legends, and in one letter to his father, asked

---

[18] The fullest account of Thackeray's illustrations is N. Pickwoad, 'Thackeray and his Book Illustrations' (D.Phil. thesis, University of Oxford, 1978). J. Buchanan-Brown, *The Illustrations of William Makepeace Thackeray* (Newton Abbot, London, and North Pomfret, Vt., 1978) is an excellent and more concise account.

[19] See, for examples of such uses of illustration by Thackeray in *Vanity Fair*: Pickwoad, 'Thackeray', i. 133–65.

[20] Ibid. i. 1–15, for Thackeray's early artistic career.

[21] See Ch. 7 for further information on James Doyle.

whether the tale of Richard I pardoning his brother could not have been invented. His attitude to great history paintings was frequently mocking, as was apparent in *Selections from the Rejected Cartoons* (1840)—a skit on the Westminister Competition cartoons of the 1840s—perhaps as a result of his own abortive wish to be a history painter, abandoned in the face of anxieties about his inadequacies.[22]

Thackeray's satire, too, must have been sharpened by a sense of artistic inadequacy: the success of his own illustrations to his works was always compromised by his poor figure drawing, his inability to portray drama and movement, and recurrent problems in translating his work into engraving media.[23] He was employed by several newspapers as an art critic, and in these articles he frequently criticized the inaccuracy of other artists' attempts at portraying historical events in the 1840s. However, his criticism was not entirely rooted in envy: as early as 1830, during a visit to Paris and before his hopes of success as an artist had been dashed, he had rejected the great historical canvases of the French school of J. L. David and his pupils—not a surprising response for the future author of *Barry Lyndon* and *Henry Esmond* (1852), novels which dispensed with traditional concepts of heroism.[24]

Critical of the grand idealism of traditional history painting, Thackeray could be equally severe on the artists of the hybrid form, historical genre, which had obviously much attracted him as a young artist: he was well-versed in the details of historical costume and armour, of which he took sketches,[25] as his art criticism showed.[26] Like many nineteenth-century artists of picturesque historical reconstruction, he was concerned with historical accuracy and the avoidance of anachronism. In 'A Pictorial Rhapsody' of 1840, he complains of the modern 'black cassock' worn by the Archbishop in Alfred Elmore's *The Murder of Thomas à Becket*, commenting that 'a painter should be as careful about his costumes as his dates'.[27] Henry Corbould's *Canterbury Pilgrims* is an improvement, but it is by no means perfect: 'the artist shows a genuine antiquarian or Walter-Scottish spirit . . . it is a pity that his ladies wear such uncommonly low dresses—they did not wear such (according to the best authorities) in Chaucer's time'.[28] In an article on the Louvre in 1841, 'On Men and Pictures' (1841), real praise is reserved for the French historical genre painters:

---

[22] Engen, *Doyle*, 28–30, 38–9, 73–4; A. Burton, 'Thackeray's Collaborations with Cruikshank, Doyle, and Walker', in P. L. Shillingsburg (ed.), *Costerus: Essays in English and American Literature: Thackeray* (Amsterdam and Columbia, SC, 1974), 152–5.

[23] Pickwoad, 'Thackeray', i, discusses these problems fully.

[24] Ray, *Uses*, 123.   [25] Pickwoad, 'Thackeray', i. 100–1.

[26] J. L. Fisher has pointed out how rarely grand painting, whether neo-classical of Romantic, whether by David, Delacroix, or Turner, met with Thackeray's approval; he preferred domestic and sentimental scenes or landscapes by artists in the Wilkie tradition. Fisher describes this as an 'aesthetic of mediocrity', a rather too condemnatory phrase; he was not the only art critic of the age calling for the painting of everyday life. See J. L. Fisher, 'The Aesthetic of the Mediocre: Thackeray and the Visual Arts', *VS* 26 (1982), 65–82.

[27] *Oxford Thackeray*, ii. 511.   [28] Ibid. ii. 531.

as upon the French stage the costume pieces are far better than with us, so also are French costume pictures much more accurately and characteristically handled than are such subjects in this country. You do not see Cimabue and Giotto in the costume of Francis the First . . . the artists go to some trouble for collecting their antiquarian stuff and paint it pretty scrupulously.[29]

However, Thackeray's art criticism, despite pungent comments, remained essentially shallow; his small criticisms of costume details did not lead to a broader attack on the viability of the picturesque historical reconstructions produced by historical genre painters. He found them fundamentally unconvincing, he detected some of the reasons why, but it was only in his novels that the problems of historical reconstruction received profound attention. There he looked not to the public theatre of dignified history, but to the real and private history that might be discerned behind the scenes.

'DIVESTED OF ITS GORGEOUS ACCESSARIES'

Gilbert A'Beckett[30] and John Leech,[31] like Thackeray, felt that Victorian picturesque reconstructions of national history were often inauthentic and inaccurate. They also shared his conviction that moral and edifying presentations of history in early nineteenth-century English history textbooks obscured truth. In the Preface to the book version of *The Comic History of England*, A'Beckett voiced both criticisms, disguising the gravity of his comments by the use of an ironic tone:

Though the original design of this History was only to place facts in an amusing light, without a sacrifice of fidelity, it is humbly presumed that truth has rather gained than lost by the mode of treatment that has been adopted. Persons and things, events and characters, have been deprived of their false colouring, by the plain and matter-of-fact spirit in which they have been approached by the writer of the 'Comic History of England'. He has never scrupled to take the liberty of tearing off the masks and fancy dresses of all who have hitherto been presented in disguise to the notice of posterity . . . Some, who have been accustomed to look at History as a pageant, may think it a desecration to present it in a homely shape, divested of its gorgeous accessaries. Such persons as these will doubtless feel offended at finding the romance of history irreverently demolished, for the sake of mere reality . . .[32]

[29] *Oxford Thackeray*, ii. 565–6.

[30] Accounts of A'Beckett's life can be found in *DNB* i. 31 and A. W. A'Beckett, *The A'Becketts of 'Punch': Memories of Father and Sons* (1903), 9–114. He was the first editor of *Figaro in London*, the precursor of *Punch*, before working on that magazine. Besides *The Comic History of England*, he also produced *The Comic History of Rome*.

[31] Three 19th-cent. accounts of Leech exist: J. Brown, *John Leech and Other Papers* (Edinburgh, 1882), 3–79; F. G. Kitton, *John Leech, Artist and Humourist* (1884); W. P. Frith, *John Leech: His Life and Work*, 2 vols. (1891). See also S. Houfe, *John Leech and the Victorian Scene* (Woodbridge, 1984) for a modern account of his life and work.

[32] G. A. A'Beckett, *The Comic History of England* (1846–8; 2 vols., 1847–8 edn.), i. pp. v–vi. The announcement of A'Beckett's *Comic History* provoked a response from Douglas Jerrold

Once again, the metaphor of the stage is used to convey the sense of the artificiality involved in early nineteenth-century attempts to reconstruct the national past. In *The Comic History*, it is frequently used to expose the artificiality of well-known and unlikely accounts of historical events. A'Beckett included, for instance, the popular textbook anecdote of Margaret of Anjou and the benevolent robber. He remarked: 'Use is second nature in literature as well as anything; and the public, being accustomed to falsehood, would regard the absence of even the most flagrant hoax as a curtailment of the fair proportions of history.'[33] He began to recount the tale:

Margaret fled with her son into the recesses of the forest, like one of those which we see on the stage . . . We fancy her advancing to slow music, laying her child on a canvas bank, and listening to the rattle of peas, accompanied by the shaking of sheet iron, which form the rain and thunder of theatrical life.[34]

He proceeded to undermine 'the scholastic versions of this little incident' of the robber's recall to virtue and his stalwart loyalty, by pointing out that his offer to share the Queen's fortunes, 'considering the desperate nature of his own, was a proposition equally indicative of self-love and loyalty'.[35] Leech's illustration to the tale used, too, the theatrical metaphor: an examination of the background reveals that the forest floor is a stage and the nearby rock, stiff board (Fig. 32).[36]

Similar treatment was accorded to textbook versions of the Battle of Bosworth, for which Shakespeare's account in *Richard III* was still the model. It was dramatic moments from Shakespeare's history plays which lent themselves most readily to the elaboration of the theatrical image by A'Beckett, as these scenes appeared not only on the Victorian stage, but were, of course, the inspiration of the earliest paintings and illustrations of English history, of the huge canvases of Boydell's Gallery and the vignettes in editions of Hume's *History* and history textbooks.[37] A'Beckett therefore described the event as if witnessing a fifth-rate

which shows that he did not grasp the seriousness of A'Beckett's aims: 'I do not [hold] very cordially with its [*Punch*'s] new spirit. After all, life has something very serious in it. It cannot be all a comic history of humanity. Some men would write a Comic Sermon on the Mount. Think of a comic History of England; the drollery of Alfred; the fun of Sir Thomas More in the Tower; the farce of his daughter begging the dear head, and clasping it in her coffin on her bosom! Surely the world will be sick of such blasphemy!' (Spielmann, '*Punch*', 277). A'Beckett's son disputed this account, claiming that Jerrold referred to Thackeray's *Miss Tickletoby's Lectures* (A'Beckett, *Memories*, 99–100).

[33] A'Beckett, *History*, i. 276.   [34] Ibid. i. 277.

[35] Ibid. i. 278.   [36] Ibid. i. 277.

[37] See Ch. 2. For Victorian stage presentations of Shakespeare, see R. Foulkes (ed.), *Shakespeare and the Victorian Stage* (Cambridge, 1986). Two essays in this work (M. Jones, 'Stage Costume and Historical Verisimilitude', 56–73, and R. Foulkes, 'Charles Keen's King Richard II: A Pre-Raphaelite Drama', 39–55) and M. R. Booth, 'Shakespeare as Spectacle and History: The Victorian Period', *Theatre Research International*, 1 (1979), 99–113, show that the debate on, and adoption of, historically authentic and reconstructive costumes and scenery, was only just beginning to affect the stage in the late 1850s (excepting the 1824 production of *King John*, for which Planché designed authentic costumes). Thus the association of sophisticated pictorial and narrative reconstructions with stage versions of Shakespeare was, in the 1840s and early 1850s, an

Fig. 32. J. Leech, *Margaret of Anjou and her Child Meeting the Benevolent Robber*, from G. A'Beckett, *The Comic History of England*, 2 vols. (1847–8), i. 277

production of *Richard III*. The crown is a 'gilt-rimmed opera hat'; the scene in which it is recovered is like one from a pantomime.[38] The description is rounded off with a complete deflation of 'one of the grandest and . . . most dramaticest battles in English history', which is, according to the author, too great an event for mere prose. The subsequent imitation of Macaulay's *Lays of Ancient Rome* relates the tale.[39] The opening lines of 'The Battle of Bosworth' parodies Macaulay's 'The Battle of the Lake Regillus'; the poem comically recounts, not a real battle, but a stage production. The accompanying illustration complements

insulting comparison. The emphasis on spectacle, however, was apparent much earlier: the dialogue of plays was often severely cut to make time for lavish presentations of scenes merely described in the script, and the popularity of dioramas and panoramas no doubt greatly encouraged this tendency.

[38] A'Beckett, *History*, i. 302–3.   [39] Ibid. i. 303–9.

Fig. 33. J. Leech, *The Battle of Bosworth Field, a Scene in the Great Drama of History*, from A'Beckett, *History*, i, facing 303

the text perfectly. We view a production of *Richard III* from backstage: while the King and Richmond fight, the bored players of bit-parts as soldiers drink beer and yawn (Fig. 33).[40] The point is clearly made: the historians' descriptions aim at the sublime, like bad productions of Shakespeare, but the shoddy reality of the events shows through on an examination of the facts—of the tin foil and soiled trains, as Thackeray would put it.

Like Thackeray, A'Beckett was concerned with what he considers to be truth and accuracy, at the expense of traditional, Romantic, or moralizing versions of history (although the author had his own moral point to make). The *gravitas* of history, but not history itself, was to be sacrificed to truth; in the Preface to the *History*, he emphasized his 'real respect for the great and the good' which made him determined to prevent the 'little and bad' from claiming admiration on 'false pretences'.[41] He ruled that 'Fidelity must not be sacrificed even to a desire for solemnity.'[42] The moral necessity which he perceived for truth and accuracy made A'Beckett highly critical of his sources, both primary and secondary. With the irony of his attack on picturesque presentations of history, came a mood of historical empiricism: A'Beckett behaved not unlike a professional historian, weighing sources and authorities against each other, trusting none fully, and

[40] A'Beckett, *History*, i. 303.   [41] Ibid. i, p. vi.   [42] Ibid. i. 103 n.

resting his critique on the foundation of common sense. In the Prospectus advert-ising *The Comic History*, he wrote:

In announcing a Comic History of England it may be necessary to observe that the levity implied in the title will relate to the manner, but by no means to the matter of the work, which will be collected with the gravest regard to the truth and accuracy that the subject requires. The aim of the writer will be to present a faithful narrative, for which the best authorities will be carefully consulted . . . The Comic History of England will not be a mere abridgement of any other work, nor will it follow servilely in the steps of any former historian . . . [it will] be an entirely original composition, the materials of which will be derived from a consultation of all the best histories already in existence, whose authority will be tested by direct reference to the most undoubted authorities.[43]

On the subject of the Battle of Falkirk in 1298, he remarked: 'the Scotch loss is vari-ously stated at ten, fifteen, and sixty thousand men. In ordinary matters, it is sometimes safe to believe half of what we hear, but it would be more judicious to limit one's trust to ten per cent in the records of history.'[44] Boldly he attacked accepted authorities of the nineteenth century; he confronted thus historians' suspicions concerning the death of Edmund Ironside, commenting that it 'has been good-naturedly suggested that Canute had murdered him', a theory spoilt by 'only one or two facts', 'the first of which is, that there is no proof of his having been killed at all . . . Hume has, without hesitation, appointed Oxford as the scene of the assassination, and has been kind enough to select two chamberlains as the perpetrators of the deed, but we have been unable to collect sufficient evid-ence'.[45] What is humorously presented here is a rough-and-ready historical methodology of a recognizably modern and scientific type.

As in Thackeray's 1840s *Punch* works, text and images both contributed to the central ironical narrative of *The Comic History of England*. A'Beckett and his illustrator, Leech, worked together closely: A'Beckett's son remembered seeing Leech at home, 'standing in the firelight, talking to my father about the newest work they [had] in hand in collaboration', and he mentioned *The Comic History* as one of the works thus planned.[46] Issues of historical accuracy exercised Leech as well as A'Beckett. While illustrating Albert Smith's historical novel, *The Marchioness of Brinvilliers*, in 1844, he wrote in despair to Morgan, an official at the publishing house of Bentley: 'Here we are at the twentieth of the month and I have only four pages of Smith's new story . . . Really, it is too much to ex-pect that I can throw myself at a moment's notice into the seventeenth century, with all its difficulties of costume etc., etc.'[47] An illustration from this work, such as *Le Premier Pas*, shows the detailed research into 'costume etc., etc.'

---

[43] The Prospectus of *The Comic History* is to be found on the covers of some of the original serial parts. A'Beckett's claim to be a serious author of history was supported by his son, who asserted that the himself had passed history examinations, in his youth, with 'the assistance of my father's Comic history' (A'Beckett, *Memories*, 83–4).

[44] A'Beckett, *History*, i. 139.   [45] Ibid. i. 44.   [46] A'Beckett, *Memories*, 74.

[47] Frith, *Leech*, i. 153. J. Leech to Morgan, 1844.

Fig. 34. J. Leech, *Battle between the Mercians and Egbert—Cotton M.S*, from A'Beckett, *History*, i. 19

which Leech carried out in the endeavour to produce a convincing picturesque reconstruction.

Such care gave Leech as keen an eye as Thackeray for visual anachronisms, and a similar delight in playing with them: he had already collaborated with Cruikshank on the illustrations to R. Barham's *Ingoldsby Legends* (1840), a comic book of mock-medieval ballads full of such anachronisms.[48] Leech helped A'Beckett to strip away the masks of several historical heroes by anachronistically portraying them as the figures they might have been in nineteenth-century England, characters of the kind Leech portrayed in his contemporary social satires: for instance, Robert Curthose, whose name was affectionately rendered as 'Bob Socks', becomes an extravagant man about town, permanently in debt.[49] Leech was as keen to satirize the visual sources of textbook histories as A'Beckett was to expose the written: when A'Beckett remarked on the peculiarity of early illustrations of a cannon, in which the cannon ball is twice the size of the cannon itself, Leech provided an apt comic illustration.[50] Sometimes, he parodied the 'authentic' metanymic illustrations used in textbooks, attaching a caption with a mock source such as 'Cotton M. S', as in the case of *Battle between the Mercians and Egbert* (Fig. 34):[51] the linear style and deliberate awkwardness of such images is highly reminiscent of Richard Doyle's *Punch* series, *Manners and Customs of ye Englyshe in 1849*. A'Beckett and Leech were as determined as their greater contemporary, Thackeray, to scrutinize critically many early nineteenth-century versions of history.

[48] Kitton, *Leech*, 51–2.   [49] A'Beckett, *History*, i. 71, 77.
[50] Ibid. i. 287–8.   [51] Ibid. i. 19.

'HISTORY FAMILIAR RATHER THAN HEROIC'

In the 1840s, Thackeray was already contemplating the creation of an alternative, and more truly authentic, form of history—one concerned with the everyday life of the past, not just the pageant-like surface of it, which empathized more than edified. Meditating on the Crusades in *A Journey from Cornhill and Cairo*, he wrote: 'When shall we have a real account of those times and heroes—no good humoured pageant, like those of the Scott romances but a real authentic story to instruct and frighten?'[52] In 1841, he began to write *The Knights of Borsellen*, an attempt to produce 'a real authentic story' of medieval Europe in which the harsh brutality of the age was not softened to suit nineteenth-century tastes.[53] It was not completed, but it probably contributed to the harshly realistic mood of *Barry Lyndon*, in which considerations of historical reconstruction are, however, much overshadowed by interest in the Newgate novel. It was not until 1852, with the writing of *The History of Henry Esmond*, that Thackeray really devoted himself to the creation of an alternative history, and explored the nature of historical reconstruction.

In *The History of Henry Esmond*—as the title suggests—real history becomes private history; the subjective memoir of an eighteenth-century gentleman-officer, not the supposedly impartial history book, becomes the vehicle of truth (remember his comments on the Duchess of Marlborough's correspondence). It is 'dignified' history which is the fiction, the play; conversely, his own historical fiction, by dint of its recreation of the reality of eighteenth-century life, is an approach to a truer history. Consider the introduction in book 1 of *Esmond*, apparently written by Esmond himself, which exploits again the theatre image:

The actors in the old tragedies . . . piped their iambics to a tune, speaking from under a mask, and wearing stilts and a great head-dress. 'Twas thought the dignity of the Tragic Muse required these appurtenances . . . The Muse of History hath encumbered herself with ceremony as well as her Sister of the Theatre. She too wears her mask and cothurnus, and speaks to measure. She too, in our age, busies herself with the affairs only of kings . . . as if she . . . had nothing to do with the registering of the affairs of the common people. I have seen in his very old age and decrepitude the old French King Lewis the Fourteenth . . . persisting in enacting through life the part of Hero; and . . . this was but a little wrinkled old man, pock-marked, and with a great periwig and red heels to make him look tall—a hero for a book if you like, or for a brass statue or a painted ceiling . . . but what more than a man for Madame Maintenon, or the barber who shaved him . . . ? I wonder shall History ever . . . cease to be court-ridden? . . . Why shall History go on kneeling to the end of time? I am for having her rise off her knees, and take a natural posture . . . In other words, I would have History familiar rather than heroic . . .[54]

This passage concerning Louis XIV is clearly a textual parallel to one of Thackeray's most successful illustrations in the *Paris Sketchbook*, 'Rex/

---

[52] *Oxford Thackeray*, ix. 166.   [53] Ray, *Uses*, 268–9.
[54] *Oxford Thackeray*, xiii. 13–14.

Ludovicus/Rex Ludovicus', where the King's royal costume and his aged and uninspiring person appear separately, in ironic contrast to each other, before the two are combined to create the picture of a haughty king.[55]

This desire to explore the private history of historical events and individuals is clearly related to the interest of the picturesque historian in explorations of social history, the history of manners and morals, court history, and biography. Ultimately, however, the author of *Esmond* went beyond the innovations inherent in Romantic picturesque historiography to challenge the very process of historical reconstruction even as he attempted it. *Esmond* owed much to Thackeray's reading for a series of lectures, *The Humourists*, delivered in 1851. In these lectures, he had pleaded for the validity of viewing the literature of an age as its true history:

What do we look for in studying the history of a past age? Is it to learn the political transactions and characters of the leading public men? Is it to make ourselves acquainted with the life and being of the time? If we set out with the former grave purpose, where is the truth, and who believes that he has it entire? . . . I . . . say to the Muse of History, 'O venerable daughter of Mnemosyne, I doubt every statement that you have made since your ladyship was a Muse! . . . You bid me listen to a general's oration to his soldiers; Nonsense! He no more made it than Turpin made his dying speech at Newgate. You pronounce a panegyric on a hero; I doubt it . . . You offer me an autobiography: I doubt all autobiographies I ever read; except those, perhaps, of Mr. Robinson Crusoe, Mariner and other writers of his class. . . . these have no motive for concealment or half-truths; these call for no more confidence than I can safely give . . . fiction contains a greater amount of truth in solution than the volume that purports to be all true. Out of the fictious book I get all the expression of the life of the time; of the manners of the moment, the dress, the pleasures, the laughter, the ridicules of society . . . Can the heaviest historian do more for me? . . . [']'[56]

Initially, this passage seems to be a denunciation of philosophical history and a celebration of the ideals and approaches of picturesque historiography. However, Thackeray adopted a more radical stance, not only advocating that history should make use of the apparatus of fiction, but that a well-written historical fiction (which honestly admits that is a constructed narrative rather than an objective record of events) may be more truthful than any history text or source.

To the reader of this passage, it is no surprise to find Thackeray producing his historical fiction in the form of memoirs, consciously copying and rivalling not such authentic autobiographies as the diary of Samuel Pepys—but the fictional autobiographies of Daniel Defoe. The conscious subjectivity of fiction is perceived as ultimately more honest and less confining than the assumed objectivity of history. While Walter Scott, the founding father of the picturesque historical romance, distanced himself from his novels by posing as an impartial antiquarian editor—for instance, Dr Dryasdust—Thackeray decided to draw closer to the historical world he creates by entering it as a character (Henry Esmond) in the

---

[55] *Oxford Thackeray*, ii. 323.   [56] Ibid. xiii. 542–3.

tale, by making himself both editor and hero, and raising doubts about his assumed objectivity.

Thackeray's first-person narrative (though it is occasionally varied by Esmond's use of the third person) was a device common to the mid-century period, and it is important to realize how much more seriously this technique was received by a mid-nineteenth-century public. By many a reader, a first-person narrative claiming to be true was taken as true: it was considered as an autobiographical work or at least a tale based on fact, not as the literary device of a fiction. As J. C. Simmons has pointed out, the early Victorian period witnessed the writing of several mock autobiographies of historical characters—such as Anne Manning's *The Household of Sir Thomas More* (1851)—which claimed to be authentic historical documents, and were, indeed, often accepted as such. Anne Manning's works, for instance, were admitted to libraries which refused to stock fiction.[57] The autobiography which Thackeray himself mentioned admiringly, *Robinson Crusoe*, was itself just such a hoax. Thus, when Thackeray spoke of a fiction truer than conventional history, he was more serious than, perhaps, his twentieth-century critics may realize. The gravity of the enterprise which he was undertaking is confirmed by his decision to publish *Esmond* in an eighteenth-century format and, importantly, to leave the work unillustrated. This decision was surely the result of his recognition that his own 1840s style of illustration, strong on the comic and the grotesque, would be inappropriate and distracting in such an essentially serious and complex work as *Esmond*.[58] It is reminiscent, too, of the post-1850 tendency to limit or dispense with the illustrations of English history textbook.

Esmond is, therefore, a work aiming to explore with a kind of radical subtlety the area between fiction and history so well traversed by the picturesque historians of the early nineteenth century. (As Jane Millgate has seen, Thackeray's admiration for Macaulay, who seemed to him to be giving history the thrill and appeal of fiction, was an acknowledgement of a fellow-traveller. Thackeray's publisher, George Smith, also recognized the connection between the work of these two men when he asked Thackeray to write a continuation of *The History of England*.[59]) *Esmond* manages to avoid the Scylla of the popular historical novel in the style of G. P. R. James, and the Charybdis of serious 'heroic' history. On the one hand, it reverses the usual devices of the historical romance: the lost heir, Esmond, is not restored to his lands and title; the heroine turns out not to be the beautiful but heartless Beatrix, whom he initially loves, but her mother Rachel. On the other hand, we are shown historical personages, not from the perspective of the history books, but the uncomplimentary viewpoint of an increasingly disillusioned contemporary. John Churchill, the celebrated Duke of Marlborough,

---

[57] J. C. Simmons, 'Thackeray's *Esmond* and Anne Manning's "Spurious Antiquities"', *VN* 42 (1972), 22–4.

[58] Pickwoad, 'Thackeray', i. 182–3.

[59] J. Millgate, 'History *versus* Fiction: Thackeray's Response to Macaulay', in Shillingsburg, *Thackeray*, 43–58.

is shown as a mercenary and treacherous character, ready to sell his country to whoever will pay the highest price, while the Pretender is a weak womanizer, who nearly dishonours his loyal supporters in his pursuit of Beatrix—'no more than a man, and not a good man'.[60] The recognition of the selfish and debased nature of the heroes of both the English political parties, Whig and Jacobite, results in Esmond's withdrawal from the stage of public and national history to the New World: America represents a sort of ahistorical paradise where those who cannot—or will not—fit into the national narrative can take refuge. The private life of Esmond and his growing love for Rachel becomes for him, and for the reader, far more significant than political issues: 'Sure, love vincit omnia: it is immeasurably above ambition, more precious than wealth, more noble than name.'[61]

The conclusion of *Esmond* came as something of a surprise to the contemporary reader, and the novel was by no means a popular success. It is a surprise, too, perhaps, for any student of Thackeray's views on the nature of history in the 1840s. For Thackeray goes beyond the advocacy of picturesque social and cultural history as real experience of the past; he asserts instead the significance of the timeless world of personal and private emotion. But he does not stop there: the ultimate message of Esmond is not the viability of an alternative version of historical reconstruction, but the insignificance and unreliability of all historical reconstruction, in the face of human emotions and the process of human memory. As several critics have perceived, *Esmond* exposes not only the subjectivity and inaccuracy of supposed impartial 'dignified' public history, but the impossibility of objective reconstruction of the past, even at the level of personal experience.[62] J. M. Rignall has argued convincingly that the novel is the result of a 'productive inner conflict' between the nihilist and deconstructionalist tendencies of Thackeray's ironic vision, and his use of narrative to derive a pattern of meaning (i.e. a historical interpretation) from life. Thackeray watches Esmond struggle to create a meaning for history and fail; the struggle is then transferred to his own private life, and, in the love of Rachel and an idyllic home in America, Esmond does succeed in creating a meaning, though a fragile one, accepted with irony, but not cynicism.[63] Here was the full awareness of the unreality, the inauthenticity of every reconstruction of the past, including that of the author, which characterizes the work of the historian utilizing ironic emplotment. The reaction of critics to the work shows a suitable sense of unease: reviewers in *The Irish Quarterly Review*, *Bentley's Miscellany*, and *The Literary Gazette* recognized his

---

[60] *Oxford Thackeray*, xiii. 420.   [61] Ibid. xiii. 462.

[62] See W. Iser, *The Implied Reader* (Baltimore and London, 1974), 123–34; M. Rosner, 'Perspectives on *Henry Esmond*', *VN* 56 (1979), 26–31; J. H. Miller, '*Henry Esmond*: Repetition and Irony', in *Fiction and Repetition: Seven English Novels* (Cambridge, 1982), 73–115; H. Shaw, *The Forms of Historical Fiction* (Ithaca, NY, and London, 1983), 56–70. All these critics offer interpretations of the historical relativism and shifting viewpoints of the novel. For a more empirical— but superficial—attribution of these features to Thackeray's careless composition after a decision to remove criticism of Marlborough, see J. Sutherland, *Thackeray at Work* (1974), 67–73.

[63] J. M. Rignall, 'Thackeray's *Henry Esmond* and the Struggle against the Power of Time', in J. Hawthorn (ed.), *The Nineteenth Century British Novel* (1986), 81–93.

success in telling the tale in a contemporary style—one said that 'no imitation could be happier'—but they were very disturbed by the appearance of the Pretender in England, at the time of Queen Anne's death, 'a palpable violation of historical truth'. This suggests a sense of the uncomfortable at such a plausible hoax, such a play with the 'dignity of history'.[64]

Thackeray's awareness of the impossibility of objectivity did not lead him, in *Esmond*, to mock the human desire to interpret and reconstruct the past to make sense. But in the 1850s, a conviction that human nature and the human condition were a constant, thus making historical reconstruction superfluous in all but matters of costume, was to grow out of the experience of *Esmond*, and to make his vision of the past more cynical. As the demands for factual accuracy increased, so the hope of an acceptable reconstruction of the past in fictive form receded. Thackeray's belief in the basic similarity of the human condition in all ages, in a mythic rather than an historicist vision, had certainly been an undercurrent in *Esmond* but had only served as a spur towards a dynamic personal reconstruction. In *The Virginians* (1857–9), it became a cynical excuse which allowed the tired and disillusioned author to avoid the complexities of reconstruction and interpretation that he had handled with such poise in *Esmond*.

'NOTHING NEW UNDER THE SUN'

By the time he began to write *The Virginians*, Thackeray was beset by work pressures, financial worries, and declining health. His decision to illustrate the work himself suggests not only a continuing commitment to combining text and image in the style of the 1840s, but also a recognition that this work, although a sequel to *Esmond*, was a rather different (and a rather dated) enterprise.[65] The picturesque historical novel was in crisis by the late 1850s. Moreover, signs of despair at the possibility of meaningful historical reconstruction had already appeared in Thackeray's work—for instance, in the 1855 lectures, *The Four Georges*. Deceptively, they open with a confident restatement of the theory of familiar rather than heroic history: 'Not about battles, about politics, about statesmen and measures of state, did I ever think to lecture you: but to sketch the manners and

---

[64] [Anon.], 'Thackeray's *Esmond*', *Irish Quarterly Review*, 2 (1852), 849–70; [Anon.], '*Esmond and Basil*', *BM* 32 (1852), 576–86; [Anon.], '*The History of Henry Esmond*', *The Literary Gazette*, 1868 (1852), 823–25, and 1869 (1852), 839–40.

[65] The illustrations of *The Virginians* are discussed at length in Pickwoad, 'Thackeray', i. 195–213. See also J. L. Fisher, 'Image and Text in the Illustrated Novels of William Makepeace Thackeray', in C. T. Christ and J. O. Jordan (eds.), *Victorian Literature and the Victorian Visual Imagination* (Berkeley, Los Angeles, and London, 1995), 60–87: it is suggested here that Thackeray used illustrations not only to 'ironize' the text, but intended both text and image to destabilize each other, exposing the impossibility of accurate and objective representation. Clearly, this interpretation is particularly relevant to a late and disillusioned publication such as *The Virginians*.

life of the old world; to amuse for a few hours with talk about the old society'.[66] But the picturesque project of reconstructing the character of George IV proved impossible, as he was all external 'pad and tailor's work': 'there may be something behind [but] we cannot get at the character; no doubt never shall'.[67] Thackeray had begun to feel the distance between himself and the period which he studied very acutely: 'He [George IV] is dead but thirty years . . . In this quarter of a century, what a silent revolution has been working! How it has separated us from the old times and manners! How it has changed men themselves!'[68]

Thus the writer of *The Virginians* was more emphatically pessimistic about the possibilities of reconstruction and the discovery of meaning than the author of *Esmond*. This lack of confidence was reflected in Thackeray's failure to establish a clear authorial voice. While *Esmond* was a memoir, *The Virginians* was a collection of letters relating to Esmond's daughter, Rachel Warrington, and her two sons George and Harry: Thackeray seems to have adopted an editorial *persona* in order not to assess critically and weigh the worth of his purported sources, but to distance himself from their inaccuracies and relativisms in a manner impossible to Esmond the autobiographer. If the earlier work was the exploration of subjectivity, this work is an open and sometimes despairing acceptance of it which allowed the editor to recognize it in both himself and his sources, and to continue his tale regardless:

The letters of the Virginians, as the reader will presently see, from specimens shown to him, are by no means full. They are hints rather than descriptions—indications and outlines chiefly: it may be, that the present writer has mistaken forms, and filled in the colour wrongly: but, poring over the documents, I have tried to imagine the situation of the writer, where he was, and by what people surrounded . . .[69]

This editor tries to empathize with the writers of the letters and to paint a full picture by filling in the gaps imaginatively, but his interrogation of the sources is fundamentally half-hearted, lacking the conviction of Esmond's self-analysis. It can come as no surprise to the reader when Thackeray largely abdicates his editorial status in favour of the world-weary autobiographical voice of George Warrington. The author of *The Virginians* seems to have no real confidence in either his ability to produce a meaningful reconstruction of the past, or the existence of a public able and willing to read it.

In *The Virginians*, Thackeray's theme of the immutability of human nature and emotions emerges fully. He attempted to play with the differences between the habits of the eighteenth and nineteenth centuries. When young Harry Warrington sees with delight the famous author, Samuel Richardson, Thackeray teasingly remarked:

Do not let any young lady trip to her grandpapa's book-case in consequence . . . and rashly take down *Clarissa* from the shelf. She would not care to read the volumes, over

---

[66] *Oxford Thackeray*, xiii. 700.   [67] Ibid. xiii. 783.
[68] Ibid. xiii. 792.   [69] Ibid. xv. 2.

which her pretty ancestresses wept and thrilled a hundred years ago; which were commended by divines from pulpits . . . I wonder if a century hence the novels of to-day will
be hidden behind locks and wires, and make pretty little maidens blush.

But a sense that 'nothing is new under the sun' underlies this rather heavy-
handed coyness; he adds 'I wonder, are our women more virtuous than their
grandmothers, or only more squeamish? If the former, then Miss Smith of New
York is certainly more modest than Miss Smith of London, who still does not
scruple to say, that tables, pianos and animals have legs.'[70] Obviously Thackeray
thought that his female contemporaries were simply more squeamish—or even
hypocritical.

   The static yet repetitive nature of human experience is suggested by the great
number of allegorical and classical figures which appear in this work, standing,
like Platonic ideals, as the essential idea from which multiplying but similar
exempla derive. They feature in the pictorial capitals which head the chapters
(the use of these small vignettes to make ironic comments on the contents of the
text was a technique for which Thackeray had a special fondness and which he
had used with great effect in *Vanity Fair* and *The Newcomes*). Examples include
the Cupid of chapter 75, which is entitled 'The Course of True Love',[71] and
Melpomene who appears at the head of chapter 63.[72] There are many allusions in
both text and image to the seventeenth- and eighteenth-century classical theatre,
a resurrection of that particular metaphor of artificiality which clearly appealed to
the novel's world-weary narrator. As illustrator Thackeray was careful to ensure
historical accuracy in his presentation of eighteenth-century dress,[73] but the allusions to the stage provide an ironical perspective which undermines this concern
for period details. Eighteenth-century actors had tended to perform classical
plays in largely contemporary, rather than historical, costumes; in portraying
these anachronistic costumes, Thackeray indicated his sense of the essentially
unaltering nature of human experience. Thus he dismissed the obsessive search
for authentic detail characteristic of picturesque historiography and its scientific
successor, even as he engaged in it to produce his illustrations. Not surprisingly,
one of the more favourable reviews of the novel came from the critic of *The Daily
News*, who appeared to share Thackeray's contention of the basic immutability
of human experience, with 'difference of drapery' merely, from age to age.[74]

   Thackeray's attraction to the classically based theatre and literature of
Augustan England was natural, since classicism was (for Thackeray and many of
his contemporaries) the cultural expression of belief in eternal values and the
immutability of human nature. These classical allusions are frequent. Pyramus
and Thisbe in eighteenth-century costume appear at the head of chapter 88, for
the subject of the chapter is their story resurrected in eighteenth-century form:
the tale of the love of George Warrington and Theo Lambert, opposed by his

[70] *Oxford Thackeray*, xv. 273.   [71] Ibid. xv. 791.   [72] Ibid. xv. 659.
[73] Pickwoad, 'Thackeray', i. 201.
[74] [Anon.], '*The Virginians*', *The Daily News* (30 Dec. 1859), 2.

mother, Madame Esmond, and her father, Mr Lambert.[75] George is the narrator; years later, finding a 'dreadful' letter to his mother in which he threw off her authority, he burns it, 'not choosing that the story of domestic grief and disunion should remain amongst our family annals for future Warringtons to gaze upon, mayhap, and disobedient sons to hold up as examples of foregone domestic rebellions.'[76] In an attempt to prevent history repeating itself, he leaves instructions for his own love letters to be burnt. But for all this, he knows that disobedient sons will rebel anyway: 'We appeal, we imprecate, we go down on our knees, we demand blessing . . . the great course of the world moves on; we pant and strive and struggle . . . we pass away and other little strugglers succeed; our days are spent; our night comes; and another morning comes, and another sun rises, which shines on us no more.'[77] He adds: 'I forget what happened stage by stage and day by day; nor, for the instruction of future ages, does it much matter. When my descendants have love scrapes of their own, they will find their own means of getting out of their troubles.'[78] Here Thackeray completely jettisoned both the essential detail beloved of the picturesque reconstructor, and the didactic function of history expounded by the philosophical historian. George narrates, with a combination of futility and concealment, the story of his own marriage (which he thinks of as a dangerous lesson for young readers) to an audience he believes will not listen anyway (his own son Miles has not read his father's poems and plays).[79] A reconstruction of his own past is surrendered by the autobiographer, who himself finds it arbitrary and uninstructive. As Rignall indicates, whereas in *Esmond* Thackeray allows the hero to create his own reconstruction of the past, however fragile and subjective, in *The Virginians* no attempt to make a real interpretation of history, however private and personal, is accepted. Rignall concludes that the later work 'capitulates to that nihilistic sense of transience which *Henry Esmond* both acknowledged and resisted, and effectively undoes the achievement of the earlier novel'.[80]

In *Esmond*, Thackeray had dismissed the public sphere of national history, finding value and meaning instead in the private sphere of personal relationships. In *The Virginians*, neither public nor private events have the potential for meaningful reconstruction: indeed, at the very beginning of the novel, a serpent enters the ahistorical paradise of *Esmond* (America) as political and national conflicts began to disturb her peace. The central focus of *The Virginians*—two brothers, George and Harry, tied by blood yet separated by the American War of Independence—suggested that Thackeray might have considered presenting a confrontation and resolution of the rival claims of the personal and the private, and the public and national, life. This promise of a reprise of *Esmond*—possibly

---

[75] *Oxford Thackeray*, xv. 823.   [76] Ibid. xv. 823.

[77] Ibid. xv. 824.   [78] Ibid. xv. 825.

[79] See J. Carlisle, *The Sense of an Audience: Dickens, Thackeray, and George Eliot at Mid-Century* (Athens, Ga., 1981), 142–65, for an able analysis of Thackeray's perception of his audience in *Esmond* and *The Virginians*.

[80] Rignall, 'Thackeray's *Henry Esmond*', 92–3.

Fig. 35. W. M. Thackeray, *Capital W*, from W. M. Thackeray, *The Oxford Thackeray*, ed. G. Saintsbury, 17 vols. (1908), xv. 242

with a less uncompromising ending—is not fulfilled: although George Warrington's rebellion against his mother initially parallels the rebellion of the American colonies against the mother country, Thackeray lacked the interest to pursue this or any other similar theme linking the personal and public spheres. Curiously, the War of Independence plays remarkably little role in *The Virginians*, where Thackeray abandoned public events in favour of private ones. But even the issue of generational conflict in domestic life seemed meaningless to him, a repeating revolution whose circle could neither be varied or broken. This adherence, even on the level of personal politics, to a pessimistic (and tradition-ally classical) view of history as circular and ever-repeating only underlines how still more futile and distant the course of the history of the nation—or nations—continued to seem to the ageing author.

    This entire disillusionment with history-making in any form is reflected in the use of historical allusions in *The Virginians*: they are intended to draw attention, not edifyingly but bathetically, to the precedents for the actions and emotions of the characters, almost as if to save the author the trouble of reconstruction, of detailing the individual case.[81] Like Pyramus and Thisbe, Rosamund and Queen

---

[81] This might well have been increased by his sense that readers were growing indifferent to historical reconstructions anyway. In a letter to W. F. Synge in 1858, he complained that *The*

Fig. 36. W. M. Thackeray, *Capital I*, from
Oxford Thackeray, xv. 843

Eleanor, the women of the eternal love triangle appear at the head of chapter 24,
clad in eighteenth-century dress (Fig. 35).[82] The allusion here is to Henry's Aunt
Bernstein and his fiancée and cousin, the elderly and unattractive Maria.
Thackeray satirically drew the parallel in the preceding chapter: 'What . . . if his
fell aunt's purpose was answered and his late love is killed as dead by her poison-
ing communications as the fair Rosamund by her royal and legitimate rival?'[83] A
similar allusion occurs in chapter 80, where the capital and the title both refer to
the Indian princess, Pocahontas, who saved the English explorer, Captain Smith,
from death at the hands of her tribe (Fig. 36).[84] The chapter draws a comparison
between Pocahontas and George's wife Theo, who shields him from the slings

Virginians 'sadly lacks story, and people wont care about old times, or all the trouble I take in
describing them'. Sutherland, *Thackeray*, 109.

[82] *Oxford Thackeray*, xv. 242.   [83] Ibid. xv. 237.   [84] Ibid. xv. 843.

and arrows of outrageous theatre critics when his tragedy, *Pocahontas*, is slated. Ironically, one reason for the failure of the play is the appearance of Miss Pritchard, the actress playing the heroine, 'dressed exactly like an Indian Princess'. Sampson, George's clerical friend, comments: 'Why . . . would you have Caractacus painted blue like an ancient Briton, or Bouduca with nothing but a cow-skin?' George adds: 'And indeed it may be that fidelity to history was the cause of the ridicule cast upon my tragedy'.[85] Here the one-time author-cum-illustrator of spoofs deriving much of their comedy from the ridicule of clumsy anachronism, envisaged the possibility of anxious accuracy being equally laughable. Historical reconstruction is dismissed with a smile as an artificial game, play-acting. Rignall's summary of the historical philosophy of *The Virginians* is illuminating: 'Instead of the positive pattern of continuity and change . . . there is a combination of sameness and loss . . . Repetition in this novel does not generate meaning so much as destroy it, hollowing out the significance of present experience. Thus life seems governed by a negative double law: nothing stands . . . and everything repeats itself.'[86]

Once again, critical opinion was uneasy, and seemed as unconvinced by historical reconstructions in a fictional form as was Thackeray himself. The reviewer of *The Edinburgh Review* stressed the incompatibility of real and fictional elements in the novel, complaining that the introduction of real characters broke the illusion of the novel in a way that the mere historical background of *Vanity Fair* did not. He suggested that Thackeray abandon 'this hybrid form of composition', and write a proper history instead.[87] Thackeray did not write the history, but his last unfinished historical novel did move in the other direction of a fictional tale to which history formed only a discreet background.

That nothing is new under the sun was an opinion which it took Thackeray some time and experiment to develop. A'Beckett arrived at this conclusion with the rapidity of a cruder intellect, which would not achieve the same depth of self-awareness of subjectivity apparent in Thackeray. For him, repetition did generate meaning. In the Preface of the book version of *The Comic History*, he wrote: 'Motives are treated as unceremoniously as men; and as the human disposition was much the same in former times as it is in the present day, it has been judged by the rules of common sense, which are alike in every period.'[88] The comparisons of historical figures to contemporary social types, verbally and visually, was not only used to deflate the Romantic views of these characters, but to point to the basic constant in history provided by human nature. One can find a good example of this technique in the treatment of the traditional anecdote of the meeting of Elizabeth Grey and Edward IV, a much illustrated subject. Both A'Beckett and Leech are ruthless in exposing the mercenary and match-making propensities of Elizabeth and her mother: the former is characterized as 'a finished pupil in the school of flirtation', while the latter is described as 'an old match-making

[85] *Oxford Thackeray*, xv. 848.   [86] Rignall, 'Thackeray's *Henry Esmond*', 93.
[87] [G. Smith], '*The Virginians*', *ER* 110 (1859), 438–53.   [88] A'Beckett, *History*, i. p. vi.

mother, who exhibited all those manoeuvring qualities which constitute, in the present day, the art of getting a daughter off to the best advantage'.[89] Leech's illustration, with its mixture of modern and medieval dress, shows Elizabeth as a flirtatious young miss, with a rather low cleavage, a silly little parasol, and a pug, and cunningly avoids inclusion of her sons (the yawning boy is surely a page), which might draw attention to more sympathetic motives for her conduct.[90]

A'Beckett and Leech were concerned to identify common 'types' across the ages, thus equating all periods of history as equally good—or bad. A'Beckett remarked, *vis-à-vis* the hunting Bishop of Ely, that 'the Fox-Parson is a character as old as the days of Richard II', and Leech, by attiring his subject in a mixture of medieval and modern dress, asserted the permanence of this social type.[91] Even when things appear to have changed, A'Beckett suggested, there is an underlying continuity. After a description of the battle by ordeal, he commented: 'it may seem unjust and ridiculous to the present generation that the strongest arm or stoutest spear should have settled a legal difference, but even in our own times it is frequently the longest purse which determines the issue of a law-suit.'[92] Like Thackeray, A'Beckett returns to the metaphor of the theatre but, like Thackeray again, uses it for a different purpose than his original one. The image here is used, not to expose the artificiality of the early nineteenth-century portrayal of national history, but to suggest the existence of eternal human types and ways of behaviour:

We have seen what our ancestors in their habits, pleasures and pursuits, none of which differed materially from those that people of the present generation are or have been in the habit of following . . . though in the drama, 'each man in his time plays many parts', there is scarcely one of which he can be called the original representative.[93]

Thackeray's last historical work, *Denis Duval*, represents a retreat from the difficulties of historical reconstruction, and the question of the constancy or otherwise of human nature. Here history has become a background, not a vital component of the novel: it is the means of escape into a more Romantic era where adventures may take place. As Ray points out, this work 'does not pretend to be more than a simple story of adventure',[94] in the same category as many of the historical romances inspired by Robert Louis Stevenson's historical novels.

In the late 1850s, A'Beckett and Leech, too, were in retreat. Their assertion of the basic similarity of human behaviour in all ages was a extension of their satire of contemporary habits and personalities to the historical past. To Leech, the clothing of present-day problems in partial historical dress, and relating past and present conduct, was less important than a more straightforward criticism of here and now: the fashion for contemporary subjects was making itself felt. The artist W. P. Frith wrote in his biography, *John Leech: His Life and Work*:

[89] A'Beckett, *History*, i. 281.   [90] Ibid. i. 282.   [91] Ibid. i. 205–6.
[92] Ibid. i. 200.   [93] Ibid. i. 206.
[94] G. N. Ray, *Thackeray: The Age of Wisdom 1847–63* (Oxford, 1958), 411.

About the year 1852 I began the first of a series of pictures from modern life, then quite a novelty in the hands of anyone who could paint tolerably. When the picture, which was called 'Many Happy Returns of the Day' . . . was finished, Leech came to see it, and expresses his satisfaction on finding an artist who could leave what he called 'mouldy costumes' for the habits and manners of everyday life.[95]

Lindsay Errington points to the importance of Leech's influence on Millais in directing his attention to subjects from modern life, rather than historical and literary ones.[96] In Leech's work, the real history was modern, as Kitton's comments show: 'His experience of our social life . . . make[s] up such a history of his time as to the future historian will be invaluable.'[97] A'Beckett, too, had earlier struck the note of a man of the day: after a description of seventeenth-century literature in *The Comic History*, he commented: 'The "palmy days of dramatic literature" are, according to the ordinary acceptation of those who use the term, any days but the present and it is not improbable that our own will be looked back upon and lamented as the genuine "palmy days" by a generation of grumblers who may come after us'.[98] Thus speaks the voice of the perceptive cynic.

CONCLUSION: A CRISIS OF TRANSITION

By the 1850s, then, a crisis in picturesque historical reconstruction was under way which frequently gave rise to contradictory convictions in the work of the same person. This crisis was caused by the continuing drive for authenticity, and the growing sense of the inadequacy and artificiality of attempts so far to revive the past. It led to a new concentration on issues of contemporary life, to the use of the past as an instrument of escapist adventure, to the assertion of the immutability of human nature in all ages—to a variety of responses, many of them manifested in the work of Thackeray and his less talented contemporaries, A'Beckett and Leech. These men, in their texts and illustrations, developed an ironic and self-conscious perspective on the historiographical modes of their age which sounds familiar to our own postmodernist generation. Thackeray's realization of the unreality of even his most self-aware reconstructions inevitably makes his analysis more significant than that of A'Beckett and Leech. But the common-sense standards of these two men, with their crude but shrewd critique of historical sources and authorities, parodied the contemporary development of source criticism then commencing in the professional academic world. If Thackeray's historical fiction predicted the mythical and escapist paths pursued by late nineteenth-century historical novelists, A'Beckett's and Leech's comic collaboration caricatured the concerns of the scientific and positivist historiography which was to dominate later Victorian history-writing.

[95] Frith, *Leech*, ii. 15.
[96] L. Errington, *Social and Religious Themes in English Art 1840–60* (New York and London, 1984), 392–401.
[97] Kitton, *Leech*, 46–7.   [98] A'Beckett, *History*, ii. 251.

9

The Abuse of Antiquity and the Uses of Myth: The Illustrated Historical Novel after 1850

'I hope it's not historical Mr Trollope? . . . whatever you do, don't be historical, your historical novel is not worth a damn [*La Vendee* (1850)].[1] Thus the foreman of Hurst and Blackett to Anthony Trollope in 1857, when the novelist presented the manuscript of *The Three Clerks* (1858) to him. Trollope achieved great literary success in the 1860s and 1870s partially because he had abandoned historical fiction in favour of novels about English contemporary life. Trollope's experience as a historical novelist was not unique:[2] one of the causes of the decline of the picturesque historical novel after 1850 was undoubtedly the public preference for novels with contemporary settings. But there were other reasons, too. Students of nineteenth-century historiography agree that, during the picturesque period of the 1830s and 1840s, there was 'greater emphasis on empathy than analysis', which had encouraged reconstructive historical fiction:[3] the focus of both historians and historical novelists 'fell upon the concept of history as a narrative rather than a dissertation'.[4] After 1850, history was developing as a discipline and its practitioners classed it more with the social sciences; their preoccupation with textual analysis of documents and scientific format worked against the picturesque historical novel. Accordingly, a fictional format became far less acceptable and less adaptable as the means by which the history of the nation was to be imbibed by its citizens.

This chapter considers the illustrated historical novel after 1850, and its response to the rise of scientific history, the creation of professional historians and teachers of history, themselves part of the expanding bureaucracy of a nation-state. The works of three writers—Elizabeth Gaskell, George Eliot, and Charlotte Mary Yonge—are discussed in the context of an examination of the problems of the illustrated historical novel after 1850, and responses to it. Chapter 10 extends the discussion to the later, feeble works of Ainsworth, in an analysis which acts as

[1] A. Trollope, *Autobiography* (1883; Oxford, 1989 edn.), 110–11.
[2] See W. Dunn, *R. D. Blackmore: The Author of Lorna Doone* (1956), 129–30. Blackmore's famous work was initially rejected by many publishers because 'the public took no interest in a time so remote'.
[3] P. Levine, *The Amateur and the Professional* (Cambridge, 1986), 72–3.
[4] J. C. Simmons, *The Novelist as Historian* (The Hague and Paris, 1973), 39.

a counterfoil to the more successful and challenging solutions of the writers considered in this chapter.

THE LATER NINETEENTH-CENTURY HISTORICAL NOVEL:
FICTION CURBED BY HISTORY

Questions of accuracy and authenticity were still at the heart of the problem of the historical novel after 1850: in a sense, it was the very success of picturesque historiography in demanding a convincing reconstruction of the national past which led to its demise. The expectations of the audience for the historical novels placed an impossible tension on authors: critics were as concerned about factual accuracy as ever, with a more profound understanding of authenticity which stressed psychological characterization of period and person, but they still insisted on—yet were dissatisfied by—copious historical details. A reviewer in *The Edinburgh Review* of 1859 recognized that 'the necessity of preserving antiquarian correctness must keep the critical judgement of the writer always in a state of vigilance incompatible with the intense and unshackled exertion of the creative imagination'. But, while he deplored the currency of novels where 'the sole object is to cram us with antiquities', he was equally critical of historical novels which were full of imaginary details, 'history written with the licence of fiction . . . dangerous to the integrity of historical truth'.[5] The contradictory demands of the critics and the public made the writing of the historical novel an extremely difficult affair.

While continuing to research their historical novels intensively, novelists used various concepts and techniques to address the problem of authenticity. Frequently, like Thackeray, they avoided the problem of historical characterization by asserting the immutability of human nature and the essential resemblance of all ages. The last paragraph of Charles Kingsley's *Hypatia* (1853) provides a classic statement of this kind: 'There is nothing new under the sun. The thing that has been, is that which will be.'[6] Such a philosophy had a multitude of virtues: in addition to relieving the historical novelist of the labours of picturesque historical reconstruction (as Thackeray had discovered), it legitimated a variety of displacements in terms of time, place, and person, and underpinned redefinitions of the identity of the historical novel itself, its purposes, and its intended audience. While many of the features considered here (such as the use of foreign settings, for example) were present in various picturesque historical novels of the 1830s and 1840s, they undoubtedly appeared with much greater frequency after 1850.

Because the concept of all ages as fundamentally the same was becoming so widespread, historical novels intended as explicit and pointed commentaries on

[5] [G. Smith], '*The Virginians*', *ER* 110 (1859), 440–1.
[6] C. Kingsley, *Hypatia, or, New Foes with an Old Face*, 2 vols. (1853), ii. 337.

contemporary national issues frequently eschewed national history itself, paradoxically addressing such issues by reference to a far distant period and a far distant culture: the past was indeed another country. Kingsley's *Hypatia*, Nicholas Wiseman's *Fabiola*, and John Henry Newman's *Callista* all used early Christian history to reflect on present religious concerns: they have rightly been seen as primarily vehicles for 'dogmatic exposition',[7] which emphasized 'the meaning and relevance of the past to the present'.[8] Other novels in which the predominant concern with current issues was more disguised—'not meditations on history itself but meditations taking place in an historical environment'[9]—included John Shorthouse's *John Inglesant* (1881) and Walter Pater's *Marius the Epicurean* (1885). *John Inglesant* is the only one set in England (and then only intermittently).

The problems of authenticity and the concept of the immutability of human nature provoked the use of various devices to structure the narrative and background history itself in the historical novel. The overwhelming preponderance of fictional, or near-fictional, characters as the main agents cannot escape notice: such picturesque novelists as Scott and Ainsworth, had, of course, used fictional heroes and heroines, but without such dread of employing real historical figures. In *The Cloister and the Hearth*, Reade chose a sixteenth-century European setting for his novel before further removing it from the arena of the national and the public by displacing the hero of his novel: he made the father of Erasmus, rather than Erasmus himself, the hero. His opening paragraph showed his reluctance to engage with well-known historical characters, for it celebrates the virtues of 'men and women of no note'. His tale was to be 'the strange history of a pair, who lived untrumpeted and died unsung'.[10] Other writers peopled their works entirely with fictional characters, as Dickens did in *A Tale of Two Cities*: his use of fictional characters mirrored his conviction that the solution to the historical evil which provoked the Revolution was essentially a private and timeless Christian one.[11] This ahistorical (and non-national) interpretation of events contrasts sharply with most popular historical treatments of the French Revolution, which smugly compared the gradual progress of the English nation towards political liberty and economic prosperity with the catastrophe which met the reactionary government and aristocracy of France.

The structure of many historical novels produced after 1850 reflected the centrality of a subject besides history, or the philosophical conviction of the author of the immutability of human experience. Historical novels rarely owned themselves as such, and emphasized their distance from history proper, and particularly national history. In *The Cloister and the Hearth*, Read saw his tale as 'fiction . . . curbed by history'; he would not describe the career of Erasmus who

---

[7] A. Fleischmann, *The English Historical Novel from Walter Scott to Virginia Woolf* (Baltimore, 1971), 150.

[8] A. Sanders, *The English Historical Novel* (1979), 147.   [9] Fleischmann, *Novel*, 151.

[10] C. Reade, *The Cloister and the Hearth*, 4 vols. (1861) i. 1–2.

[11] Fleischmann, *Novel*, 126.

'belongs not to Fiction but to History'.[12] R. D. Blackmore, in the Preface to *Lorna Doone* (1869), also disclaimed the traditional role of the historical novelist, classifying his work as 'a romance' and avoiding 'the dignity or . . . the difficulty of an historic novel'.[13] Blackmore identified his novel with the narrative form of legend, when he commented that, for 'any son of Exmoor', it 'cannot fail to bring to mind the nurse-tales of his childhood' on which it was based.[14] Frequently the structure of the narrative of historical novels of the period was provided, as with *Lorna Doone*, by legend or myth; also typical is the retreat to the marginal, the provincial, the isolated, for the setting of the novel.

Historical novelists writing in the latter half of the nineteenth-century often seemed to anticipate a diminished audience for the traditional picturesque fiction. Some historical novels were simply presented as adventure stories for young people: Kingsley's *Westward Ho!* (1855), a celebration of English Protestantism and nationhood, was nevertheless intended only for a juvenile audience. Older historical novels were already suffering relegation to the juvenile market: Leslie Stephen claimed that *Ivanhoe* had 'rightly descended from the library to the schoolroom', as it was 'the most amusing nonsense',[15] but another critic could still view it as a suitable book to 'place before the mind of a young student of history vivid . . . picture of life in England in the time of the Crusades'.[16] The two motives here suggested propelled the historical novel of the juvenile market: amusement and—though less frequently—instruction. By the end of the century, new historical novels were often written for young readers, and most aimed to amuse only, dispensing with much concern for the traditional claims of historical reconstruction. R. L. Stevenson's *Kidnapped* (1886) and *Catriona* (1893) are the best examples of this genre. In the dedication of *Kidnapped*, Stevenson confessed 'how little I am touched by the desire of accuracy', describing his tale with a deliberate artlessness as 'a book for the winter evening schoolroom when the tasks are over'.[17]

Meanwhile, illustration, too, was not unaffected by movements which emphasized modernity as an important characteristic of art. The impetus given to illustration by the Romantic movement, with its emphasis on associations of the sister arts,[18] faltered after 1850 with the rise of Realism and Impressionism, movements interested in contemporary life and the insights of science.[19] Even the Pre-Raphaelites—devotees of historical and Romantic subject-matter—were at this time turning towards the portrayal of contemporary life and the 'Modern Moral

[12] Reade, *Cloister*, iv. 430, 434.

[13] R. D. Blackmore, *Lorna Doone: A Romance of Exmoor*, 3 vols. (1869), i, preface.

[14] Ibid.

[15] L. Stephen, 'A Few Words about Scott', in *Hours in a Library* 2 vols. (1874–9), 1. 245–6.

[16] [H. Lawrance], 'Novels and Novelists', *QR* 30 (1859), 460. It is significant that the reviewer was one of the women historians considered earlier.

[17] R. L. Stevenson, *Kidnapped and Catriona* (1886, 1893; Oxford, 1986 edn.), p. xii.

[18] W. Vaughan, *Romantic Art* (1978), 273–6.

[19] P. Pool, *Impressionism* (1967), 11–19; L. Nochlin, *Realism* (1971), 23–33.

subject'.[20] While historical genre continued to be popular until the close of the century, it was increasingly rivalled by paintings of contemporary subjects. Historical novels in particular suffered from this emphasis upon the modern, and became less frequently illustrated than other contemporary works. Illustrations were notably absent in book editions of many historical novels, except those which had appeared earlier as serials in magazines. In such cases as these, one suspects that the illustrations often appeared as much as an automatic feature of the magazine format as a matter of conscious choice.

Illustration, like historical text, was subject to internal changes. With the advent of the 'Sixties Style' of illustration came a less intimate association between author and illustrator, and signs that both author and illustrator were more absorbed in their respective artistic aims than in collaborative enterprises.[21] To some extent, illustrations appeared as an unimportant but traditional appendage to the text. This might well explain why little attention has been paid to the illustrated historical novel after 1850, despite the fact that those novels which still carried illustrations offer particularly interesting opportunities to study the decline of the picturesque historical novel. For the avoidance of issues of authenticity apparent in some historical fictions extended to the illustrations of such novels. The illustrator of *A Tale of Two Cities*, H. K. Browne, showed the same indifference to historical details as Dickens: E. G. Kitton pointed out, for instance, that there was 'little attempt at archaeological accuracy in the costumes'.[22] Clearly, like Dickens, he was concentrating on the timeless, personal, human elements of the tale: one of the features of his work in its final chapter.

In fact, with textual avoidance of the problems of historical authenticity and antiquarian detail came a diminished type of historical illustration, which only mimicked the imagery of the picturesque publications of the 1830s and 1840s: it is apparent in an illustrated edition of *Lorna Doone*, which appeared in 1883. Some of the illustrations were straightforward metaphoric illustrations of episodes from the text,[23] but these were not reconstructions so much as genre scenes with fictional characters in some period costume. The vast majority of illustrations, however, were topographical views of Exmoor in its present state.[24] The artist, F. Armstrong, reflected the Romantic emphasis of the text, as Blackmore recognized, with some confusion: 'Mr Armstrong has indulged in fiction almost as freely as I have . . . my mind misgave me about the wrong impression which must ensue, but . . . I was told, "Why, the work is a romance, and the pictures must be romantic".'[25] A half-hearted throwback to the topographical preoccupations of picturesque illustration, they seemed old-fashioned and inaccurate in the brave new world of scientific authenticity. The features of this work's illustrations—the use of genre-like and intimate domestic subjects, rather than historic set pieces,

[20] T. Hilton, *The Pre-Raphaelites* (1970), 133–59.
[21] J. R. Harvey, *Victorian Novelists and their Illustrators* (1970), 162–6.
[22] F. G. Kitton, *Dickens and his Illustrators* (1899), 112.
[23] e.g. R. D. Blackmore, *Lorna Doone: A Romance of Exmoor* (1883), facing 134.
[24] e.g. ibid. 34, 25.   [25] W. Dunn, *R. D. Blackmore* (1956), 140.

and the lack of real collaboration and sympathy between author and illustrator—
will be seen in these last two chapters.

Works for the juvenile market, however, most frequently carried illustrations:
the implication is, unmistakably, that illustrations were only really suitable for
youth or the frivolous reader. The illustrations of some works betrayed a didactic
purpose. The A. and G. Black edition of Scott's novels of 1868 included some
original plates from the Magnum Opus edition of 1830–1, but added others which
seem to be educational. In *The Fair Maid of Perth*, William Allan's plate of
St Valentine's Day is included, but there is a variety of other illustrations such
as *Candlestick of Robert the Bruce; Abbotsford* and *Ancient Salt-dish*.[26] These
metanymic illustrations suggest a lurking didactic impulse, but even more clearly
indicate a slapdash attitude to illustration: unlike the best examples of such illustrations in picturesque publications, they often have only the most tenuous
relationship to the text. Many historical novels with illustrations for children,
however, aimed entirely at their amusement rather than their edification. Lavish
illustrations appear with Henty's *At Agincourt: A Tale of the White Hoods of Paris*
(1897), an adventure story for boys.

SYLVIA'S LOVERS: FACTS AND FABLES, PUBLIC AND PERSONAL, TIME AND ETERNITY

Elizabeth Gaskell's *Sylvia's Lovers* was published in February 1863; the fourth
edition, which incorporated the novelist's corrections and was illustrated by
George Du Maurier, appeared in December of that year. A tragic love-story, it
represented something of a departure from Gaskell's established territory as a
writer of contemporary industrial and domestic fictions (although her shorter
tales were sometimes historical). The historical period she chose for the novel—
the Napoleonic Wars—was the source of deep personal nostalgia: it was the
period of her parents' youth, and her father's experiments as a scientific farmer
and his later position as a keeper of Treasury records—not to mention the loss
of Gaskell's only brother at sea—all left traces in *Sylvia's Lovers*. No doubt
influenced by the conviction evidenced in her *Life of Charlotte Bronte* (1857) that
Yorkshire was a sequestered and almost barbaric region, Gaskell seems to have
deliberately selected a setting far from the political and historical centres of
national life: the provincial is here a metaphor for the parochial and the personal.
In *Sylvia's Lovers*, a conflict between the claims of the emerging nation-state and
the rights of the individual was to play a major part. Ultimately the public history
of the nation—indeed, history itself—was dwarfed by Gaskell's affirmation of the
personal and the spiritual, reflected in the presence of myth and eternity.

This essentially ahistorical perspective was not immediately apparent in
Gaskell's preparations for the writing of *Sylvia's Lovers*, which exhibited her

---

[26] W. Scott, *The Fair Maid of Perth* (1824; 2 vols., Edinburgh, 1868 edn.), i, frontispiece, 93;
ii. 187.

participation in the contemporary concern for historical authenticity; the historical and topographical background of the novel was carefully researched. In
November 1859, just after she had conceived the idea for *Sylvia's Lovers*, Gaskell
paid a visit to the port of Whitby, the Monkshaven of the book.[27] After this initial
survey, she 'took all possible pains to obtain such details as were procurable' from
a variety of sources. One of these was George Young's *History of Whitby* (1817), a
work lent to her by George Corny, a resident of the town.[28] This supplied the
names of most of the characters in the novel—Robson, Wilson, Dixon, Fishburn,
Coulson, and Dawson—as well as those of genuine Whitby ships such as *The
Resolution* and *The Aimwell*.[29] In the novel, Philip (one of the heroine Sylvia's
two lovers and eventually her husband) was employed by the Foster brothers:
their business and banking concern was inspired by the Whitby bank founded by
the Sanders brothers in 1779.[30] It was no doubt in Young's *History* that Gaskell
first read about the press-gang riot of 1793, the historical crux of the novel. It was
described as the 'most serious riot now remembered in Whitby', and an 'old man'
was mentioned, who was later executed for his part in 'encouraging the rioters':[31]
this old man was the model for Sylvia's father, Daniel Robson. Another important source was William Scoresby's *An Account of the Arctic Regions* (1820).
Gaskell used several of Scoresby's whale-fishing anecdotes in the novel: his tale
of a Dutch harpooner who rode on the back of a whale was the source for
Robson's similar story.[32] Gaskell also studied Admiralty records and the reports
of the trials of the Whitby rioters of 1793.[33] She corresponded with General
Perronet Thompson on the subject of press-gangs, visited the British Museum,
and consulted Sir Charles Napier.[34]

Nevertheless, the historical background of the novel remains a background
indeed: the national politics of the 1790s often seem to form a mere backdrop to
events in the personal lives of the main characters, as a brief summary of the plot
shows. The novel tells the Romantic tale of Sylvia Robson, courted by two lovers,
the flamboyant sailer Charley Kinraid and the quiet shopman Philip Hepburn.
Charley, whom she loves, is press-ganged and, after the execution of her father for
participation in a rising against the press-gang, she reluctantly marries Philip.
The revelation that Philip has known of her lover's fate and concealed his message to Sylvia leads her to reject her husband, who in despair joins the army. At
the siege of Acre he saves Charley's life and returns to Monkshaven, being reconciled to his wife and daughter on his deathbed. Reviews of the novel naturally
concentrated on this central tale. The reviewer for *The Athenaeum* described
Sylvia as 'charming' and Philip as 'as wise and excellent and disagreeable a young

[27] W. Gerin, *Elizabeth Gaskell: A Biography* (Oxford, 1976), 212–15.

[28] A. W. Ward, 'Introduction', to E. Gaskell, *Sylvia's Lovers* (1863; 1906 edn.), p. xxiii.

[29] G. Young, *A History of Whitby and Streonshalh Abbey; with a Statistical Survey of the
Vicinity*, 2 vols. (Whitby, 1817), ii. 524, 548, 549, 566–7, 570.

[30] Ibid. ii. 581.   [31] Ibid. ii. 605 n.

[32] W. Scoresby, *An Account of the Arctic Regions, with a History and Description of the Northern
Whale-Fishery*, 2 vols. (Edinburgh, 1820), ii. 365–7.

[33] Gerin, *Gaskell*, 216–17.   [34] Ward, 'Introduction', p. xxv.

man as can well be imagined'. The analysis of Philip's married life was considered a work of 'genius', and the ending was 'finely worked up and as true as it is powerful'.[35] The critic of *The Westminster Review*, although interested in the account of the conflict between the people of Monkshaven and the press-gang, gave priority to a sketch of the plot, commenting on Gaskell's 'cordial sympathy with all things human'.[36]

That the Romantic plot indicated in the title is the centre of the novel was reflected by the illustrator, George Du Maurier. His illustrations neatly encapsulate the principal elements of the plot: the first shows Philip teaching Sylvia to read, catching both the pedantry of his courtship and the repulsion of Sylvia; the second shows Sylvia and Charley Kinraid declaring their mutual love; the third illustrates the moment when the despairing Philip finds his wife in the arms of Kinraid, newly returned from sea; and the last shows little Bella—Philip and Sylvia's daughter—giving her (as yet unrecognized) father some bread in an unconscious gesture of reconciliation.[37] The generic eighteenth-century costume in which the characters are dressed and the simple backgrounds against which they are projected would not have demanded overmuch historical research. These illustrations are close to many anecdotal historical genre paintings produced in the later nineteenth century, of which works such as H. S. Marks's *What is it?* and Frederick Goodall's *Puritan and Cavalier* (1886) are the most extreme and frivolous examples, portraying fictional characters in everyday situations in standardized historical dress.[38]

But although *Sylvia's Lovers* is fundamentally a domestic drama, peopled with fictional characters—except for Sir Sidney Smith, who appears very briefly at the siege of Acre—Gaskell's relationship with her historical material was not simplistic. At significant junctures, the history of the nation acts a catalyst in the personal lives of the Robson family and Sylvia's two suitors. Indeed, the novel embodies Gaskell's reflections on the interactions between the public history of the nation and the private life of the individual, especially the effect of government on society. The first chapter represents the conflict between the needs of government and the rights of the individual, in the seizure of returning sailors from their families by the press-gang: Gaskell stressed the private angle which made this act of government 'tyranny'.[39] This was not because she was unable to appreciate the government's justification. Similarly, the debate on the press-gang between Robson and Philip was not an opportunity to voice criticism, but a further study of the effects of government on the personal experience of the governed. Philip's argument that empressment is 'for the good of the nation' is not wrong, but it exhibits an ignorance of the personal dimensions of this act. Scornfully bidding

---

[35] [Anon.], 'New Novels: *Sylvia's Lovers*', *The Athenaeum*, 1844 (1863).

[36] [Anon.], 'Belle Lettres', *WR* 23 (1863), 622–33.

[37] E. Gaskell, *Sylvia's Lovers* (1863), frontispiece, 93, 194, 481.

[38] See Edward Morley and Frank Milner, '*And When Did You Last See Your Father?*' (1992), 50, 64.

[39] Gaskell, *Lovers*, 7.

the 'nation, go hang!', Robson challenges him to find a law against 'pleasing our lass' in the matter of a new cloak.[40] It is a palpable hit, as Philip will later use the press-gang law to secure the removal of Kinraid, thus depriving Sylvia of choice in the matter of her suitors. Gaskell's angle is not that of an opposition member, but a personal, private view. As the matter of the press-gang is for Robson, so for Gaskell law and government are 'personal in some unspoken way'.[41]

The conflict of public and personal is evident in Gaskell's treatment of the funeral of Darley, a seaman shot by the press-gang. She entered the mind of Dr Wilson, the vicar, a man already aware of the discrepancies between public and private morality. While Wilson's 'sympathies as a man' are with Darley's father, as a local magistrate he is aware of the necessity of empressment and the 'interests of the service'.[42] He avoids both sides of the issue in his sermon. The vicar's ability to view the death of Darley from both angles contrasts with the later reaction of Sylvia and her mother to Robson's arrest as the leader of a rising which destroys an inn serving as the press-gang's headquarters. The insignificance to them of national events which do not affect their personal lives has already been indicated: 'a little bit of York news, the stealing of a few apples out of a Scarborough garden that they knew, was of far more interest to them than all the battles of Nelson and the North'.[43] They are unable to appreciate that 't'justices will be all on the t'Government's side and mad for vengeance' in the affair of the Rendez-vous.[44] Robson's execution, a public act, is only reported in its effect on the family, and the novel retreats into the private sphere of Sylvia's marriage to Philip. Even the siege of Acre becomes less an important public event than the occasion for a significant private one, as Philip redeems his infidelity to Kinraid by saving his life. Alice Rose's religious misapprehension of Philip's whereabouts at the time—'Jerusalem . . . is a heavenly and a typical city'—captures the transcendental and ahistorical meaning of the Palestine passage.[45]

The solutions offered by Gaskell to the problems posed by the intrusion of public on private life are private, personal, and spiritual. As Andrew Sanders writes: 'Mrs Gaskell finds no answer to the human condition in the movement of history; she proposes no trust in political progress, in a social dialectic, in evolution, or in a far-off divine event, but in a present, private and spiritual assent to God and man.'[46] Underlying time is the eternal realm of personal feeling and religious experience. Repetition was fundamental to the moral and personal history which Gaskell was writing. She had already alerted the reader to the difficulties of understanding the past: she had shown how smuggling was morally acceptable, and moral self-examination uncommon.[47] She was ironic at the expense of those who interpreted the past critically in terms of the present: 'In looking back to the last century, it appears curious how little our ancestors had the power of putting two things together. Is it because we are further away from those times and have, consequently, a greater range of vision? Will our descendants have a wonder

---

[40] Gaskell, *Lovers*, 41–3. [41] Ibid. 41. [42] Ibid. 66. [43] Ibid. 95.
[44] Ibid. 272. [45] Ibid. 448. [46] Sanders, *Novel*, 202. [47] Ibid. 98, 74.

about us . . . as we have about the inconsistencies of our forefathers . . . ?'[48] Lack of ability to understand the past leads to repetition, though the eternal nature of human experience already makes it likely. The moral and personal history which Gaskell documented is ever different, yet ever the same. The contrast of the eternal and the transient is established early in the novel, by the contrast of the port itself and the sea. The port and the sea are 'the types of time and eternity': the church and the churchyard, where the 'dead of many generations' lie, link the two.[49] At Phillip's deathbed, the sea is again representative of eternity—he loses all sense of time to awaken to the sound of 'the waves lapping against the shelving shore'.[50] In the present, when Monkshaven is a bathing-place, the same waves, with 'the same ceaseless, ever-recurrent sound' that Phillip heard, still lap the shore.[51] In view of this use of the image of the sea, it is not surprising to find that the one illustration which makes an attempt to portray Whitby itself (Fig. 37), instead of the central characters of the drama, shows a view, not of the port, which represents life and history, but facing out to sea—the symbol of eternity and the eternal similarity of the human lot—from the town.[52] This marginalization of the port might have been due to the fact that Du Maurier, despite his later love of Whitby, had not yet visited the town and was working from photographs,[53] perhaps rather uncertainly. But it seems likely that it was a suggestion of Gaskell's.

The impossibility of fully understanding the past, and the recurrent nature of human experience leads to the repetition of errors arising from human passions. Philip is visited by this insight when his employer, John Foster, outlines to him the love story of his landlady, old Alice Rose, which is 'something of the same kind' as his own: 'Then he went on to wonder if the lives of one generation were but the repetition of the lives of those who had gone before . . . would those circumstances which made the interest of his life now, return, in due cycle, when he was dead and Sylvia forgotten?'[54] History does repeat itself, though the 'memory of man fades away', as indeed the story of Philip and Sylvia does through its transmission in a distorted form.[55] The true history of human experience is private, a part of eternity, as Philip discovered when he found out that the old fable of Guy of Warwick and Phillis his wife, which he 'did not quite believe the truth of . . . because of the fictitious nature of some of the other champions of Christendom' in the same volume, turns out to be true to his own experience. The fable—fiction, not history—is not 'at fault': he, like Guy, dies in his wife's arms with 'many sweet and holy words'.[56]

Mrs Gaskell's assertion of the mythic and eternal significance of personal human emotion, an emphasis reflected in the illustrations to *Sylvia's Lovers*, can be compared fruitfully with Eliot's more complex use of myth in her historical novel, *Romola*, a work in which much of the apparatus of the picturesque historical novel, most of which Gaskell had often chosen to discard, was all too present.

---

[48] Gaskell, *Lovers*, 67.   [49] Ibid. 63–4.   [50] Ibid. 497.
[51] Ibid. 498.   [52] Ibid., title-page.
[53] G. Du Maurier, *The Young George Du Maurier: Letters 1860–67*, ed. D. Du Maurier (1951), 237; L. Ormond, *George Du Maurier* (1969), 148, 156.
[54] Gaskell, *Lovers*, 239–40.   [55] Ibid. 498.   [56] Ibid. 463.

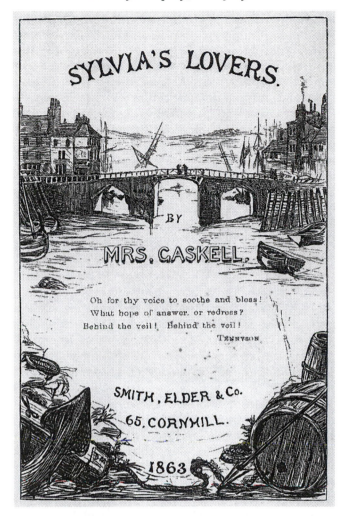

Fig. 37. G. Du Maurier, from E. Gaskell, *Sylvia's Lovers* (1863), title-page

ROMOLA: 'IMPOSSIBLE EXPECTATIONS'

Romola was first published in the *Cornhill Magazine* from July 1862 to August 1863 with twenty-three illustrations by Frederic Leighton.[57] Set in late-fifteenth-century Florence, it tells the story of Romola, the daughter of a classical scholar who marries the newly arrived Greek stranger, Tito Melema. He has already abandoned his adopted father, Baldassare, whom he has left in slavery. He

---

[57] The novel was not published in book-form with its illustrations: therefore it has been necessary to examine it in its serial appearance.

betrays both the expectation of Romola's father that he will preserve his antiquarian collection, and the love of Romola herself, taking a peasant mistress.
In her flight both from Florence and her unhappy marriage, Romola is arrested
by the religious reformer, Savonarola, and joins his radical revival movement, assuaging her personal misery in the public service of others. Finally,
Savonarola's increasingly tyrannical and extreme conduct alienates Romola. His
downfall inevitably comes; Tito is murdered by Baldassare; Romola floats away
in a boat, in a state of complete apathy, but arrives in a plague-stricken village,
where human neediness awakes her to life again. She eventually returns to
Florence, to establish a home for Tito's mistress and her children.

The idea for the novel came from the suggestion of George Lewes, Eliot's
common-law husband, while they were visiting Florence in May 1860, that
the life and times of Savonarola, would afford 'fine material for an historical
romance'.[58] Lewes's opinion of English nineteenth-century historical novels in
general was low: in an 1846 article in *The Westminster Review*, he commented
that 'the historical novel is one wherein mediocrity is at its ease'.[59] Superficial
knowledge, or else facts 'crammed' for the occasion, were displayed by the historical novelist, he argued, instead of 'that mastery of the subject which long
familiarity alone can give'.[60] However, he was convinced that Eliot would 'probably do something rather different in character from what has been done before'.[61]

Throughout the writing of *Romola* Eliot was by no means confident of success,[62] and after its completion, she felt 'great, great facts' were only able to 'speak
brokenly' through her text.[63] If Eliot fell short of her aim, it was due to the mag-
nitude of her conception: for she seems to have aimed at the creation of an
epic novel of mythical form, which was, paradoxically, the vehicle of a world-
historical view expressed symbolically through an astonishingly ambitious reconstruction of a past society. *Romola* was a multi-levelled novel in which the author
confronted both picturesque and scientific historiographies, while also addressing the problems presented by the rival claims of the personal and the social,
within a broader mythical and spiritual context. It stands out as an oddity in the
œuvre of an author whose famous works were all set in nineteenth-century
England, but, as in other historical novels of the 1850s and 1860s, a setting distant
both chronologically and geographically served as the arena for an exploration of
contemporary and national issues.

The scenario of *Romola* was that of a typical picturesque historical novel: a
period of political and religious upheaval formed the background to a plot involving both fictional and non-fictional characters. But Eliot's concern with historical detail in *Romola* is legendary and her researches, while reminiscent of
the efforts of the more conscientious of her picturesque predecessors, greatly

    [58] G. Eliot, *The George Eliot Letters*, ed. G. S. Haight, 6 vols. (1954), iii. 295. G. H. Lewes's
Journal, 21 May 1860.
    [59] [G. H. Lewes], 'The Historical Novel', *WR* 45 (1846), 34.   [60] Ibid. 35.
    [61] *Eliot Letters*, iii. 339. G. Eliot to J. Blackwood, 28 Aug. 1860.
    [62] Ibid. iv. 58. G. H. Lewes to S. S. Hennell, 12 Sept. 1862.
    [63] Ibid. iv. 97. G. Eliot to R. H. Hutton, 8 Aug. 1863.

exceeded theirs. A month after Lewes first voiced his suggestion, Eliot had already realized that 'it will require a good deal of study and labour'.[64] The next year and a half were passed in a course of intensive study. In October 1861, for instance, Lewes told John Blackwood (at that time the intended publisher) that: 'Mrs Lewes is . . . buried in musty old antiquities, which she will have to vivify.'[65] Visits to the British Museum became habitual, though Eliot felt it 'a painful way of getting knowledge'.[66] A second visit to Florence was necessary in spring 1861, during which Lewes and Eliot visited the Magliabecchian Museum.[67] Blackwood lent assistance: in March 1861, Eliot wrote to his subordinate, J. M. Langford, to thank him for 'those nice old fashioned costumes you were so good as to look up for me' and to ask him to look out for 'a good book on medieval costume',[68] a circumstance which confirms the degree to which Eliot felt the challenge by the picturesque ideal. The information thus gleaned was noted down in a series of notebooks known as the 'Quarry'. Material in one of these notebooks ranged from 'Dantesque phrases' from the *Divine Comedy* to the names of members of Savonarola's party.[69] An examination of this notebook shows how carefully the most minor details were researched and worked into the text. Eliot noted, for instance, that 'Brescia [was] celebrated for the manufacture of arms'; in *Romola*, Niccolo Caparra comments that the coat of mail which the hero, Tito, purchases is 'fine work of Maso of Brescia'.[70]

Driven by her own desire to achieve 'as full a vision of the medium in which the character moves as of the character itself',[71] Eliot was also, no doubt, conscious of the increasing demands for factual authenticity made of the later Victorian historical novelist. Her researches had been prolonged far beyond those of the early Victorian picturesque novelist, and Lewes grew concerned that her research was preventing her starting writing, and would weigh down the narrative with unnecessary facts. In December 1861, he wrote to Blackwood in some alarm: 'Polly is still deep in her researches . . . At present she remains immovable in the conviction that she can't write the romance until she has knowledge enough . . . When you see her, mind your care is to discountenance the idea of a Romance being the product of an Encyclopaedia.'[72] Lewes's fears were justified, and the Florentine street scenes of *Romola* are particularly static, weighed down by historical details. Eliot's obsessive concern for authenticity was, however, reflected in more subtle ways within the plot itself: as a recent critic, Jim Reilly, has pointed out, the heroine's relationship to her father's antiquarian collection seems to echo Eliot's own anxieties in the face of the oppressively enormous body of historical materials

[64] *Eliot Letters*, iii. 307. G. Eliot to J. Blackwood, 23 June 1860.
[65] Ibid. iii. 457. G. H. Lewes to J. Blackwood, 9 Oct. 1861.
[66] Ibid. iii. 472. G. Eliot to Mrs T. A. Trollope, 10 Dec. 1861.
[67] Ibid. iii. 414. G. H. Lewes to C. L. Lewes, 17 May 1861.
[68] Ibid. iii. 393–4. G. Eliot to J. M. Langford, 27 Mar. 1861.
[69] Oxford, Bodleian Library: MS Don. g. 8, fos. 24–7, 34^v–35^r.
[70] Bod. MS. Don g. 8, fo. 39^r; G. Eliot, *Romola*, in *The Cornhill Magazine*, 6 (1862), 604.
[71] *Eliot Letters*, iv. 97. G. Eliot to R. H. Hutton, 8 Aug. 1863.
[72] Ibid. iii. 473–4. G. H. Lewes to J. Blackwood, 14 Dec. 1861.

which she was so painfully attempting to transform into a novel. Aiming at a total historical reconstruction of late fifteenth-century Florence, Eliot's nerve often failed and these failures are reflected, Reilly suggests, by paradoxical interludes of non-representations or non-events, such as the procession of the 'Unseen Madonna' or Savonarola's aborted trial by fire.[73]

The illustrator of *Romola* seems to have been chosen with a view to the creation of a picturesque historical novel. After George Smith's offer for the novel had been accepted in early 1862,[74] Frederic Leighton was invited to illustrate it. Lewes described him as 'by far the best man to be had in England',[75] and later commentators, such as Hugh Witemeyer, have agreed.[76] Leighton seemed an ideal illustrator for *Romola* because of his earlier career as a painter of works set in medieval and Renaissance Italy, historical reconstructions which were as carefully detailed as *Romola*. While studying at Frankfurt, influenced by the Nazarene school and the Cronberg landscape school, he had painted the early works, *Preparing for a Festa* (1851) and *The Death of Brunelleschi* (1852). His best known work at this date was *Cimabue's Celebrated Madonna is carried in Procession through the Streets of Florence* (1855), a massive historical reconstruction of a Florentine religious event which naturally invites comparison with the procession of the 'Unseen Madonna' in *Romola*.[77]

Eliot was enthusiastic, and she and Leighton immediately started an exchange of ideas as he read the text: an Ainsworth–Cruikshank style collaboration seemed likely.[78] Eliot suggested a picture of the old Florentine, an imaginary spectator whom she utilized in the Proem, for the Proem's capital letter, instead of a view from San Miniato church, Leighton's initial suggestion.[79] The final version, a tail-piece, showing the Florentine contemplating a crucifix, with a view of the church in the background,[80] represents an intelligent compromise. In the same letter, Eliot approved Leighton's suggestions of further subjects for plates, including

[73] J. Reilly, *Shadowtime: History and Representation in Hardy, Conrad, and George Eliot* (London and New York, 1993), 97–104. Reilly perceptively suggests that Casaubon in *Middlemarch* (Eliot's next novel) is essentially a self-portrait of Eliot as the author of *Romola*.

[74] See R. F. Anderson, ' "Things Wisely Ordered": John Blackwood and the Publication of *Romola*', *PH* 11 (1982), 5–39, for a full account of this transaction.

[75] *Eliot Letters*, iv. 37. G. H. Lewes to C. L. Lewes, 21 May 1862.

[76] H. Witemeyer, *George Eliot and the Visual Arts* (New Haven, Conn., and London, 1979), 158.

[77] L. and R. Ormond, *Lord Leighton* (New Haven, Conn., 1975), 9–12, 15–25, 49. Another excellent, and more recent, assessment of Leighton's career can be found in the catalogue for the 1996 Royal Academy of Arts exhibition, *Frederic Leighton*: some of the illustrations to *Romola* are considered, pp. 130–2.

[78] Leighton's initial relationship with the engravers for *Romola*, Joseph Swain and W. J. Linton, was less harmonious than his interactions with Eliot: the artist complained to the publisher Smith that the engravers were leaving out some essential lines and putting in other inessential ones. Smith took photographs of the original woodblocks to prove the accuracy of the engravers and Leighton seems to have become used to the idiosyncrasies of the medium and was satisfied with the later engravings. *Frederic Leighton*, 130.

[79] *Eliot Letters*, iv. 39. G. Eliot to F. Leighton, 26 May 1862.

[80] Eliot, *Romola*, *CM* 6 (1862), 7.

Fig. 38. F. Leighton, '*You didn't think it was so pretty, did you?*', from G. Eliot, *Romola*, *The Cornhill Magazine*, 7 (1863), facing 1

the barber Nello's sanctum (this plate is '*Suppose you let me look at myself?*').[81] Leighton shared her concern for historical detail: he made reference to sketches taken earlier in Florence while designing the illustrations. The view of San Miniato in the Proem illustration derived from a notebook sketch of 1852: the lantern in the plate of *Niccolo at Work*[82] was based on an 1852 sketch of one in the Strozzi Museum.[83] Further letters between author and artist confirm this impression. In September 1862, Eliot replied to what was no doubt a request for the whereabouts of any known portraits of Piero di Cosimo: 'My copy of Vasari has a profile of Piero di Cosimo; but it is of no value . . . There is probably a portrait of Piero di Cosimo in the portrait room of the Uffizi.'[84] She received information in return, valuing Leighton's knowledge of the setting of the novel.[85] She greeted many of the plates with delight, including '*Suppose you let me look at myself?*' and '*You didn't think it was so pretty, did you?*' (Fig. 38).[86]

---

[81] Eliot, *Romola*, *CM* 6, facing 27; *Eliot Letters*, iv. 39. G. Eliot to F. Leighton, 26 May 1862.
[82] Eliot, *Romola*, *CM* 6 (1862), facing 603.   [83] Ormond, *Leighton*, 58–9.
[84] *Eliot Letters*, iv. 55. G. Eliot to F. Leighton, 10 Sept. 1862.
[85] Ibid. iv. 49. G. Eliot to S. S. Hennell, 14 July 1862.
[86] Ibid. iv. 41, 63: G. Eliot to F. Leighton, 5? June, and 25? Nov. 1862; Eliot, *Romola, CM* 7 (1863), facing 1.

Despite Eliot's and Leighton's efforts, even the supportive Lewes could not disguise the fact that the novel was 'flatly received by the general public'.[87] Eliot's attempt not only to rival but to surpass the picturesque historical novelist in her realist historical reconstruction of Savonarola's Florence only invited a critical identification of *Romola* with the very sort of historical fiction she was challenging. The critic of *The Saturday Review* wrote that:

if a sketch of Florence were her main object, she . . . has mastered every detail that could give reality and picturesqueness to her representation . . . [but] sometimes the antiquarian quite drowns the novelist . . . It is not without a pang that we come to passages in *Romola* such as that where an authoress known and respected . . . actually goes off like Becker, or G. P. R. James . . . for two pages of cram.[88]

He found the period Eliot had chosen 'remote and uninteresting', and believed that the political intrigues of the novel interfered with the working out of the personal drama of Tito, Romola, and Baldassare.[89] The critic in *The Westminster Review* was of much the same opinion: he felt that all Eliot's labour had resulted only in 'an accumulation of details', which oppressed 'the human interest of the tale'.[90] Both these post-1850 critics mistakenly treated the novel as merely the tale of a failed marriage in fancy dress, failing to grasp the links between the political and historical details and the central plot of the novel. But they rightly recognized that excessive detail injured the novel. Ironically, like Eliot, they too suggested a new concept of authenticity, one imbued with a greater appreciation of historical relativism and leading to more convincing psychological characterization.

In the same spirit, *Romola*'s reviewers criticized the characters as merely contemporary figures in Renaissance dress: the critic of *The Saturday Review*, for instance, felt that the characters and situations were too familiar and that they 'evolve the same moral problems . . . [and] encounter the same difficulties in life' as contemporary characters in Eliot's novels.[91] R. H. Hutton felt that Romola was 'the least perfect figure in the book . . . a shade more modernized than the others, several shades less individual'[92]—a criticism which Eliot herself admitted[93]— and the critic of *The Westminster Review* made similar reflections on the characters.[94] But what the reviewers perceived to be a failure of Eliot's imagination was intimately linked to her ambitious design for the novel, which none of her contemporary critics fully understood. The reviewer for *The Westminster Review*, for instance, dismissed Eliot's important assertion in the Proem of the 'broad

---

[87] *Eliot Letters*, iv. 102. G. H. Lewes's Journal, 21 Aug. 1863.

[88] [Anon.], 'Review of *Romola*', *The Saturday Review*, 16 (1863), repr. in G. S. Haight (ed.), *A Century of George Eliot Criticism* (1965), 21–2.

[89] Ibid. 23–4.

[90] [Anon.], '*Romola*', *WR* 80 (1863), repr. in G. S. Haight (ed.), *A Century of George Eliot Criticism* (1965), 27–8.

[91] 'Review of *Romola*', 23.

[92] R. H. Hutton, 'Eliot's *Romola*', *The Spectator*, 36 (1863), 2265–7, repr. in D. Carroll (ed.), *George Eliot: The Critical Heritage* (1971), 203–4.

[93] *Eliot Letters*, iv. 103–4. G. Eliot to S. S. Hennell, 23 Aug. 1863.   [94] '*Romola*', 30.

sameness of the human lot, which never alters in the main headings of its history',[95] which she had compared to the enduring nature of the great geographical features.[96] Like other critics, he also deplored the rather symbolic episode when the heroine 'drifts away' and arrives in a plague-stricken village, which he thought: 'strangely disconnected with the rest of the tale . . . All sense of probability is here sacrificed for a moral effect'.[97] These parts of *Romola* look sketchy and improvised in comparison with the detailed earlier sections of the novel, but Eliot, in a letter to her cousin, Sara Hennell, explained that they were fundamental to her original conception: they 'were by deliberate forecast adopted as romantic and symbolic elements'.[98]

The 'ideal' and 'symbolic' elements of *Romola* have remained perplexing to many modern critics. Romola's withdrawal from Florence after her clash with Savonarola has been seen as a rejection of history and political life, a retreat like Henry Esmond's into a private world to seek the higher life,[99] or as an exposure of 'the yawning gap between the world of historical experience and the world of fulfilled human desire'.[100] The ideal aspects of *Romola* seemed, and still seem, out of place in a novel apparently intended to be a model of realist historical fiction. This is due to a frequent misunderstanding, on the part of Eliot's critics, of the relationship which she envisaged between the 'real' and 'ideal' aspects of this novel.

The ideal aspects of Leighton's illustrations are apparent too, and are equally perplexing. It is as well to remember Witemeyer's caution to the commentator on text and image, on the danger of forgetting that illustrations must be seen, not only in relation to the text, but also to the entire *œuvre* of the artist, and the artistic milieu of the period.[101] In the early 1860s, Leighton's art was 'in a transitional state, and it belonged to no recognizable school or movement'.[102] Despite his enthusiasm for historical reconstruction, Leighton seems to have been driven by other concerns. Opportunities for ostentatious authenticity were missed— Witemeyer has noted that he 'positively avoided the well-known features of Savonarola'.[103] In plates such as *The Dying Message* and *'Father, I will be guided'*, a hood hides Savonarola's face or his back is turned.[104] Leighton was evolving into a neo-classical painter, whose best known works would be *The Garden of Hesperides* and *Flaming June*. For an academically trained artist with a strong sense of the sculptural, this was perhaps a natural development. Significantly, Leighton had admired the work of the neo-Greek French artists such as Cabanel, Gérôme, and Bourgereau,[105] whose works were echoed by the English-based

[95] Eliot, *Romola, CM* 6 (1862), 1.   [96] '*Romola*', 30.   [97] Ibid. 32.

[98] *Eliot Letters*, iv. 104. G. Eliot to S. S. Hennell, 23 Aug. 1863.

[99] Fleischmann, *Novel*, 162–3.

[100] J. K. Gehazi, '*Romola* and the Myth of Apocalypse', in A. Smith (ed.), *George Eliot Centenary Essays and an Unpublished Fragment* (1980), 79–80.

[101] Witemeyer, *Eliot*, 160–1.   [102] Ormond, *Leighton*, 55.

[103] Witemeyer, *Eliot*, 159.

[104] Eliot, *Romola, CM* 6 (1862), facing 433; 7 (1863), facing 145.

[105] Ormond, *Leighton*, 34.

artist, Alma-Tadema. Many of his works of the 1860s and 1870s came very close to those of these artists, who produced anecdotal subjects in a classical setting—Leighton's many figures of solitary women such as *Ariadne Abandoned by Theseus* (1868), or groups of women such as *Greek Girls Picking up Pebbles* (1871), for instance—and suggested, in their unpretending subject-matter and concentration on form rather than content, his attraction to the Aesthetic movement. Single figures of this type, or groupings of two or three, are frequent in the illustrations to *Romola*. In fact, most commentators are agreed that these—rather than the Florentine street scenes in which the artist of *Cimabue's Madonna* might have been expected to excel—are the best of the plates.[106] Possibly the success of these plates, contrasted with the failure of the Florentine street scenes, betrays his growing lack of interest in medieval reconstructions.

Many of the successful plates are of iconographical importance when seen in the context of both his contemporary and his later works. The Ormonds have noticed, for instance, how the many cloaked figures in the series—as in the plates *The Dying Message* and *A Dangerous Colleague*[107]—derive from Leighton's fresco of *The Wise and Foolish Virgins* in Lyndhurst church, on which he had recently been working.[108] Leighton's attempt to achieve statuesque dignity in many of the illustrations can be seen not only in the context of his own progress towards neo-classicism and Aestheticism, but also of the development of Sixties illustration. The black-and-white illustrators who dominated the field in the late 1850s and 1860s aimed to avoid the comical-satirical style of Cruikshank, Leech, and Browne, and to exhibit a classical sense of form, incorporating naturalist and symbolic elements from the Pre-Raphaelites.[109] The Florentine street scenes—such as, for instance, *A Florentine Joke*[110]—may represent occasions when Leighton did not fully succeed in exorcising the ghost of early Victorian illustrations.

Leighton's separate concerns, although related like Eliot's to issues of idealization and classicism, seem to have led to a relationship between text and image less cohesive than Eliot had hoped for. As early as June 1862, she wrote to Leighton: 'I feel for you as well as for myself in this inevitable difficulty—nay, the impossibility of producing perfect correspondence between my intention and the illustration.[111] The source of this concern was Eliot's dissatisfaction with the first plate of *Romola*, which showed the heroine and her father, Bardo: *The Blind Scholar and his Daughter*.[112] Eliot wrote to the artist that, although it was 'charming', if they had 'talked a little together after you had read the proof the only

---

[106] Ormond, *Leighton*, 59.
[107] Eliot, *Romola, CM* 6 (1862), facing 433; 7 (1863), facing 306.
[108] Ormond, *Leighton*, 56–7.   [109] Harvey, *Novelists*, 161.
[110] Eliot, *Romola, CM* 6 (1862), facing 450.
[111] *Eliot Letters*, iv. 40. G. Eliot to F. Leighton, 4? June 1862.
[112] Eliot, *Romola, CM* 6 (1862), facing 1.

important discrepancy might have been prevented'.[113] The 'discrepancy' was the 'listening look' of Bardo which the artist in *Romola*, Piero di Cosimo, did catch. The novelist soon realized, however, that her expectations might have been too high, since 'the exigencies of your art must forbid perfect correspondence between the text and the illustration'.[114] She was still aiming to achieve a fuller collaboration, proposing 'a little conversation' after Leighton had read the text.[115] By September 1862, she was convicted that, realistically, the illustrations could not be expected to encapsulate the text: 'I am convinced that illustrations can only form a sort of overture to the text. The artist who uses the pencil must otherwise be tormented to misery by the deficiencies or requirements of the one who uses the pen, and the writer on the other hand, must die of impossible expectations.'[116]

The juxtaposition of realistic detail and ideal and symbolic elements in *Romola* has recently attracted attention among modern critics. Recognition that the mode of *Romola* was 'fable, not realistical novel' has brought the reader, at last, nearer Eliot's conception.[117] But the historical details were not simply the irrelevant remains of the picturesque tradition. As Andrew Sanders recognizes, *Romola* proposes 'a parallel between the progress of the individual towards self-awareness and enlightenment, and the forward movement of the broad mass of humanity in a wider, creative historical process'.[118] *Romola* was not only intended to be a realistic historical reconstruction, but also—and simultaneously—an epic and mythological work. The Proem, as Felicia Bonaparte claims, tells us to read the novel not only as a tale of Florence in 1492, but 'the whole history of Western civilization, of which late fifteenth century Florence must somehow be the symbolic representation'.[119] For: 'It was only in mythology that Eliot could express in one image both the historical and universal levels, since it is the peculiar character of mythology that it embodies both.'[120]

Once the full dimensions of Eliot's project are recognized, the choice of Renaissance Italy for setting by this contemporary English novelist need not be seen as a deliberate avoidance of the national historical narrative. Instead, it can be seen as a multifaceted attempt to consider the progress of civilization itself, both national and supra-national, and the role of the individual within it. One source for this perspective, at once particular and universal, is obvious: many critics have rightly observed that *Romola* was much influenced by Eliot's

[113] *Eliot Letters*, iv. 40. G. Eliot to F. Leighton, 4? June 1862.
[114] Ibid. iv. 41. G. Eliot to F. Leighton, 5? June 1862.
[115] Ibid. iv. 42. G. Eliot to F. Leighton, 6? June 1862.
[116] Ibid. iv. 55–6. G. Eliot to F. Leighton, 10 Sept. 1862.
[117] G. Levine, '*Romola* as Fable', in B. Hardy (ed.), *Critical Essays on George Eliot* (1970), 82.
[118] Sanders, *Novel*, 170.
[119] F. Bonaparte, *The Triptych and the Cross: The Central Myths of George Eliot's Poetic Imagination* (Brighton, 1979), 12–13.
[120] Ibid. 24–5.

involvement with Frederic Harrison and other English Positivists, disciples of the French secular philosopher, Auguste Comte, and their call for the regeneration of the social state through 'order and progress'.[121]

One recent reading of *Romola* suggests that it is one of series of novels which address the issue of the emergence of the nation-state and the individual's role within it still more profoundly than Mrs Gaskell's *Sylvia's Lovers*. Bernard Semmel reads *Romola* as a sequel to *Felix Holt*, Eliot's novel about English radical utopian politics: he sees it as a deliberate exploration of the dangerous and ruthless absolutism of 'republics of virtue' advocated by Savonarola's kind. The 'drifting away' sequence, Semmel argues, represents the prelude to her next novel, *Daniel Deronda*, in which a distinction is made between 'the state, on the one hand, and the nation (that is, the people, the society, the nationality) on the other'.[122] A true democrat (and, apparently, a supporter of the gradual political and social amelioration characteristic of English national history), Romola identifies herself with the needs of the people, but not the generalities of state politics.[123]

Semmel's interpretation of *Romola* leads him to conclude that it is 'an *anti*-Positivist novel, describing the transformation of an one-time sympathizer into a clear opponent'.[124] His analysis of the political implications of Positivism obscures Eliot's wider sympathy with its universal historiographical perspective. While Semmel's interpretation explores only one aspect of *Romola*'s engagement with history—the national—Felicia Bonaparte offers a far more profound analysis of the novel. She postulates that *Romola* is a mythical parable of the historical progress of Western civilization, loosely based on the ideas of Auguste Comte, and in particular his law of the three stages (the theological, metaphysical, and the Positive). Classical ideals are represented by Romola's father and Tito (who is identified with Bacchus); Christian ones by Savonarola (who is identified with Christ) and Romola's brother: both are to be superseded by the emergence of a future Positivist society, represented by Romola's community of women and children.[125] Romola's rejection of both classical and Christian approaches to life invites the evolution of a humanist faith of sympathy and duty, symbolized by the figure of a motherly woman, the Madonna.[126] In this scheme of things, Romola's flight is reinterpreted as 'not a rejection of history, but a return to a mainstream of history'. The plague-stricken village is simply Florence, stripped of its narrow politic dimensions and 'symbolically represented in its most essential features . . . a world in which time is perceived in the context of eternity'.[127] Romola

---

[121] See G. S. Haight, *George Eliot, a Biography* (Oxford, 1968) and M. S. Vogeler, *Frederic Harrison: The Vocations of a Positivist* (Oxford, 1984) for Eliot's relationships with English Postivists.

[122] B. Semmel, *George Eliot and the Politics of National Inheritance* (New York and Oxford, 1994), 77.

[123] Ibid. 67–77.   [124] Ibid. 67.

[125] Bonaparte, *Triptych*, 34–71, 73, 177–202, 240–55.   [126] Ibid. 203–39.

[127] Ibid. 231.

experiences the strength of the simple call of human need, and, responding with uncomplicated love, creates an apolitical community of women and children, a community symbolized by a child.[128] Viewed from this perspective, *Romola* offers a historical dimension which is mythical but, unlike *Sylvia's Lovers*, does not suggest retreat into a private and spiritual realm of personal feeling: instead, it presents the inhabitants of this realm as the community of the future.

Bonaparte's analysis invites a re-examination of the illustrations of the novel. It was clearly impractical of Eliot to expect Leighton to represent the depths of this historical yet mythical creation. However, whether by discussion or insight or artistic chance, Leighton came nearer to representing the symbolic complexities of the novel than Eliot's resigned disappointment suggests. A case in point is Leighton's portrayal of Tito, whom Eliot identifies with Bacchus. Both author and artist must have been familiar with Caravaggio's *Bacchus*, to whom Tito, often plump-cheeked and curly-haired, as in the plate *The Escaped Prisoner*,[129] bears a striking resemblance. There are also similarities to Michelangelo's statue of Bacchus. The figure of Romola is clearly modelled by Leighton, as by Eliot, on the Renaissance style of madonnas—for instance, Raphael's Sistine Madonna. One wonders too if Eliot's delight with the plate '*You didn't think it was so pretty, did you?*' (Fig. 38)[130] was increased by a recognition that it caught nicely the underlying meaning of the text. Baldasarre, Tito's adopted father, shares his name with one of the three Magi, the one who brought myrrh—a symbol of sorrow—to the infant Christ; Lillo, the baby in the plate, is the son of Tito, whom Baldasarre is to murder. Lillo is later to function as the child of the Madonna, Romola. The framework of the plate where Tessa presents Lillo to Baldasarre is very reminiscent of paintings of the visit of the Magi, suggesting that Leighton exploited an established iconographical tradition, with some understanding of its relevance to the text. Another parallel example is *A Supper in the Rucellai Gardens*.[131] This event is seen, in Bonaparte's interpretation, as a Bacchic parody of the Last Supper, complete with a betrayal and followed by the death of the god-figure.[132] Comparison with Leonardo da Vinci's *Last Supper* suggests that this was another iconographical framework in which Leighton worked.

Proof of Eliot's astonishingly ambitious design for *Romola* is found in such recent readings of the novel; she herself confirmed the complex integrity of the work in her comment to R. H. Hutton: 'there is scarcely a phrase, an incident, an allusion that did not have its supposed subservience to my main artistic objects'.[133] However, several questions arise. Why has it taken so long for Eliot's depth of purpose to be acknowledged and explored? In the light both of contemporary incomprehension and the variety of modern critical interpretations of the novel, Felicia Bonaparte's contention that Eliot is successful in *Romola* is indeed

---

[128] Bonaparte, *Triptych*, 231–55.   [129] Eliot, *Romola, CM* 6 (1862), facing 577.
[130] Ibid. 7 (1863), facing 1.   [131] Ibid. 7 (1863), facing 153.
[132] Bonaparte, *Triptych*, 110–76.
[133] *Eliot Letters*, iv. 97. G. Eliot to R. H. Hutton, 8 Aug. 1863.

over-optimistic.[134] The union of real and mythical elements is perhaps not as fully successful as intended. Eliot's decision to use her reconstruction of Florentine society not only for the philosophical examination of government and the individual's relationship to it, but also as a symbol of the vast movement of Western history and the progress of the human soul, moves the novel out of the mainstream of historical fiction. While Scott's characters represented social forces within society at one period, Eliot's *Romola* is representative of centuries of change, telescoped into six years of human life, and the heroine is a symbol of an ideal state of human existence. *Romola*, similar to other historical novels of the period in its anxious authenticity and its (apparent) use of an escape from public to private history by the main character, used myth to its fullest potential not to escape history but to rise above it in order to understand it. But the significance of the work has not been readily understood, and to that extent the novel is a failure; however, it is evident that the illustrator reflected more of the meaning of its symbolism than even Eliot seems to have realized.[135]

C. M. YONGE: 'THE MEEK HANDMAID OF CLIO'?

C. M. Yonge, writes Alice Fairfax Lucy, 'has as strong a claim to be remembered as an interpreter of history as of her own century'.[136] For over forty years, she published historical novels (as well as history textbooks) from *The Little Duke* (1854) to *The Release, or Caroline's French Kindred* (1895). These works were intended for children and young people rather than adults: it has been suggested that they 'represent a side of her genius that never quite outgrew adolescence'.[137] However, it is equally probable that this orientation was a wise decision in the uncertain post-1850 era. In fact, Yonge's historical romances reflect the dilemmas of the period and the resolutions which were found for them with striking clarity: concern with accuracy and authenticity and the use of fictional characters and of legendary and even mythical elements, for instance, all feature in her mediocre historical fictions. The following discussion will focus on these aspects, and will attempt to show how the little-known illustrators of her novels responded, sometimes with Yonge's assistance, to the texts. Clearly, this minor author, generally excluded from the literary canon, found the picturesque historical novel and its engagement with national history as problematic as did Eliot and Gaskell.

---

[134] Levine, '*Romola* as Fable', 96–7; H. Shaw, *The Forms of Historical Fiction* (Ithaca, NY, and London, 1983), 106–9.

[135] Several publications which deal with *Romola* have been published too recently to be considered in this analysis of the novel and its illustrations, in particular T. Barringer and E. Prettejohn, *Frederic Leighton* (New Haven, Conn., 1999) and M. Turner and C. Levine, *From Author to Text: Re-reading George Eliot's 'Romola'* (Aldershot, 1998).

[136] A. F. Lucy, 'The Other Miss Yonge', in G. Battiscombe and M. Laski (eds.), *A Chaplet for Charlotte Yonge* (1965), 97.

[137] Ibid. 90.

Yonge was brought up with an ever-present sense of history. One of her earliest reading-books was Rollin's *Ancient History*: in her autobiography, she recalled that she was allowed 'a chapter a day of the Waverley novels', after she had read a portion of 'Goldsmith's "Rome" or some equally solid book':[138] a close association of fictional and factual history which reflected the predominance of picturesque historiography. History, both national and European, was both her lesson and her leisure activity; histories and historical novels ran in tandem. Besides her beloved Scott, she read Alessandro Manzoni's masterpiece *The Betrothed* (first published in 1827 and set in seventeenth-century Italy), and the historical novels of G. P. R. James, Ainsworth, and Edward Bulwer Lytton.[139] She wrote and acted in historical plays intended for family and friends.[140] History even haunted her sleep—as a child, she was afraid of 'being smothered like the Princes in the Tower or blown up with gunpowder'.[141] Historical images, too, were a part of this education, for her father took a keen interest in art. In a letter of 1839, she recorded the highlight of a visit to a nearby house, which was 'a beautiful picture of King Charles the martyr . . . with the beautiful forehead we sometimes see him drawn with'.[142] When the young Charlotte saw the Duke of Wellington in Christ Church Meadows, during a visit to Oxford in 1834, she characteristically described him to her parents as 'a man with a nose like the Duke of Bedford i.e. the brother of Henry V in Vertue's heads'.[143]

To such a keen student of history, factual accuracy was bound to appear almost as important as it did to Eliot, especially in view of her acceptance of the standard justification of the historical novel as an instrument of education. By the second half of the nineteenth century, with scientific historiography becoming predominant, factual accuracy was expected as the bare minimum from a historical novelist, although other legacies of the tradition of the picturesque historical novel were repudiated. In the Preface to *The Prince and the Page* (1866), Yonge herself recognized that 'in these days of exactness even a child's historical romance must point to what the French term its pieces justificatives':[144] she then proceeded to list her sources.

The extent of her desire for accuracy was well illustrated by a close examination of *The Caged Lion* (1870). In the Preface, she strikes a familiar note when she promises to 'avow what liberties have been taken, and how much of the sketch is founded on history'.[145] The rest of the Preface was a justification of her use of historical information. The tale is set in the time of James I of Scotland and

---

[138] C. Coleridge, *Charlotte M. Yonge: Her Life and Letters* (1903), 111.

[139] Lucy, 'Yonge', 93–4.

[140] G. Battiscombe, *Charlotte Mary Yonge: The Story of an Uneventful Life* (1943), 79–80. A more recent biography, B. Dennis, *Charlotte Yonge (1823–1901), Novelist of the Oxford Movement* (Lewiston, Me., 1992), exists.

[141] Coleridge, *Yonge*, 60.

[142] Ibid. 140. C. M. Yonge to A. Yonge, 1839.   [143] Ibid. 103–4.

[144] C. M. Yonge, *The Prince and The Page* (London and Cambridge, 1866), p. iii.

[145] C. M. Yonge, *The Caged Lion* (1870), p. v.

P. 96.

Fig. 39. [A. Hughes?], *Costly Fuel*, from C. M. Yonge, *The Caged Lion* (1870), facing 96

Henry V of England. The shifting of an event involving the knighting of Richard Whittington was excused on the grounds that 'nature could not resist an anachronism of a few years for such a story'.[146] But what really strikes the modern reader is the lack of such departures from historical fact. Yonge did not sacrifice history to the demands of her fictional plot; instead, she fitted the plot round the given

[146] C. M. Yonge, *The Caged Lion* (1870), p. vi.

historical facts. In the course of the story, James of Scotland, imprisoned in England by Henry IV, is temporarily released by Henry V and pays a secret visit to his own kingdom, where he makes the acquaintance of the imaginary hero, Malcolm of Glenuskie. After referring to 'the almost unique relations' between the two kings, as a justification for the release on parole of a major political figure, Yonge explained that the expedition to Scotland was 'wholly imaginary, though there appears to have been space for it during Henry's progress to the North'. Malcolm too is 'likewise invention, though as Froissart ascribes to King Robert II "eleven sons who loved arms", Malcolm may well be supposed to be the son of those unaccounted for in the pedigree of Scotland'.[147] A possible ancestry is thus discovered for the hero which links him to the king he serves. Clearly, the absence of any evidence which might show her to have departed from the historical facts was something of a relief to Yonge. Similarly, the destruction of the convent of St Abbs—where some early scenes occur—meant that she was 'the less constrained by the inconvenient action of fact upon fiction'.[148] History, the inspirer of Scott, had become an exacting monitor for his disciple, a monitor whose absence could be as welcome as its presence.

The illustrator of *The Caged Lion* shared Yonge's concern for historical accuracy.[149] The illustration entitled *Costly Fuel* repays careful examination (Fig. 39).[150] It shows a civic reception at which the newly knighted Sir Richard Whittington burns the contracts of loans owed to him by Henry V and the King tries to rescue them. The likeness of Henry has clearly been taken from the authentic portrait in the Royal Collection.[151] But this was not all: among the guests can be seen James I of Scotland and the Duke of Bedford, with whose likeness Yonge was familiar at an early age (Fig. 40). It is tempting to imagine her supplying the artist with information concerning these likenesses. That of James was repeated in the illustration *The Parliament of Perth*.[152] All the illustrations in *The Caged Lion* show an unusual degree of accuracy in details of costume: it is clear that the artist had consulted works such as Planché's *The History of British Costume* (1834) and Fairholt's *Costume in England* (1846). Lady Whittington's headdress in *Costly Fuel*, for example, is very similar to fifteenth-century headdresses illustrated in Planché's *History*,[153] while the hero's sister, Lilias, in *The Parliament of Perth*, wears a hat with a curled centre-piece which is undoubtedly

[147] C. M. Yonge, *The Caged Lion* (1870), p. v.   [148] Ibid., p. vii.

[149] The illustrator signed himself or herself with 'A' and another illegible initial. It seems possible that the unknown artist is Arthur Hughes, a Pre-Raphaelite painter who frequently illustrated children's books; certainly the style of the illustrations resembles that of his other work. *The Caged Lion* is not listed among the works illustrated by Hughes in L. Roberts, *Arthur Hughes: His Life and Works: A Catalogue Raisonne* (Woodbridge, 1997), but Hughes did work on occasion for Yonge's publisher, Macmillan.

[150] Yonge, *Lion*, facing 96.

[151] This was a well-known portrait, utilized by William Kent in one of the earliest attempts by a painter to reconstruct a scene from English history. R. Strong, *And When Did You Last See Your Father? The Victorian Painter and British History* (1978), 15–16.

[152] Yonge, *Lion*, facing 335.

[153] J. R. Planché, *The History of British Costume* (1834), 188–9.

Fig. 40. G. Vertue, *John, Duke of Bedford*, from G. Vertue, *The Heads of the Kings of England, proper for Mr. Rapin's History* (1736), plate 27

derived from Fairholt's *Costume*.[154] It is probable that the works of Strutt were consulted too: several of the plates in his *Dress and Habits* seem to have contributed to the appearance of Queen Catherine in *Costly Fuel*, particularly plate 97, which shows a lady of rank wearing a coronet very similar to Catherine's, and an identical hair coif with a double plait.[155]

---

[154] F. W. Fairholt, *Costume in England* (1846), 186, fig. 5.

[155] J. Strutt, *Dress A Complete View of the Dress and Habits of the People of England*, 3 vols. (1796–9), ii, plates 94–7.

The Caged Lion is, however, unusual among Yonge's historical novels in its willingness to focus on, and deal directly with, major historical figures and events. A later and aptly named work, *Stray Pearls* (1886), which attempted to concentrate on important historical figures and events, was an aesthetic disaster. The sequel to *The Chaplet of Pearls, Stray Pearls* (which struggled to adapt itself to its English and French seventeenth-century background) led Yonge to make the following perceptive comments:

Formerly the Muse of the historical romance was an independent and arbitrary personage, who could . . . make the most stubborn facts subservient to her purpose. Indeed her most favoured son [i.e. Scott] boldly asserted her right to bend time and place to her purpose . . . But the critics have lashed her out of these erratic ways, and she is now become the meek handmaid of Clio . . . never venturing on more than colouring and working up the grand outlines that her mistress left undefined. Thus, in the present tale, . . . it had been found necessary . . . to be at least consistent with the real history, at the entire sacrifice of the plot.[156]

Though authenticity was a fundamental concern for Yonge, she was fully aware of the problems which a preoccupation with its demands could create. It is no surprise to find that, in other historical romances, she attempted to evade these problems as far as she was able within a framework of historical fact.

By the 1860s, Yonge's correspondence with her publisher, Alexander Macmillan, reveals that she was losing confidence in her ability to handle authentic events and characters with conviction. In October 1864, she wrote to Macmillan:

I have a short story by me . . . about a son of Simon de Montfort, but I have not touched it up . . . partly because, since the Little Duke's time, I have come to have less faith in my own knowledge of ancient customs . . . I have hopes of making something of another story, but I must get some information about Germany under Maximilian I before I can set to work on it.[157]

Yonge here exhibited signs of the same fear of inaccuracy which drove Eliot to spend so many months in research and to delay the writing of *Romola*. The latter of the two stories referred to in this letter was eventually published as *The Dove in the Eagle's Nest* (1866): unlike the former of the tales, it was set in Germany rather than England. But despite the use of this classic displacement device, its writing and publication were plagued by Yonge's constant striving for a greater degree of authenticity and her concern in the face of inaccuracies and anachronisms. On 21 November 1864, she wrote to her publisher Alexander Macmillan, wishing for 'more authorities';[158] in May 1865, she confessed to her publisher: 'what is so heavy on my soul is that I must have made Maximilian too old and antedated the Swabian League . . . and that I regaled the travellers on pasty, when they should

---

[156] C. M. Yonge, *Stray Pearls* (1883; 1900 edn.), pp. v–vi.
[157] London, British Library: Additional MS 54920, fo. 50^{r-v}. Hereafter, BL Add. MS 54920. C. M. Yonge to A. Macmillan, 24 Oct. 1864.
[158] BL Add. MS 54920, fo. 55^r. C. M. Yonge to A. Macmillan, 21 Nov. 1864.

have eaten sausage'.[159] This painful (and bathetic) concern for authenticity, which found the history of the Swabian League and the gastronomic anachronism of pasties of equal gravity, extended to the illustrations: Yonge strongly urged her publisher to consider the use of reproduced authentic images, a means of bypassing the problems of picturesque reconstruction altogether.[160] She wrote to him in August 1865, proposing a meeting in the British Museum to view 'some of the wonderful woodcuts of Maximilian's time. In the Nuremberg Chronicle, there is a woodcut of Ulm which would make a delicious frontispiece . . . I fancy a few facsimiles (reduced) of those curious woodcuts such as this and one or two from the Thenesdank and the Weise Konig would be very attractive.'[161] Eventually—and perhaps significantly—the first edition of *The Dove in the Eagle's Nest* was published without any illustrations.

Although Yonge's correspondence with her publisher reveals much of the tension which the demands of authenticity created for the writer, the texts of her works are still more revealing. One obvious result of her concern for historical accuracy was the displacement of her main characters. While the early and popular tale for children, *The Little Duke*, took as its hero an authentic and important historical figure, Richard the Fearless of Normandy, practically none of the later novels do so. As Reade did in *The Cloister and the Hearth*, Yonge was prone to displace her major characters by making them not important historical figures, but their relatives, generally fictitious. Many problems of authenticity were thus avoided. When Yonge did select an authentic hero or heroine—as in the case of Richard de Montfort, son of the famous Simon, the hero of *The Prince and the Page*—she chose one whose 'history cannot be traced'.[162] Even this choice is no real exception to the rule: Richard de Montfort did indeed exist, but Yonge had originally written the tale in ignorance of his existence, using an entirely imaginary son of the great Simon called Wilfred. Then, in July 1865, she wrote to Macmillan of this discovery, adding: 'I suspect Wilfred's name ought to be changed all through . . . People did not mind such things when Sir Walter Scott called Aubrey de Vere Arthur, but they are more particular now.'[163] There is apparent here both Yonge's preference for fictional heroes and her fear of inaccuracies, which, she recognized, were no longer as acceptable as in Scott's day.

But it is not just Yonge who ran away from history; her characters followed suit. In the preface to *The Chaplet of Pearls*, which she stressed was not 'a controversial tale' despite its setting during the religious crises of the sixteenth century,[164] she suggested a contrast between the world of history (English and French), of controversy and conflict, and the timeless world of unrecorded and private

---

[159] BL Add. MS 54920, fos. 78ᵛ–79ʳ. C. M. Yonge to A. Macmillan, 4 May 1865.

[160] See, however, ibid., fos. 105ᵛ–106ʳ. C. M. Yonge to A. Macmillan, 2 Aug. 1865. In this letter, Yonge did recognize that the authentic images she wished to include 'would not illustrate the whole story, as the events come in only incidently'.

[161] Ibid., fo. 108ʳ⁻ᵛ. C. M. Yonge to A. Macmillan, 13 Aug. 1865.   [162] Yonge, *Prince*, p. vi.

[163] BL Add. MS 54920, fo. 103ʳ⁻ᵛ. C. M. Yonge to A. Macmillan, 28 July 1865.

[164] C. M. Yonge, *The Chaplet of Pearls* (1868), p. iv.

human emotions, a better and purer sphere. She sounded a retreat from history itself, venturing into 'historical matters' only 'so far as my story became involved with them'.[165] Although the crux of *The Chaplet* was the French Massacre of St Bartholomew's Eve, it was on the private tragedy of a young husband, supposedly murdered under the cover of that night's events, that the text centred. The suggestion of two worlds, implicit in this work, occurred in many of Yonge's historical novels. The contrast between the two worlds became a conflict in one late work, significantly entitled *Unknown to History* (1882), where an (imaginary) daughter of Mary, Queen of Scots, concealed from birth in an obscure family, is forced to choose between her private and domestic identity as Cecily Talbot and a public and historical role as the Princess Bride: effacing herself from national history, she prefers an obscure and virtuous existence as the wife of her foster brother, in self-imposed exile in the Low Countries.

The escape of both Yonge and her characters from history is, however, apparent before the later novels, and so too is the use of a particular narrative device to lessen involvement with historical matters. A brief analysis of *The Lances of Lynwood*, a story for children published in 1855 with seven illustrations, will be helpful. Set during the Hundred Years War, it is the tale of Eustace Lynwood and how he comes to true knighthood by conquering the evil nature of his hereditary enemy, Fulk de Clarenham, and forgiving him. Although the Black Prince plays a part in the story, Yonge's preoccupation is not with medieval history, but medieval romance, as this plot summary suggests. Indeed, twice the course of events is interrupted by the telling of a romantic tale: one is the tale of Orthon, a spirit-bearer of news, lifted straight from Jean Froissart's *Chronicles*;[166] the other is the life-history of Eustace's page, Gaston d'Aubricour, which he saves the reader the trouble of tracing by indicating its similarity to the history of the 'Quatre Fils Aymon'.[167] The illustrations show the same preoccupation with medieval romance: the illustrator was the bird and animal painter, Jemima Blackburn,[168] who had already illustrated *The Little Duke* and with whom Yonge was clearly on amicable and open terms, as she corresponded with her on Macmillan's behalf when he proposed to publish another edition of *The Little Duke*.[169] Their good working relationship was founded on similar ages, educations, and backgrounds: born in 1823, Blackburn came from a upper middle-class Scottish family and had been an enthusiast for the Waverley novels, which soon

---

[165] Yonge, *Chaplet*, p. vii.

[166] C. M. Yonge, *The Lances of Lynwood* (1855), p. i.　　　[167] Yonge, *Lances*, 88.

[168] Mrs Hugh Blackburn, née Jemima Wedderburn, was a painter of animals, who, though she only exhibited three works at the Royal Academy, was admired by Ruskin for her *Illustrations of Scripture* (1855). See R. Fairley (ed.), *Jemima: The Paintings and Memoirs of a Victorian Lady* (Edinburgh, 1988).

[169] BL Add MS 54920, fos. 16ʳ, 17ᵛ, 18ʳ, 20ʳ. C. M. Yonge to A. Macmillan, 25 and 27 Jan., 1 and 17 Feb. 1864. Yonge was not entirely satisfied with Blackburn's illustrations for *The Little Duke*, but those for *The Lances of Lynwood* she described as 'much better'. She added, however, the perceptive comment that Blackburn was 'never really at home without animals as her subject'. Ibid., fos. 16ᵛ, 21ᵛ–22ʳ. C. M. Yonge to A. Macmillan, 25 Jan., 26 Feb. 1864.

Fig. 41. J. Blackburn, *The Disgraced Knight*, from C. M. Yonge, *The Lances of Lynwood* (1855), facing 259

became 'favourite subjects for illustration'.[170] It seems likely that Yonge and Blackburn agreed the subjects for illustration together, without the intervention of the publisher. Their choice is revealing: of the seven, no less than three[171] illustrate the tales within the text, and Blackburn seems to have used several as an opportunity to create nightmarish and Gothic images in 'atmospheric, almost claustrophobic engravings of an uneven quality'.[172] Scenes of picturesque historical reconstruction seem to have been avoided: the subject of the last illustration, entitled *The Disgraced Knight* (Fig. 41), would give latitude for the artist to depict Fulk's public degradation before the Black Prince and his court. But the historical was neglected in favour of the religious theme: Eustace is shown

[170] Fairley, *Jemima*, 101. [171] Yonge, *Lances*, frontispiece, facing 89, 93.
[172] Fairley, *Jemima*, 44.

rescuing Fulk from a stoning by the townsfolk, a church and a cross in the back-ground pointing the moral.[173]

The medieval romance as an escape device is more fully integrated into the text in the later novel, *The Prince and the Page* (1866), which was published with six amateurish illustrations by A. Farren.[174] The tale takes as its hero Richard de Montfort, as has been already mentioned. The future Edward I, in a spirit of for-giveness towards the family of his father's foe, elevates him from outlaw to royal page. Henry de Montfort, Richard's eldest brother and now the rightful Earl of Leicester, is believed slain at Evesham, but is found by the young page as a contented beggar, the widower of his old love whom he has secretly married and the father of a young girl. He refuses overtures of reconciliation and restora-tion from Edward, declaring (somewhat improbably) that his vagrant existence has afforded him 'happier days than ever I passed as Lord de Montfort at Kenilworth'.[175] Richard's further career includes a visit to Palestine on the Crusades, and a heroic death while saving Edward from the attacks of other, more vengeful Montfort brothers. Meanwhile, Henry remains a beggar, and accepts as son-in-law the only suitor of his daughter who will take her just as she is, without dowry. This strange conclusion derives from 'the old ballad of the Blind Beggar of Bethnal Green':[176] a mere tradition, rather than historical fact, has taken charge of Henry de Montfort as soon as he has been emancipated by his apparent death from the constraints of national history. This is the less surprising in view of the fondness for anecdotal traditions which Yonge has already manifested. The tale opens with what she confesses to be 'one of the stock anecdotes of history': the story of Edward and the outlaw, Adam de Gourlay.[177] When the assassin attacks Edward in the Holy Land, she recounts the old tale of Eleanor sucking the poison from the wound before the arrival of a physician, and remarks sadly that: 'Eleanor's devoted deed, the true saving of her husband, has lived on as a mere delusive tradition, weakly credited by the romantic, while the credit of his recov-ery has been retained by the Knight Templars' leech.'[178] History here has become the bearer of falsehood; tradition, the real truth, the truth of private and personal experience.

Do the illustrations reflect these aspects of *The Prince and the Page*? It seems likely that Yonge exercised some influence in the choice of the illustrations. Initially, in June 1865, she even proposed an illustrator, Miss Johns,[179] informing Macmillan that she has been 'promised some illustrations, the first of which is excellent'.[180] After seeing some more designs, Yonge was a little less enthusiastic,

[173] Yonge, *Lances*, facing 259.

[174] This artist was possibly a (female) relative of R. B. Farren, a landscape artist with a Cambridge address who was born in 1832. Wood, *Dictionary*, 150.

[175] Yonge, *Prince*, 79.   [176] Ibid., p. v.   [177] Ibid., p. iv.

[178] Ibid. 176. Yonge as a textbook writer was altogether more cautious. See Ch. 3.

[179] Miss Johns was active in 1859, when she exhibited a watercolour of a bird's nest at the Royal Society of British Artists at Suffolk Street. Wood, *Dictionary*, 255.

[180] BL Add. MS 54920, fos. 97ᵛ–98ʳ. C. M. Yonge to A. Macmillan, 23 June 1865.

Fig. 42. A. Farren, *Richard at the Bedside of Henry*, from C. M. Yonge, *The Prince and the Page* (1866), facing 69

although she had seen other works of the artist which were 'really very well executed'. She added 'I thought of having six illustrations if it seemed prudent and manageable.'[181] Six illustrations there were indeed, but the illustrator was A. Farren. Charlotte Yonge was, on the whole, satisfied, finding them 'full of life', although she was critical of the appearances of Queen Eleanor and Richard de Montfort in certain plates.[182] The coincidence of the number of illustrations suggests that, once again, Yonge selected the subjects. Strikingly, none of them is an authentic historical incident (or even a standard anecdotal subject), with the possible exception of the first, which illustrates the capture of Adam de Gourlay by

[181] BL Add. MS 54920, fo. 100[r-v]. C. M. Yonge to A. Macmillan, 1 July 1865.
[182] Ibid., fo. 115[r-v]. C. M. Yonge to A. Macmillan, 30 Oct. 1865.

Edward. The illustration, which shows Richard at the bedside of Henry, is typical (Fig. 42).[183] The least historical part of the book is, in fact, the most illustrated. The section devoted to the retelling of the ballad constitutes less than a fifth of the book, yet two of the six illustrations are given to it, probably because such simple and undemanding subjects as a pretty girl standing by a well were less intimidating for an artist clearly of no very high calibre than one such as the death of St Louis, a historical event which also occurs in the story.[184] The avoidance of some eminently appealing subjects, such as Edward repelling his assassin (with a well-established pictorial tradition), suggests that different, ahistorical priorities dominated the book and its illustrations.

From the inclusion of fables and legends as a sort of light relief in an historical novel, Yonge moved towards the simple telling of such tales—perceived as the repository of the eternal and recurring in human experience—in historical dress. Yonge's critics, however sympathetic, have rarely appreciated that this was the infirmity of nobler minds, and have tended to attribute this attitude to the parochial nature of her own experience.[185] A later work such as *Love and Life* (1880) took the immutability of human nature as an accepted premiss. The novel was subtitled 'an old story in Eighteenth Century costume': the old story was the Greek myth of Cupid and Psyche. Yonge commented disingenuously that it seemed to be 'one of those legends of such universal property that it was quite fair to put it into eighteenth century English costume'.[186] In the opening chapter, she justified the apparent anachronism involved in the transfer of a myth to a later age and another country: if 'times differ, human nature and national character vary but little'.[187] In this rejection of both nationality and history as significant forces shaping human experiences, Yonge expresses a weariness with both the picturesque historiography of her youth and the imperatives of contemporary scientific history.

THE LATER NINETEENTH-CENTURY HISTORICAL NOVEL:
OUT OF THE NATIONAL ARENA

The evolution of Yonge's novels thus reflected most facets of the development of the historical novel in the post-1850 period. Forging alliances of fact and fiction, text and image, the early nineteenth-century historical novel had engaged with national history: Scott had been preoccupied with the evolution of Britain from a medieval into a modern society, while Ainsworth had concerned himself with the picturesque reconstruction of the face of the national past. The later nineteenth-century historical novel confronted a new historiographical emphasis which marginalized narrativity and illustration as means of representing the national

---

[183] Yonge, *Prince*, facing 69.   [184] Ibid., facing 224, 228.
[185] See Battiscombe, *Yonge*, 131.   [186] C. M. Yonge, *Love and Life* (1880; 1882 edn.), p. x.
[187] Ibid. 1.

past, thus sidelining the historical novel itself. A new and more problematic relationship between the historical novel and national history thus resulted: while historical novelists remained committed to an ever more demanding standard of authenticity and research, typical of scientific historiography, their tales and the images which accompanied them emphasized the mythical and legendary rather than the historical, the private and personal rather than the public. Gaskell's triumphant and transcendent answer to the problem of the historical novel, the over-ambitious, intriguing, but ultimately flawed resolution of Eliot, and the varied attempts and partial successes of Yonge, all throw into contrast the gradual but inevitable decline of the picturesque antiquarian novel in the later works of one of its leading proponents, W. H. Ainsworth.

10

Experiments with History: The Later Novels of
W. H. Ainsworth and their Illustrations and
the Decline of the Picturesque Historical Novel

During a conversation with John Forster in 1870, Robert Browning mentioned meeting the novelist William Harrison Ainsworth; the biographer of Dickens exclaimed 'Good Heavens! . . . is he still alive ?'[1] The obscurity of the novelist who had once been seen as the rival of Dickens reflected the difficulties of continuing to write the picturesque historical fiction typical of the 1830s and 1840s after the middle of the century. Chapter 9 considered the extraordinary historical novels of successful writers, whose careers were built on their reputations as writers of contemporary novels: it showed how they turned from history to myth, from Romantic to Positivist philosophies, from engagement with the public narrative of national history to diverse and almost anti-national narratives of the private lives of obscure individuals. This chapter concentrates instead on the decline of an author whose *œuvre* was principally and almost entirely historical fiction of a type quintessentially of the 1840s.

Ainsworth's historical fiction collapsed under both internal and external pressures. Study of his 1844–6 novel, *Auriol Darcy*, reveals tensions and doubts already manifesting themselves within Ainsworth's traditional reconstructive fiction. These aspects of the novel are admirably illustrated by an artist whose style, like Ainsworth's, was typical of the 1830s and 1840s: H. K. Browne. Analysis of Ainsworth's later novels reveals the external pressures which the decline of the Romantic historical novel placed upon Ainsworth, and his struggles to adapt his work. It also shows his vain attempts to retain control over his illustrations, and to ensure a pattern of illustration which looked back to his heyday in the 1840s. This endeavour was doomed as his reputation declined and the power of his publishers increased proportionately, and as the rage for illustration characteristic of the 1840s was replaced by a new approach to the inclusion of imagery. Failure here reflected the failures of his later texts.

---

[1] S. M. Ellis, *William Harrison Ainsworth and his Friends*, 2 vols. (London and New York, 1911), ii, 264.

AURIOL DARCY: 'THE MOST FANTASTIC DISORDER'

Auriol Darcy, or, The Elixir of Life, first published in 1844–6 as *Revelations of London* in *Ainsworth's Magazine* and *The New Monthly Magazine*, was by far the most confusing novel Ainsworth ever wrote. Critics are usually at a loss to explain it. S. M. Ellis described it as 'the most extraordinary romance . . . a veritable night-mare and amazing jumble of antithetical incidents', adding that, although it contained 'the germ of a very fine plot' and was 'singularly picturesque', it was 'carelessly constructed and incomplete'.[2] George Worth sees it as 'the most disjointed of Ainsworth's novels and probably unfinished'.[3] More recently, John Sutherland has attempted to untangle the plot of the work, but describes it as 'a cobbled-together narrative' which ends with a return to the location and time of the first scene, and a dismissal of all preceding events as a hallucination of the hero.[4] Even Ainsworth himself dismissed it as 'merely a fragment of a romance'.[5] How did he come to write such an extraordinary and confused work?

Was Ainsworth forced to conclude the novel in an abrupt manner because of external pressures? He had occasionally succumbed to the pressure of time and finished a work so suddenly that substantial parts of the plot were left unresolved. *The Admirable Crichton* (1837), for instance, was finished very hurriedly: it concludes with an unlikely marriage, leaving the fate of two main characters unresolved.[6] While writing *Auriol*, Ainsworth was undoubtedly under considerable pressure, due to an argument with John Mortimer, the owner of *Ainsworth's Magazine*, which led to the author's resignation from the editorship, and his purchase of *The New Monthly Magazine*.[7] Ainsworth's resignation from *Ainsworth's Magazine* dissolved his partnership with Cruikshank:[8] the break-up of this significant creative relationship must have bruised his confidence. But this pressure could not be compared with that which he must have experienced in 1840, when he was planning and writing three novels, as well as carrying out the duties of an editor.[9] None of these works—the three considered in Chapter 4—suffered from the severe structural weaknesses which seem to characterize *Auriol*. Advocates for Cruikshank's primary role in the creation of the *Tower of London*, *Windsor Castle*, and *Old St Paul's* might initially seem to have strengthened their case by Ainsworth's apparent collapse as narrative author. However, the quality of several passages of description in *Auriol Darcy*, not to mention Ainsworth's

---

[2] S. M. Ellis, *William Harrison Ainsworth and his Friends*, 2 vols. (London and New York, 1911), ii. 110–11.

[3] G. Worth, *William Harrison Ainsworth* (New York, 1972), 120.

[4] J. Sutherland, *The Longman Companion to Victorian Fiction* (Harlow, 1988), 33.

[5] MCL MS vii, fo. 71ʳ. W. H. Ainsworth to J. Crossley, 6 Dec. 1869.

[6] Ellis, *Ainsworth*, i. 300–3; Worth, *Ainsworth*, 55–6.   [7] Ellis, *Ainsworth*, ii. 111.

[8] R. L. Patten, *George Cruikshank's Life, Times and Art*, 2 vols. (Cambridge, 1992 and 1996), ii. 174–5.

[9] Ellis, *Ainsworth*, i. 392–3.

relative return to form in a select number of novels of the late 1840s including *The Lancashire Witches*, militates against this conclusion.

It seems, therefore, that the elements of the novel itself—not external circumstances—were the real cause of most of the problems Ainsworth encountered. In *Auriol*, Ainsworth examined, probably not fully consciously, the problems of understanding the national past, and of bridging the gap between past and present by the sorts of imaginative reconstructions which he was producing in the 1840s. While he was doing this, the problems seem to have overwhelmed him, leading him to conclude the work ambiguously. A close examination of the text and of the marvellous illustrations provided by H. K. Browne, who seems to have realized the nature of Ainsworth's dilemma acutely, suggest what *Auriol* might be saying.

In 1844, Ainsworth had just completed the best of his historical reconstructions, works such as *Windsor Castle*, which combined text and image fully. He never published after this date any work which was quite as popular as these achievements of the early 1840s.[10] It seems that, in the mid to late 1840s, Ainsworth began to experience difficulty in producing the historical reconstructions in which he specialized: rather feeble novels, such as *James the Second, or, The Revolution of 1688* (1848), started to appear. Problems even at the peak of his achievement explain a tentative collaboration with Catherine Gore, the silver-fork novelist, in writing a contemporary novel, *Modern Chivalry, or a New Orlando Furioso* (1843), although the extent of his involvement is uncertain.[11]

This was the literary context within which Ainsworth wrote *Auriol*. Although his vision of the past was essentially Gothic and he frequently used Gothic elements in his fiction, *Auriol* represented a new departure in this field: historical elements embellish a Gothic argument rather than vice versa, as was the case in a novel such as The *Tower of London*. *Auriol* is entirely structured round the idea of immortal life, sustained from the sixteenth century to the nineteenth. As Sutherland has indicated, the most probable immediate source for the elixir of life motif was Edward Bulwer Lytton's *Zanoni* (1842).[12] Eugene Sue's *Mysteries of Paris* (1842–3) and his later *The Wandering Jew*, a copy of the former of which Ainsworth owned,[13] are likely sources for both the theme of immortality and the underworld scenes. For the latter, Dickens's *Oliver Twist* (1838) and G. W. M. Reynolds's *Mysteries of London* (1845–55) were also possible models.

---

[10] In 1881, the most popular novels of Ainsworth in the Manchester libraries were *The Tower of London*, *The Lancashire Witches*, *Old Saint Paul's*, *Windsor Castle*, *The Miser's Daughter*, and *The Manchester Rebels*. *The Lancashire Witches* and *The Manchester Rebels* were both boosted by local interest, and are therefore unrepresentative. A letter from Routledge and Sons to the editor of *The Manchester Guardian*, dated 10 Jan. 1905, elicited the information that the most profitable of Ainsworth's novels were still *The Tower of London*, *Windsor Castle*, and *Old Saint Pauls*. Ellis, *Ainsworth*, ii. 324–5; MCL MS xi, fo. 37ʳ.

[11] Ellis, *Ainsworth*, ii. 66–7.   [12] Sutherland, *Fiction*, 33.

[13] *Catalogue of the Library of the Late Celebrated Novelist, William Harrison Ainsworth* (1882), 17.

Ainsworth's illustrator, H. K. Browne, was, like the author, in a period of artistic evolution. Edward Hodnett has justly praised his illustrations to a new edition of Ainsworth's *The Admirable Crichton*, published in 1853, and those he
later produced for Ainsworth's *Mervyn Clitheroe* (1858), an autobiographical novel
set in contemporary England.[14] The illustrations to *Crichton* were quintessential
Browne of the 1840s: detailed and picturesque in manner, full of an antiquarian
interest in the costumes and architecture of the past. Some plates in *Auriol* are
very similar to these: *The Elixir of Life* (Fig. 43),[15] for example. Nevertheless,
Hodnett describes the illustrations to this novel as 'examples of his [Browne's]
in-between work'. A plate such as *Signing the Compact*[16] is in a different, more
classical and experimental manner, showing signs of change and growth.[17]
Browne's illustrations to Dickens's *Barnaby Rudge* (1841) had already shown use
of naturalistic graphics in the portrayal of Sir John Chester and Luke.[18] However,
Hodnett's criticism of the illustrations to *Auriol Darcy*—he comments that
Browne's attempts at sensational illustration are 'as dreadful as Ainsworth's
prose'[19]—show little appreciation of the variety and excellence of the plates, or of
the extent to which their eccentricities are explained by close consideration of the
text. The artist's attempt to experiment with a style closer to that which was to
dominate in the 1860s made him a very suitable illustrator for a novelist who was
similarly concerned about his artistic techniques. We can postulate a fairly high
degree of collaboration between author and artist: Ainsworth was a powerful
author, with a tradition of working closely with his illustrators; Browne was usually 'unspectacular because he always put the author's interests before his own'.[20]
It is not surprising to find a considerable correspondence between text and illustrations in this novel.

Auriol opens in 1599 in the chamber of Dr Lamb, an alchemist, who has been
trying to discover the elixir of life for half a century. Dr Lamb's quest to achieve
'the volatilisation of the fixed and the fixing of the volatile', to enter 'perpetual
life',[21] contrasts with the New Year's Eve activities outside, where there is 'an universal wish . . . among the citizens to see the new year in and [to] welcome the
century accompanying it'.[22] They welcome and accept the passage of time and its
natural consequences. By contrast Lamb, who seeks to preserve life unnaturally,
lives in a chamber full of death:

In one corner was a terrestrial globe . . . On the other side lay a black, mysterious-
looking book . . . Near this, was the leather bag containing the two decapitated heads
. . . Near it were two parchment scrolls . . . One of the scrolls was kept in place by

[14] E. Hodnett, *Image and Text* (1982), 158.
[15] W. H. Ainsworth, *Auriol, or the Elixir of Life* (1844–6; 1875 edn.), facing 20.
[16] Ibid., facing 135.   [17] Hodnett, *Image*, 158.
[18] J. R. Cohen, *Charles Dickens and his Original Illustrators* (Columbus, Ohio, 1980), 78.
[19] Hodnett, *Image*, 158.
[20] E. Hodnett, *Five Centuries of English Book Illustration* (Aldershot, 1988), 113. Some recent
critics stress Browne's relative independence from Dickens. See J. H. Miller, *Illustration*
(Cambridge, Mass., 1992), 96–111.
[21] Ainsworth, *Auriol*, 15.   [22] Ibid. 2.

a skull. An ancient and grotesque-looking brass lamp, with two snake-headed burners, lighted the room. From the ceiling depended a huge, scaly sea-monster . . . The chimney piece . . . was laden with various implements of hermetic science. Above it were hung dried bats and flitter-mice, interspersed with the skulls of birds. Within the room were two skeletons, one of which, placed behind a curtain in the deep embrasure of the window, where its polished bones glistened in the white moonlight, had a horrible effect . . .[23]

The portents for Lamb's project are ominous, as he has already failed once in an attempt to preserve life against the advance of time: he tells his great-grandson, Auriol, how his earlier efforts to preserve the beauty of his young wife led to her death.[24]

The elixir is not unsuccessful: it does indeed impart immortal life—but what life. Ainsworth, who, like Lamb, has tried to defy time by reanimating what is consigned to death, seems alarmed at the methods by which he has reconstructed the past. The very fires of the elixir have a terrifying effect on the dead and inanimate objects about the room, which

seemed to take on other forms, and to become instinct with animation. The gourd-shaped cucurbites were transformed into great bloated toads bursting with venom; the long-necked bolt-heads become monstrous serpents; the worm-like pipes turned into adders; the alembics looked like plumed helmets; the characters . . . on the parchments . . . seemed . . . to be ever changing; the sea-monster bellowed and roared, and, flapping his fin, tried to burst from his hook; the skeletons wagged their jaws, and raised their fleshless fingers in mockery, while blue light burnt in their eyeless sockets; the bellows became a prodigious bat fanning the fire with its wings; and the old alchemist assumed the appearance of the archfiend . . .[25]

The reanimated objects of death, of the past, become monsters. Ironically, Lamb dies before he can take the elixir, which Auriol snatches from his corpse and drinks. Once again, the dead objects in the room take on a ghoulish life: 'Every object reeled and danced around him . . . the skeletons grinned and gibbered; so did the death's-head on the table; so did the skulls against the chimney; the monstrous sea-fish belched forth fire and smoke . . . while the dead alchemist shook his hand menacingly'.[26] Flapdragon, a dwarfish servant of Lamb, who also swallows some of the potion, experiences the same hallucinogenic sense of the dead objects being endowed with a menacing and unnatural appearance of life.[27] Browne encapsulated the message of this prologue to the novel in the illustration *The Elixir of Life* (Fig. 43). In this plate, the dead and inanimate objects show signs of life, particularly the skeletons, the skull on the table, the mask above the mantlepiece, and the fish hanging from the ceiling. Browne was, in fact, an ideal illustrator for this subject: he perceptively used the well-worn techniques of early nineteenth-century caricature to personify inanimate objects.

But unnatural life carries a curse, as Flapdragon soon discovers: he is doomed to live in 'poverty and distress', haunted by visions of his dead master.[28] Auriol, too, carries the same curse with him: it is a flaw of which Lamb's teachers had

---

[23] Ainsworth, *Auriol*, 11.   [24] Ibid. 17–18.   [25] Ibid. 12–13.   [26] Ibid. 20–1.
[27] Ibid. 58.   [28] Ibid.

Fig. 43. H. K. Browne, *The Elixir of Life*, from W. H. Ainsworth, *Auriol, or The Elixir of Life* (1875), facing 20

warned their pupil, 'the *one* vulnerable point, by which, like the heel of Achilles, death might reach' the drinker of the elixir.[29] This Achilles' heel metaphor is carried through the novel by both author and artist: they remind the reader of it when Auriol, now living in 1830 and in the torments of a compact with an agent of the Devil, Cyprian de Rougemont—which he has made to escape the eternal poverty and misfortune entailed by the curse—is forced to meet his foe in Hyde Park. The meeting takes place beneath the Achilles statue, erected after the Napoleonic Wars to celebrate the victory of the Duke of Wellington at Waterloo and a potent symbol of pride in the national past; Browne provides an illustration

[29] Ainsworth, *Auriol*, 14.

of the scene to reinforce this point, allowing the statue to dominate a good two-thirds of the plate.[30]

Ainsworth's almost unconscious suspicions about bridging time and reanimating the national past, an attempt which might produce gibbering skeletons rather than realistic reconstructions, were compounded by almost contradictory doubts of the feasibility of reconstruction of any sort. At times, for the author, the past seemed too hopelessly fragmented for meaningful reconstruction. Dr Lamb's chamber, a room full of the past, is in complete disarray: everything is 'scattered about without any attempt at arrangement',[31] as Browne's illustration shows (Fig. 43). But a more compelling example of the fragmentation of the national past is presented by the ruined house in Vauxhall Road, where Auriol is ambushed by two robbers, as he goes to meet Rougemont. One of the two, the Sandman, looks round the 'tumble-down' property as they await Auriol's arrival:

[An] extraordinary and incongruous assemblage of objects . . . met the gaze of the Sandman . . . he beheld huge mill-stones, enormous water-wheels, boilers of steam-engines, iron vats, cylinders, cranes, iron pumps . . . a gigantic pair of wooden scales, old iron safes, old boilers, old gas-pipes, old water-pipes, cracked old bells, old bird-cages, old plates of iron, old pulleys, ropes and rusty chains, huddled and heaped together in the most fantastic disorder. In the midst of the chaotic mass frowned the bearded and colossal head of Neptune, which had once decorated the forepart of a man-of-war. Above it, on a sort of framework, lay a prostrate statue of a nymph, together with a bust of Fox, the nose of the latter being partially demolished, and the eyes knocked in. Above these, three garden divinities laid their heads amicably together. On the left stood a tall Grecian warrior, minus the head and right hand.[32]

Once again, a fine illustration by Browne (Fig. 44) reinforced the point, centralizing the most obvious fragments of the past—the busts and statues.[33] The national past is in ruins here, and lies irrevocably jumbled with the debris of a destructive industrial present. As Richard Maxwell points out, the house epitomizes specifically 'the plight of the modern city whose past is being swept away while its present and future seem to lack coherent form'.[34] Anne Humphreys, examining the genre of the Victorian mysteries novel, to which *Auriol* partly belongs, also identifies the sharply felt loss of the old in a time of transition as a concern of all authors working in this genre: 'The mysteries novel could not come into being until the modern city itself was visible, until the effects of rapid expansion and change were evident in the disappearance of the old'.[35] As she points out, in these works the Gothic castle or abbey is here replaced by empty and

---

[30] Ainsworth, *Auriol*, frontispiece.   [31] Ibid. 11.   [32] Ibid. 27.

[33] Ibid., facing 31.

[34] R. Maxwell, 'City Life and the Novel', *Comparative Literature*, 30 (1976), 160.

[35] A. Humphreys, 'Generic Strands and Urban Twists: The Victorian Mysteries Novel', *VS* 34 (1991), 456. Visual aspects of the interpretation of London, and its changing appearance, are considered in A. Potts, 'Picturing the Modern Metropolis: Images of London in the Nineteenth Century', *HWJ* 26 (1988), 28–56.

Fig. 44. H. K. Browne, *The Ruined House in Vauxhall Road*, from
Ainsworth, *Auriol*, facing 31

ruinous buildings in the city.[36] Ruined and fragmented houses are indeed the
motifs of the text and illustrations of *Auriol*. Meditating on this ruin of the past at
the very heart of national history—the city of London, the historic appearance of
which he had rebuilt in *The Tower of London* and *Old St Paul's*—Ainsworth

---

[36] Humphreys, 'Victorian Mysteries Novel', 459.

seems to have abandoned his agenda for the picturesque reconstruction and preservation, both literal and figurative, of the architecture of the national past.

In *Auriol*, Ainsworth seems driven to ask questions about his own role as a narrator of the national past and about the response of his public. Is a truthful reconstruction from these fragments of the past possible, or is the past already too destroyed to allow it, so that the reconstructor will seem a liar? This is Flapdragon's experience when he attempts to describe old London to a circle of underworld friends. He waxes eloquent, in a speech reminiscent of Ainsworth's own nostalgic reconstructions of the London of Tudor and Stuart England:

The whole aspect of the place is altered. The Thames itself is unlike the Thames of old. Its waters were . . . once . . . clear and bright . . . and its banks . . . were edged with gardens . . . all are gone! . . . London is a mighty city . . . but in point of beauty it is not to be compared with the city of Queen Bess's days.[37]

Here is the usual Ainsworthian sense of an irretrievable picturesque past. However, one of Flapdragon's auditors, Ginger, replies that he speaks 'like one o' them smart chaps they calls, and werry properly, penny-a-liars . . . You've seen some picters o' Old Lunnon, and they've haunted you in your dreams, till you've begun to fancy you lived in those days.'[38] Here Ainsworth exposed his own practices unerringly, and suggested that his reconstructions contain a risk of falsehood. To judge by the response of Flapdragon's audience, the novelist was doubting his ability to reconstruct fragments of the past into a truly authentic and convincing picture.

In a later chapter focused on the statue of Charles I at Charing Cross, this theme continues. Flapdragon tells the antiquary, Loftus, how John Rivers preserved the Hubert LeSueur statue of the King, which Parliament ordered to be sold and broken up:

we digged a great pit, secretly, in the cellar . . . and buried it . . . my master [Rivers] collected together all the pieces of old brass he could procure. These he afterwards produced, and declared they were the fragments of the statue . . . And plenty of 'em he sold too, for the Cavaliers bought them 'em as memorials of their martyred monarch, and the Roundheads as evidences of his fall. In this way he soon got back his outlay.[39]

The statue was brought out at the Restoration, but Rivers got no reward. The image of the past buried whole, the false fragments, and the opposing interpretations of the past which they represent to their purchasers, suggest Ainsworth's unease with his own reconstructive practices. Ironically, the statue itself is, in a sense, a fraud, as its construction signalled the final destruction of an older relic of the past, the Eleanor Cross, which Loftus significantly would have preferred.[40] Loftus is that rare phenomenon, a man who recognizes historical truth and is interested in it: Ainsworth clearly identifies with the antiquary as well as the dwarf. Few others besides Loftus give Flapdragon a sympathetic hearing, or care to see the past revived. When the two study the statue at Charing Cross, an

---

[37] Ainsworth, *Auriol*, 52–3.   [38] Ibid. 54.   [39] Ibid. 106.   [40] Ibid. 105.

uncomprehending crowd joins them, more interested in the antiquaries than in the statue:[41] this moment is chosen for illustration, which suggests its importance to the author.[42] The crowd's mockery and failure to realize why Loftus is fascinated by the statue may reflect Ainsworth's unconscious concern with the lack of knowledge and interest about the past in his readers, his sense of himself as a figure of ridicule, and even his fear that his style of historical fiction (dependent on the antiquarian approach of such gentlemen-scholars as Loftus) was losing popularity. Did Ainsworth consider the reading public as imitators of the Tinker, who is 'content vith Lunnon as it is . . .' specially as there ain't much chance o' the ould city bein' rewived'?[43]

Both the dangers and the difficulties of attempts to bridge the gap between the past and the present, and to reconstruct and reanimate the past, are finally exposed in the much debated conclusion. In the last two chapters we witness the final breakdown of Auriol's sense of time, aided by Rougemont. Auriol wakes up from a drugged sleep to find himself in Elizabethan dress. He is unable to decide whether the events of the last 230 years are a dream or a reality, experiencing the passage of national history as violently and traumatically changeful and essentially alienating: such a perception contradicts the dominant and optimistic nineteenth-century interpretation of national history as a process of gradual and gentle progress. He asks himself:

Have I endured a long and troubled dream, during which I have fancied myself living through more than two centuries? . . . Methought I lived in the reigns of many sovereigns . . . saw revolutions convulse the kingdom—old dynasties shaken down, and new ones spring up. Fashions seem to me to have so changed, that I clean forgot the old ones; while my fellow-men scarcely appeared the same as heretofore.[44]

Whether or not Auriol has been dreaming is not made very clear, but (despite Sutherland's contention) all the indications that there are suggest that he has not, and is in fact being deceived by Rougemont. It is unnatural to defy time, it seems, and Auriol's attempt has left him open to the collapse of sanity which his foe wishes to engineer. Rougemont's presence and suppressed laughter as Auriol postulates the theory of a dream; the suspicious potion administered before Auriol is taken to visit the supposed Dr Lamb; Lamb's refusal to let Auriol touch him, and the final ambiguous paragraph of the book all suggest this conclusion. The final paragraph reads

It was very dark, and objects could be only imperfectly distinguished. Still he fancied he could detect the gleam of the river beneath him, and what seemed a long line of houses on the bridge. He also fancied he discerned other buildings, with the high roofs, the gables, and the other architectural peculiarities of the structures of Elizabeth's time. He persuaded himself, also, that he could distinguish through the gloom the venerable Gothic pile of Saint Paul's Cathedral . . . After a while, he returned from the window, and said to his supposed grandsire, 'I am satisfied. I have lived centuries in a few nights.'[45]

[41] Ainsworth, *Auriol*, 108–9.   [42] Ibid., facing 107.   [43] Ibid. 53.
[44] Ibid. 188.   [45] Ibid. 200–1.

The use of 'seemed', 'fancied', 'persuaded', and 'supposed' are clearly intended to alert the reader. Browne's illustration to this section also carries clues to what has happened—both in Rougemont's hidden, laughing presence, and the possible resemblance of Auriol's figure to Delacroix's 1824 representation of the (mad) Tasso imprisoned in the hospital of St Anna.[46]

The novel ended abruptly, with the fate of all the characters unresolved. But it fulfilled one purpose: it expressed Ainsworth's deep, perhaps unconscious, recognition of the dangers and difficulties of imaginative reconstructions of national history. The unfinished nature of the novel suggests Ainsworth's desire to evade further consideration of the nature of his historical fiction. However, struggles with the form of historical fiction which he practised in the 1840s were not to be avoided after 1850, as Ainsworth experienced the same external problems as other historical novelists. *Auriol* was only a foretaste of the problems which lay ahead.

AINSWORTH'S LATER NOVELS: FAR FROM THE MADDING CROWD

The internal difficulties which Ainsworth experienced writing *Auriol* were exacerbated by the financial problems of writing historical fiction after 1850. Commentators agree that Ainsworth's decline arose from an inability to write anything but the style of historical fiction which had made him famous. Andrew Sanders argues that descent into obscurity was the result of his outlasting his public, and failing to regain their attention with sequels.[47] However, as both Ellis and Sutherland have recognized, it was not for want of trying to break out of his established mode of fiction. The early numbers of his contemporary autobiographical novel, *Mervyn Clitheroe*, were unpopular. The novelist wrote: 'I cannot understand why it has not found favour with the general public, because I have written carefully, and I think there is interest in the story—But I could not go on at a loss'.[48] As Ellis indicates, the reading public expected only one sort of novel from the author of *The Tower of London*.[49] Sutherland has accurately assessed the problems which the Victorian publishing system imposed on the writer: although there was a brief period in the early 1840s when Ainsworth was powerful enough to have experimented with other sorts of novels, his continuation of historical novel-writing at that point meant that, eventually, he had to 'write historical romances or starve'.[50]

Nevertheless, Ainsworth's later work was not simply a repetition of the format of the 1840s. The inferiority of his late novels was not purely the result of the

---

[46] Ainsworth, *Auriol*, facing 192; L. Johnson, *The Paintings of Eugene Delacroix: A Critical Catalogue, 1816–31* (Oxford, 1981), i. 91; ii, plate 92.

[47] A. Sanders, *The English Historical Novel* (1979), 45.

[48] MCL MS v, fo. 19ʳ. W. H. Ainsworth to J. Crossley, 4 Mar. 1852.

[49] Ellis, *Ainsworth*, ii. 177–8.

[50] J. A. Sutherland, *Victorian Novelists and Publishers* (1976), 161.

increasing pressures of low returns, shortage of time, old age, and inability to secure collaborative illustrators of the calibre of Cruikshank.[51] It was the result, too, of a struggle for a form of historical fiction so severe, that—despite all adverse circumstances—Ainsworth several times attempted to rival the success of sensationalist novelists such as William Wilkie Collins with a modern novel. These attempts—*Old Court* (1867), *Myddleton Pomfret* (1865), and *Hilary St Ives* (1870)—were unsuccessful; Sutherland describes the last of the three as 'a pathetic attempt' which 'failed miserably'.[52] Ainsworth's later historical novels, meanwhile, fall roughly into two classes. The first class—examples of which include *The Spendthrift: A Tale* (1856), *Ovingdean Grange, A Tale of the South Downs* (1860), and *The Lord Mayor of London, or, City Life in the Last Century* (1862)—are centred round mainly or wholly fictitious characters and plots set against an historical background. The second class includes novels such as *Cardinal Pole; or the Days of Philip and Mary* (1863), *The Constable of the Tower: An Historical Romance* (1861), *Boscobel; or The Royal Oak: A Tale of the Year 1651* (1872), *The Goldsmith's Wife: A Tale* (1875), and *The Fall of Somerset* (1878). In these novels, history itself provides the plot, historical characters predominate, and the fictional heroes and heroines are disposed of in a very peremptory fashion. Some novels appear to fall between the two categories, such *The Manchester Rebels* (1873). Ainsworth's uneasy vacillation between these two forms suggests his lasting anxiety concerning authenticity and the feasibility of continuing to reconstruct the national past as he had done. His attempts to reform the traditional structure of his historical fictions shows the use (generally without success) of many techniques already discussed in Chapter 9. The accompanying illustrations by Browne, Frederick Gilbert, and J. H. Rimbault show the author struggling to retain control over the images published with his text, and they act as an revealing variation on the same theme of the breakdown of picturesque historical reconstruction.

  The Spendthrift (1856) is described by Ellis as a tale of 'little merit . . . [in which] both plot and incident are weak'.[53] It is clearly in the tradition of *The Miser's Daughter*—a plot set against a historical background. But while *The Miser's Daughter* does contain historical characters, and makes an attempt at engagement with the past though in an unusual way, *The Spendthrift* is a purely fictional tale of private concerns. It is a Rake's Progress, fortunately and suddenly arrested: Gage de Monthermer, the spendthrift, is cheated by his steward, Fairlie, rejected by Fairlie's daughter Clare, and falls into a career of debauchery, a circumstance exploited by various unscrupulous card-sharpers. The friendship of

---

[51] Ainsworth was clearly experiencing these pressures. While, according to Ellis's estimation, Ainsworth received £1,500 from the sale of *Guy Fawkes* in 1842, a late novel such as *Preston Fight; or the Insurrection of 1715* (1875) was purchased by his publisher, Tinsley, for £125. Ainsworth worked during the last twenty years of his working career at a breakneck speed. As early as 1864, he wrote to Crossley: 'For several years I have been obliged to work exceedingly hard, and the strain is almost too much for me . . . It is only prudent . . . to relax these excessive exertions, but as I now stand, I cannot do so.' Ellis, *Ainsworth*, i. 405; ii. 296, 251.

[52] Sutherland, *Novelists*, 159.   [53] Ellis, *Ainsworth*, ii. 223.

Arthur Poynings and the love of Poynings's sister, Lucy, with the loyalty of his tenants, save his estates and his life. The illustrations are, once again, by H. K. Browne, and they interpret the text very accurately: they are dramatic and comic scenes in eighteenth-century dress. *Sword-Play*, for instance, is a picture of a duel set against the backcloth of an ivy-covered ruined castle;[54] *A Night at the Groom-Porters* is a gambling scene.[55] Although Browne has taken care to include all the correct characters in each scene, the treatment is sketchy. The artist frequently avoids the trouble of creating an entire eighteenth-century backcloth by the use of screens: four of the eight illustrations include one. Clearly the purpose of these images is not to reconstruct an authentic image, but to evoke an atmosphere by the use of charming vignettes. In view of the existence of a blindingly obvious visual precedent—Hogarth's *Rake's Progress*—and the tradition of reliance upon Hogarth and the caricature school among the illustrators of the 1830s and 1840s, analysed by J. R. Harvey,[56] it is startling that Browne draws so little upon this source. In fact, the illustrations as a whole show Browne's work in a moment of transition and experimentation.[57] The elements of the comic and the grotesque, which are commonly associated with his style, are toned down. The sense of structure inherent in an illustration such as that of Hugh for Dickens's *Barnaby Rudge* is faintly apparent, but the artist is clearly struggling in his attempt to change and develop his style. This is reflected in his failure to find one standard figure to represent Gage, who appears in six of the seven illustrations.

When he illustrated Ainsworth's *Ovingdean Grange* (1860), Browne achieved a more consistent, if still more sketchy style. This novel is the best of Ainsworth's later works: Ellis has described it as 'the prettiest of Ainsworth's stories: it . . . is simply a charming, unaffected tale of English life in the days of Cavalier and Roundhead'.[58] Its plot is better than most of Ainsworth's later works, no doubt partly because it is so closely modelled on Scott's *Woodstock* (1826). The opposition of the old Cavalier, Colonel Maunsel, his son Clavering, the High Church vicar Ardingley Beard, and his daughter, to the encroachments of the Puritan minister, Increase Micklegift, and the parliamentary general, Stelfax, may be lacking in subtlety, but it is structurally sound. The absence of any real historical character (as opposed to than 'types'),[59] except the Earl of Rochester and (briefly) Charles II, freed Ainsworth from some of the restrictions of historical

---

[54] W. H. Ainsworth, *The Spendthrift: A Tale* (1856), frontispiece.   [55] Ibid., facing 211.

[56] Harvey, *Novelists*, 19–75.

[57] See J. Buchanan-Brown, *Phiz! The Book Illustrations of Hablot Knight Browne* (Newton Abbot, London, and Vancouver, 1978), 23–4.

[58] Ellis, *Ainsworth*, ii. 231.

[59] The use of types of characters in historical opposition may suggest that Ainsworth was considering an approach to historical fiction closer to Scott's, by creating typical characters representing social groups within an historical conflict. If so, Ainsworth is not successful, both because the situations in which the characters clash are not historically typical, and (paradoxically) because the characters are so general, so lacking in particularities, that they lack real and historical substance. Ainsworth might have developed his novel as Gaskell did *Sylvia's Lovers*, to present real history as ultimately private and transcendent, but this was undoubtedly beyond his powers of characterization.

authenticity. Even the visit of the King himself to the Grange is an invention, as it was in *Woodstock*, although, as Ellis points out, there was a tradition of such a visit.[60]

Two aspects of the novel are of particular interest. *Ovingdean Grange* highlights the appearance, in Ainsworth's novels, of the theme of retreat from history, a retirement from the passage of time and events. Whereas, in earlier works, Ainsworth's imagination and indignation often centred on urban change and the stark contrast of the national past and present presented in the city, here, by selecting a secluded village, he avoided many of these concerns: 'Since the year 1651, but slight change has taken place in the sequestered little village of Ovington . . . notwithstanding its contiguity to the queen of watering places, Brighton, [it] seems quite out of the world.'[61] It had, he wrote, a peaceful little church, already old in 1651 which 'Time has dealt kindly with', and which possessed a 'peculiar air of privacy and tranquillity': 'Truly, a quiet resting place after the turmoil of life'.[62] It is in this quiet and unchanging hamlet that Clavering Maunsel decides to remain at the close of the novel. Charles II, now restored, asks him to 'quit his seclusion and come to court', but he 'respectfully declined the honour'.[63] The King (who represents history and change) is associated with Brighton, which, Ainsworth noted, was to see 'wondrous and inconceivable changes'.[64] This provision of an ahistorical home for the fictional characters, safe from the passage of historical change, is not the only sign of Ainsworth's unease with imaginative historical reconstruction. A centrepiece of the novel is 'The Legend of Devil's Dyke', an unconnected fiction reminiscent of Barham's *Ingoldsby Legends*. This tale proved very popular, and was reprinted, with illustrations of the Dyke, in 1862 and 1876.[65] In the legend, St Cuthman saves the Downs from being flooded by the Devil. Ainsworth appeared to view the Downs (as he had earlier viewed the Tower of London and other great national monuments) as an uncorrupted record of the national past, placed in danger. The Downs at night, he wrote in the first chapter, 'seem . . . to mutter secrets of the Past. Of most other places in the land the ancient features are changed, disfigured; or wholly obliterated; but the old visage of the South Downs is unaltered . . . What wonder that such ancient hills . . . should sometimes discourse of the great people they have known.'[66] The legend, then, is a representation of Ainsworth's old anxiety for the preservation of historical remains; what is unusual is his reticence in calling for the protection of the Downs. The disguising of his anxiety in legend—which, in later Victorian historical novels, suggests avoidance of history—seems to indicate confusion and loss of confidence. The implication that the past is concealed in muttered 'secrets', rather than presented in readable texts, may suggest, too, that it is difficult to approach and unavailable to reconstruction.

  [60] Ellis, *Ainsworth*, ii. 232–3. As has been shown, later 19th-cent. historical novelists often preferred to rest their tale on a tradition, legend, or myth, rather than an authenticated and detailed historical event.

  [61] W. H. Ainsworth, *Ovingdean Grange: A Tale of the South Downs* (1860), 7.

  [62] Ibid. 9.   [63] Ibid. 357.   [64] Ibid. 331–2.

  [65] Ellis, *Ainsworth*, ii. 232 n.   [66] Ainsworth, *Grange*, 5.

Fig. 45. H. K. Browne, *Clavering Sets out to Join the King*, from
W. H. Ainsworth, *Ovingdean Grange: A Tale of the South Downs*
(1860), facing 16

The illustrations of *Ovingdean Grange* reflect uncannily Ainsworth's use of
fictional characters who represent 'types' of historical ones: General Stelfax, for
instance, is presented by Ainsworth as the type of a parliamentary general,
loosely derived from Fairfax. The illustrations are well-drawn, but in a stylized
way: characters' features are sketchy and impersonal, if not concealed. A clear
example of this absence of facial definition is in the plate *Clavering Sets out to Join
the King* (Fig. 45).[67] Dulcia, the heroine, and her maid, Patty, have their backs

---

[67] Ainsworth, *Grange*, facing 16.

to the viewer, and no one could tell from the presentation of Clavering and his servant, John Habergeon, that the latter is supposed to be fifty years older than the hero. The plate *Hawking on the Downs*[68] is a similarly stylized genre scene, completely different from the scenes portrayed by Cruikshank for *The Tower of London*, where specific historic events had taken place with identifiable characters. In this plate, although we know the riders are Colonel Maunsel and Dulcia, this is irrelevant to the enjoyment of a pleasing old world social occasion. Even where the artist had a clear portrait model—in the plate *Charles II at Ovingdean Grange*[69]—the King remains an undistinguishable type of the Cavalier. Only Stelfax and Micklegift have anything like a distinctive appearance. The illustrations represent Browne's attempt to come to terms with the Sixties style, which was clearly not fully compatible with his own. Where John Millais is statuesque, he is stylized and sketchy. But then Ainsworth, as a novelist, was equally tried.

Ovingdean Grange was the last of Ainsworth's novels to be illustrated by Browne; the Gilberts, Sir John and his son Frederick,[70] monopolized the illustration of this novelist from 1861. Ainsworth produced other novels of this kind—for instance, *The Lord Mayor of London* (1862), which, like *The Spendthrift*, was set in the eighteenth century. Although it did include more real historical characters than *Ovingdean Grange*, the plot centres round the 'imaginary' mayor, Sir Gresham Lorimer, and his equally fictive family.[71] The novel remained unillustrated until it was reprinted by Routledge and Sons, with four illustrations by Frederick Gilbert, in 1880. One wonders if this absence of illustrations is linked to Ainsworth's deteriorating position with his publishers, Edward Chapman and William Hall, despite the fact that they were old friends: Chapman refused to give Ainsworth the same terms as he had offered the author for his 1861 novel, *The Constable of the Tower*, on the grounds of this novel's disappointing sales.[72] The publishers may well have wished to economize on the illustrations too.

AINSWORTH'S LATER NOVELS: RESPECTING
THE 'AUTHORITY OF HISTORY'

The second format adopted by Ainsworth in his later historical novels is apparent in this very novel, *The Constable of the Tower* (1861). Here Ainsworth

---

[68] Ainsworth, *Grange*, facing 83.   [69] Ibid., facing 322.

[70] Sir John Gilbert was a painter and watercolourist of historical genre, a successor to the sentimental and Romantic tradition of George Cattermole. His initial career was as an illustrator, particularly to *The Illustrated London News*; after 1850, however, he concentrated mainly on his watercolours. His son was an exhibitor at Sussex Street, whose work included subjects from Shakespeare and Tennyson. Wood, *Dictionary*, 175.

[71] W. H. Ainsworth, *The Lord Mayor of London, or, City Life in the Last Century*, 3 vols. (1862), i, p. iv.

[72] Sutherland, *Novelists*, 155–6; for the firm of Chapman and Hall, see Sutherland, *Fiction*, 115–16. In the 1840s, they had produced cheap reprints of Ainsworth's works.

intended to make history itself the entire plot, at the cost of any fictional and romantic subplot. The reader is initially perplexed by the title of the novel—the constable, Sir John Gage, serves as a moral touchstone in a corrupt world, but is otherwise a very minor element in the novel. It is focused instead on the career of Sir Thomas Seymour, brother of Protector Somerset, from the last days of Henry VIII to his own execution. Even this focus is a dim one: Ainsworth moved from one court anecdote or event to the next with so little discrimination that chronology often appears to be the sole ordering principle. The tale of Catherine Parr's near arrest for Protestant sympathies, for example, touches only tangentially on the career of Seymour (later her fourth husband), and could easily have been excluded.

Although, as Andrew Sanders notes, many of Ainsworth's novels are 'moulded round historical crises which oblige the novelist to follow a line of development close to his sources',[73] there are substantial differences between *The Tower of London*, which Sanders has examined, and *The Constable*. *The Tower of London* can rely on the events of the life of Lady Jane Grey from her accession to her execution to provide the plot because 'Lady Jane Grey is more than just the centre of a political plot, she is the moral centre of the novel'.[74] Thomas Seymour is portrayed as charming but villainous. *The Tower of London* may appear to be nothing more than an arbitrary chunk of history; it closes abruptly, but it does achieve unity by its concentration of all action around the Tower. *The Constable*, meanwhile, shifts between London, Sudeley, Whitehall, and Windsor. The accession and execution of Lady Jane Grey are two linked events; but the novelist could easily have taken up the career of Thomas Seymour at any number of earlier points. While the events of all but the subplot of *The Tower* relate, in some way, to the fate of the central character, this is not true in the case of *The Constable*. In this work, Ainsworth digresses to describe at great length Henry VIII's funeral, for no better reason than that 'the obsequies were the most magnificent ever celebrated in this country, or perhaps any other, [so] we may be excused for dwelling upon them at some length; . . . [the event presents] a very striking illustration of the customs of an age that delighted in show and solemnities of all kinds'.[75] The coronation of Edward VI is a similar event.[76]

The illustrations to *The Constable*, which were by John Gilbert, showed some attention to the text, but none of the research which characterizes Cruikshank's, or even Browne's, collaboration with the novelist. In the title-page illustration for volume i, *Sir Thomas Seymour Vowing Fidelity to Prince Edward* (Fig. 46),[77] Henry VIII, a particularly pleasing grotesque figure, is clearly derived from Holbein's portraits. But in the plate *The Earl of Hertford and Sir Anthony Brown Announcing his Father's Death to the Prince Edward*,[78] the figure of the Princess

---

[73] Sanders, *Novel*, 35.   [74] Ibid. 41.

[75] W. H. Ainsworth, *The Constable of the Tower: An Historical Romance*, 3 vols. (1861), ii. 132–94.

[76] Ibid. ii. 242–87.   [77] Ibid. i, frontispiece.   [78] Ibid. i, facing 157.

Fig. 46. J. Gilbert, *Sir Thomas Seymour Vowing Fidelity to Prince Edward*, from W. H. Ainsworth, *The Constable of the Tower: An Historical Romance*, 3 vols. (1861), i, frontispiece

Elizabeth, despite the existence of a well-known portrait of her at the appropriate age, is not derived from any source. In the plate *The Meeting between King Edward and the Lady Jane Gray* [sic] *in the Tower Gardens*,[79] Edward resembles his portraits, but Lady Jane does not resemble any of hers. Gilbert's plates are rather splendid, and when the artist had a chance to produce a really melodramatic image, he exploited the opportunity—as in the plate, *The Meeting between*

[79] W. H. Ainsworth, *The Constable of the Tower: An Historical Romance*, 3 vols. (1861), i, facing 223.

Sir Thomas Seymour and the Princess Elizabeth Interrupted by the Queen Dowager.[80] But clearly Gilbert's preoccupations were very different from those of Cruikshank and Ainsworth himself. As Gilbert was renowned as a hack artist who worked at an incredible pace, it seems unlikely that Ainsworth was able to exercise much control over the illustrations. Indeed, he might well have been able to publish the book edition of his novel with illustrations only because they were already provided for the magazine version.

Like *The Constable*, Ainsworth's 1863 novel, *Cardinal Pole*, marginalized the titular hero, who only appeared in the second third of the book; once again, it was a chunk of history which formed the main plot. Unlike *The Constable*, however, this novel had a fictional subplot, but the hero and heroine of this are inexplicably sacrificed to the main plot: this is the first case in the 1860s of Ainsworth's historical plot taking over and destroying the fictional subplot, a motif which occurs in other novels written in this format. Once again, the text was unillustrated when the novel was published in book-form: Chapman and Hall, who published it, might well have been economizing once again.

Boscobel or, The Royal Oak (1872), the tale of Charles II's escape after the Battle of Worcester, is, however, the novel in this group which best repays attention. As Ellis points out, this work displayed much of the intense research and examination of the localities which had characterized his best work in the 1840s.[81] Ainsworth's correspondence with James Crossley shows that he sought and received much assistance from other enthusiasts, and did indeed visit many of the places at which Charles stayed after his escape from Worcester. In April 1872, he wrote to his friend: 'Tomorrow, I go to Wolverhampton to see Mr Parker, a bookseller of that town . . . who has furnished me with a great deal of material relative to Worcester and Boscobel. On Thursday I am going with him to Boscobel and Moseley.'[82]

The main source for the novel was J. Hughes's *The Boscobel Tracts* (1830), a collection of documents relating to Charles II's escape typical of the antiquarian publications of the heyday of picturesque historiography. Passages from Ainsworth's work accord very closely with many in *The Tracts*. Charles's journey to Moseley, for instance, was very clearly derived from Clarendon's account in his Diary.[83] The meeting of Charles II and Richard Penderell with the Miller of Evelith, while travelling at night to Madeley, was evidently drawn from Charles's own account of his adventures to Samuel Pepys.[84] A comparison of the Miller's speech in the novel and the *Tracts* shows the closeness of the fictional account to its source. Pepys informed the reader that the Miller shouted out: 'If you be

[80] W. H. Ainsworth, *The Constable of the Tower: An Historical Romance*, 3 vols. (1861), ii, facing 74.

[81] Ellis, *Ainsworth*, ii. 278.

[82] MCL MS ix, fos. 37ᵛ–38ʳ. W. H. Ainsworth to J. Crossley, 23 Apr. 1872.

[83] W. H. Ainsworth, *Boscobel, or, The Royal Oak: A Tale of the Year 1651*, 3 vols. (1872), iii. 237–48; J. Hughes, *The Boscobel Tracts, Relating to the Escape of Charles II after the Battle of Worcester and his Subsequent Adventures* (1830), 46–7.

[84] Ainsworth, *Boscobel*, ii. 113–15; Hughes, *Tracts*, 137–8.

neighbours, stand, or I will knock you down.'[85] Ainsworth's Miller shouts out: 'If you be friends, stand and give an account of yourselves, or sure as I'm an honest man, and you are a couple of rogues, I knock you down.'[86] This careful reproduction of the body of his sources may not initially appear as in any way different from the picturesque reconstructions of the 1840s. In fact, it is even more intensive than in the earlier reconstructions. Furthermore, *Boscobel* is remarkable for the absence of any fictional characters, apart from two Puritan soldiers and Dame Gives, Careless's sweetheart, who is conveniently removed from the novel by a sudden death, so as to avoid the necessity of an inauthentic marriage to Charles's companion. It is as if Ainsworth were carrying to extremes the reconstructive techniques of his novels of the 1840s in a last vain attempt to regain the style and success of that time.

The slavish adherence to the sources might be further explained by a connection between the Introduction to the *Tracts* and the Preface to the novel. Hughes attributed his intention to collate the tracts to a letter from Bishop Copleston of Llandaff, in which the bishop attacked Scott's then recently published novel, *Woodstock*, for its use of an impossible and inauthentic visit by Charles II to Woodstock:

Whenever his [i.e. Scott's] pen is employed in filling up the vacant outline of historical truth, in clothing the bare skeleton of recorded facts with natural and probable circumstances, in giving warmth of colouring to the portrait of personages long since deceased, and introducing to our familiar acquaintance those stately characters who must always wear some degree of stiffness in the hand of the historian, I feel . . . the highest admiration of his enchanting powers. But the transaction of which I am speaking [i.e. the escape of Charles II] would not admit of the exercise of those powers, even if the authority of history had been respected. For the truth is here preserved in the minutest detail . . . The fertility of invention would, in this case, have been thrown away . . .[87]

Ainsworth might well have read this as a kind of challenge—to rewrite *Woodstock* in a form in which the authority of history was respected and the 'minutest detail' was introduced. The existence of such details, too, saved him from accusations of inaccuracy: 'fertility of invention' to reconstruct the fragments of evidence was unnecessary. History itself supplied the entire text for *Boscobel*.

Paradoxically, the very subject-matter of *Boscobel* also allowed him to avoid history. In the Preface, Ainsworth agreed with the Bishop of Llandaff that the tale of Charles II's escape after Worcester was 'by far the most romantic piece of English history we possess'.[88] History became a romance without the assistance of the historical novelist. Ainsworth quoted Hughes's own comment: 'the occurrences in question are calculated to present one of those pleasing episodes in history, distinct from the wearying details of bloodshed and political intrigue . . . The reality here presents all those features of romance which the imagination

---

[85] Hughes, *Tracts*, 135.   [86] Ainsworth, *Boscobel*, ii. 114.
[87] Hughes, *Tracts*, 3–4.   [88] Ainsworth, *Boscobel*, i, p. v.

chiefly supplies in the Partie de Chasse d'Henri IV, or the incognitos of Haroun Allraschid.'[89] It is ironic that Ainsworth's most successful novel of the 1870s focused on a romantic excursion set in the provinces, outside the main course of English political history, and detailing the escape of a disinherited prince into temporary exile on the Continent.

The illustrations of this work are particularly significant, as they were prior to the text and inspired Ainsworth to write the novel.[90] In the Preface to *Boscobel*, he explained that he had long wished to write a tale on the subject of Charles II's wanderings after Worcester, but 'I deferred my design, and possibly might have never executed it, had I not seen a series of views depicting most graphically the actual state of the different places visited by Charles, and privately published by Mr Frederick Manning, of Leamington'.[91] J. H. Rimbault engraved eight of the plates from Manning's work, *A Series of Views Illustrative of the Boscobel Tracts, published in 1660, shewing the Present State of the Places visited by King Charles II* (1861) for inclusion in the novel. A Captain Archer 'sketched on the spot' a further three: *The Site of Fort Royal*, *The Room in the Commandery*, and *The Old Bridge at Powick*.[92] A comparison of the plates of Manning's *Views* with Rimbault's copies show no alterations other than the addition of a few small figures in seventeenth-century dress, intended to connect the illustration with the text. When Charles arrives at Moseley Hall, for instance, he is pursued by two Commonwealth soldiers, Ezra and Manmannah. Accordingly, in the plate *Moseley Old Hall* (Fig. 47), two figures surveying the house are included and a few silhouettes at the windows.[93] The plates are thus a reflection of the text: almost entirely metanymic and lifted very directly from one source, rather than careful metaphoric reconstructions like Cruikshank's steel-engravings. There is only minimal touching up to link the illustration to the fiction. Their initial resemblance to some of Franklin's illustrations to *Old Saint Paul's* is rather deceptive: unlike Franklin, Rimbault was a mere copyist, not an artist of some reputation engaged in researching and creating a series of detailed reconstructions, including some plates concentrating on figures, from a number of different sources. In fact, the very inclusion of Rimbault's illustrations might well be due to the ease with which they could be prepared.

Later attempts to write novels adhering rigidly as far as possible to the historical text were much less successful than *Boscobel*. *The Goldsmith's Wife* (1875), purporting to be the tale of Jane Shore, only really focused on the heroine at the beginning and end of the novel. *The Fall of Somerset* (1877), the sequel to *The Constable*, was similar to that earlier work in its meandering succession of incidents, but it lacked the focus of even a central character such as Thomas Seymour. Somerset's career after the death of his brother does not serve to unify

---

[89] Ainsworth, *Boscobel*, i, p. ix; Hughes, *Tracts*, 12–13.

[90] Book versions of *Boscobel*, as studied here, lack five of the original illustrations to the work, which originally appeared in *The New Monthly Magazine* in 1872. Ellis, *Ainsworth*, ii. 354.

[91] Ainsworth, *Boscobel*, i, pp. v–vi.   [92] Ibid. i, p. vi n.; facing 21, 171, 286.

[93] Ibid. ii, facing 288.

Fig. 47. After F. Manning, engraved J. H. Rimbault, *Moseley Old Hall*, from W. H. Ainsworth, *Boscobel, or, The Royal Oak: A Tale of the Year 1651*, 3 vols. (1872), ii, facing 288

the book, the first volume of which deals with the 1549 Revolt in East Anglia, thus preventing the entrance of the titular hero until the second volume. The hero and the heroine of the fictional subplot, as in *Cardinal Pole*, seem to be entirely at the mercy of the vagaries of national history. The heroine perceptively comments to her suitor that they 'must await the course of events';[94] she is, in fact, to die later to keep company with Somerset. Both these rather dismal novels were illustrated by the undistinguished Frank Gilbert at their initial publication in the minor periodical, *Bow Bells*.[95] Clearly it was not thought worth reproducing these illustrations for the first book editions.

A novel which falls between the two main categories of Ainsworth's later novels also suffers severely. *The Manchester Rebels* (1873) combines a sensational tale, based upon a local legend, with the events of the 1745 Rising in Manchester and the regiment formed to fight for Charles Edward Stuart. The result was not satisfactory: towards the end of the novel, in order to disengage himself from the historical plot, the fictional hero, the pro-Jacobite Atherton Legh 'pusillanimously forswears prince and principles to gain his freedom'.[96] The combination of two formats, the fictional tale against an historical background, and the

---

[94] W. H. Ainsworth, *The Fall of Somerset*, 3 vols. (1877) iii. 212.
[95] Ellis, *Ainsworth*, ii. 355.   [96] Ibid. ii. 289.

history-as-text romance, where historical sources are rigidly followed, was not happy. After the deaths of various of his friends, Legh, like Clavering Maunsel, retreats from the stage of national history, avoiding 'all dangerous politics' and remaining 'well affected towards the Government'.[97] But Ainsworth's failure to characterize Atherton fully means that this retreat has none of the significance of that of the hero of *Waverley* (1814), in spite of the clear parallels between the two books: it appears to be simply the device of an author attempting to disengage two plots which have never really coalesced.

The textual failure of this attempt to create a novel similar to those of the 1840s is matched by a failure with regard to the illustrations. *The Manchester Rebels* was unillustrated in the first edition; Ainsworth wished to see the second illustrated in much the same way as *Boscobel*. But by now his wishes had no weight with his publisher, who was at this time the rather disreputable William Tinsley (Chapman and Hall had let the ageing author go). In February 1874, Ainsworth wrote to Tinsley, who is pungently described by Sutherland as 'a vulgar man who dropped his "h's" and patronised the proud old dandy':[98] 'As I mentioned to you in a former letter, I can get you some very curious views of old houses in Manchester, if you mean to give illustrations.'[99] To Crossley, the novelist wrote that, with these illustrations, the work would sell well in a cheap edition.[100] Ainsworth's hesitant tone, and the fact that he did not even suggest original illustrations, merely the reproduction of pre-existing ones, shows how fallen the author now was. Tinsley obviously did not think it worth the trouble to provide even these illustrations: the book never appeared with illustrations. It was the last impulse of Ainsworth's keenly picturesque vision, an enthusiasm to preserve a little of the lost appearance of his native city and the national heritage in the face of accelerating industrial change.

PICTURESQUE HISTORY: A SEA-CHANGE

Ainsworth's later career symbolizes the fate of his form of picturesque historical reconstruction in mid-Victorian Britain: the doubts of *Auriol Darcy* were realized. The potential of *Ovingdean Grange*, the possibility of writing fictional plots with a vague historical background, failed in the face of Ainsworth's obsessive desire for a plot provided by national history itself. Ainsworth's lack of 'fertility of invention' in this department is amply proved by his letters to Crossley in his later years. They are full of such requests as this: 'Is there any of the Chetham Society publications that you think would furnish me with material for a Tale?'[101] Ainsworth could not bring himself to escape history, but, in the new atmosphere of scientific history-writing, with its heavy demands for authenticity, his old

---

[97] Ainsworth, *Rebels*, iii. 270–1.   [98] Sutherland, *Novelists*, 159.
[99] Ellis, *Ainsworth*, ii. 290. W. H. Ainsworth to W. Tinsley, 11 Feb. 1874.
[100] MCL MS ix, fo. 58ᵛ. W. H. Ainsworth to J. Crossley, 2 Oct. 1873.
[101] Ibid., x, fo. 23ᵛ. W. H. Ainsworth to J. Crossley, 12 Oct. 1876.

formula was not viable. Nor were his works accompanied with illustrations like those of his earlier novels—H. K. Browne's work became the sympathetic reflection of his own vain but brave endeavour to adapt the old formula, for the artist was as troubled by the necessity of changing his style as was the author. Later, with the advent of the Gilberts and the reversal of his position with publishers, Ainsworth appears to have lost control over the illustrations to his works.

Symptomatic of his problems was *Boscobel*, the best of his last novels, a strange mixture of an annal and an adventure story. Historical events, thinly described, succeed each other swiftly, with nothing more interpretative than chronology to structure the novel. The illustrations, borrowed from another work, metanymic images clumsily adapted to be metaphoric representations of scenes in the novel, reflect Ainsworth's own methods in the text and his inability to create and supervise picturesque reconstructions like those of the 1840s. *Boscobel* was neither history nor romance. Ainsworth had armed himself against the criticism of reviewers, but, *Boscobel* was no model for the late Victorian historical novelist. The fully fledged national historical romancer of the last part of the nineteenth century, R. L. Stevenson, turned to the novels of Scott, not, as Ainsworth had done, to learn reconstructive techniques, but to study character and adventure in an historical setting.

But, in addition to the novels of Scott, Stevenson also found in his father's library one novel by Ainsworth, that perennial favourite, *The Tower of London*.[102] While picturesque history was never again to achieve the prestige it enjoyed in the 1830s and 1840s, the emergence of scientific history could not extinguish the popular enthusiasm for imaginative reconstructions of the English past first awakened in the early and mid-nineteenth-century. The historiographical crisis of the 1850s may have signalled the ruin of Ainsworth's career and the decline of his picturesque historical reconstructions in text and image, but the impulse to revive the past in other media, by other means, was to resurface. The big Hollywood costume drama and the 'living history' theme park are distant relatives of the 1840s novels of Ainsworth.

[102] G. Balfour, *The Life of Robert Louis Stevenson*, 2 vols. (1901), i. 64.

Conclusion

The presentation of national history in nineteenth-century Britain was both pervasive and varied. Popular novelists and antiquaries, educational authors and the obscure writers of amusing stories for children, all produced works which helped to form the historical and national consciousness of the Victorian middle-class public. Educated as a child with Mrs Markham's *History of England* and then Hume's still better known *History*, the contemporary (male) reader might well have digested the works of Lingard and Knight at university. His sister, meanwhile, might be listening to Strickland's *Lives of the Queens of England*, as she sewed, or reading Yonge's historical tales to her siblings. The family circle would enjoy the arrival of Ainsworth's lively novels and A'Beckett's *Comic History* from Mudie's Library, or hear together, from the pages of *The Cornhill Magazine*, Eliot's latest and oddest work, *Romola*. And although the analysis of such publications contributes mainly to an understanding of middle-class culture, it is worth remembering that such novels as Ainsworth's reached a wider public, in pirated editions and as popular plays, and that Knight published *The Penny Magazine*, which was intended for a working-class readership, as well as *A Popular History*.

The importance of this rich historical culture to the nineteenth-century public is well-known. But it is only recently that much attention has been paid to the role of text and image in combination, in the creation of this national culture. The contemporary reader may well have viewed the 1843 exhibition of cartoons submitted for the Houses of Parliament competition, depicting scenes from the nation's history, or seen on the wall of the Royal Academy such paintings of historical genre as William Dyce's *George Herbert at Bremerton* (1861). But there was no need to visit an art gallery in order to absorb images of the English past. Illustrated history books, history textbooks, and historical novels were more significant purveyors of this form of education and entertainment, and they deserve further study. The fact that the most important standard work of national history for the nineteenth-century reader (Hume's *History of England*) was frequently illustrated suggests the necessity of such analysis. This book shows that a great diversity of nineteenth-century presentations of text and image can be found in such works, where text and image interpret each other, and/or reinforce a common message. Examples such as the illustrated works of women historians,

and Dolman's 1854–5 edition of Lingard's *History of England* show how complicated the interaction of historical texts and images could be, and display
the significance of their relationship to an understanding of each work as a whole.
In an age when concepts of literary criticism have increased the range and sophistication of our interpretations of many other texts and images, it is indeed time for
historiography to benefit more fully from new analytic approaches.

The messages of the illustrated texts may differ widely; representations of
national history may vary, and inevitably—as this book suggests—the presentation of the national narrative is always ambiguous and essentially protean. But a
common form—a structure beneath the surface content—seems to shape the earlier works here examined: picturesque historical reconstruction was clearly the
principle guiding many writers in the first half of the nineteenth century. For
many works of this period, illustrations were considered vital, as the discussion
here of Ainsworth's 1840s novels and early nineteenth-century textbooks has
shown. After the middle of the century, although this mode of presentation continued to be important, it was challenged by the development of history as a formal academic discipline. In history books and textbooks, the dramatic narrative
texts and metaphorical illustrations of picturesque reconstruction began to give
way to a more scientific format and apparently objective metanymic images.
Illustrations became dispensable, and were often considered inappropriate: they
ceased to appear in many textbooks, for instance. Illustrations were often being
relegated to works intended for a very juvenile audience, or to texts considered
inferior as history. The dilemma of the historical novel, once the vehicle of
national edification, has shed further light upon this mid-century transition. A
variety of solutions were attempted by novelists and their illustrators. While
Thackeray adopted the opinion that all ages were essentially the same, and
Ainsworth and Browne struggled unsuccessfully to adapt their picturesque
styles, women novelists—Gaskell, Eliot, and Yonge—turned from the national
narrative to various forms of myth to structure their fictions. Their illustrators
played down or avoided the claims of picturesque reconstruction in favour of
other concerns.

The models suggested here for the changes in the rhetoric and strategies of
nineteenth-century presentations of illustrated history—the evolution from
philosophical to picturesque to scientific—may seem too rigid. It is possible to
suggest that they were, and are, a matter of individual choice by author and/or
illustrator, rather than stages in a historical development. Certainly picturesque
historiography continues to flourish, even though its scientific successor has
long since claimed the universities and schools. But it is evident that an important
change in the historical consciousness of the age took place after 1850, which has
received little of the attention which it deserves in this context. Examination of
this change may aid understanding of the present state of historical education in
this country, for our own historical culture and sense of national identity has been
shaped by these nineteenth-century developments. To the many practitioners of
picturesque history we owe countless colourful versions of our national history,

our island story: it is retold now by the heirs of Ainsworth and Knight in the reconstructions and representations of the heritage industry, from the stately home belonging to the National Trust to the historical theme park. Meanwhile, academic historians, successors of the new professional and scientific historians of the late nineteenth century, are now questioning and examining the very concept of the nation and national history enshrined in most picturesque reconstructions, both past and present, of English history.

Our understanding of these issues is necessarily complicated by this gulf between professional and popular historiographies, an abyss which first began to open in the 1850s. It is undoubtedly right for the academic historian to question the idea of national history, and to interrogate the narratives and images which have shaped our consciousness of this community's past. As this book shows, challenges to the predominance of the national narrative were inherent in its nineteenth-century formation and expression. It is also right, however, for the practitioners of picturesque historiography to employ all the rhetoric of narrative and imagery, now vastly enhanced by new media and technologies, to capture the popular imagination. Their enterprise to produce and purvey reconstructions and representations of the national past may not always be scholarly but it is essential and valuable. Surely, if academic history is to survive, the professional historian needs to learn to communicate with a wider, non-academic audience, while the popular historian must benefit from an increased access to the results of scholarly research and a fuller awareness of its critical disciplines. To both the history of the nation (our imagined community and the interpretations of its past we have constructed) are of central importance. Picturesque and scientific history, however they may differ, are both children of Clio.

BIBLIOGRAPHY

The place of publication is given, unless it is London. Articles published anonymously, for which no author is attributable, are listed under the first letter of the title; where an author has been attributed, the article is listed under that name, which is given in square brackets.

PRIMARY SOURCES: MANUSCRIPT

London, British Library: Additional MSS, 44727, 44792, 54920.
London, John Murray Archives: Callcott, Penrose and Scharf MSS.
London, University College Library: SDUK Correspondence.
London, Westminster Diocesan Archives: The Bagshawe Papers.
Manchester, Manchester Public Libraries: MS 928. 23. A8.
Oxford, Bodleian Library: Phillipps-Robinson MSS; MS. Don. g. 8.
Oxford, Harris Manchester College Library: The Shepherd Letters.
Reading, University Library: The Bell Archives, MS 308.

PRIMARY SOURCES: PRINTED

A'Beckett, G. A., *The Comic History of England* (1846–8; 2 vols., 1847–8).
Ainsworth, W. H., *Auriol, or the Elixir of Life* (1844–6; 1875 edn.).
—— *Boscobel, or, The Royal Oak: A Tale of the Year 1651*, 3 vols. (1872).
—— *Cardinal Pole, or, The Days of Phillip and Mary*, 3 vols. (1863).
—— *The Constable of the Tower: An Historical Romance*, 3 vols. (1861).
—— *The Fall of Somerset*, 3 vols. (1877).
—— *The Goldsmith's Wife*, 3 vols. (1875).
—— *The Good Old Times: The Manchester Rebels of the Fatal '45*, 3 vols. (1st edn., 1873).
—— *The Good Old Times: The Manchester Rebels of the Fatal '45* (n.d).
—— *Guy Fawkes, or, The Gunpowder Treason*, 3 vols. (1841).
—— *The Lord Mayor of London, or, City Life in the Last Century*, 3 vols. (1862).
—— *The Miser's Daughter* (1844; 1848 edn.).
—— *Old Saint Paul's: A Tale of the Plague and the Fire*, 3 vols. (1841).
—— *Ovingdean Grange: A Tale of the South Downs* (1860).
—— *Rookwood: A Romance* (1834; 1878 edn.).
—— *The Spendthrift: A Tale* (1856).
—— *The Tower of London: An Historical Romance* (1840).
—— *Windsor Castle* (1843; 1891? edn.).
[Allen, J.], 'Lingard's *History of England*', *ER* 42 (1825).
[——], 'Lingard's *History of England*: The Massacre of St Bartholomew', *ER* 44 (1826).
Anecdotes of Kings, selected from History, or Gertrude's Stories for Children (1837).
Austen, J., *Northanger Abbey* (1818; Harmondsworth, 1982 edn.).

Beale, D., *The Student's Textbook of English and General History* (1858).

'Belle Lettres', *WR* 23 (1863).

Bennett, W., *Popery Set Forth in Scripture: Its Guilt and its Doom* (1850).

Beverley, M., *Romantic Passages from English History* (1863).

Birkby, T., *The History of England* (1870).

Blackmore, R. D., *Lorna Doone: A Romance of Exmoor*, 3 vols. (1869).

—— *Lorna Doone: A Romance of Exmoor* (1883).

[Bowyer, R.], *A Series of One Hundred and Ninety-One Engravings (in the Line Manner) by the First Artists in the Country Illustrative of 'The History of England'* (1812).

Brodie, G., *A History of the British Empire from the Accession of Charles I to the Restoration . . . including a Particular Examination of Mr Hume's Statements Relative to the Character of the English Government*, 2 vols. (Edinburgh, 1822).

Callcott, M., *Little Arthur's History of England* (1835; 1856 edn.).

Carlyle, T., *On Heroes and Hero-Worship, and the Heroic in History*, 2 vols. (1837–9; Oxford, 1927 edn.).

Catalogue of the Library of the Late Celebrated Novelist, William Harrison Ainsworth . . . which will be sold by auction (1882).

A Catalogue of the Pictures in the Shakespeare Gallery, Pall-Mall (1810).

The Children's Picture-Book of English History (1859).

Cobbett, W., *A History of the Protestant Reformation in England and Ireland* (1824–6; 2 vols., 1857 edn.).

Collier, W., *Pictures of the Periods: A Sketch-Book of Old England* (1865).

Craik, G. L., and Macfarlane, C., *The Pictorial History of England*, 4 vols. (1837–50).

Dickens, C., *The New Oxford Illustrated Dickens*, 21 vols. (1958).

Doyle, J. E., *A Chronicle of England BC 55–AD 1485* (1864).

[Eastlake, E.], 'Illustrated Books', *QR* 74 (1844).

Eliot G., *The George Eliot Letters*, ed. G. S. Haight, 6 vols. (1954).

—— *Romola, Cornhill Magazine*, 6 and 7 (1862–3).

[Empson, W.], 'J. H. Burton's *Life and Correspondence of David Hume*', *ER* 85 (1847).

'*Esmond* and *Basil*', *BM* 32 (1852).

Fairholt, F. W., *Costume in England: A History of Dress* (1846).

Farr, E., *The Collegiate, School and Family History of England* (1848).

Foxe, J., *The Acts and Monuments of John Foxe*, ed. S. R. Cattley, 8 vols. (1837).

Gaskell, E., *Sylvia's Lovers* (1863).

Gosse, E., *Father and Son* (1907; 1983 edn.).

Green, M. A. E, *The Lives of the Princesses of England from the Norman Conquest*, 6 vols. (1849–55).

Greig, G. R., *A School History of England* (1872).

Grimaldi, S., *A Synopsis of English History* (1871).

Grose, F., *A Treatise of Ancient Armour and Weapons* (1786).

Hall, Mrs M., *The Lives of the Queens before the Conquest*, 2 vols. (1854).

Hallam, H., *The Constitutional History of England from the Accession of Henry VII to the Death of George II*, 3 vols. (1823; 1867 edn.).

—— 'Lingard's *History of England*', *ER* 53 (1831).

Hays, M., *Female Biography; or, Memoirs of Illustrious and Celebrated Women of All Ages and Countries*, 6 vols. (1803).

'*The History of Henry Esmond*', *The Literary Gazette*, 1868–9 (6 and 13 Nov. 1852).

Horne, R. H., *A New Spirit of the Age* (1844; Oxford, 1907 edn.).

[Hosack, J.?], 'Miss Strickland's *Lives of the Queens of Scotland*', *Tait's Edinburgh Magazine*, NS 18 (1851).

Hughes, J., *The Boscobel Tracts, Relating to the Escape of Charles II after the Battle of Worcester and his Subsequent Adventures* (1830).

Hughes, M. V., *A London Child of the 1870s* (1934; Oxford, 1977 edn.).

Hume, D. (with T. Smollett and T. A. Lloyd), *The History of England*, 12 vols. (1754–62; 1793–4 edn.).

—— (with T. Smollett and T. S. Hughes), *The History of England*, 21 vols. (1834–6).

—— (with T. Smollett and H. Stebbings), *The History of England*, 10 vols. (1838).

—— (with T. Smollett and J. C. Campbell), *The History of England*, 3 vols. (1848: Kelly edn.).

—— (with T. Smollett and W. Farr), *The History of England*, 3 vols. (1848: Virtue edn.).

—— *The Student's Hume*, ed. anon. (1859).

—— *The Student's Hume*, ed. J. S. Brewer (1880).

Hutton, R. H., 'Eliot's *Romola*', *The Spectator*, 36 (1863), repr. in D. Carroll (ed.), *George Eliot: The Critical Heritage* (1971).

'Illustrated Gift-Books', *The Spectator*, 30 (1857).

Ince, H., and Gilbert, J., *Outlines of English History* (1865).

Jameson, A., *The Beauties of the Court of Charles the Second*, 5 parts (1831).

—— *Memoirs of Celebrated Female Sovereigns* (1869).

[Johnstone, C.], 'Hannah Lawrance's *Historical Memoirs of the Queens of England*', *Tait's Edinburgh Magazine*, NS 5 (1833).

Kingsley, C., *Hypatia, or, New Foes with an Old Face*, 2 vols. (1853).

Knight, C., *Capital and Labour* (1830; 1845 edn.).

—— *et al.*, *London*, 6 vols. (1841).

—— *Old England: A Pictorial Museum*, 2 vols. (1845).

—— *Once Upon a Time*, 2 vols. (1850).

—— *Passages of a Working Life During Half a Century: With a Prelude of Early Reminiscences*, 3 vols. (1864).

—— *The Pictorial Shakspere*, 8 vols. (1837).

—— *The Popular History of England: An Illustrated History of Society and Government*, 8 vols. (1856–62).

Laurie, J. S., *Outlines of English History* (1865).

Lawrance, H., *The Historical Memoirs of the Queens of England from the Commencement of the Twelfth Century to the End of the Fifteenth Century*, 2 vols. (1838).

—— *The History of Woman in England and her Influence on Society and Literature from the Earliest Period to the Year 1200* (1843).

[——], 'Novels and Novelists', *QR* 30 (1859).

Legg, W., *A Reading Book in English History*, ed. R. K. Brewer (1863).

[Lewes, G. H.], 'The Historical Novel', *WR* 45 (1846).

Lingard, J., *The Antiquities of the Anglo-Saxon Church* (1806; Newcastle, 1810 edn.).

—— *Documents to Ascertain the Sentiments of British Catholics in Former Ages Respecting the Power of the Pope* (1812).

—— *The History of England* (1819–30; 13 vols., 1837–9 edn.).

—— *The History of England*, 10 vols. (1854–5).

—— *Observations on the Laws and Ordinances which Exist in Foreign States Relative to the Religious Concerns of their Roman Catholic Subjects* (1817), in *A Collection of Tracts on Several Subjects, Connected to the Civil and Religious Principles of Catholics* (1826).

—— *A Vindication of Certain Passages in the Fourth and Fifth Volumes of the History of England* (1826).

[Linton, W. G.], 'Illustrative Art', *WR* 51 (1849).

Lockhart, J. G., *Narrative of the Life of Sir Walter Scott* (1836–8; 1906 edn.).

Lodge, E., *Portraits of Illustrious Personages of Great Britain*, 12 vols. (1821–34).

Lytton, E. B., *The Last Days of Pompeii* (1834; 2 vols., 1850 edn.).

Macaulay, T. B., 'History' (1828), in *Miscellaneous Essays and the Lays of Ancient Rome* (1926), 36–9.

—— *The History of England*, 4 vols. (1807).

—— *The History of England*, 4 vols. (1840).

—— *The History of England*, 4 vols. (1849–55).

[McMahon, P.], 'Dr Lingard's *History of England*', *The Dublin Review*, 12 (1842).

Manning, A., *The Cottage History of England* (1861).

Maurier, G. Du, *The Young George Du Maurier: Letters 1860–67*, ed. D. Du Maurier (1951).

[Merivale, H.], '*The Pictorial History of England*', *ER* 74 (1842).

Meyrick, S. R., *Specimens of Ancient Furniture* (1836).

More, H., *Hints Towards Forming the Character of a Young Princess*, 2 vols. (1805).

'New Novels: *Sylvia's Lovers*', *The Athenaeum*, 1844 (1863).

Nichols, C. H. S., *Outlines of English History* (1850).

[Palgrave, F.], '*The History of England* by Hume: A New Edition, 1825', *QR* 34 (1826).

—— 'Hume and his Influence upon History', *QR* 73 (1843).

[Patmore, P. G.], 'Ainsworth's *Windsor Castle*', *The New Monthly Magazine*, 67 (1843).

The Penny Magazine (1832–5).

Penrose, E. ('Mrs Markham'), *A History of England from the First Invasion of the Romans to the End of the Reign of George IV* (1823; 1846 edn.).

—— *A History of England*, ed. anon. (1853).

—— *A History of England*, ed. M. Howitt (1865).

—— *A History of England*, ed. anon (1875).

—— *The New Children's Friend*, 2 vols. (1832).

Planché, J. R., *The History of British Costume* (1834).

Reade, C., *The Cloister and the Hearth*, 4 vols. (1861).

'Review of *Romola*', *The Saturday Review* 16 (25 July 1863), reprinted in G. S. Haight (ed.), *A Century of George Eliot Criticism* (1965).

Rodwell, A., *The Child's First Step to English History* (1844).

'*Romola*', *WR* 80 (Oct. 1863), repr. in G. S. Haight (ed.), *A Century of George Eliot Criticism* (1965).

Ruskin, J., *The Seven Lamps of Architecture* (1849; 1905 edn.).

Scoresby, W., *An Account of Arctic Regions, with a History and Description of the Northern Whale-Fishery*, 2 vols. (Edinburgh, 1820).

Scott, W., *The Fair Maid of Perth* (1824; 2 vols., Edinburgh, 1868 edn.).

—— *The Letters of Sir Walter Scott*, ed. H. J. C. Grierson, 12 vols. (1932–7).

—— *Sir Walter Scott: On Novelists and Fiction*, ed. I. Williams (1968).

—— *The Waverley Novels*, 48 vols. (Edinburgh, 1829–33).

Sewell, E. M., *A Cathechism of English History* (1872).

[Smith, G.], '*The Virginians*', *ER* 110 (1859).

Smyth, W., *Lectures on Modern History from the Irruption of the Northern Nations to the Close of the American Revolution*, 2 vols. (1840).

Stephen, L., 'A Few Words about Scott', in *Hours in a Library*, 2 vols. (1874–9).

Stevenson, R. L., *Kidnapped* and *Catriona* (1886, 1893; Oxford, 1986 edn.).

[Stone, E.], *The Art of Needlework from the Earliest Ages* (1841).

Strickland, A., *Tales and Stories from History* (1870).

—— [and E.], *The Lives of the Queens of England* (1840–8; 12 vols., 1845–8).

—— *The Lives of the Queens of Scotland and Princesses Connected to the Royal Succession*, 8 vols. (Edinburgh, 1850–8).

—— *The Lives of the Tudor Princesses including Lady Jane Grey and her Sisters* (1868).

Strickland, J. M., *Life of Agnes Strickland* (Edinburgh and London, 1886).

Strutt, J., *A Complete View of the Dress and Habits of the People of England*, 3 vols. (1796–9).

—— *Gli-gamena Anjel-deod, or, The Sports and Pastimes of the People of England* (1801).

—— *Horda Anjel-cynna, or, A Compleat View of the Manners, Customs, Arms, Habits etc of the Inhabitants of England*, 3 vols. (1775–6).

Taylor, E., *England and its People: A Familiar History* (1821; 1860 edn.).

—— *Historical Prints, Representing Some of the Most Memorable Events in English History* (1821).

Thackeray, W. M., *The Oxford Thackeray*, ed. G. Saintsbury, 17 vols. (1908).

'Thackeray's *Esmond*', *Irish Quarterly Review*, 2 (1852).

Todd, H. J., *A Reply to Dr Lingard's Vindication of his History of England as far as respects Archbishop Cranmer* (1827).

—— *A Vindication of the Most Reverend Thomas Cranmer . . . and therewith of the Reformation in England* (1826).

'The Tower of London', *Fraser's Town and Country Magazine* 23 (1841).

Trimmer, S., *A Description of a Set of Prints of English History* (1817).

—— *A Series of Prints Designed to Illustrate English History* (1817).

Trollope, A., *Autobiography* (1883; Oxford, 1989 edn.).

A True Account of the Gunpowder Plot (1851).

Turner, S., *The History of the Anglo-Saxons* (1799–1805).

—— *The History of the Anglo-Saxons*, 2 vols. (1807).

—— *The History of the Anglo-Saxons*, 3 vols. (1840).

Uncle William's Concise History of England for the Use of Schools and Families (1880s?).

Vertue, G., *The Heads of the Kings of England, Proper to Mr Rapin's History* (1736).

'The Virginians', *The Daily News* (30 Dec. 1859).

Yonge, C. M., *Aunt Charlotte's Stories of English History for Little Ones* (1873).

—— *The Caged Lion* (1870).

—— *The Chaplet of Pearls, or, The White and Black Ribaumont* (1868).

—— *The Dove in the Eagle's Nest*, 2 vols. (1866).

—— *Heartsease; or, The Brother's Wife* (1854; 1877 edn.).

—— *The Kings of England* (1852).

—— *The Lances of Lynwood* (1855).

—— *Love and Life* (1880; 1882 edn.).

—— *The Prince and the Page* (London and Cambridge, 1866).

—— *Stray Pearls* (1883; 1900 edn.).

—— *That Stick* (1892).

—— *Unknown to History*, 2 vols. (1882).

Young, G., *A History of Whitby and Streonshalh Abbey; with a Statistical Survey of the Vicinity*, 2 vols. (Whitby, 1817).

SECONDARY SOURCES: MANUSCRIPT

Cherry, A. C., 'A Life of Charles Knight (1791–1873) with Special Reference to his Political and Educational Activities' (MA thesis, University of London, 1945).

Fox, C. A., 'Graphic Journalism in England during the 1830s and 1840s', 2 vols. (D.Phil. thesis, University of Oxford, 1975).

Pickwoad, N., 'Thackeray and his Book Illustrations', 2 vols. (D.Phil. thesis, University of Oxford, 1978).

SECONDARY SOURCES: PRINTED

A'Beckett, A. W., *The A'Becketts of 'Punch': Memories of Father and Son* (1903).

Aldrich, M., *A. W. N. Pugin: Master of Gothic Revival* (New Haven, Conn. 1995).

Altick, R. D., *The English Common Reader: A Social History of the Mass Reading Public 1800–1900* (Chicago, 1957).

—— *Paintings from Books: Art and Literature in Britain, 1760–1900* (Columbus, Ohio, 1985).

—— *Punch 1841–51: The Lively Youth of a British Institution* (Columbus, Ohio, 1997).

—— *The Shows of London* (Cambridge, Mass., 1978).

—— *Writers, Readers and Occasions: Selected Essays on Victorian Literature and Life* (Columbus, Ohio, 1989).

Anderson, B., *Imagined Communities: Reflections on the Origin and Spread of Nationalism* (1983; 1991 edn.).

Anderson, J., *Sir Walter Scott and Society* (Edinburgh, 1971).

Anderson, P., *The Printed Image and the Transformation of Popular Culture, 1790–1860* (Oxford, 1991).

Anderson, R. K., ' "Things Wisely Ordered": John Blackwood and the Publication of *Romola*', *PH* 11 (1982).

Anthias, F., and N. Yuval-Davis, *Women–Nation–State* (1989).

Atterbury, P., and C. Wainwright, *Pugin: A Gothic Passion* (New Haven, Conn., and London, 1994).

Austen, Z., 'Elizabeth Rigby Eastlake', in E. Mitchell (ed.), *Victorian Britain: An Encylopedia* (New York and London, 1988).

Balfour, C. L., *A Sketch of Mrs Trimmer* (1854).

Balfour, G., *The Life of Robert Louis Stevenson*, 2 vols. (1901).

Bann, S., *The Clothing of Clio* (Cambridge, 1984).

—— *The Inventions of History* (Manchester, 1990).

—— *Romanticism and the Rise of History* (New York, 1995).

Barthes, R., 'The Discourse of History', trans. S. Bann, in E. S. Shaffer (ed.), *Comparative Criticism: A Yearbook* (Cambridge, 1981).

—— 'The Photographic Image' (1961), in *Image–Music–Text*, trans. S. Heath (1977).

—— 'The Reality Effect', in T. Todorov (ed.), *French Literary Theory Today: A Reader*, trans. R. Carter (Cambridge, 1982).

—— 'The Rhetoric of the Image' (1964), in *Image–Music–Text*, trans. S. Heath (1977).

Battiscombe, G., *Charlotte Mary Yonge: The Story of an Uneventful Life* (1943).

Benjamin, W., 'The Work of Art in the Age of Mechanical Reproduction', in *Illuminations*, ed. H. Arendt, trans. H. Zohn (1970), 219–53.

Bennett, S., 'The Editorial Character and Readership of *The Penny Magazine*: An Analysis', *VPR* 17/4 (1984).

Bhabha, H. K., 'Introduction: Narrating the Nation', in H. K. Bhabha (ed.), *Nation and Narration* (London and New York, 1990).

Bhalla, P., *The Cartographers of Hell: Essays on the Gothic Novel and the Social History of England* (New Delhi, 1991).

Blaas, P., *Continuity and Anachronism: Parliamentary and Constitutional Development in Whig Historiography and in the Anti-Whig Reaction between 1890–1930* (The Hague, Boston, Mass., and London, 1978).

Black, J. B., *A Study of Four Great Historians of the Eighteenth Century* (1926).

Boase, T. S. R., 'Illustrations of Shakespeare's Plays in the Seventeenth and Eighteenth Centuries', *JWCI* 10 (1947).

—— 'Macklin and Bowyer', *JWCI* 26 (1963).

Bonaparte, F., *The Triptych and the Cross: The Central Myths of George Eliot's Poetic Imagination* (Brighton, 1979).

Booth, M., 'Shakespeare as Spectacle and History: The Victorian Period', *Theatre Research International*, 1 (1979).

Bossy, J., *The English Catholic Community 1570–1850* (1975).

Bowler, P. J., *The Invention of Progress: The Victorians and the Past* (Oxford, 1989).

Braudy, L., *Narrative Form in History and Fiction: Hume, Fielding and Gibbon* (Princeton, 1970).

Breuilly, J., *Nationalism and the State* (Manchester, 1993).

Brown, D., *Walter Scott and the Historical Imagination* (1989).

Brown, J., *John Leech and Other Papers* (Edinburgh, 1882).

Bruntjen, S. J., *John Boydell, 1719–1804: A Study of Art Patronage and Publishing in Georgian London* (New York and London, 1985).

Bryson, N., *Vision and Painting: The Logic of the Gaze* (1983).

Buchanan-Brown, J., 'British Wood-Engravers, c.1820–1860: A Checklist', *JPS* 17 (1982/3).

—— *The Illustrations of William Makepeace Thackeray* (Newton Abbot, London, and North Pomfret, Vt., 1978).

—— *Phiz! The Book Illustrations of Hablot Knight Browne* (Newton Abbot, London, and Vancouver, 1978).

Burrow, J. W., *A Liberal Descent: Victorian Historians and the English Past* (Cambridge, 1981).

Burton, A., 'Thackeray's Collaborations with Cruikshank, Doyle and Walker', in P. L. Shillingsburg (ed.), *Costerus: Essays in English and American Literature: Thackeray* (Amsterdam and Columbia, SC, 1974).

Butler, M., 'Romanticism in England', in R. Porter and M. Teich, *Romanticism in National Context* (Cambridge, 1988).

Campbell, J., 'The United Kingdom of England: The Anglo-Saxon Achievement', in A. Grant and K. J. Stringer, *Uniting the Kingdom? The Making of British History* (1995).

Cannadine, D., 'British History as a "New Subject": Politics, Perspectives, and Prospects', in A. Grant and K. J. Stringer, *Uniting the Kingdom? The Making of British History* (1995).

Cannon-Brookes, P. (ed.), *The Painted Word: British History Paintings 1750–1830* (Woodbridge, 1991).

Carlisle, J., *The Sense of an Audience: Dickens, Thackeray, and George Eliot at Mid-Century* (Athens, Ga., 1981).

Chancellor, V. E., *History for their Masters: Opinion in the English History Textbook 1800–1914* (Bath, 1970).

Chandler, A., *A Dream of Order: The Medieval Ideal in Nineteenth Century English Literature* (1971).

Chapman, H., *Lady Jane Grey* (1962).

Chapman, R., *The Sense of the Past in Victorian Literature* (1986).

Chase, M., and C. Shaw, 'The Dimensions of Nostalgia', in C. Shaw and M. Chase (eds.), *The Imagined Past: History and Nostalgia* (Manchester and New York, 1989).

Chatto, W., and J. Jackson, *A Treatise of Wood-Engraving, Historical and Practical* (1839).

Chinnici, J. P., *The English Catholic Enlightenment: John Lingard and the Cisalpine Movement 1780–1850* (Shepherdstown, 1980).

Christensen, A. C., *Edward Bulwer Lytton: The Fiction of New Regions* (Athens, Ga., 1976).

Clive, J., *Macaulay: The Shaping of an Historian* (Cambridge, Mass., 1987).

Clowes, A. A., *Charles Knight, a Sketch* (1892).

Coates, C., 'Thackeray's Best Illustrator', in P. L. Shillingsburg (ed.), *Costerus: Essays in English and American Literature: Thackeray* (Amsterdam and SC, 1974).

—— 'Thackeray's Editors and the Dual Text of Vanity Fair', *Word and Image*, 9 (1993).

Cohen, J. R., *Charles Dickens and his Original Illustrators* (Columbus, Ohio, 1980).

Cole, W., 'The Book and the Artist: Rethinking the Traditional Order', *Word and Image*, 8 (1992).

Coleridge, C., *Charlotte M. Yonge: Her Life and Letters* (1903).

Colley, L., *Britons: Forging the Nation 1707–1837* (1992; 1994 edn.).

Connolly, G., 'The Transubstantiation of Myth: Towards a New Popular History of Nineteenth Century Catholicism in England', *Journal of Ecclesiastical History*, 35 (1984).

Cressy, D., *Bonfires and Bells: National Memory and the Protestant Calendar in Elizabethan and Stuart England* (1989).

—— 'The Fifth of November Remembered', in R. Porter (ed.), *Myths of the English* (Cambridge, Mass., 1992).

Crosby, C., *The Ends of History: Victorians and 'the Woman Question'* (New York and London, 1991).

Culler, A. D., *The Victorian Mirror of History* (New Haven, Conn., 1985).

Curwen, H., *A History of Booksellers, the Old and New* [1873].

Dahl, C., 'History on the Hustings: Bulwer Lytton's Historical Novels of Politics', in R. C. Rathburn and M. Steinmann (eds.), *From Jane Austen to Joseph Conrad* (Minneapolis, 1958).

Daiches, D., 'Sir Walter Scott and History', *Études anglaises*, 24 (1971).

Dalziel, E., and G., *The Brothers Dalziel: A Record of Fifty Years' Work* (1901).

Dalziel, M., *Popular Fiction one Hundred Years ago: An Unexplored Tract of Literary History* (1957).

Davidoff, L., and C. Hall, *Family Fortunes: Men and Women of the English Middle Classes, 1780–1850* (1987).

Davies, N. Z., 'Gender and Genre, Women as Historical Writers, 1400–1820', in P. Labalme (ed.), *Beyond their Sex: Learned Women of the European Past* (New York and London, 1980).

Day, P. W., *In the Circles of Fear and Desire: A Study of Gothic Fantasy* (Chicago and London, 1985).

Delheim, C., *The Face of the Past: The Preservation of the Medieval Inheritance in Victorian Britain* (Cambridge, 1982).

Delorme, M., ' "Facts not Opinions": Agnes Strickland', *History Today*, 38 (1988).

Dennis, B., *Charlotte Yonge (1823–1901): Novelist of the Oxford Movement* (Lewiston, Me., 1992).

The Dictionary of National Biography, ed. L. Stephen and S. Lee, 63 vols. (1885–1904).

Douglas, D., 'Thackeray and the Uses of History', *The Yearbook of English Studies*, 5 (1975).

Duffy, E., 'Ecclesiastical Democracy Detected, II: 1787–1796', *RH* 10 (1970).

—— 'Ecclesiastical Democracy Detected, III: 1796–1800', *RH* 13 (1975).

Duncan, I., *Modern Romance and the Transformation of the Novel: The Gothic, Scott, and Dickens* (Cambridge, 1982).

Dunn, W., *R. D. Blackmore: The Author of Lorna Doone* (1956).

Ellis, S. M., *The Solitary Horseman, or The Life and Adventures of G.P.R. James* (1927).

—— *William Harrison Ainsworth and his Friends*, 2 vols. (London and New York, 1911).

Engen, R., *A Dictionary of Victorian Engravers* (Cambridge and Teaneck, NJ, 1979).

—— *A Dictionary of Victorian Wood Engravers* (Cambridge and Teaneck, NJ, 1985).

—— *Richard Doyle* (Stroud, 1983).

Errington, L., *Social and Religious Themes in English Art 1840–60* (New York and London, 1984).

Fairley, R. (ed.), *Jemima: The Paintings and Memoirs of a Victorian Lady* (Edinburgh, 1988).

Fay, B., P. Pomper, and R. T. Vann (eds.), *History and Theory: Contemporary Readings* (Oxford, 1988).

Feather, J., 'Publishers and Politicians: The Remaking of the Law of Copyright in Britain, 1775–1842: Part I: Legal Deposition and the Battle of the Literary Tax', *PH* 24 (1988).

—— 'Publishers and Politicians: The Remaking of the Law of Copyright in Britain, 1775–1842: Part II: The Rights of Authors', *PH* 25 (1989).

Finlay, G., *Landscapes of Memory: Turner as Illustrator to Scott* (1980).

Fischer, D. H., *Historians' Fallacies: Towards a Logic in Historical Thought* (1971).

Fisher, J. L., 'The Aesthetic of the Mediocre: Thackeray and the Visual Arts', *VS* 26 (1982).

—— 'Image and Text in the Illustrated Novels of William Makepeace Thackeray', in C. T. Christ and J. O. Jordan (eds.), *Victorian Literature and the Victorian Visual Imagination* (Berkeley, Los Angeles, and London, 1995).

Flaxman, R. L., *Victorian Word-Painting and Narrative: Towards the Blending of the Genres* (Ann Arbor, Mich., 1983).

Fleischmann, A., *The English Historical Novel from Walter Scott to Virginia Woolf* (Baltimore, 1971).

Fletcher, A., 'The First Century of English Protestantism and the Growth of National Identity', in S. Mews (ed.), *Religion and National Identity* (Oxford, 1982).

Forbes, D., *Hume's Philosophical Politics* (Cambridge, 1975).

Foster, R., *Paddy and Mr Punch: Connections in Irish and English History* (1993).

Foulkes, R. (ed.), *Shakespeare and the Victorian Stage* (Cambridge, 1986).

Fox, C., 'The Development of Social Reportage in English Periodicals during the 1840s and Early 1850s', *Past and Present*, 74 (1977).

Frank, F. S., *The First Gothics: A Critical Guide to the English Gothic Novel* (1987).

Frederic Leighton 1830–1896 (Royal Academy of Arts exhibition catalogue, New York, 1996).

Frith, W. P., *John Leech: His Life and Work*, 2 vols. (1891).

Furtado, P., 'National Pride in Seventeenth-Century England', in R. Samuel (ed.), *Patriotism: The Making and the Unmaking of the British National Identity*, 3 vols. (1989).

Garside, P. D., 'Scott and the Philosophical Historians', *Journal of the History of Ideas*, 36 (1975).

Gehazi, J., '*Romola* and the Myth of Apocalyse', in A. Smith (ed.), *George Eliot Centenary Essays and an Unpublished Fragment* (1980).

Gellner, E., *Nations and Nationalism* (Oxford, 1983).

Gerin, W., *Elizabeth Gaskell: A Biography* (Oxford, 1976).

Gilbert, S. M., and S. Gubar, *The Madwoman in the Attic: The Woman Writer and the Nineteenth Century Literary Imagination* (New Haven, Conn., and London, 1984).

Gilley, S., 'John Lingard and the Catholic Revival', in D. Baker (ed.), *Renaissance and Renewal in Christian History* (Oxford, 1977).

—— 'Nationality and Liberty, Protestant and Catholic: Robert Southey's Book of the Church', in S. Mews (ed.), *Religion and National Identity* (Oxford, 1982).

Glover, J., 'Juvenile Researches, or the Diligent Dudleys', *Sussex County Magazine*, 22 (1948).

Goldman, P., *Victorian Illustrated Books, 1850–1870: The Heyday of Wood-Engraving* (1994).

—— *Victorian Illustration: The Pre-Raphaelites, the Idyllic School, and the High Victorians* (Aldershot, and Brookfield, Vt., 1996).

Gooch, G. P., *History and Historians in the Nineteenth Century* (1952).

Gordon, C., 'The Illustration of Sir Walter Scott: Nineteenth Century Enthusiasm and Adaption', *JWCI* 34 (1971).

Gotch, R. B., *Maria, Lady Callcott: The Creator of 'Little Arthur'* (1937).

Greenfield, L., *Nationalism: Five Roads to Modernity* (Cambridge, Mass., 1992).

Greenhalgh, P., *Ephemeral Vistas: The Expositions Universelles, Great Exhibitions, and World's Fairs, 1851–1939* (Manchester, 1988).

Grene, M., 'Hume: Sceptic or Tory?', in D. Livingston and M. Martin, *Hume as Philosopher of Society, Politics and History* (Rochester, NY, and Woodbridge, Suffolk, 1991).

Haggerty, G. E., *Gothic Fiction/Gothic Form* (Philadelphia, 1989).

Haight, G. S., *George Eliot, a Biography* (Oxford, 1968).

Haile, M., and E. Bonney, *The Life and Letters of John Lingard, 1771–1851* (1912).

Harris, E. M., 'Experimental Graphic Processes in England, 1800–1859', *JPS* 4 (1968).

—— 'Experimental Graphic Processes in England, 1800–1859', *JPS* 5 (1969).

—— 'Experimental Graphic Processes in England, 1800–1859', *JPS* 6 (1970).

Harrison, J. F. C., *Learning and Living: A Study in the History of the Adult Education Movement* (1961).

Hart, F. R., *Scott's Novels: The Plotting of Historic Survival* (Charlottesville, Va., 1966).

Harvey, J. R., *Victorian Novelists and their Illustrators* (1970).

Haskell, F., *History and its Images: Art and the Interpretation of the Past* (New Haven, Conn., and London, 1993).

Hastings, A., *The Construction of Nationhood: Ethnicity, Religion, and Nationalism* (Cambridge, 1997).

Heimann, M., *Catholic Devotion in Victorian England* (Oxford, 1995).

Hennessy, B., *The Gothic Novel* (Harlow, 1978).

Hill, B., *The Republican Virago: The Life and Times of Catherine Macaulay, Historian* (Oxford, 1992).

Hill, C., 'The Norman Yoke', in *Puritanism and Revolution: Studies in the Interpretation of the English Revolution of the Seventeenth Century* (1958).

Hill, J. E., 'Cruikshank, Ainsworth and Tableau Illustration', *VS* 3 (1980).

Hilton, T., *The Pre-Raphaelites* (1970).

Hobsbawm, E., *Nations and Nationalism since 1780* (Cambridge, 1990).

—— and T. Ranger, (eds.), *The Invention of Tradition* (Cambridge, 1983).

Hodnett, E., *Five Centuries of English Book Illustration* (Aldershot, 1988).

—— *Image and Text: Studies in the Illustration of English Literature* (1982).

Holcomb, A. M., 'Turner and Scott', *JWCI* 34 (1971).

Hollis, P., 'Women in Council: Separate Spheres, Public Space', in J. Rendall (ed.), *Equal or Different? Women's Politics, 1800–1914* (Oxford, 1987).

Holt, J. C., *Robin Hood* (1982).

Honour, H., *Romanticism* (Harmondsworth, 1979).

Houfe, S., *The Dictionary of British Book Illustrators and Caricaturists 1800–1914* (Woodbridge, 1981).

—— *John Leech and the Victorian Scene* (Woodbridge, 1984).

Hughes, L. K., and M. Lund, *The Victorian Serial* (Charlottesville, Va., and London, 1991).

Humphreys, A., 'Generic Strands and Urban Twists: The Victorian Mysteries Novel', *VS* 34 (1991).

Hunnisett, B., *Steel-Engraved Book Illustration in England* (1980).

Hutchinson, J., and A. D. Smith (eds.), *Nationalism* (Oxford, 1994).

Hyde, R., *Panoramania* (1989).

Iser, W., *The Implied Reader: Patterns of Communication in Prose Fiction from Bunyan to Beckett* (Baltimore and London, 1974).

Jackson, P., *George Scharf's London: Sketches and Watercolours of a Changing City, 1820–50* (1987).

James, L., *Fiction for the Working Man, 1830–50: A Study of the Literature Produced for the Working Classes in Early Victorian England* (1963).

Jann, R., *The Art and Science of Victorian History* (Columbus, Ohio, 1985).

Johnson, L., *The Paintings of Eugene Delacroix: A Critical Catalogue, 1816–31*, 2 vols. (Oxford, 1981).

Jones, E., *The English Nation: The Great Myth* (Stroud, 1998).

—— 'John Lingard and the Simancas Archives', *The Historical Journal*, 10 (1967).

Kedourie, E., *Nationalism* (1960; Oxford, 1993 edn.).

Ker, I., *John Henry Newman* (Oxford, 1988).

Kerr, I., *Fiction against History: Scott as Storyteller* (Cambridge, 1989).

Kidd, C., *Subverting Scotland's Past: Scottish Whig Historians and the Creation of an Anglo-British Identity, 1689–c.1830* (Cambridge, 1993).

Kilgour, M., *The Rise of the Gothic Novel* (1995).

Kitton, F. G., *Dickens and his Illustrators* (1899).

—— *John Leech, Artist and Humourist* (1884).

Kliger, S., *The Goths in England: A Study in Seventeenth and Eighteenth Century Thought* (Cambridge, Mass., 1952).

Knowles, D., *Great Historical Enterprises and Problems in Monastic History* (Edinburgh, 1963).

Lambert, S., *The Image Multiplied: Five Centuries of Printed Reproductions of Paintings and Drawings* (1987).

Lang, T., *The Victorians and the Stuart Heritage: Interpretation of a Discordant Past* (Cambridge, 1995).

Leavis, Q. D., *Fiction and the Reading Public* (1932).

Le Quesne, A. L., *Carlyle* (Oxford, 1982).

Levine, G., '*Romola* as Fable', in B. Hardy (ed.), *Critical Essays on George Eliot* (1970).

Levine, P., *The Amateur and the Professional: Antiquarians, Historians and Archaeologists in Victorian Britain, 1838–1886* (Cambridge, 1986).

Levy, M., *Le Roman 'gothique' anglais* (Toulouse, 1968).

Linker, R. W., 'The English Roman Catholics and Emancipation: The Politics of Persuasion', *Journal of Ecclesiastical History* 27 (1976).

Loades, D., 'The Origins of English Protestant Nationalism', in S. Mews (ed.), *Religion and National Identity* (Oxford, 1982).

Lowenthal, D., *The Heritage Crusade and the Spoils of Modern History* (Cambridge, 1997).

Lucy, A. F., 'The Other Miss Yonge', in G. Battiscombe and M. Laski (eds.), *A Chaplet for Charlotte Yonge* (1965).

Lukas, G., *The Historical Novel*, trans. H. and S. Mitchell (Harmondsworth, 1962).

McLean, R., *George Cruikshank: His Life and Work as a Book-Illustrator* (1948).

—— *Victorian Book Design and Colour Printing* (1963; 1972 edn.).

Macpherson, G., *Memoirs of the Life of Anna Jameson* (1878).

Madigan, L. (ed.), *The Devil is a Jackass* (Leominster and Stratton on the Fosse, 1995).

Maidment, B. E., *Reading Popular Prints 1790–1870* (Manchester and New York).

Maitzen, R., ' "This Feminine Preserve": Historical Biographies by Victorian Women', *VS* 38 (1995).

Mandler, P., *The Fall and Rise of the Stately Home* (New Haven, Conn., 1997).

—— ' "In the Olden Time": Romantic History and the English National Identity', in L. Brockliss and D. Eastwood (eds.), *A Union of Multiple Identities: The British Isles, c.1750–c.1850* (Manchester and New York, 1996).

Marie, A., *Alfred et Tony Johannot: Peintres, graveurs et vignettistes* (Paris, 1925).

Mason, M., 'The Way We Look Now: Millais's Illustrations to Trollope', *Art History*, 1 (Sept. 1978).

Mavor, E. (ed.), *The Captain's Wife: The South American Journals of Maria Graham 1821–23* (1993).

Maxwell, R., 'City Life and the Novel: Hugo, Ainsworth and Dickens', *Comparative Literature*, 30 (1976).

Meisel, M., *Realizations: Narrative, Pictorial and Theatrical Arts in Nineteenth Century England* (Princeton, 1983).

Miele, C., ' "Their Interest and Habit": Professionalism and the Restoration of Medieval Churches, 1837–77', in C. Brooks and A. Saint (eds.), *The Victorian Church: Architecture and Society* (Cambridge and New York, 1995).

Miller, J. H., '*Henry Esmond*: Repetition and Irony', in *Fiction and Repetition: Seven English Novels* (Cambridge, 1982).

Miller, J. H., *Illustration* (Cambridge, Mass., 1992).

Millgate, J., 'History *versus* Fiction: Thackeray's Response to Macaulay', in P. L. Shillingsburg (ed.), *Costerus: Essays in English and American Literature: Thackeray* (Amsterdam and Columbia, SC, 1974).

—— *Scott's Last Edition: A Study in Publishing History* (Edinburgh, 1987).

—— *Walter Scott: The Making of a Novelist* (Edinburgh, 1984).

Mitchell, J., *Scott, Chaucer and Medieval Romance: A Study in Scott's Indebtedness to the Literature of the Middle Ages* (Lexington, Ky., 1987).

Mitchell, W. J. T., *Iconology: Images, Text, and Ideology* (Chicago and London, 1986).

Morbey, C. C., *Charles Knight: An Appreciation and Bibliography of a Great Victorian Publisher* (Birmingham, 1979).

Morgan, P., 'Early Victorian Wales and its Crisis of Identity', in L. Brockliss and D. Eastwood (eds.), *A Union of Multiple Identities: The British Isles, c.1750–c.1850* (Manchester and New York, 1996).

Morley, E., and Milner, F., *'And When Did You Last See Your Father?'* (1992).

Morris, K. L., 'John Bull and the Scarlet Woman: Charles Kingsley and Anti-Catholicism in Victorian Literature', *RH* 23 (1996).

—— 'Kenelm Henry Digby and English Catholicism', *RH* 20 (1991).

Mossner, E. C., 'Was Hume a Tory Historian? Facts and Reconsiderations', in D. Livingston and M. Martin, *Hume as Philosopher of Society, Politics and History* (Rochester, NY, and Woodbridge, 1991).

Muir, P., *Victorian Illustrated Books* (1971).

Nead, L., *Myths of Sexuality: Representations of Women in Victorian Britain* (Oxford, 1988).

Newman, G., *The Rise of English Nationalism: A Cultural History, 1740–1830* (1987; 1991 edn.).

Nochlin, L., *Realism* (1971).

Norman, E. R., *Anti-Catholicism in Victorian England* (1967).

—— *The English Catholic Church in the Nineteenth Century* (Oxford, 1984).

Nunn, P. G., *Problem Pictures: Women and Men in Victorian Painting* (Aldershot, 1995).

—— *Victorian Women Artists* (1987).

Oddie, W., *Dickens and Carlyle: The Question of Influence* (1972).

Ormond, L., *George Du Maurier* (1969).

—— and R., *Lord Leighton* (New Haven, Conn., 1975).

Ousby, I., *The Englishman's England: Taste, Travel and the Rise of Tourism* (Cambridge, 1990).

Pantazzi, S., 'Author and Illustrator: Images in Conflict', *VPN* 9 (1976), 42.

Parker, R., *The Subversive Stitch: Embroidery and the Making of the Feminine* (1984).

Parsons, I., 'Copyright and Society', in A. Briggs (ed.), *Essays in the History of Publishing* (1974).

Patten, R. L., *George Cruikshank's Life, Times and Art*, 2 vols. (Cambridge, 1992 and 1996).

Peardon, T. P., *The Transition in English Historical Writing 1760–1830* (New York, 1933).

Pears, I., 'The Gentleman and the Hero: Wellington and Napoleon in the Nineteenth Century', in R. Porter (ed.), *Myths of the English* (1992).

Phillips, P., 'John Lingard and *The Anglo-Saxon Church*', *RH* 23 (1996).

Phillipson, N., *Hume* (1989).

Piggott, S., *Ruins in a Landscape* (Edinburgh, 1976).

Pocock, J. G. A., *The Ancient Constitution and Feudal Law* (1957; Cambridge, 1987 edn.).

Pointon, M., *William Dyce, 1806–1864: A Critical Biography* (Oxford, 1979).

Pool, P., *Impressionism* (1967).

Pope-Hennessy, U., *Agnes Strickland, Biographer of the Queens of England, 1796–1874* (1940).

Potts, A., 'Picturing the Modern Metropolis: Images of London in the Nineteenth Century', *HWJ* 26 (1988).

Punter, D., *The Literature of Terror* (London and New York, 1980).

Ray, G. N., *The Illustrator and the Book in England from 1790 to 1914* (Oxford, 1976).

—— *Thackeray: The Age of Wisdom 1847–63* (Oxford, 1958).

—— *Thackeray: The Uses of Adversity, 1811–1846* (1955).

Reed, J., *Sir Walter Scott: Landscape and Locality* (1980).

Reid, F., *Illustrators of the Sixties* (1928).

Reilly, J., *Shadowtime: History and Representation in Hardy, Conrad, and George Eliot* (London and New York, 1993).

Rendall, J., *The Origins of Modern Feminism: Women in Britain, France, and the United States, 1780–1860* (1985).

Richard Doyle and his Family (Victoria and Albert Museum exhibition catalogue, 1983–4).

Richter, D. H., *The Progress of Romance: Literary Historiography and the Gothic Novel* (Columbus, Ohio, 1996).

Rignall, J. M., 'Thackeray's *Henry Esmond* and the Struggle against the Power of Time', in J. Hawthorn (ed.), *The Nineteenth Century British Novel* (1986).

Roberts, H. E., 'Marriage, Redundancy and Sin: The Painter's View of Women in the First Twenty-Five Years of Victoria's Reign', in M. Vicinus (ed.), *Suffer and be Silent: Women in the Victorian Age* (Bloomington, Ind., and London, 1973).

Rosenberg, J. D., *Carlyle and the Burden of History* (Cambridge, Mass., 1985).

Rosner, M., 'Perspectives on *Henry Esmond*', *VN* 56 (1979).

Ross, A. M., *The Imprint of the Picturesque in Nineteenth Century British Fiction* (Ontario, 1986).

Rowlands, M., 'The Education and Piety of Catholics in Staffordshire in the Eighteenth Century', *RH* 10 (1969).

Sadleir, M., 'Aspects of the Victorian Novel' (1937), *PH* 5 (1979).

Sambrook, W., *William Cobbett* (1973).

Samuel, R., *Theatres of Memory, i. Past and Present in Contemporary Culture* (1994).

Sanders, A., *The English Historical Novel 1840–1880* (1979).

Schnorrenberg, B. B., 'The Brood-Hen of Faction: Mrs Macaulay and Radical Politics, 1765–75', *Albion*, 11 (1979).

Semmel, B., *George Eliot and the Politics of National Inheritance* (New York and Oxford, 1994).

Seton-Watson, H., *Nations and States* (1977).

Shaw, H., *The Forms of Historical Fiction* (Ithaca, NY, and London, 1983).

Shea, D. F., *The English Ranke: John Lingard* (New York, 1969).

Sheets, R., 'Anna Murphy Jameson', in S. Mitchell (ed.), *Victorian Britain: An Encylopedia* (New York and London, 1988).

Showalter, E., *A Literature of their Own: From Charlotte Bronte to Doris Lessing* (1977; 1982 edn.).

Simmons, J., 'The Writing of English County Histories', in Simmons (ed.), *English County Histories* (Wakefield, 1979).

Simmons, J. C., *The Novelist as Historian: Essays on the Victorian Historical Novel* (The Hague and Paris, 1973).

—— 'Thackeray's *Esmond* and Anne Manning's "Spurious Antiquities" ', *VN* 42 (1972).

Slee, P., *Learning and a Liberal Education: The Study of Modern History in the Universities of Oxford, Cambridge and Manchester, 1800–1914* (Manchester, 1986).

Smith, A. D., *National Identity* (1991).

Smith, B. G., 'The Contribution of Women to Modern Historiography in Great Britain, France and the United States, 1750–1940', *American Historical Review*, 89 (1984).

—— 'Gender and the Practices of Scientific History: The Seminar and Archival Research in the Nineteenth Century', *American Historical Review*, 100 (1995).

Smith, H. W., *German Nationalism and Religious Conflict: Culture, Ideology, Politics* (Princeton, 1995).

Smith, R. J., *The Gothic Bequest: Medieval Institutions in British Thought, 1688–1863* (Cambridge, 1987).

Soffer, R., *Discipline and Power: The University, History and the Making of the English Elite, 1870–1930* (Stanford, Calif., 1994).

Spencer, J., *The Rise of Woman Novelist from Aphra Behn to Jane Austen* (Oxford, 1986).

Spielmann, M. H., *The History of 'Punch'* (1895).

Sprigge, S. S., *The Methods of Publishing* (1890).

Staley, A., *et al.*, *The Post Pre-Raphaelite Print: Etching, Illustration, Reproductive Engraving, and Photography in England in and around the 1860s* (New York, 1995).

Stanton, P., *Pugin* (1971).

Steadman, C., ' "The Mother Made Conscious": The Historical Development of a Primary School Pedagogy', *HWJ* 26 (1985).

Steig, M., 'The Critic and the Illustrated Novel: Mr Turveydrop from Gillray to *Bleak House*', *The Huntingdon Library Quarterly*, 36 (1972–3).

Stevens, J., 'Thackeray's Capitals', in P. L. Shillingsburg (ed.), *Costerus: Essays in English and American Literature: Thackeray* (Amsterdam and SC, 1974).

—— ' "Woodcuts Dropped into the Text": The Illustrations in *A Tale of Two Cities* and *Barnaby Rudge*', *Studies in Bibliography*, 20 (1967).

Strong, R., *And When Did You Last See Your Father? The Victorian Painter and British History* (1978).

—— *The National Portrait Gallery: Tudor and Jacobean Portraits*, 2 vols. (1969).

Sunderland, J., 'Mortimer, Pine, and Some Political Aspects of English History Painting', *Burlington Magazine*, 116 (1974).

Sutherland, J., 'Henry Colburn, Publisher', *PH* 19 (1986).

—— *The Longman Companion to Victorian Fiction* (Harlow, 1988).

—— *Thackeray at Work* (1974).

—— *Victorian Novelists and Publishers* (1976).

Sweet, R., *The Writing of Urban Histories in Eighteenth-Century England* (Oxford, 1997).

Thomas, C., *Love and Life Enough: The Life of Anna Jameson* (Toronto, 1967).

Todd, J. (ed.), *A Dictionary of British and American Women Writers, 1600–1800* (1984).

Trumpener, K., *Bardic Nationalism: The Romantic Novel and the British Empire* (Princeton, 1997).

Twymman, M., *Lithography 1800–1850* (Oxford, 1970).

Vaughan, W., *German Romanticism and English Art* (New Haven, Conn., and London, 1979).

—— *Romantic Art* (1978).

Vergo, P. (ed.), *The New Museology* (1989).

Vickery, A., 'Golden Age to Separate Spheres: A Review of the Categories and Chronology of English Women's History', *Historical Journal*, 36 (1993).

Vogeler, M. S., *Frederic Harrison: The Vocations of a Positivist* (Oxford, 1984).

Wakeman, G., *Victorian Book Illustration: The Technical Revolution* (Newton Abbot, 1973).

Ward, A. W., 'Introduction', to E. Gaskell, *Sylvia's Lovers* (1863; 1906 edn.).

Warren, J., '*The Dublin Review* (1836–75), its Reviewers and a "Philosophy of Knowledge"', *RH* 21 (1992).

Warrington, B., 'The Bankruptcy of William Pickering in 1853: The Hazards of Publishing and Bookselling in the First Half of the Nineteenth Century', *PH* 27 (1990).

Webb, R. K., *Harriet Martineau: A Radical Victorian* (New York, 1960).

The Wellesley Index to Victorian Periodicals, 1824–1900, ed. W. E. Houghton and J. L. Slingerland, 5 vols. (Toronto, 1966–89).

Wertz, S., 'Hume, History and Human Nature', in D. Livingston and M. Martin, *Hume as a Philosopher of Society, Politics and History* (Rochester, NY, and Woodbridge, 1991).

Wexler, V. G., *David Hume and the History of England* (Philadelphia, 1979).

Whalley, J. I., *Cobwebs to Catch Flies: Illustrated Books for the Nursery and the Schoolroom 1700–1900* (1974).

White, H., *Metahistory: The Historical Imagination in Nineteenth Century Europe* (Baltimore and London, 1973).

Wind, E., 'The Revolution of History Painting', in Wind., *Hume and the Heroic Portrait: Studies in Eighteenth-Century Imagery*, ed. J. Anderson (Oxford, 1986).

Witemeyer, H., *George Eliot and the Visual Arts* (New Haven, Conn., and London, 1979).

Wood, C., *The Dictionary of Victorian Painters* (Woodbridge, 1978).

Woolf, D. R., 'A Feminine Past? Gender, Genre, and Historical Knowledge in England, 1500–1800', *American Historical Review*, 102 (1997).

Wootton, D., *The Illustrators: The British Art of Illustration 1780–1996* (1996).

—— with L. Coleman and A. Horne, *The Illustrators: The British Art of Illustration 1780–1996* (1997).

[Worsley, A.?], *A Sketch of Emily Taylor by a Friend* (private circulation, 1872).

Worth, G., *William Harrison Ainsworth* (New York, 1972).

INDEX

Please note that the dates given in the index for books etc are those of their first publication. Subsequent editions appear under the same heading.

Printed in the United States
45014LVS00002BA/129